D0932459

The CIVILIAN *and the* MILITARY

The Civilian and the Military: A History of the American Antimilitarist Tradition

E-70

ARTHUR A. EKIRCH, JR.

RALPH MYLES, PUBLISHER

COLORADO SPRINGS

1972

To Merle Curti

First published in 1956 by
Oxford University Press

First paperbound edition
copyright, 1972, by Arthur A. Ekirch, Jr.

International Standard Book Number: 0-87926-007-6
Library of Congress Card Number: 72-80273

Ralph Myles, Publisher, Inc.
Box 1533
Colorado Springs, Colo. 80901

Printed in the United States of America

Contents

Preface, vii

Introduction, xv

Acknowledgments, xix

I The Anglo-American Heritage, 3

II The Founding Fathers Reaffirm Civil Supremacy, 18

III The Defeat of the Federalist Military Plans, 32

IV The Jeffersonian-Republican Surrender, 45

V A More Militant Nationalism and Growing Pacifism, 60

VI A Military Hero and Manifest Destiny, 74

VII The Menace of Civil War, 90

VIII The Reconstruction of Civil Society, 107

IX The New Threat of Imperialism and Navalism, 124

X Theodore Roosevelt and Modern American Militarism, 140

XI European Militarism and American Preparedness, 156

XII Conscripting America for War, 176

XIII Disillusionment and Partial Disarmament, 195

XIV Militarism in Education, 217

XV The Hope of Isolation and Neutrality, 234

XVI Immersion in Total War, 254

XVII Toward the Garrison State, 271

Bibliographical Comment, 291

Notes, 293

Index, 329

Preface

In the decade and a half since the publication of *The Civilian and the Military* in 1956, the American antimilitarist tradition has slowly emerged from the nadir of the post-World War II years. Military institutions and military men are no longer sancrosanct, and the aggressive American foreign policy of the Cold War, which has been the constant excuse and rationale for the military's tremendously expanded role, is now itself under growing popular attack. This resurgence of historic American antimilitarism should not, however, blind us to certain continuing realities.

Objective assessment of the relative strengths and weaknesses of the civilian and military sectors of American society makes it clear that the latter's influence is still overwhelmingly strong and pervasive. Close to three million men and women in the armed forces, conscription under the guise of Selective Service, and direct military spending amounting to almost one half of the entire federal budget, with the additional indirect costs of past or future wars pushing the total still higher, all combine to put the United States in first place among the nations of the world in the percentage of its Gross National Product devoted to military expenditures. Current annual United States military expenses per capita (well over $300) are, in turn, nearly double those of the Soviet Union or of any other nation. Antimilitarism, indeed, could hardly be the major issue that it is today were it not for the provocation that it continues to receive from the presence of a military machine without a parallel or precedent in the peacetime history of the United States. Thus the revived public concern over the dangers of militarism merely underscores the necessity of restoring a proper balance in civil-military relations.

It is naive, of course, as *The Civilian and the Military* demonstrates, to think of modern militarism and military interests in the old-fashioned sense of their identification with a stylized Prussian officer corps. Although ostentatious military display has not been wanting in twentieth-century America, present-day attitudes among the younger generation suggest the waning popular appeal of such events as Army, Navy, or Air Force "days." However, public relations and propaganda techniques much more subtle than brass bands or formal parades are now the military order of the day. And even more significant is the fact that military personnel and military values have become an integral part of what was formerly taken for granted as a civilian way of life. Many of the historic distinctions between military and civilian areas in American life have accordingly become less and less real. Military leaders, as J. W. Masland and L. I. Radway, authors of *Soldiers and Scholars*, point out, are now "called upon to work closely with foreign affairs experts, industrial managers, scientists, labor leaders, and educators. They participate in the drafting and promotion of legislation, in the preparation of a national budget, and in the determination of the American position on a wide variety of foreign policy issues. . . . They are called upon to evaluate the motivations and capabilities of foreign nations and to estimate the effects of American action or inaction upon these nations. And above all, the new role of military leaders requires of them a heightened awareness of the principles of our democratic society."

In the twentieth-century world, military organizations are an integral part of the Leviathan state, and military men are vital components of modern bureaucracies. As personal rights are subordinated to the needs of the state, power and responsibility, in turn, are transferred from the individual to society. Governed by its chain-of-command psychology, the military ethos of implicit obedience and loyalty to the institutional foundations of the status quo now serves also as one of the essential characteristics of a profoundly conservative American society. Thus the military ethos, in contrast to its old conflict with liberal values, is currently a part of the new consensus of a status-directed society.

Today, however, along with "duty-honor-country," the governing maxims in American life are those of a crude power politics, backed up by a military establishment and by a weaponry unprecedented in the annals of mankind. The arts of diplomacy have been subordinated, as perhaps never before, to those of preparedness and war. In the new policy-making offices of the nation, particularly in the National Security Council, the Joint Chiefs of Staff, and the Central Intelligence Agency, a military point of view has been able to exercise a major, and even decisive and determining, influence upon a succession of American Presidents and Secretaries of State. Thus it is now hardly true that military men or their particular philosophy remain neglected or subordinate to a liberal or civilian view of world affairs.

Military life, in itself a pragmatic sort of socialism, is well attuned to the varieties of state socialism or state capitalism characteristic of the present-day warfare-welfare economy, while military men, accustomed to a lifetime of government salaries, allowances, and pensions, are well equipped to assume positions of leadership in a paternalistic environment. The social and economic planning characteristic of American democracy today is therefore closer to a military way of life than it is to the older laissez-faire liberalism of the nineteenth century. Thus military men can live happily in the contemporary world, accepting its values and not feeling themselves a caste set apart by the opposed ideals of the American liberal and antimilitarist tradition.

The whole extraordinary complex of values and interests underlying the influence of the military establishment in modern American society has reached what appears to be a climax or plateau in the course of the war in Vietnam. Increasing disillusionment over America's role in that conflict has been the greatest single factor in the willingness of more and more Americans to take a critical view of the military establishment. Doctrines of containment, limited war, liberation, police action, and counter-insurgency, all advanced by America's "cold warriors" as palatable substitutes for nuclear

warfare, have had their supreme test in Vietnam. America's undeclared war in Southeast Asia, according to its protagonists, was to
revitalize our interventionist world diplomacy while it persuaded
the American people to continue to shoulder the burden of ever-
larger military expenditures. Since nuclear weapons make all-out
war unthinkable, the architects and technicians of the Cold War
hoped to find in areas and operations like Vietnam the means to a
stronger Pax Americana. The struggle in Vietnam has proved, of
course, to be an odd type of limited war. Restricted so far only by
the absence, or at least the non-use of nuclear weapons, it has become in all other respects a major conflict with more bombs
dropped and exploded than in all World War II, with hundreds of
thousands of civilian casualties, and with more American soldiers
killed and wounded than in any previous war, excepting only the
Civil War and Second World War.

Open protest against the role of the military in American foreign
and domestic affairs, so conspicuously absent during the Korean
War and the Truman administration, has gradually mounted in
volume and intensity. Far from remaining an exclusive pacifist
preserve, the voices of dissent have even included a surprising number of military men. It was President Eisenhower, for example, who
used the prestige of his high office to warn the nation against the
danger of militarism in his Farewell Address of January 1961.
Thus the contention of C. Wright Mills and other critics of American postwar foreign policy that the United States is fastened in the
grip of a "power elite" composed of high governmental officials, big
businessmen, and top military commanders won the affirmation of
the President of the United States who, more than any of his pre-
decessors, had devoted his life to a professional military career.
"America's adventure in free government," Eisenhower declared,
could be menaced by the rise of a "military-industrial complex. . . .
We must never let the weight of this combination endanger our
liberties or democratic processes. We should take nothing for
granted. Only an alert and knowledgeable citizenry can compel
the proper meshing of the huge industrial and military machinery
of defense with our peaceful methods and goals, so that security and
liberty may prosper together."

In a recent echo of Eisenhower's considered advice, two former high-ranking Marine officers, Commanding General David M. Shoup and Colonel James A. Donovan, have explicitly levied the charge of militarism against United States postwar policies. In Colonel Donovan's words: "America has become a militaristic and aggressive nation embodied in a vast, expensive and burgeoning military-industrial-scientific-political combine which dominates the country and affects much of our daily life, our economy, our international status and our foreign policies."

The grave dangers in the misplaced powers of the military-industrial complex, of which Eisenhower spoke, have become the subject of repeated warnings in the last decade. Concerned scholars, well-informed journalists, and a few courageous Congressmen and Senators have documented the interrelation of the modern American military and industrial establishments and their pervasive impacts upon society and the individual. Curiously one of the latest and most authoritative accounts is that of a close associate of former Defense Secretary Robert S. McNamara. Adam Yarmolinsky, author and research director of the Twentieth Century Fund's volume *The Military Establishment,* provides a detailed analysis of the military's influence upon President and Congress, its direct involvement in intelligence, propaganda, public relations, and foreign policy, its alliance with science, industry, and education, and its role in civil affairs and the domestic economy. Much, though not most, of the military's undoubted influence has been indirect—a result of the fact that top-level statesmen and diplomats like President Johnson and Secretaries of State Dean Acheson, John Foster Dulles, and Dean Rusk, together with such behind-the-scenes advisers as McGeorge Bundy, Walt Rostow, and Henry Kissinger have been men thoroughly imbued with a military point of view. They are convinced that America must exercise its role in global affairs through its military might, including the stockpiling of missiles and anti-missiles more than sufficient to annihilate not only the Soviet Union and Red China but the entire civilized world. Thus, despite the halting attempts at a diplomatic rapprochement with the Soviet Union by Presidents Eisenhower and Kennedy, the United States has made little effort and less progress toward the goal of resolving the tensions of the Cold War.

Our continued insistence on achieving our national ends through military means requires, of course, the expenditure of more and more billions of dollars in the never-ending quest for what is mistakenly regarded as the National Security. Thus we continue to place our faith in massive nuclear deterrents, rather than in disarmament or even in arms control. And we condone the imprisonment of conscientious objectors and draft resisters as a means of coercing young men into the armed services for overseas duty in Vietnam. Indeed, we have moved so far along the road to a garrison state that even the minuscule groups of non-deferred youths who choose jail rather than the Army may be counted "in the service of their country." As the psychiatrist author of a recent study of American war resisters in prison point out, "They are the innocent minority who must be sacrificed to insure the efficiency of the punishment system." For, Dr. Willard Gaylin notes, "When a government does not trust itself, its purposes, or its population, it dare not depend on a volunteer army." Meanwhile the American political-military establishment resists every effort to end the draft or reduce substantially America's military commitments abroad.

Historically an arms race and militarization on the vast scale that is now characteristic of a number of countries, and especially of the United States, has had as its most likely outcome war, revolution, and national bankruptcy. Although some economists see in what Kenneth Boulding aptly calls "the world war industry" merely another means to full production and employment, it is plain that "the permanent war economy" of the United States has not been a sure road to even a minimum sort of welfare state, and much less surely to one that is gaining in the effort to eliminate poverty. Most serious of all is the still largely unspoken possibility that the militarization of America has now gone so far that even a peaceful resolution of the Cold War and the fighting in Vietnam will not be sufficient to release the American people from the power of the Pentagon and its corporate allies. Thus the purported secret, and perhaps apocryphal, governmental *Report from Iron Mountain* argues that peace is no longer an economical, psychological, or politically feasible or desirable outcome for the United States.

Nuclear weapons may well have achieved what Walter Millis has termed the hypertrophy of war. War, in his words, can no longer be deemed to serve the national interest. Less certain is the question of whether its current high degree of militarization will permit the United States to return to a traditionally civilian society and a normal peaceful world. Failure to find some way to curb the militarization of America offers the grim prospect of a future society which, if not a true garrison state, may still be so Spartan and totalitarian in its demands that it will hurry America along the road to 1984—perhaps even before the clock runs out on George Orwell's dire prediction.

Introduction

THE TRADITION of antimilitarism has been an important factor in the shaping of some two hundred years of American history. This tradition, with its emphasis upon civil as against military authority, is accepted as an essential element of American freedom and democracy. Though involved in numerous wars, the United States has avoided becoming a militaristic nation, and the American people, though hardly pacifists, have been staunch opponents of militarism.

Unlike the complete pacifist, who is opposed to all use of force, the antimilitarist may accept war and armies as a sometimes necessary evil, although he regards a large military establishment and conscript armies, even when needed, as a threat to the preservation of civil institutions of government. Fortunately, the United States throughout most of its history has been largely isolated from the danger of foreign invasion. Reluctant to yield this heritage of peace and security, the antimilitarist, together with the pacifist and anti-imperialist, has opposed expansion overseas or intervention in world affairs. In the course of our history, antimilitarists have often co-operated with other liberal and reform groups, and these in turn have not hesitated to invoke the antimilitarist tradition to further their own ends. The rise and decline of the antimilitarist tradition thus mirrors American life and thought, just as it has reflected the character of past civilizations throughout history.

The origins of the conflict between a civil and a military way of life may be traced back to the attempt of primitive peoples to free themselves from subjection to a warrior class. Later, the Greek and Roman, as well as other ancient civilizations, were confronted by this problem and succumbed ultimately to Caesarism. Following the decline of Greece and Rome, Western Europe was governed in military fashion by a succession of barbarian invaders, feudal overlords, and absolute monarchs. Gradually, however, with the rise of modern civilization and the restoration of civil order and the rule of law, the military class lost some of its influence and was relegated to a position of relative inferiority.

Though professional standing armies succeeded the old feudal array, they were motley bodies of men held in contempt by the nonmilitary classes of Europe during the era of the eighteenth-century Enlightenment. Under capitalism, the growing national economies no longer tolerated the removal of the useful classes of the population from civil life. Only the surplus nobility, who received the officer's commissions, and the dregs of society, who made up the bulk of the soldiery, could be spared for the pursuit of war. Under the spell of the Enlightenment and the idea of progress, people believed once more in a coming era of peace and felt that an army was a comparatively useless burden.[1]

The eighteenth-century hope of peaceful progress was rudely shattered by the outbreak of the French Revolution and the rise of Napoleon. The Emperor Napoleon exemplified in dramatic fashion the renaissance of the militarist state, but the fast-ripening forces of nationalism, democracy, and industrialism also contributed their share to its rebirth. It was, after all, the early Revolutionary leaders who revived the Ancients' concept of total war, marshaling both the industry and the manpower of France in the national cause. Napoleon then showed how easily a war of peoples could be transformed into the tyranny of a militarist dictatorship. Although not so well recognized at the time, or even later, it is certainly one of the paradoxes of modern civilization that the assertion of the rights and liberties of man was followed almost immediately by his regimentation and conscription for military purposes. In the words of a recent student of the spirit of the French Revolution, 'the new individualism on its militaristic side was not the purely liberating force that it first seemed.' [2] The Revolutionary *levée en masse*, with its conscription of the population and workshops of France, was not only the negation of liberty in the name of liberty but also an unpleasant foretaste of things to come.

The full impact of the Revolutionary variety of total militarism was delayed, however, until the onset of the First World War. During the hundred years that intervened between Waterloo and Sarajevo there was, except perhaps in the case of the American Civil War, no recurrence of war and militarism on the vast scale that had characterized the era of the French Revolution. The 'century of progress' witnessed, on the whole, a return to many of the liberal and humane values cherished in the eighteenth-century Enlightenment, including the renewed growth of an anti-militarist tradition. But during these years militarism in a limited sense endured. Instead of encompassing the whole economy and society as it had in Revolutionary France, militarism in the nine-teenth century became a 'caste and cult, authority and belief,' adhered to by a small, but nevertheless influential, minority of the population. As Alfred Vagts has pointed out, it served the army, and not war, and flourished in time of peace.

> Militarism is thus not the opposite of pacifism; its true counter-part is civilianism. Love of war, bellicosity, is the counterpart of the love of peace, pacifism; but militarism is more, and sometimes less, than the love of war. It covers every system of thinking and valuing and every complex of feelings which rank military institutions and ways above the ways of civilian life, carrying military mentality and modes of acting and decision into the civilian sphere.[3]

In the process of two world wars, militarism as a nineteenth-century Prussian phenomenon, replete with brass bands and an arrogant officer class, has been superseded by the French Revolutionary variety of total militarism. To the old French Revolutionary *levée en masse* has been added the enormous productive capacity of modern industrialism and the incessant propaganda of the masses. With the power of the military extended to all phases of national life, its contrast and conflict with the civil authority has also become less apparent. In other words, military power is able to dominate civil authority to the point where the latter becomes a willing dupe of military men, overwhelmed by their prestige, and confused as to the validity of the experts' opinions on questions of larger policy.

The threat of militarism seems, therefore, to be far greater today in all countries than it was a hundred years ago when the chief dispute between the military and civil authority was over the size of the standing army. With virtually the whole population enrolled in some military capacity or dependent upon the military office, all conflict with civil society is necessarily eliminated. The resulting extinction of strong antimilitarist sentiments is not, however, proof of the absence of militarism. Thus, as a recent writer has pointed out, it is

> possible that, in the United States as elsewhere, the technological implications of modern warfare may make possible a new type of militarism unrecognizable to those who look for its historic characteristics. . . . Anyone who thinks for one moment of the effort involved in building the atomic bomb will not find it difficult to realize that, in the new warfare, the engineering factory is a unit of the army, and the worker may be in uniform without being aware of it. The new militarism may clothe itself in civilian uniform; and, if the present relations of production are maintained, it may be imposed upon a people who see in its development no more than a way to full employment.[4]

The inability, or refusal, of the world to recognize the existence of this militarism, which has so increasingly penetrated all phases of twentieth-century civilization, imperils the future of both liberalism and democracy. In the United States, where the antimilitarist tradition has been a conspicuous part of our history, it is especially pertinent to recall our national heritage and re-examine its implications for the future.

Acknowledgments

THE IDEA FOR THIS BOOK began to take form during World War II, although serious research was not started until 1946. Since that time I have profited greatly from the generous counsel of several friends and colleagues. I wish to thank William Neumann, Elton Atwater, and Rudolph Von Abele for their careful reading of the manuscript in its early stages, and for their valuable suggestions as to its style and content. To Merle Curti I am deeply indebted for past instruction, and for his sympathetic reading of the completed manuscript.

Libraries whose resources furnished materials include the Library of Congress, New York Public Library, Carnegie Library, and the libraries of Columbia University, American University, and Swarthmore College. To the staffs of each of these institutions, and especially to the Stack and Reader Division of the Library of Congress, and to the Curators of the Swarthmore College Peace Collection, I wish to express my appreciation.

For permission to examine the Oswald Garrison Villard Papers I am indebted to Konrad Mueller and the Directors of the Houghton Library of Harvard University.

The final preparation of the manuscript was facilitated by a grant-in-aid from the Social Science Research Council. Mrs. Marion Gardell and Mrs. Kermit L. Culver deserve credit for the care with which they typed successive drafts of the manuscript.

I

The Anglo-American Heritage

THE AMERICAN TRADITION of civil supremacy and of opposition to
militarism goes back in its origins to English history and experience. Great Britain, the homeland of the thirteen American colonies, was of all the European nations the most favorably situated
for the development of a strong antimilitarist tradition. In comparison with the powers on the Continent, she was practically free
of the danger of invasion and the consequent need to maintain a
large army. The English people also enjoyed in greater measure
than their neighbors the advantages of a government of laws
and the privileges of individual freedom. Though English constitutional government was severely threatened during the seven-
teenth-century revolutions, it survived the ferment of civil strife
and gained new prestige with the ultimate triumph of the principle
of parliamentary supremacy. Meanwhile the American colonies,
which had been founded during this time of troubles, were able
to profit from the mother country's experience in establishing a
proper balance in civil-military relations.

The backbone of the English military organization was not a
standing army but the ancient militia, descended from the days of
Alfred the Great. This militia was purely a local and defensive
force, in which by the time of the seventeenth century all Englishmen owed their nominal and infrequent services as a compulsory

duty. Unlike a regular army, the militia could not easily be used to undertake a war of conquest or to suppress domestic discontent among a great body of the people. The effort of the English Stuart kings to raise an army for such purposes succeeded only in touching off a storm of disapproval and helping to provoke an open revolt.

As early as 1628, in the Petition of Right, the English people protested King Charles's policy of martial law, army impressments, and billeting troops among the inhabitants. The Petition of Right, 'the charter of the most civilian nation of Europe,' was a notable landmark in parliamentary efforts to protect civil society against military dominance.[1] Expressing Parliament's jealousy of the standing army of the Stuarts, the Petition was also one of the steps that led to the Puritan Revolution of the 1640s. Unfortunately, Oliver Cromwell's victorious but unruly army transformed itself from oppressed to oppressor and intimidated the new Puritan Parliament with a show of force.

Under Cromwell's rule only the more radical Puritans championed a thorough-going democracy in which the people would be protected against any exercise of military tyranny. John Lilburne and his fellow Levellers made much use of the argument that Cromwell had usurped the powers of government and elevated the military over the civil authority. Their protests, written into the various drafts of The Agreement of the People, affirmed that no person was to be impressed for military service in a foreign war, nor for service at home, except to repel invasion. Even then no man was to be compelled to serve against his conscience, nor if he could procure another to fill his place.[2]

The Stuart Restoration, which succeeded Cromwell's military regime, witnessed new attempts to fasten a standing army upon the English nation, but the final downfall of the Stuarts in the Glorious Revolution of 1688 opened the way for the development of permanent parliamentary authority over the army. In an England where Tories remembered the military despotism of Cromwell and Whigs the large personal forces of the Stuarts, a standing army was not destined to be popular. At the close of the seventeenth century, when the Crown sought a permanent standing army to thwart the designs of France on the Continent, there was intense opposition both in Parliament and throughout the realm. Although a regular army was established, it was provided that the Mutiny Act, which authorized its support, must be re-enacted yearly, and no permanent barracks were to be erected.[3]

The chief defense of England continued, as in the past, to rest with her navy and militia. But despite the popularity of the latter as a source of potential strength, the average Englishman had little desire to subject himself to the rigors and restraints of organized military life. Accordingly, when William Pitt and Charles Townshend sought to create a national militia during the Seven Years War, the scheme produced an 'ominous discontent' with severe riots in some of the rural areas. Regular troops had to be used to force the people into the militia for which they had been clamoring as an alternative to a standing army.[4] The militia was popular only when it remained an idealized or sentimentalized kind of paper army; organized into a trained body of semi-regular troops, it was no more acceptable than a professional army and, indeed, was little different from such a force.

The English aversion to military service of any type, and to military interference with or control of the civil machinery of government, had been strengthened during the seventeenth century when war and civil strife absorbed much of the time and energy of the English people. Americans during the colonial period also lived in an environment of war and violence, and they were as little inclined as their English cousins to accept a military pattern of life or to spend overmuch of their time in training or preparation.[5] In the colonies subordination of military to civil power became the cardinal principle it was in England. Few Americans, after all, had seen service in European armies, and they could take pride in the knowledge that their settlements had been founded without the aid of an English regular army. While military experience of a sort was gained in fighting the Indians, this sporadic frontier strife did not result in the establishment of a standing army of professional soldiers. The colonists, already accustomed to the use of weapons, had little time or inclination for unnecessary training. The scarcity of labor, coupled with the need of hard work to subdue the wilderness, contributed to the development of a type of colonial economy in which an elaborate military organization had no place.

Militia service, it is true, was required of all able-bodied male colonists, but the exceptions were so numerous and the training days so few that there was little interruption of normal peacetime pursuits. In Massachusetts, for example, after 1679 the number of training days was reduced from six to four.[6] The colonial militia laws, and the compulsory service they exacted, were designed to meet the occasional emergency of an Indian raid rather than a long-drawn-out war. Colonial militia service thus differed from modern military conscription, and instead of fostering a military tradition it seems to have had the opposite effect.

In the colonial period, the most determined opposition to war and military service was that carried out by the Society of Friends or Quakers. With the founding of William Penn's colony of Pennsylvania the Quakers were afforded a real opportunity to escape persecution and apply their pacifist doctrines. Peace with the Indians was secured for over half a century under Penn's original policy of fair dealing, but the Pennsylvania colony could not avoid being drawn into the North American phase of the mother country's wars with her European rivals. The first period of Pennsylvania settlement took place during the era of the Anglo French wars from 1689 to 1713, and the Quakers were soon forced to vote the war supplies sought by Great Britain, although they were able to hold fast to their refusal to raise a militia. After William Penn's descendants abandoned the Quaker faith, the Pennsylvania proprietors came to favor a more aggressive frontier defense against both the Indians and their French allies. Finally, the growing differences between the Penn family and the Quaker Assembly in regard to military matters reached a crisis during the French and Indian War. In 1755 the Assembly, following the withdrawal of several Quaker members, enacted a militia law that ended the long period of Quaker ascendancy in Pennsylvania politics The Friends never regained control of the Assembly after 1756 and in that year the first warlike action of Pennsylvania against the Indians was begun in reprisal for the uprisings after Braddock's defeat.[7]

In Pennsylvania, the matter of defense had been complicated by the difficulties between the Quakers and the proprietors, but in almost every colony outside New England there was strong opposition to the British plans for fighting the French. The New England colonies, close to the seat of hostilities, voted money freely and, in the case of Massachusetts, offered liberal bounties and enacted a militia draft. But in Maryland, where conditions were much like those of Pennsylvania, the militia law compelled service only in the case of invasion. The Assembly was cautious about voting funds for defense and insisted upon retaining exclusive control of all troop movements. Virginia's militia law passed in 1748 stated that men could not be taken from the colony, and though the new act of 1754 provided for a draft, it contained such broad exemptions that almost the only persons affected were propertyless vagrants. The North Carolina law drafting unmarried men was openly defied.[8]

How much of the failure of the colonial assemblies to co-operate more vigorously with British plans for prosecuting the French and Indian War was based on antimilitarist sentiments, and how much on opposition to imperial authority, is difficult to say. In the course of fighting the Revolution, Americans were to demonstrate their aversion to all militarism, but, in the decade preceding independence, British militarism, as a part of the mechanism of imperial control, was the immediate issue facing the colonies. Colonial feelings became clear in the outcry that was raised against British notions of a standing army of ten thousand men to protect her North American empire. The difficulty in securing American help against the French in Canada may have strengthened the British resolve to keep a postwar standing force in the colonies, but that so vast an army was actually needed for defense after 1763 was doubtful. From the standpoint of the mother country though, the proposal undoubtedly had other advantages, including the fact 'that the army thus maintained formed the base of a control of wide-reaching importance.'[9]

The wisdom of keeping a standing army in North America was questioned immediately by influential colonial statesmen. Daniel Dulany of Maryland, a leading colonial lawyer and opponent of British taxation who later became a Loyalist, raised the issue of why, if the money was to be used to maintain an army in America, the taxes had to be paid directly to the British Treasury.[10] Governor William Pitkin of Connecticut asserted, in 1768, that 'maintaining troops in the Colonies now, in this time of profound peace, would be an unnecessary expense, and have an unhappy tendency to produce uneasiness among the people, hurt their morals, and hinder their industry.' [11] From England, where he was acting as colonial agent, Benjamin Franklin compared colonial opposition to the presence of a British army to the outcry that would be raised in England were the King to import troops from North America or Ireland for use against the homeland. 'As to the Standing Army kept among us in time of Peace, without the Consent of our Assemblies,' he declared, 'I am clearly of Opinion that it is not agreeable to the Constitution.' [12] Thomas Pownall, Franklin's fellow colonial agent, expressed the view that the American people, already oppressed with the British taxation policy, now 'apprehend and think they feel a military power established among them, independent of, and paramount to, their civil jurisdiction; by which . . . they do think it is meant to throw a kind of military net over them. And have they not foundation, Sir, for these fears?' [13]

The colonials' anxiety at having a British standing army permanently quartered in their midst was not lessened with the news in 1765 of the extension of the British Mutiny Act to America. This measure, which was the annual appropriation bill for the British army, had not previously been directly applied to the American colonies. It included provisions that enabled the British to require greater colonial co-operation in the matters of quartering troops, furnishing transportation, or apprehending the numerous deserters from the British ranks. These affairs were a source of conflict between civil and military authorities throughout the colonies, but the first test of the Mutiny Act came in New York, which General Thomas Gage had selected as the British headquarters. For refusing to comply in full with the provisions of the act requiring the quartering and supply of troops, the New York Assembly was suspended in 1767, and its legislative powers were renewed only after it had yielded to the British demands.

Friction between the military and the civil power reached its climax in Boston, where the British troops were transferred from New York in 1768, remaining until 1775. Having a British army in their city was deeply resented by Bostonians, who viewed it as a threat to American liberties. This American prejudice against British redcoats balked any attempt to integrate the troops with the community and insured a series of provocative incidents, culminating in the so-called Massacre of 1770. Months before this event, Massachusetts newspapers had been full of sensational accounts of misdeeds on the part of the British soldiery. A contemporary journal describing events in Boston from September 1768 to August 1769, which was published in many colonial newspapers, stressed the evil effects of military rule in a city like Boston — the demoralization of the soldiers, and the mistreatment of civilians. 'Along with this,' in the words of a recent editor of the journal, 'goes a constant stream of evidence that the military rule was illegal, that the local authority was subservient to the military, that soldiers and officers were encouraged to be insolent, abusive, and criminal; and that, so long as they remained in the city, there was no effective remedy at civil law.' [14]

One of the most unrelenting critics of the British soldiery was Samuel Adams, who had the greatest ability and strongest desire to arouse the anti-English feelings of his fellow Americans. Beginning in December 1768 he contributed to the *Boston Gazette* a celebrated series of letters, signed 'Vindex,' devoted to an attack upon the institution of a standing army. Predicting that the troops would foment rather than prevent disorder, Adams asked: 'Are we a garrison'd town or are we not?' If so, he demanded to know by what authority, and he reminded his readers of the rights of British subjects to be free of a standing army in time of peace except by the consent of their representatives. 'It is a very improbable supposition,' he declared,

> that any people can long remain free, with a strong military power in the very heart of their country. . . .
> Even where there is a necessity of the military power, within the land, which by the way but rarely happens, a wise and prudent people will always have a watchful & a jealous eye over it; for the maxims and rules of the army, are essentially different from the genius of a free people, and the laws of a free government.[15]

In the spring of 1769, the selectmen of the town of Boston pro
tested the necessity of conducting an election while British troop
were quartered in the city and stated that they wished to make i
clear that they were not accepting the election, held under the
shadow of the military, as a precedent for the future. A year later
the long-predicted, violent incident between troops and inhabi
tants took place when, on the evening of 5 March, a group of
soldiers, following a taunt from an apprentice boy, fired on an
assembly of the citizens, killing three and wounding eight, two of
whom later died. This so-called Boston Massacre furnished idea
political capital for colonial patriots, and Samuel Adams resumed
writing his Vindex articles. After summarizing the larger issues
involved in the Massacre and giving an account of the trial of the
British soldiers, he went on to say: 'And let me observe, how fata
are the effects, the danger of which I long ago mention'd, of post
ing a standing army among a free people!' In 1722 Boston pre
sented a list of grievances drafted by Adams affirming that 'In
troducing and quartering standing Armies in a free Country in
times of peace without the consent of the people either by them
selves or by their Representatives, is, and always has been deemed
a violation of their rights as freemen.' [16]

During the era of the American Revolution, beginning in 1771
the people of Boston gathered each 5 March to hear an oration
commemorating the famous Massacre. Sam Adams is supposed to
have commented that 'This Institution in a great Measure answer
the Design of it, which is, to preserve in the Minds of the Peopl
a lively Sense of the Danger of standing Armies.' [17] James Lowell
delivering the first Massacre oration, asked: 'What check have we
upon a British army?' A year later Dr. Joseph Warren contrasted
military and civilian modes of life. 'Soldiers,' he declared, 'are als
taught to consider arms as the only arbiters by which every disput
is to be decided between contending states.' The discipline of im
plicit obedience to their officers made the soldiers ready instru
ments of tyranny and oppression, and the result of such trainin
became especially apparent, Warren felt, when troops were sta
tioned, as in Boston, 'to overawe the inhabitants.' In 1773 Dr. Ben
jamin Church, who two years later was to be found guilty of 'hold
ing criminal correspondence with the enemy,' concluded his effor

with a call to 'manly rage, against the foul oppression of quartering troops in populous cities in times of peace.' John Hancock, the following year, recommended to the colonies the substitution of their own militia as a defense force. In the midst of the Revolution, when opposition to standing armies might have proved embarrassing, Jonathan W. Austin carefully distinguished between the 'fatal effects of standing armies in time of peace,' and armies raised for the defense of a country unjustly invaded. In 1783, with the conclusion of hostilities, Dr. Thomas Welsh, giving the last of the Massacre orations, paid tribute to the militia as the most adequate protection for a new nation separated from Europe by the vast ocean.[18]

After the bloody events of the Massacre, faithfully re-portrayed each year on 5 March, Governor Thomas Hutchinson yielded to popular pressure and transferred the British troops from the city proper to Fort Castle William in Boston Harbor. This removal alleviated the tense situation in Boston, but four years later the Coercive Acts included the stipulation that British troops again be stationed within the town. If the available barracks were inadequate, they might be housed in taverns, alehouses, and unoccupied buildings. With an army billeted in the town and with the appointment of General Gage, commander of the British forces in America, as Governor of Massachusetts, Boston was now ruled by an arbitrary government backed up by military force.

Formal colonial protest against the new British military measures followed immediately. The Declaration of Rights, adopted by the First Continental Congress on 14 October 1774, included the resolution 'That the keeping a Standing army in these colonies, in times of peace, without the consent of the legislature of that colony, in which such army is kept, is against law.' This attack upon a standing army was restated, a few days later, in the petition of Congress to the King. Among the long list of grievances laid before King George, mention was made of the fact that:

A standing army has been kept in these colonies, ever since the conclusion of the late war, without the consent of our assemblies; and this army with a considerable naval armament has been employed to enforce the collection of taxes.
The Authority of the commander in chief, and, under him, of

the brigadiers general has in time of peace, been rendered supreme in all the civil governments in America.

The commander in chief of all your majesty's forces in North America has, in time of peace, been appointed governor of a colony.[19]

For the peacetime 'defence protection and security of the colonies,' the American petitioners proposed to rely on their colonial militias, supplemented in time of war by volunteers. American jealousy of centralized power, whether in the hands of the British government, Continental Congress, or Patriot army, encouraged a reliance upon militia and volunteers in preference to regular troops. Actually the Revolution was to be fought by a combination of forces that included the regular Continental army created by Congress, militia units temporarily under Washington's authority and separate state militia and irregular troops that remained under state control. Meanwhile Congress in 1775 adopted a resolution suggesting 'that all able bodied effective men, between sixteen and fifty years of age in each colony, immediately form themselves into regular companies of Militia.' This recommendation of a militia draft was tempered by the suggestion that after four months service the men might be replaced by new levies. Congress also advised the states that those 'people, who, from religious principles cannot bear arms in any case,' be asked to contribute other type of service.[20] Reliance upon an army enlisted for only a few month duty was in many ways a hazardous expedient, but strong fears of any sort of standing army prevented Congress from adopting a plan to enroll men for a longer period. John Adams stated his belief that New England was averse to an aristocratic army in which large sums of money would be paid the officers. Roger Sherman of Connecticut declared, 'Long enlistment is a state of slavery' while James Wilson of Pennsylvania pointed out that enlistment for the duration of the war was open to question on the ground that it would create the danger of a standing army.[21]

It may seem strange that the method of fighting a revolution should have occasioned so much debate, even before the Revolution was in effect consummated by a declaration of independence. It was not to be expected that Americans, even under the duress of war, would yield their old colonial prejudices against a standing army. An important argument for independence had been that it would free the American people from involvement in the wars of Europe and from the necessity of helping to support a British army. The Declaration of Independence itself contained the well-known provisions asserting that the King 'has kept among us, in times of peace, Standing Armies without the Consent of our legislature. He has affected to render the Military independent of and superior to the Civil Power.' This charge, along with the complaint of 'quartering large bodies of armed troops among us' and 'protecting them, by a mock trial, from punishment for any Murders which they should commit on the Inhabitants of these States,' was repeated in broader and more inclusive form in the various state constitutions adopted in 1776 or soon thereafter.

These new state constitutions were usually prefaced by a Declaration of Rights in which the opposition to standing armies in time of peace, the superiority of the civil over the military authority, the right of a people to freedom from having troops quartered in their homes, and the necessity of limiting the length of time for which military appropriations could be made were set forth as general principles. A provision in the Pennsylvania Constitution, which served as a model for that of other states, claimed:

> That the people have a right to bear arms for the defence of themselves and the state; and as standing armies in the time of peace are dangerous to liberty, they ought not to be kept up; And that the military should be kept under strict subordination to, and governed by, the civil power.[22]

The Virginia Declaration of Rights, drafted by George Mason, included a similarly worded resolution. The New York Constitution of 1777 exempted Quakers from militia duty upon the payment of a fee, and the New Hampshire Constitution of 1784 provided in a Bill of Rights that 'No person who is conscientiously scrupulous about the lawfulness of bearing arms, shall be compelled thereto, provided he will pay an equivalent.' Several state constitutions made some provision for conscientious objectors, and without exception restraints of one sort or another were placed upon the military office.[23]

There was also some attempt by the states to include in the draft

of the Articles of Confederation the provision that no standing
armies be kept up in time of peace. In June 1778, a time of crisi
for the Revolutionary armies, the Continental Congress received
reports from Massachusetts, New Jersey, and Pennsylvania sug
gesting limitations on the military powers of Congress under th
proposed Articles of Confederation. A memorial from the legisla
ture of New Jersey affirmed that 'A standing army, a military es
tablishment, and every appendage thereof, in time of peace, i
totally abhorrent from the ideas and principles of this State.' Re
minding Congress of the attack upon standing armies written int
the Declaration of Independence, the memorial concluded wit
the wish that 'the Liberties and happiness of the people may by th
confederation be carefully and explicitly guarded in this respect
Massachusetts took much the same stand as New Jersey, and Penn
sylvania suggested that the states be allowed to withhold a part o
their militia from the central government.[24] Congress, howeve
was ill-disposed to consider any changes that might further dela
the presentation of the Articles to the States, and all proposals fo
amendments were voted down. It is important to note that a
though the power to establish a standing army in peacetime wa
not denied to Congress under the Articles, neither was it specifi
cally granted, and this question was raised again after the wa
when Congress turned to consider the problem of a peacetim
army.[25]

During 1777 and 1778 much dissatisfaction was expressed i
Congress and in the states over the course of the war. In large par
this was a natural result of the decline in revolutionary enthusias
after the exciting events of 1775 and 1776. Despite the encourag
ment of large bounties, it became difficult for the states to fill the
militia quotas. Although a militia draft was authorized by Co
gress, and by some of the states, it was a highly distasteful measur
Thomas Jefferson, writing to John Adams in May 1777, declared '
ever was the most unpopular and impracticable thing that cou
be attempted.' To avoid a draft some Massachusetts towns raise
money for bounties by taxation or sought permission to hire me
from outside the community. The wealthier class generally pr
ferred hiring substitutes, despite the cry raised against this pra
tice.[26]

Once in the Continental army, the American soldier was often too deeply imbued with revolutionary ideas of individual liberty and equalitarian democracy to take kindly to strict military discipline. This leveling spirit interfered with distinctions in rank and hindered the development of an officer caste. An even more serious threat to the maintenance of any army was the prevalence of desertion and mutiny among the soldiers. The extreme hardships and privations suffered by the army throughout the Revolution help to explain the large number of such incidents which occurred in the years from 1777 to 1783. At the same time the American distaste for organized military life must have been an additional motivating factor in the breakdown of morale and discipline.[27]

The reluctance of Congress and the states to provide a more efficient military establishment, despite the perilous nature of the revolutionary cause, was a continual reminder of the strength of the popular opposition to any concentration of power in the hands of military men. This feeling expressed itself most frequently in a jealousy of standing armies, but during the Revolution it was also exemplified in the concern of civilian leaders lest they become subordinate to some form of military authority or even, perhaps, to outright military dictatorship. In the several states, army commanders were almost immediately involved in disputes with civil authorities touching upon the matter of supplies, test oaths, and control of the militia. At first, local Committees of Safety and later, wartime governors and legislatures, filled with a distrust of military power, resisted any encroachment upon their prerogatives. Although under officers were apt to be insolent, Washington and most of the general officers were respectful and aware of the importance of securing state co-operation and assistance in meeting the needs of the Continental army. In return the state governors often lent aid more readily to Continental officers than to Congress itself.[28]

The clashes between civil and military authorities in the states were paralleled by an even more serious antagonism between Congress and the army. Washington himself was careful to respect the wishes of Congress, but he never ceased to complain of what he felt to be its inadequate military policy. While his army was in retreat in the fall of 1776, he sent several emphatic letters to Congress.[29] In December that body, with Philadelphia threatened by a probable British attack, granted Washington dictatorial powers for six months. Later there was a disposition in the Continental Congress to minimize this abrogation of its authority; and the members never ceased to be on guard against any possible usurpation of powers by military personnel. Early in 1777, when a motion was presented in Congress to refer to Washington for advice in the appointment of three major generals, Benjamin Rush made a sarcastic notation in his diary that, if the motion were passed, he would 'move immediately afterwards that all the civil power of the continent may be transferred from our hands into the hands of the army, and that they may be proclaimed the highest power of the people.' [30] John Adams at this time expressed dissatisfaction with the number of officers holding the rank of general, and while he did not include Washington, he wrote that many others were incompetent and 'I wish they would all resign. For my part I will vote upon the genuine principles of a republic for a new election of general officers annually.' [31]

By the winter of 1777–8, Washington's dwindling army was in danger of falling apart, a prey to dissension, maladministration and the severe winter at Valley Forge. New recruits were impossible to secure, and Washington was forced to urge repeatedly that Congress lengthen the term of enlistment and secure from the states some form of an effective militia draft. Congress, mindful of popular hostility to both of these measures, sought some compromise. Following the report of a committee that visited the army at Valley Forge early in 1778, it resolved that the states, except in cases where they were actually menaced by invasion, should be required to fill their quotas in the Continental army by a draft from their militia forces. All persons so conscripted were to serve nine months, although the states were advised to secure enlistments for the longer term of three years or for the duration of the war. As soon as voluntary recruits from the respective states joined the army, those drafted from the militia were to be discharged. This Congressional recommendation accomplished little, and some members at once predicted opposition in the states. Washington never yielded his preference for longer enlistments but by 178 here was a countermovement in Congress, led by Robert R. Livingston and John Penn, to reduce the size of the army.[32]

As the period of active hostilities gave way to the armed truce that succeeded the American and French victory at Yorktown, the attention of Congress and the country was diverted to a consideration of the problems of peace and demobilization. Americans could pride themselves on the fact that they had fought the Revolution and made good their independence without the sacrifice of the ideals and interests that had originally inspired them to break away from the mother country. The lack of military efficiency, of which Washington and the other commanders often complained, had been more than compensated by the preservation of popular liberties and civil procedures of government. The argument that the Revolution could have been effected more readily by a regular army of trained conscripts overlooks the fact that the Americans of 1776 were not willing to exchange a British yoke for one of their own contriving. Thus the colonial aversion to a vast military machine, which was an important part of the English heritage transmitted to America, was in turn strengthened by the revolt against the mother country.

II

The Founding Fathers
Reaffirm Civil Supremacy

THE PERIOD AFTER the American Revolution marked the young republic's first venture in demobilization. In the brief span of years stretching from the Treaty of Paris to the ratification of the new Constitution, military questions occupied a conspicuous place among the problems facing the new nation. Radicals and conservatives waged a sharp struggle for political power. In general, the conservative upper classes favored the creation of a highly centralized government with a strong military establishment under national rather than state control. Radical groups, in contrast, wanted to keep political and military authority within the states and they favored a militia as against a regular standing army.[1]

Conservative dismay at such evidences of continued revolution as Shays' Rebellion was paralleled by an equal concern on the part of radical and popular groups lest they be subjected to a counterrevolution of discontented and politically ambitious army officers. These officers, clamoring for their pensions, could lend material support to the conservative business and mercantile classes' demand for a government strong enough to pay its debts. Thus, apprehensive of a popular uprising of penniless veterans, and alarmed at the pretensions of an influential officer caste, it is easy to see why the American feeling of gratitude toward those who had fought the Revolution gave way after 1783 to distrust and suspicion.

With the Revolution at an end, the wartime problem of raising an army was succeeded by the question of how to disband an ill-paid and dissatisfied body of soldiers who insisted that they should not be discharged until the states had granted pensions and separation allowances. Alexander Hamilton, noting the danger of keeping an army together in a state of inactivity, pointed out that unless the states complied with a requisition for funds from Congress, the country would be faced with 'a standing army during peace.' The attitude of the debt-ridden states was expressed in a letter to Congress from the Massachusetts legislature. The legislature, desirous of carrying out the measures of Congress, and not insensible to the bravery and sufferings of the soldiers 'wished that they may return to the bosom of their country, under such circumstances, as may place them in the most agreeable light with their fellow-citizens.' [2]

The pension demands of the Revolutionary army officers, as distinct from those of the common soldiers, attracted more attention and also greater opposition. The officers concentrated upon a proposal for half pay for life, to which Washington had persuaded a reluctant Congress to agree in October 1780.[3] Disappointed after the war by the failure of Congress to raise sufficient revenue for carrying out this provision, various officers took matters in their own hands. For example, in 1783, General Nathanael Greene, still commanding in South Carolina, in a letter to the governor, argued the case of the financial needs of the army and advised against any state interference with Congressional efforts to secure the requisite funds. When this letter was referred to the South Carolina legislature, that body promptly rebuked Greene for his intervention and charged him with aspiring to become another Cromwell.[4]

More serious was the scheme popular with certain groups of officers to establish a monarchy in the United States. In 1782, Colonel Lewis Nicola wrote to Washington suggesting that he lead an army revolt and make himself king. Then, in the spring of 1783, an anonymous petition was circulated among the officers at Newburgh. This petition contained a veiled threat to overthrow Congress and substitute some sort of military dictatorship or monarchy headed, if possible, by Washington himself. The real danger of such a plan, nourished by the prevailing discontent in the army, was largely removed by the rebuke to those involved which Washington delivered in his celebrated Newburgh Address.[5] Washington also enclosed a full report of the affair to Congress, where James Madison commented that 'The steps taken by the General to avert the gathering storm & his professions of inflexible adherence to his duty to Congress & to his Country, excited the most affectionate sentiments toward him.' Despite the strong opposition of the New England states, Congress on 22 March 1783, a few days after the Newburgh Address, passed an act commuting its earlier provision of half pay for life to full pay for a period of five years.[6]

Washington in his 'Farewell Order to the Armies of the United States' recommended that, despite any seeming injustices suffered by the veterans of the Revolution, 'they should carry with them into civil society the most conciliating dispositions; and that they should prove themselves not less virtuous and useful as Citizens, than they have been persevering and victorious as Soldiers.' Tendering his resignation to Congress on 23 December 1783, Washington received their congratulations in person and was commended by Elias Boudinot, the President of Congress, for having 'conducted the great military contest with wisdom and fortitude, invariably regarding the rights of the civil power through all disasters and changes.' [7]

Washington's resignation and exemplary words of advice to his troops were a concrete expression of his own desire to cast aside the trappings of the soldier and return to the peaceful pursuits of civilian life. While he retired gladly to Mount Vernon, his countrymen turned to the postwar problems besetting the Confederation. In these years after 1783, two questions especially stirred the antimilitary feelings of the people. The one concerned the power of the government to establish and maintain a peacetime army, and the other was related to the founding of the Society of the Cincinnati.

As early as April 1783, Congress appointed a committee to draw up plans for a peacetime military establishment. To Alexander

Hamilton, chairman of this committee, Washington sent his 'Sentiments on a Peace Establishment,' recommending a small regular army for the frontier and a well-regulated militia. He renewed his advice in a personal appearance before Congress and also in a circular letter addressed to the governors of the states. A large standing army Washington represented as unnecessary and impossible 'without great oppression of the people,' while the militia, in contrast to his wartime criticism, was referred to 'as the Palladium of our security.' In his suggestions for a militia force Washington went farther than most of his contemporaries by advocating regular training, uniform arms, and the instilling of a military spirit among the youth of the nation.[8]

The idea of any sort of a regular army in peacetime at once met with strong opposition in Congress. James Madison, another member of the committee appointed by Congress to look into such an establishment, was uncertain that Congress had the necessary powers. James Monroe, Madison's fellow delegate from Virginia, wrote Richard Henry Lee that the question of a peace establishment to meet the threat of a war in the West might lead 'to the ingrafting a principle in our constitution which may in its consequences, as it ever hath done with other powers, terminate in the loss of our liberty.' To this Lee replied that a standing army always abrogated the liberties of a people. 'It has not only *been* constantly so, but I think it clear from the construction of human nature, that it will always *be* so.' The report of the Hamilton committee, however, interpreted the Articles of Confederation as giving Congress the power to set up a peacetime standing army. At the same time, it urged that Congress should not overlook the militia and the advantages of giving it a uniform organization and training, while it added that military academies and a general staff were unnecessary.[9]

In May 1784, Congress debated the practical question of whether to enlist an army of 896 men for three years service defending the frontiers, each state contributing its fair share. Amended to require only 450 men, the plan was still defeated, and instead Congress agreed to call out 700 militia from Connecticut, Pennsylvania, New York, and New Jersey for the purposes of taking over the British forts in the Northwest, and of protecting the frontier against Indian attack. This plan was adopted over the negative votes of New York and New Jersey, two of the four states whose militia was involved. Then, on 2 June, Congress voted to discharge all armed forces except 25 privates at Fort Pitt and 58 more at West Point, as well as an appropriate number of officers. None of the latter was to be above the rank of captain.[10]

Congress's fear of a standing army was shared by other prominent Revolutionary leaders in the postwar period. From Paris, Thomas Jefferson wrote to his friend James Monroe that the Confederation must have some power of coercion. For this, he preferred a naval force which 'can never endanger our liberties, nor occasion bloodshed; a land force would do both.'[11] Benjamin Franklin also adjusted very quickly to the ways of peace. Justice, he felt, was due between nations as clearly as between individuals. The tradition that military men by the nature of their calling were not allowed to question the rightness of a war, Franklin believed, led to tyranny and, in the case of the common soldier, to a servitude worse than that of a Negro slave. The conscientious officer might resign 'rather than be employ'd in an unjust War; but the private Men are Slaves for Life.' Even the supposed advantages of war might be gained more cheaply with money, for an army was 'a devouring monster.'[12]

In the midst of this general postwar revulsion against all military pretensions, a group of Revolutionary army officers in the spring of 1783 launched the Society of the Cincinnati and thus fanned the flames of antimilitarist sentiment in the American states. Baron von Steuben and Major General Henry Knox, who wished to see some honorary award granted to those who had fought in the cause of independence, were the chief authors of the idea, while George Washington was prevailed upon to become president of the new organization. Almost at once the Society was criticized as an attempt to establish the former Revolutionary officers as a hereditary aristocracy, and the volume of protest soon reached impressive proportions.[13] The most systematic of these early attacks upon the Cincinnati came from the pen of Aedanus Burke, one of the Chief Justices of South Carolina and himself a veteran of the Revolution. Published late in 1783 under the pen name Cassius, Burke's pamphlet attracted much attention and undoubtdly stimulated the popular outcry against the Society. Although he American people as a whole had fought in the Revolution, Burke pointed out that the Cincinnati would commemorate only he officer class. Recalling the fate of Rome and the examples of Caesar and Cromwell, Burke asserted his belief 'that military commanders acquiring fame, and accustomed to receive the obedience of armies, are generally in their hearts aristocrats, and enemies to the popular equality of a republic.' [14]

In Europe as well as in America the Cincinnati was looked upon as an anomalous institution and a strange departure from the declared ideals of the new nation. At home, its opponents included he two Adamses, Elbridge Gerry, John Jay, and Thomas Jefferson. Jefferson, for example, believed it an undemocratic institution, incompatible with the Revolutionary spirit of liberty and equality. It emphasized the military as a separate caste, so that 'a distinction is kept up between the civil & military, which it is for the happiness of both to obliterate.' [15] Washington, who was especially influenced by Jefferson's criticism, took pains to explain to him his reasons for accepting the presidency of the Society. Although he felt popular fears unwarranted, like Jefferson he did not wish to see a line drawn between military men and their fellow citizens. At the first general meeting of the Cincinnati in Philadelphia in 784, Washington suggested fundamental changes in its constitution. These were designed to keep the Society out of politics, to remove the hereditary feature of membership, to admit no more honorary members, to place its funds under the supervision of the state legislatures, and to discontinue the general meetings. The delegates themselves testified to the widespread suspicion and fear of the Cincinnati entertained by the plain people. Reports of this popular terror were made by both Washington and Knox for their states of Virginia and Massachusetts. In the latter state, the General Court passed resolutions condemning the Society, and in Rhode Island and North Carolina there were movements to deprive members of the franchise or right to hold office. In Connecticut the state Society was unable to secure a charter from the legislature.[16]

While the furor over the Cincinnati may seem, in retrospect, to have been exaggerated, it did serve the good purpose of dramatizing, as nothing else could have, the importance of subordinating the military to the civil power. At the time of its founding, the Society was a potential vehicle for conservative military elements, but three years later, when its triennial general meeting at Philadelphia coincided with the Constitutional Convention, the Cincinnati had already lost much of its original political force, although its members comprised as much as half the delegates to the Convention.

In the Constitutional Convention, which began its work on 25 May 1787, there was little direct discussion of military affairs until the middle of August, although at the outset an attack was made upon the deficiencies of the Articles of Confederation in time of war. Edmund Randolph, in his speech presenting the Virginia Plan, drafted by his fellow delegate James Madison, urged that the central government be given authority to raise a regular army exclusive of militia or volunteers. Randolph, mindful of the unhappy Revolutionary experience, explained: '*Draughts* stretch the string of government too violently to be adopted. Nothing short of a regular military force will answer the end of war, and this only to be created and supported by money.' [17] Because of the weaknesses of the Articles, the Convention periodically discussed the practicability of using force against a state to compel its compliance with federal laws. Madison, Hamilton, and others, however, opposed as unrealistic the notion that the federal government could coerce the states through the exercise of superior force.[18] Instead, by enabling the federal government to act directly upon citizens as individuals, the danger of military coercion would be diminished.

The general opposition of the people to anything that resembled military domination was illustrated in the Constitutional Convention by the attempt to circumscribe both the President's control of the army and navy and his influence in deciding the question of peace or war. The Convention, although it desired to endow the President with authority to enforce the laws, was greatly concerned at the possibility of executive usurpation. To satisfy the general feeling that the power of the purse and the sword should never be concentrated in the same hands military affairs were divided between the Congress, which was to provide funds for an army, and the President who would be commander in chief. A hough permitted to call out the militia to repel invasion, the President, despite some sentiment to the contrary, was denied the right o declare war, that power being lodged in both houses of Congress. Debating this question, Elbridge Gerry of Massachusetts leclared that he 'never expected to hear in a republic a motion to mpower the Executive alone to declare war.' And George Mason of Virginia asserted that neither the President nor the Senate was o be trusted. 'He was for clogging rather than facilitating war; but or facilitating peace.' [19]

The power to declare war presumed authority to raise an army. uch authority was less readily conceded to Congress than some f its other powers, and the discussion of the question also emphasized anew the traditional Anglo-American hostility to the maintenance of a standing army in time of peace. Early in the Convention, James Madison warned the small states that if they continued o think in terms of the security of each individual state, their nutual rivalries would drive them to the introduction of large nilitary forces patterned after the example of Europe. He then vent on to picture the final results of such a policy:

> In time of actual war, great discretionary powers are constantly given to the Executive Magistrate. Constant apprehension of War, has the same tendency to render the head too large for the body. A standing military force, with an overgrown Executive will not long be safe companions to liberty. The means of defense agst. foreign danger, have been always the instruments of tyranny at home. Among the Romans it was a standing maxim to excite a war, whenever a revolt was apprehended. Throughout all Europe, the armies kept up under the pretext of defending, have enslaved the people.[20]

n 18 August, Luther Martin of Maryland and Elbridge Gerry ffered a motion to amend and limit the power of Congress to raise n army by the addition of a clause providing that 'in time of peace he army shall not consist of more than —— thousand men.' 'his motion was defeated, and the Convention then turned to ebate the relationship of the state militia to the federal government.[21]

Among the advocates of federal regulation and discipline of the nilitia were men like George Mason who hoped in this way to

avoid the creation of a standing army. Unlike Mason, most of those
who feared a standing army also raised objections to the establishment of a uniform system of militia training and discipline under
federal control. The Convention itself provided that the President
should command the militia only 'when called into the actual service of the United States.' The appointment of officers and training
of the men, subject to rules prescribed by the United States, was
reserved to the states, and an amendment by Madison to permit
the states to appoint only those officers below the rank of general
was rejected.[22]

One other endeavor to constrain the military power should be
mentioned. This was part of an effort to add to the Constitution a
bill of rights, and with that in mind, Charles Pinckney of South
Carolina on 20 August made a motion to submit to the Committee
of Detail a series of propositions stating that the liberty of the press
shall be preserved, that the writ of habeas corpus shall not be
suspended except by the legislature and then only in time of pressing need and for a limited period, and that:

> No Troops shall be kept up in time of peace, but by consent of
> the Legislature.
> The military shall always be subordinate to the civil power, and
> no grants of money shall be made by the Legislature for support-
> ing military land forces for more than one year at a time.
> No Soldier shall be quartered in any house in time of peace with-
> out consent of the Owner.

Although no action was taken on the Pinckney proposal, the Convention on 5 September, as an amendment to the clause empowering Congress to raise and support an army, added the words: 'But
no appropriation of money to that use shall be for a longer term
than two years.'[23]

Three members of the Convention who refused to sign the final
draft of the Constitution, Edmund Randolph, George Mason, and
Elbridge Gerry, gave as one of their reasons its failure to set any
limitation on a standing army.[24] In other respects the document
was not unsatisfactory to opponents of a strong military establishment. Civil control was emphasized in the provision that the President shall be commander in chief of the army and navy. Congress
controlled military appropriations, which were also limited to two

years, and the authority to declare war was lodged with the two houses of Congress in the hope of insuring that so grave a decision would always rest upon the popular will. The lack of more specific limitations, such as might be included in a bill of rights, plus the failure to prohibit a standing army in time of peace, were viewed as the two chief defects of the Constitution from the antimilitarist point of view. Both of these matters were brought up again in the contest over ratification of the Constitution by the states.

In the state ratifying conventions, considerable apprehension was expressed over the clauses of the Constitution relating to standing armies, Congressional control of the state militia, and personal command of the army by the President. Pennsylvania, one of the first states to complete ratification, saw these issues vigorously debated in the newspaper press, where anti-Federalist editors and correspondents attacked the authorization of a standing army and the improper safeguards for the rights of the Quakers and other sects that objected to bearing arms.[25] In Massachusetts, where the ratifying vote was especially close, the arguments against the Constitution in contemporary newspapers and pamphlets complained of the dangers of a standing army and of centralized military control. Samuel Nason, a member of the state convention, recalled that when 'Britain attempted to enforce her arbitrary measures by a standing army,' she had been thwarted by the resolute Massachusetts and colonial patriots. 'What occasion have we for standing armies?' he inquired. 'We fear no foe. If one should come upon us, we have a militia, which is our bulwark. . . . A standing army! Was it not with this that Caesar passed the *Rubicon*, and laid prostrate the liberties of his country?'[26]

Several states ratified the Constitution only after adopting resolutions or amendments calling for changes in some of the clauses pertaining to military affairs. New Hampshire, New York, North Carolina, and Rhode Island all urged that some limits be placed upon the power of Congress to raise a standing army in time of peace. North Carolina and Rhode Island in identical resolutions also suggested: 'That any person religiously scrupulous of bearing arms ought to be exempted, upon payment of an equivalent to employ another to bear arms in his stead.' Rhode Island, where the Quakers and advocates of state rights were strong, further proposed an amendment to the Constitution to provide: 'That no person shall be compelled to do military duty otherwise than by voluntary enlistment, except in cases of general invasion. . . .' [27]

Virginia, the tenth state to ratify the federal Constitution, was also the scene of the most thorough debate of its provisions. In the Old Dominion, opponents of the Constitution included such outstanding Revolutionary figures as Richard Henry Lee, George Mason, and Patrick Henry. Lee, early in October 1787, published a widely read series of letters containing his observations on the late Convention. Unlike *The Federalist*, Lee's *Letters* were printed in time to have a considerable effect on the debate over the Constitution. They are, perhaps, the best contemporary expression of the opposition to the Constitution. In his third letter, Lee gave an able analysis of his reasons for opposing certain of its military clauses. Because the central government had the power of taxation, its military powers were rendered all the more dangerous. Once an army was raised, it would not be difficult, he predicted despite the two-year limit on appropriations, to secure from Congress the necessary funds to keep it on a permanent basis. Many men in America were already fond of the idea of a standing army, the officering of which would provide an agreeable place of employment for young gentlemen. Admitting the necessity of lodging the power to raise armies somewhere in the government, he argued that it should not reside exclusively in Congress without some check on the part of the people. Also, it was undoubtedly desirable that the government should try to administer its laws fairly and honestly without resorting to an expensive army.[28]

The Virginia convention itself, meeting in June 1788, heard Patrick Henry and George Mason deliver long attacks on the principle of standing armies. Henry declared that 'Congress, by the power of taxation, by that of raising an army, and by their control over the militia, have the sword in one hand, and the purse in the other. Shall we be safe without either?' Mason especially desired some restrictions on federal control over the state militia, a body which he believed the central government, under the existing Constitution, would find the means to destroy. James Madison, replying to Mason, agreed that 'a standing army is one of the greatests mischiefs that can possibly happen,' but he concluded

The most effectual way to render it unnecessary, is to give the general government full power to call forth the militia, and exert the whole natural strength of the Union, when necessary.' Madison's answer gave Patrick Henry the opportunity to ask why the federal government needed the power to raise a standing army if it also had full authority over the militia. 'It demands a power, and denies the probability of its exercise. There are suspicions of power on one hand, and absolute and unlimited confidence on the other. I hope to be one of those who have a large share of suspicion.' [29]

After a month's debate, the Virginia convention ratified the Constitution by the close vote of 89 to 79, proposing at the same time amendments to the Constitution in the form of a bill of rights, reminiscent of its own state Declaration of Rights drafted in 1776 by George Mason. The Virginia suggestions for a bill of rights included a declaration attacking a peacetime standing army as dangerous to liberty, and favoring a militia as 'the proper, natural, and safe defence of a free state.' No soldiers were to be quartered on the inhabitants in time of peace, and conscientious objectors to military service were to be exempted upon the payment of an equivalent fee. A separate amendment affirmed, 'That each state respectively shall have the power to provide for organizing, arming, and disciplining its own militia, whensoever Congress shall omit or neglect to provide for the same.' [30]

Thomas Jefferson, the most famous of the Virginians who had not played a role in either the drafting or ratification of the new Constitution, listed among the features that he disliked the omission of a bill of rights with 'protection against standing armies.' [31] In his desire to see a bill of rights added to the Constitution, he expressed a general feeling which won increasing acceptance, even among those who had originally felt such a measure superfluous. In the first session of Congress, James Madison introduced a series of amendments to the federal Constitution. Included among these Madison amendments was a proposal to insert in Article I Section 9 of the Constitution a provision guaranteeing freedom of conscience:

> The civil rights of none shall be abridged on account of religious belief or worship. . . .

> The right of the people to keep and bear arms shall not be infringed; a well armed and well regulated militia being the best security of a free country; but no person religiously scrupulous of bearing arms shall be compelled to render military service in person.

Although this amendment failed in the Senate and was never adopted in its entirety as a part of the Bill of Rights, it is worthy of note that it passed the House of Representatives by the close margin of two votes.[32]

New York, the last of the states to ratify the Constitution except for North Carolina and Rhode Island, furnished the setting for the publication of the celebrated *Federalist* papers, in which Alexander Hamilton and his fellow contributors, James Madison and John Jay, sought to refute the anti-Federalist arguments. Hamilton's defense of the military provisions of the Constitution is especially interesting. In his discussion Hamilton showed that he was aware of the need of conciliating the strong antimilitarist sentiments of the people, and traced back these feelings to the Glorious Revolution in England, and to the Americans' own experiences in the late Revolution. Throughout *The Federalist*, Hamilton, repeating Madison's argument in the Convention against the possibility or desirability of coercing individual states, emphasized the point that a strong government would prevent both foreign and internecine wars. On the other hand, a combination of strong state militias, together with state rivalries and the weak central government of the Confederation, would lead inevitably to civil war and foreign attack.[33]

Defending the value of a standing army as against an untrained militia, Hamilton was careful to stress the fact that the Constitution did not create such a force. Moreover, the ability of Congress to raise an army was confined by the two-year limit to its appropriations. Hamilton also took advantage of the popular aversion to standing armies to gain support for the provision of the Constitution that gave the federal government the authority to train and discipline the militia. Finally, he pointed out that the ability of Congress to raise a standing army was limited by the as yet meager financial resources of the country, 'and as the means of doing this increase, the population and natural strength of the community will proportionally increase,' thus providing an automatic check against any possible military tyranny.[34]

Madison joined Hamilton's literary efforts in *The Federalist*, arguing that every government must have the means of defense. The Constitution, he believed, established a just balance in the matter of raising an army. Although the legions of Rome had made her mistress of the world, still it was not the less true, he warned

> that the liberties of Rome proved the final victim to her military triumphs; and that the liberties of Europe, as far as they ever existed, have, with few exceptions, been the price of her military establishments. A standing force, therefore, is a dangerous, at the same time that it may be a necessary, provision. On the smallest scale it has its inconveniences. On an extensive scale its consequences may be fatal. On any scale it is an object of laudable circumspection and precaution.[35]

The authors of *The Federalist* thus assured their readers that the new Constitution provided satisfactory safeguards against the dangers of a standing army. Although Hamilton and others maintained that a well-trained militia would make such a force unneeded, after the Constitution was adopted, its staunchest supporters readily forgot the interpretation of the document that they had offered in the heat of the struggle for ratification. While the proponents of a strong centralized government lost no time in presenting to Congress their plans for a regular military establishment, the anti-Federalist opponents of the Constitution united to prevent the creation of a standing army.

Debate on this issue would presently occupy the attention of the new Congress. However the First Congress decided the question of a militia versus a standing army, at least the founding fathers at Philadelphia had carefully provided that the military power be kept subordinate to civil control. There is much point to the conclusion of an eminent historian that the 'Leaders among the framers of the Constitution regarded the resort to constitutional government instead of a military dictatorship as their greatest triumph.'[36]

III

The Defeat of the Federalis

Military Plans

As THE FIRST President of the United States, George Washingto
was head of a government in which, on questions of militar
policy as well as on other issues, there was increasing divergenc
between Federalists and Republicans. The Federalists, proponent
of a strong centralized government, wished to see the nation:
power supported by a well-disciplined army of trained men, an
as the party of the commercial seaboard region, they also desire
a naval establishment to protect and encourage American oversea
trade. Their Republican opponents, deriving their political suppo:
primarily from the agricultural areas of the interior, viewed
permanent army or navy as instruments chiefly for the benefit (
the merchant and trader class. Furthermore, a large standing arm
could be used to coerce the separate states and to augment th
powers of the national government.

Between the Federalists and the Republicans, Washington :
first attempted to pursue an impartial course, but his sympathie
were clearly with the Federalist element within his administratio
This was especially the case in all matters of army or navy polic
On this subject Washington had already expressed himself in h

Sentiments on a Peace Establishment,' which he had presented to the Continental Congress in 1783. Introduced in Congress as a measure to create a regular army and to bring the state militia under federal control, Washington's scheme had been rejected along with the more comprehensive plans drawn up by Generals Steuben and Knox.[1]

In his capacity as President of the new national government, Washington was somewhat reluctant to enter into the direct discussion of military matters, preferring rather to voice his opinions through friends and cabinet officers, especially Alexander Hamilton and Henry Knox. In 1789, Secretary of War Knox, with the full support of Hamilton as well as of the President, drew up a new project for organizing the militia. When introducing his design for the militia, Knox set forth the desirability of having some republican system of defense to counter the standing armies of Europe. 'An energetic national militia is to be regarded as the *capital security* of a free republic, and not a standing army, forming a distinct class in the community.' [2] Knox also placed much stress on the obligation of all male citizens to perform some military service, even though as a practical matter, since all those eligible could not be trained in arms, his plan divided the militia into classes. The ones in the youngest age group, from eighteen to twenty years, were to receive an advanced course of military drill which, Knox asserted, 'will at the same time mould the minds of the young men to a due obedience of the laws.' Knox similarly believed the training of this age group was desirable because:

> Youth is the time for the State to avail itself of those services which it has a right to demand and by which it is to be invigorated and preserved. In this season the passions and affections are strongly influenced by the splendor of military parade. The impressions the mind receives will be retained through life.[3]

Despite Washington's repeated recommendations, Congress was slow to take positive action regarding Knox's plan. In December 1790, a bill 'to establish a uniform militia throughout the United States' was debated in the House of Representatives, but the members were suspicious of the measure and desired to limit its extent. Considerable discussion was directed toward the question of

whether Quakers and other religious groups opposed to war should
be required to pay fines in lieu of military service. Aedanus Burke
of South Carolina reasoned that it was not 'consonant with the
principles of justice to make those conscientiously scrupulous of
bearing arms pay for not acting against the voice of their con
science.' James Jackson of Georgia, a strong advocate of the state
militia, in reply to Burke raised the question of how to decide
'what persons were really conscientiously scrupulous.' Even if the
exemption were confined to Quakers, he feared 'that the opera
tion of this privilege would be to make the whole community turn
Quakers.' James Madison, seconded by Roger Sherman of Con
necticut, proposed the insertion of an amendment to the Militia
Act specifically exempting 'persons conscientiously scrupulous of
bearing arms.' 'It is the glory of our country,' he asserted, 'that a
more sacred regard to the rights of mankind is preserved than has
heretofore been known.' Throughout the period when Congress
was considering this first Militia Act, the Quakers themselves sent
numerous petitions to Congress, praying to be relieved of militia
duties or any penalties on that account.[4]

Although the Madison motion was tabled, the Militia Act that
finally passed Congress in April 1792 was an extremely mild meas
ure which left the matters of training, discipline, and exemption
to the states and failed to include the Knox scheme of a classifica
tion by age groups. Lacking this last feature and also requiring
individuals to furnish their own arms, the act did not provide a
workable basis for any system of compulsory service or training,
and it added little to the nominal service traditionally required
of the citizen militia in England and the American colonies. All
further attempts of the Washington administration and of the
military element in Congress to strengthen federal control of the
militia and to provide some sort of systematic training or draft
proved fruitless.[5]

The situation with respect to a trained militia was equally un
satisfactory in the states, although, in response to the federal act of
1792, the various states gradually passed their own militia laws.
These measures, which in part complied with the federal law,
were calculated to interfere as little as possible with normal civil
life. For example, the Virginia law, first state measure to be

enacted, required the militia to meet once every three months, but exemptions were numerous and included all ministers, professors, and Quakers.[6] On the evidence of actual legislation, both federal and state, it seems reasonable to conclude that the people were disinclined to accept the Washington and Knox pleas for pre-paredness by means of an effective militia system.

Somewhat more successful were the efforts of the Federalists to raise a standing army. In January 1790, the same month in which Washington submitted his militia plan, Secretary of War Knox appeared before Congress with a confidential report from the President urging that an army of five thousand men be raised to resist the depredations of the Creek Indians along the southern frontier. The previous year Congress had authorized the continu-ance of the small army of 840 men and 46 officers inherited from the Confederation, but this force Knox now proposed to increase more than six times.[7] Knox's measure, despite pressure on its behalf by the Washington administration, met with either indiffer-ence or opposition in Congress. In the Senate, where the numbers called for were immediately reduced to 1600, William Maclay of Pennsylvania 'spoke against the whole bill as an egg from which a standing army would be hatched.' With regard to a report that the Spanish were stirring up the Southwest Indians, Maclay com-mented: 'New phantoms for the day must be created.' [8] Although not able to defeat the bill, Maclay and his colleagues in the Senate were successful in further reducing the authorized size of the army to 1,216 men and 57 officers, a total figure not far above that of the army of the Confederation, and much below Knox's request for five thousand men.

In the course of the Senate debate in 1790, Maclay had pre-dicted: 'Give Knox his army, and he will soon have a war on hand.' This expectation was presently realized when Washington in 1791 informed Congress that 'offensive operations' had been taken against the Indians on the western frontiers.[9] The President and Secretary Knox again requested Congress to provide a larger military establishment. The House of Representatives, debating a bill to increase the army by three regiments, listened to a bitter attack upon every aspect of the administration's Indian policy. The advantages of westward extension were questioned, the whites were accused of despoiling the Indians, and the opinion was expressed that peace with the Red Men could be secured more easily and cheaply than their defeat in war. It was noted that the British had overawed the Indians in United States territory with only one thousand men, and that Washington himself had never had under his command during the Revolution more than ten thousand troops. In view of this, it appeared 'a strange policy, indeed, to raise five or six thousand men to oppose a handful of Indian banditti. . . . We are preparing to squander away money by millions; and no one, except those who are in the secrets of the Cabinet, knows for what reason the war has thus been carried on for three years.' [10] Thomas Jefferson, in discussing this legislation, ventured the opinion that '12, or 1500 woods men would soon end the war, and at a trifling expence.' [11]

.Although Knox and Washington finally received Congressional approval of their call for an army of five thousand men, it is important to note that the bill was passed following the defeat of the American armies under Generals Josiah Harmar and Arthur St. Clair. Congress had acted only under the pressure of military necessity after the executive had first launched offensive operations against the Indians. In this way, the President had helped to create a situation in which Congress was compelled to grant the increase of the army that it had earlier rejected.[12]

With the expansion of the army and passage of the Militia Act of 1792 there was a temporary lull in military affairs. Two years later, however, the attacks of Algiers pirates upon American citizens and new difficulties with England provided the basis for seeking further increases in both the army and the navy. To meet the threat of the Algerine pirates Congress created a small naval establishment of six ships. Republican opposition to this measure was allayed somewhat by a provision promising that if peace were concluded with Algiers, the navy would engage in no further activity. Not satisfied with this, Abraham Clark of New Jersey suggested that the United States hire the Portuguese navy for duty in the Mediterranean. He was against 'the establishment of a fleet because, when once it had been commenced, there would be no end of it. We must then have a Secretary of the Navy, and a swarm of other people in office, at a monstrous expense.' Sharing the view, William B. Giles of Virginia predicted: 'The sending of American armed ships into the midst of the fleets of Europe would certainly produce a quarrel.' [13]

The Federalists, though averse to war, were not unwilling to use the strained diplomatic relations with Great Britain as a pretext for securing a provisional army of ten or fifteen thousand men. Both James Madison and James Monroe wrote to Jefferson, manifesting considerable alarm lest the Federalist army bill pass Congress. Madison informed Jefferson: 'This is the 3rd or 4th effort made in the course of the Session to get a powerful military establishment, under the pretext of public danger and under the auspices of the President's popularity.' [14] Despite the fears of the Jeffersonians, the army increase was not voted by Congress, and later, after General Anthony Wayne's successes against the Northwest Indians, the authorized strength of the army was reduced to somewhat over three thousand men, a figure much smaller than that originally contemplated by the Federalist leaders.

Support for this last reduction came from Republican Congressmen, some of whom attacked the whole idea of a military establishment. Representative John Williams of New York objected to the costs of a large peacetime army, and the retention in the army of useful citizens, who would be otherwise employed in pursuits of much more benefit to the United States.' William B. Giles and John Nicholas of Virginia attacked the special provision of the army law enabling General Wayne to keep his wartime rank. Nicholas saw no use for a general in peacetime and complained of the inconsistency of the army advocates who at one time sought to make our Establishment as large as possible, and when more favorable circumstances appeared, they were not to reduce it. Where were the benefits of peace,' he asked, 'if they were still to keep up our war establishments?' [15]

This question of the size of the regular military establishment was temporarily put aside when, in the summer of 1794, the anti-army Republicans perceived that their political enemies were about to raise a vast militia force to stamp out the so-called Whiskey Rebellion along the Pennsylvania western frontier. To prevent the spread of the disorders and to overawe the Whiskey rebels, Washington, with the enthusiastic support of Alexander

Hamilton and to the embarrassment of the Jeffersonians, asked
Congress for authority to call out some twelve thousand state
militia. This step immediately aroused much suspicion and hos
tility. Thomas Mifflin, the Federalist Governor of Pennsylvania
at the outset of the disorders had advised Washington against such
a use of force. Gratified to hear that Washington regretted the
possible necessity of an appeal to arms, Mifflin wrote: 'I, too, shall
ever prefer the instruments of conciliation to those of coercion
and never, but in the last resort, countenance a dereliction of
judiciary authority, for the exertion of military force.' Past ex
perience, Mifflin felt, dictated the wisdom of pursuing a lenien
course, but if 'it is necessary to call forth the Military power for
the purpose of executing the laws, it must be shewn that the
Judicial power has in vain attempted to punish those who violate
them.' Averse to calling out his state militia, and preferring to
assemble the legislature to deal with the question, Mifflin asked
Washington: 'Will not resort to force, inflame and cement the
existing opposition?' [16]

An especial source of alarm to opponents of military coercion
were rumors of Hamilton's ambitions in connection with the
projected militia expedition against the Whiskey rebels. Although
the chief command was given to Governor Henry Lee of Virginia
Hamilton accompanied the troops in his capacity as Secretary of
the Treasury. Washington himself rode part way with the militia
and before returning to Philadelphia he warned them 'that every
officer and soldier will constantly bear in mind that he comes to
support the laws, and that it would be peculiarly unbecoming in
him to be in any way the infractor of them.' [17] Washington, by his
temperate advice, allayed somewhat the fears of the opposition
and the distrust inspired by Hamilton. James Madison, for ex
ample, in the fall of 1794 expressed the conviction that only lack
of support by Washington and some of the New Englanders pre
vented Congress from attempting to establish the principle that
large standing army was necessary to enforce the laws.[18]

The fact that militia, instead of a contingent of the regular army
was used against the Whiskey rebels was in itself a victory for
the opposition. The militiamen, moreover, were not recruited with
out difficulty, especially in frontier districts where the levie

aroused an outburst of popular resentment and of sympathy with
the rebels. Once enrolled, the militia were accused of bad conduct
along the line of their march and of meting out excessively cruel
treatment to their prisoners. William Findley, a member of the
House of Representatives from Pennsylvania and one of the
deputation that had urged Washington to withdraw the troops,
in his contemporary *History of the Insurrection* described the fear
of the western Pennsylvania people lest they be slaughtered by
the advancing soldiery. Included among the supposed victims,
Findley wrote, were those

> who had reasoned in favour of the subjection of the military to
> the civil law, or suggested that those who killed a citizen in cold
> blood should answer to the proper courts, and that the army was
> only employed to aid the Judiciary in the exercise of its proper
> functions, and not to usurp or exercise those functions them-
> selves. . . .[19]

Washington, while pleased to learn 'that the general conduct and
character of the Army has been temperate and indulgent,' warned
his officers to impress upon the men that 'they have no other
authority, than other citizens . . . and that the whole country is
not to be considered as within the limits of the camp.'[20]

The vigorous countermeasures against the Whiskey rebels
carried out by the Washington administration were in accord
with the movement toward a stronger centralized government.
Furthering that trend was the establishment of a regular army and
its use against the Indians on the frontier. On the other hand, the
military elements within the Federalist party had not been able
to detach the militia from the states nor to inaugurate the practice
of compulsory military service or training. However far in a
militarist direction a Knox or a Hamilton might have wished to
go, their ambitions had not been realized as Washington himself
refused to countenance their more extravagant schemes. In his
Farewell Address at the close of his Presidency, he advised the
American people that by a policy of peace, at home and abroad,
they will avoid the necessity of those overgrown military establishments which, under any form of government, are inauspicious to
liberty, and which are to be regarded as particularly hostile to
republican liberty.'[21]

This valedictory advice, as the American people presently dis
covered, was not always easy to follow. In its foreign relations
the young republic became more and more involved in seriou
difficulties with both England and France. At home the bitte
struggles of the Federalists and their Jeffersonian antagonists soo
found a parallel in the private strife of the Federalists within th
Adams administration. This quarrel between the Adams and Ham
ilton factions was in large part a result of their conflicting view
in regard to a proper military and foreign policy for the Unite
States.

In the course of the effort to protect American neutral right
from violation by both Great Britain and France, America cam
close to war during the 1790s. In 1794, threatened hostilities wit
England were averted only by the unsatisfactory Jay Treaty. Thi
agreement contributed in turn to the deterioration in United State
relations with France, and by 1798 the situation had reached th
point of an undeclared naval war. The prospects of such a conflic
were especially abhorrent to the Jeffersonian Republicans, wh
had sympathized with France in its struggle against Europe, an
who were also against a policy of large-scale military or nava
preparedness. In contrast to the Jeffersonians, the Federalist
overwhelmingly pro-English and conservative in their feeling
were not averse to the idea of a United States war upon Revolu
tionary France. Alexander Hamilton led that faction of the Fed
eralist party which saw, in the possibility of a foreign war, an op
portunity to secure from Congress the creation of a larger army
Such a force, whether or not it was needed for war purposes, migh
prove useful in connection with the Federalist sedition legislatio
that was being invoked against the Democratic-Republican so
cieties and other opponents of the government's policies. A larg
army raised by Congress would also help to set a precedent fo
federal control of the militia and would make further inroads upo
the military powers of the states.[22]

No less threatening from a Republican point of view wer
Federalist plans for strengthening the navy. Jeffersonian Republi
cans from the interior of the country believed that a large nav
force was an aggressive instrument which, instead of providin
protection for the United States, would provoke Europe to coun

eraction and war. Of economic advantage only to the Eastern seaboard, a navy would prove a heavy tax burden upon the rest of the United States. Accordingly Congress, despite the imminent danger of war with France in 1798, almost defeated the creation of a separate Navy Department. The first report of the new Secretary of the Navy, suggesting the political advantages of naval expenditures, did little to allay this Republican resentment. Rendered temporarily powerless by the outbreak of the naval war with France, the opposition was able after the war to accomplish the defeat of the Federalist plans for naval expansion.[23] The Virginia state legislature in 1799 attacked a navy as of little use to the country, and in Congress Albert Gallatin expressed alarm 'at the idea of creating a navy with a view of throwing our weight into the political scales of Europe.' [24]

In addition to strengthening the navy in 1798, President Adams recommended a series of some twenty measures affecting the army. Eighty thousand militia, detached from state control, were to be held in a state of war-readiness, and the regular army was to be increased temporarily by an additional twenty thousand men. Washington was called from retirement to become head of the army, while Alexander Hamilton, the leading exponent of military nationalism, was appointed second in command, and was expected to become the active field general.[25]

These Federalist war plans drew a bitter, but unsuccessful, protest from Republican party leaders. Philip Freneau, the foremost Republican newspaper editor of the day, in an attack on the selfishness of the proponents of a war policy had commented in 1797: 'It is to be suspected that providing for friends in an American army and navy contributed in some degree to the thirst of certain persons for a war with France.' [26] For requesting Congress to place so vast an army at his disposal in time of peace, Adams was accused of desiring to create an executive despotism. Even in the event of war it was felt that there was no real danger of invasion at the hands of a French army. Nathaniel Macon of North Carolina asked why, if the Federalists wanted war, they did not admit as much instead of trying to raise an army by subterfuge. Albert Gallatin saw the bill as the culmination of a long-continued Federalist drive 'to give to the President of the United States a

standing army, or select corps of militia.' Republican spokesmer
reasoned that the preparations called for by Adams had no legiti
mate basis as defensive measures. Alleging their equal uselessnes
as a means of coercing France, they argued that such devices as a
large army would only cause a war. The Republicans also were
fearful lest a successful war augment the powers of the nationa
government and further enhance the reputations of Alexande
Hamilton and his fellow officers.[27]

Suspicion of Hamilton's intentions and ambitions was not con
fined to the Republican opposition. President Adams himself, in
contrast to Hamilton, Secretary of State Timothy Pickering, and
Secretary of War James McHenry, represented the antimilitaris
wing of the Federalist party. Co-operating temporarily with the
Hamilton program for a vast army, President Adams was eithe
carried away by the hysteria of 1798 or felt that he could in such
fashion impress the French government. Yet the President mani
fested no real enthusiasm for military preparedness. Unlike Hamil
ton he was not especially perturbed at the slow progress in re
cruiting the large force authorized by Congress, and he expresse
little surprise that men would not volunteer for five dollars a montl
when common labor brought fifteen. In a communication to th
Secretary of War, Adams explained very well the basic dilemm
of the Federalist preparedness program:

> There has been no national plan, that I have seen, as yet formed
> for the maintenance of the army. One thing I know, that regiments
> are costly articles everywhere, and more so in this country than
> any other under the sun. If this nation sees a great army to main-
> tain, without an enemy to fight, there may arise an enthusiasm that
> seems to be little foreseen. At present there is no more prospect
> of seeing a French army here, than there is in Heaven.[28]

Much concerned over Hamilton's schemes, and imbued with
New Englander's distrust of a standing army, Adams in 179
effectively forestalled any incipient militarism by abruptly placin
before Congress the nomination of a new envoy to France.

With peace in the offing, a motion was made in Congress to re
duce the army as a means of economy. To the contention that
might lessen the effectiveness of the American diplomatic missio
in France, Representative John Nicholas of Virginia replied tha

he United States was already weakened in world opinion because
f an increased debt stemming from a large army. Restating the
eed for economy and bitterly attacking the entire principle of a
tanding force, John Randolph in a famous antimilitarist speech
sserted that reduction of the army would remove a prime cause
f popular dissatisfaction.

> The military parade which meets the eye in almost every direc-
> tion excites the gall of our citizens; they feel a just indignation at
> the sight of loungers, who live upon the public, who consume the
> fruits of their honest industry, under the pretext of protecting them
> from a foreign yoke. They put no confidence, sir, in the protection
> of a handful of ragamuffins.[29]

Although not so vehement as the Republican critics of the army,
President Adams continued throughout his long life to entertain
a healthy distrust of the military office. Looking back upon his
areer, he strongly denied the monarchist and militarist sympa-
hies attributed to him, and in 1807 he informed a correspondent
hat, although in favor of a certain necessary amount of prepared-
ess, 'Armies were always my aversion, however, I may have been
elied.' In his later years, he expressed the desire to be remem-
ered by the epitaph: 'Here lies John Adams, who took upon him-
elf the responsibility of the peace with France in the year 1800.' [30]
The difficulties that Adams had faced in his efforts to preserve
eace emphasized the timeliness of the 'Plan for a Peace-Office
or the United States,' which was proposed again in 1798 by
Benjamin Rush, the celebrated physician, whom Adams had ap-
ointed to a post as Treasurer of the United States Mint. Al-
hough Rush had in mind particularly the recurrent wars with
he Indians, his plan was also a thorough attack on other evidences
f militarism. He urged the repeal of all capital punishment and
nilitia laws, and the avoidance of any sort of military displays
nd titles. Finally, he recommended the establishment of a peace
nuseum in Federal Hall to offer a favorable contrast to another
oom, inscribed 'National Glory,' in which the horrors of war
vould be depicted. Over the portals of the Department of War
here would be painted the captions: 'An office for butchering the
uman species,' 'A Widow and Orphan making office.' [31]
Benjamin Rush's plan for a peace office came close to realiza-

tion when Thomas Jefferson succeeded John Adams as President. Jefferson's victory was partially a result of the fact that President Adams had resisted the demand of his own party for war. In thus 'pulling down the pillars' of his administration, Adams had shown real courage and a true understanding of popular feelings. Placing country above party, he had preserved civil government and left the way open for the peaceable triumph of the Jeffersonian Republicans in 1800.

IV

The Jeffersonian-Republican Surrender

THE VICTORY of the Republicans in the election of 1800 and Jefferson's elevation to the Presidency seemed to promise a dramatic reversal of the Federalist policies that had dominated the first twelve years of government under the Constitution. Far-reaching changes were especially anticipated in connection with the army and the navy. Proponents of simplicity and economy, the Republicans were staunch foes of a strong centralized government and a large military establishment. Primarily agricultural and agrarian in their interests, they could be expected to take little responsibility for building up a navy to protect American overseas commerce.

Jefferson himself was conspicuously and essentially a man of peace. As an individualist and democrat, he shunned an excess of military discipline. In the constitution which he proposed for his native state, he intrusted responsibility for military affairs to the legislature, the body that controlled the purse strings. Carrying this principle still further, he expressed a desire to see the federal government's borrowing power confined within certain natural limits as a means of bridling the spirit of war.[1] The Society of the

Cincinnati, Jefferson particularly feared and detested as a po
tential source of division between the military and civil order
In the Washington and Adams administrations, he had used hi
influence to help prevent the establishment of a standing army an
a permanent navy. Though a friend of France and in sympath
with the ideals of the French Revolution, he was as alarmed a
the Federalists at the usurpation of civil authority by Napoleor
Disappointed in his hope that Bonaparte would follow the ex
ample of a Washington instead of a Cromwell, Jefferson saw i
Napoleon's coup against the Directory 'a lesson against the dang
of standing armies.' [2]

In the course of a long public career, Jefferson had many oppor
tunities to voice an opinion on military affairs. That he at all time
adhered to a strictly consistent position is too much to expect o
a statesman and philosopher who was also a political realist. Minc
shifts in his thinking have resulted, in extremely varied interpre
tations of what may be regarded as his well-considered views o
national defense. Perhaps the best summary of the policy he wa
later to put into practice as President was that described by Jeffe
son himself in 1799:

> I am for relying, for internal defence, on our militia solely, till
> actual invasion, and for such naval force only as may protect our
> coasts and harbors from such depredations as we have experi-
> enced; and not for a standing army in time of peace, which may
> overawe the public sentiment; nor for a navy, which, by its own
> expenses and the eternal wars in which it will implicate us, will
> grind us with public burthens, & sink us under them. I am for free
> commerce with all nations; political connection with none; & little
> or no diplomatic establishment.[3]

Transferred from the ranks of the opposition to the exercise o
full responsibility as President of the United States, Jefferson i
his inaugural address continued to attack the doctrine of forc
as 'the vital principle and immediate parent of despotism.' R
ferring to a 'well-disciplined militia' as 'our best reliance in peac
and for the first moments of war,' Jefferson indicated that h
administration would give unqualified support to the doctrine o
'the supremacy of the civil over the military authority.' A standin
army, which Jefferson never ceased to indict as dangerous i

rinciple, he now attacked as a useless extravagance in time of
eace, and as an inadequate defense against invasion in time of
ar.[4]

In carrying out the Jeffersonian program of economy and re-
enchment, Congress drastically curtailed the costs of the military
nd naval establishment. The army, already cut back at the close
f the Adams administration to slightly over four thousand men,
as now further reduced by about one-fourth. During the general
eace in Europe that characterized the first Jefferson administra-
on, Congress exceeded even the President in its indifference to
ilitary affairs, refusing, for example, to authorize the improve-
ents in the militia system he had recommended.

Jefferson, despite the lack of interest by Congress, continued
urge the cause of an organized militia, hoping that it would
ove a desirable substitute for the unpopular, peacetime stand-
g army. In his scheme, the younger single men would be trained
provide an emergency force that could be called out whenever
cessary.[5] Otherwise, Jefferson's proposed militia differed little
om the traditional informal and unorganized militia existing in
merica since colonial times. Militia service of this type involved
minimum of training, no rigorous discipline, and usually made
eral provisions for exemptions or substitutes. Performed in such
manner, the militia duty of the early days of the republic bore
ght resemblance to the type of military service actually exacted
ter in the United States under the conscription and selective
rvice laws. To argue that Jefferson would have supported uni-
rsal military training in peacetime [6] overlooks the fact that his
ongest advocacy of a trained militia came during the years
en the United States was embroiled in difficulties with France
d England. Even then he coupled his enthusiasm for a strong
ilitia with hostility toward a standing army.

As President of the United States and especially in his second
ministration, Jefferson, it is true, allowed himself to pursue
licies hardly consistent with his individualist, pacifist philoso-
y. Students of his Presidency, including Henry Adams, have
und his firm resolve to maintain peace the clue to these Jeffer-
ian compromises with principle. Adhering to this purpose,
fferson was careful to still the war fever in Congress after Na-

poleon's acquisition of Louisiana, and again when the Britis
fired on the *Chesapeake*. The peaceful purchase of Louisian
Jefferson hoped, would keep the United States immune to Eur
pean strife; and the non-intercourse and embargo measures h
conceived as means of securing American neutral rights withou
resort to war. Though intended to preserve peace, the enforc
ment of the embargo and non-intercourse policy led Jefferson an
the country to the brink of war. Still unwilling to give his san
tion to a navy, Jefferson instead called upon Congress to me
the crisis by fortifying the principal harbors of the Eastern se
board and by building an additional fleet of small gunboats.[7]

Despite Jefferson's caution in recommending preparedne
measures, his critics accused him of departing from tradition
Republican policies. Earlier, in 1806, John Randolph in a brillia
speech had denounced the non-importation bill as a step towa
offensive war, inconsistent with the Constitution. Already, he d
clared, war contractors and commissaries were overrunning t
House. Now, in 1807, Randolph was joined by a group of Co
gressmen who attacked the entire idea of peace by preparednes
Rather than see the people 'reduced to beggary and want' in ord
to provide a large army and harbor fortifications, Republican Co
gressmen from the interior of the country preferred to see 'all t
towns in the United States prostrate.' John Eppes, Jefferson's so
in-law, declared in Congress, 'If there is any principle which oug
to be hooted at in a Republican Government,' it is the princip
'that to preserve peace we ought to be prepared for war.' Repr
sentative James Holland of North Carolina argued that the nav
weakness of the United States was the chief means of keepi
her at peace. 'If we had a few ships-of-the-line,' he asserted, '
should have been at war before now.' [8] Randolph himself affirm
that gunboats were useless and that the whole naval establishme
had been for years 'a moth in the public purse.' The gravity
the crisis, which Jefferson used to justify his conduct, only prov
Randolph asserted, 'the more clearly . . . the necessity of co
vening Congress.' [9]

Jefferson incurred still further denunciation when, in the l
year of his administration, he asked Congress to increase the reg
lar army by six thousand men and to authorize calling out twent

our thousand volunteers. His critics now recalled the President's earlier depreciation of all rumors and threats of conflict, and especially his message of December 1806, when he told Congress that, although the situation in Europe called for reasonable preparations, 'Were armies to be raised whenever a speck of war is visible in our horizon, we never should have been without them.' [10]

By the close of his administration Jefferson's efforts to enforce the Embargo Act gave even the Federalists an opportunity to denounce the Republicans in terms that they had long heard applied to themselves. Various New England towns, for example, included in their resolutions of protest against the Embargo and Force Acts the charge that the measure elevated the military over the civil power.[11] Given a further extension of time and a greater willingness on the part of the people to accept the economic sacrifices required, the embargo might have secured European recognition of American neutral rights. As it was, Jefferson, despite the attacks on his policies, was able to retire to Monticello consoled by the fact that the country was still at peace.

For a brief period at the outset of his administration, it seemed though Jefferson's friend and successor, James Madison, would be able to carry out his announced intention of returning to the traditional Republican pursuit of peace and economy. The short interval between the repeal of the Embargo Act in March 1809 and the rise of an ardent war party in the fall of 1811 saw a momentary check in the drive for preparedness and a reassertion of the old Republican hostility toward the army and the navy. The regular army had also become somewhat discredited in this period because of the dubious role that its commanding officer, General James Wilkinson, had played in the Burr Conspiracy. John Randolph, the most bitter antagonist of Wilkinson in Congress, resumed his former attacks upon the regular army with a series of resolutions calling for its reduction and the substitution of an armed militia. Supporting these resolutions, he charged that the evidence in the Burr trial proved the army to be ridden with corruption. Led on by Randolph and Nathaniel Macon, the Republican party was returning to its old suspicious attitude in regard to a standing army. In June 1809, Congress stopped further enlistments, and at the same time it authorized the President, in

the event of a favorable change in foreign relations, to make re
ductions in the existing naval force.[12]

Toward the navy, Republican policy continued consistentl
hostile. Until the War of 1812 had actually begun, President Mad:
son manifested a Jeffersonian indifference to building up a large
naval force. In Congress, Republican 'War Hawks,' intent on th
invasion of Canada, saw no inconsistency in uniting their approvɛ
of going to war with their opposition to a powerful navy. Th
argument was made that a navy 'will be the means of excitin
many wars' and 'will create a new and dangerous interest in ou
country.' Republican Representatives Richard M. Johnson an
Samuel McKee of Kentucky pointed out that the high costs c
building a navy would lead to an increased debt and furthe
taxation. Expressing views typical of its Republican back countr
opponents, McKee declared that the benefits of a large naval forc
would accrue to the mercantile class, while the burden of th
expense would fall mainly on the agricultural class. Congress,
few months before its declaration of war, voted down that sectio
of the naval bill providing for the construction of large frigate
thus proclaiming its adherence to the Jeffersonian policy of coa
defense by a fleet of gunboats.[13]

Although the War Hawks of the Twelfth Congress were relu
tant to provide a navy capable of waging offensive operations o
of protecting American maritime commerce, in the matter of a
army their enthusiasm led them to exceed President Madison
original recommendations. William B. Giles, a veteran Republica
legislator from Virginia, introduced in December 1811 a bill t
increase the standing army by enlisting twenty-five thousand me
for five years. Such a measure was necessary, he asserted, 'b
cause an impression appeared to be almost universally entertaine
that Congress could not constitutionally command the services o
the militia beyond the limits of the United States. . . .' Skeptic
of the efficiency of short term volunteers, Giles deprecated all fea
of a standing army. The recruits, he pointed out, would be draw
from the whole people, who would retain the security and prote
tion of their own state militia.[14]

Giles's bill was not passed by Congress until after John Randol
had first had the opportunity to berate his colleagues once aga

or their betrayal of Republican principles. Pointing out that the
arty had formerly 'shrunk at standing armies,' he asked sarcas-
cally, 'what is the object now — defence? . . . to be protected
y ten thousand vagabonds who were fit food for gunpowder?'
'robing into 'the ulterior views of the committee on this point,'
andolph accused his fellow Republicans of preparing for ag-
ression against Canada. In the light of the Jeffersonian stand
gainst war in 1798, he could not understand 'how gentlemen,
alling themselves Republicans, could advocate such a war.' He
oncluded sadly:

> This war of conquest, a war for the acquisition of territory and
> subjects, is to be a new commentary on the doctrine that Repub-
> lics are destitute of ambition — that they are addicted to peace,
> wedded to the happiness and safety of the great body of their peo-
> ple. . . .
> We had vaunted of paying off the national debt, of retrenching
> useless establishments; and yet had now become as infatuated with
> standing armies, loans, taxes, navies, and war, as ever were the
> Essex Junto. What Republicanism is this? [15]

Randolph's bitter speech, the delivery of which had taken up
he greater part of three days, was in vain as Congress passed a
ill authorizing the President to call for fifty thousand volunteers
rom the state militia to serve for twelve months alongside the
egular army. Congress, however, failed to provide specifically
or militia duty beyond the United States borders. This setback
o the militarism of the War Hawks was probably a result of the
act that few of the members believed that the militia could con-
titutionally be used for purposes of invasion. Even excepting
his state militia, the authorized strength of United States forces
n the eve of the War of 1812 was large, including a regular army
f almost thirty thousand men plus fifty thousand volunteers, al-
hough neither figure was achieved in the course of actual re-
ruiting.[16]

The small size of the existing federal army, and the resulting
ecessity of using state militia, has led to the charge, particularly
y military historians, that the United States was woefully unpre-
ared for war in 1812. The lack of preparedness in 1812 was not
s is usually implied a result of Congressional neglect or ignorance.

The unfilled ranks in the armies of the United States were due
rather, to the bitter internal opposition to the declaration and
prosecution of the War of 1812. This opposition, except in the
case of the Quakers and a few other religious groups, was much
less a pacifist objection to all wars than a profound conviction of
the folly of the particular war in question. This feeling was shared
not only by New England Federalists, but also by those Jeffersonian Republicans who could not forget the traditions of their
party, even when they voted with the western War Hawks in
support of Madison's war message. The moral to be drawn from
the War of 1812 is not the necessity of extensive preparedness so
that war may be an ever-ready resort; rather it is the wisdom of
not embarking upon a war that is either staunchly opposed or
only grudgingly supported by the bulk of the population.

The closeness of the vote on the war resolution — 79 to 49 in the
House, with 14 absent, and 19 to 13 in the Senate — indicated the
lack of unity in the country in June 1812. This disunity received
added illustration when a group of thirty-four members of the
House published an address to their constituents, accusing the
Madison administration of exerting pressure upon Congress for
a declaration of war. The war itself, they predicted, was to be
fought for the purpose of invading Canada and would result
only in tremendous costs and taxes.[17]

The opposition by eastern Congressmen to the expansionist
schemes of the War Hawks illustrated the extraordinary political
transformation that had taken place in the country since 1798
when the Federalists had been the ones clamoring for war. The
proponents of a militant foreign policy when it was directed
toward the enforcement of American neutral rights on the high
seas, the Federalists became peace-minded in the face of actual
war with the British navy. The prospect of gaining Canada made
the war all the more distasteful, creating as it did the possibility
of new areas for western expansion and weakening the political
importance of the Eastern seaboard. Thus, however appealing a
war for Canada might seem to expansionists in the West, to New
England Federalists it indicated only the imminent destruction
of their maritime commerce and the invasion of their coastal towns
by the British navy. Confronted with the probable loss of political

and economic power, Federalist leaders took a pessimistic view of the future of the country. During Jefferson's Presidency, Fisher Ames, an old-school Federalist, had gloomily predicted: 'A democracy cannot last. Its nature ordains that its next change shall be into a military despotism, of all known governments, perhaps, the most prone to shift its head, and the slowest to mend its vices.' Seeing much to compare between the course of events in the United States and in Ancient Rome and Revolutionary France, Ames warned: 'A military government may make a nation great, but it cannot make them free.' [18] In similar fashion, three days after the declaration of the War of 1812, John Adams wrote:

> The danger of our government is, that the General will be a man of more popularity than the President, and the army possess more power than Congress. The people should be apprised of this, and guard themselves against it. Nothing is more essential than to hold the civil authority decidedly superior to the military power.[19]

In Massachusetts there was intense opposition to the War of 1812. The day after the declaration of war, the state House of Representatives, fearful of coming restrictions upon freedom of speech, hastened to 'lift up a warning voice to our constituents, and apprise them of their danger . . . while our Chamber is not yet encompassed by a standing army and the writ of habeas corpus is not suspended. . . .' Believing the war to be an unjust conflict without cause, but accepting the fact that the United States must be defended against invasion, the Massachusetts legislature sought a remedy in an aroused public opinion and in the organization of a peace party. 'If your sons must be torn from you by conscription,' the legislators declared, 'consign them to the care of GOD; but let there be no volunteers except for defensive war.' [20] In July, the Boston town meeting declared the war would be opposed by all means short of force. In August, a convention of delegates from forty-one towns in Worcester County advised the people to pay their taxes but to refuse all loans to the government. Affirming that the governors of the states were empowered to decide when an emergency existed that would justify the President calling out the militia, the Worcester delegates concluded: 'The president has not power to levy an army of conscripts — and let there be no volunteers in this ungrateful service.' [21]

The Governor of Massachusetts, backed up by a ruling from the state supreme court that there was no reason to warrant the President's request for the Massachusetts militia, refused to make the state forces available. Joined in his stand by Connecticut and Rhode Island, the governor in a long and bitter correspondence with the War Department maintained that, since no actual invasion had occurred, there were no grounds for the states yielding control of their militia to the federal government.[22] Success in the fall elections encouraged the New England Federalists to continue their obstructionist policy of withholding the men and money desired by the pro-war element in the South and West.

Although thoroughgoing opposition to the war was confined largely to the New England area, even in the West bounties had to be offered in order to secure recruits. Much of this hostility to the war was based on a popular fear of some sort of military despotism. A people accustomed to Indian warfare, and for whom the appeal to arms in the late Revolution was still a fresh memory, were not pacifists. But the Revolution itself, the actions of John Adams in 1799, and the later triumph of Jefferson were all illustrations of strong American oppositions to centralized power, and especially to authority concentrated in the hands of a military class. During the War of 1812 the expansionist and militarist schemes of the War Hawks were very largely forestalled by the lack of co-operation received from the state militia, and by the refusal of Congress to authorize strong military measures.

Although the Federalists no doubt exaggerated the danger of the war to American institutions, their partisan opposition may have exercised a restraining influence upon the more extravagant plans of the War Hawks. Josiah Quincy of Massachusetts warned that a successful conquest of Canada would result in the return of 'a veteran army, under a popular leader, flushed with victory' which would not be disbanded until a King or Emperor were crowned. Laban Wheaton of Massachusetts, invoking the example of Greece, Rome, and Napoleonic France, predicted that liberty could not withstand a war for foreign conquest. Harmanus Bleecker, elected as an antiwar Federalist from New York, told Congress that he had opposed the war 'because I thought it might expose our happy form of Government — our excellent political nstitutions — to a dangerous trial.' Bleecker also explained that he United States was unable to raise an army because the people vere contented and prosperous at home and included few of that lepressed class of the population which generally made up an rmy. Daniel Sheffey, a Federalist from Staunton, Virginia, deounced the attempt to still the minority. 'Uniformity of action,' le declared, 'is only desirable where there is uniformity of sentilent; and that, on most subjects, will only exist where the mind s enchained by the fear which despotic power inspires.' Agreeing vith the Federalists in their opposition to the war, John Ranolph, who because of his views had been defeated for re-election y John Eppes, Jefferson's son-in-law, told Congress in his farevell speech that his alleged desertion of the Republican party vas a result of the party's own desertion of the principles of Jefferon's first administration.[23]

Although Randolph and the Federalists were not able to prevent the passage of a wartime bill increasing the regular army, le problem of recruiting troops to the number authorized by ongress was by no means solved. The traditional alternative to standing army, the resort to the state militia, was rendered diffiilt by the lack of co-operation in the northern states and by the lefficiency of the militia in actual service. Instead the Madison lministration turned to the old idea of classifying the militia ith the significant added feature that if the number of volunteers ere not sufficient to fill the ranks, a federal militia draft could e instituted. Accordingly in November 1814, James Monroe, as cretary of War, despite some misgivings as to the political reperssions of a draft, sent a report to Congress in which he recomended four possible plans for improving and increasing the my. The first of these was a scheme to divide the militia into oups of one hundred men between the ages of eighteen and venty-five. Each of these groups would then be required to rnish, and keep replaced, a total of four men in actual service. If cessary, the federal government would be able to draft these ur men although substitutes would be allowed.[24]

Thomas Jefferson, who regretted that Congress during his esidency had not approved a similar system of classifying and aining the militia, was an early proponent of the Monroe plan.

Aware of the obstructions to the conduct of the war interposed
by the Federalists, and believing the country imperiled by the
British, while at the same time American citizens were too pros
perous 'to be shot at for a shilling a day,' he wrote to Monroe of
'the necessity of obliging every citizen to be a soldier.' In the
same letter to Monroe, Jefferson, despite the gravity of the war
situation, repeated his old belief that the United States was for
tunate in lacking a standing army.[25] The clue to the seeming mili
tarism of Jefferson's espousal of a militia conscription rests on
his concept of a citizenry trained to arms as the best alternative
to a standing army. The use of the militia draft would in all
probability be confined to a time when the country was actually
at war. In peace, the militia service contemplated by Jefferson
would certainly not have been the onerous year or more of duty
envisaged by those later advocates of peacetime military training
who quote Jefferson's wartime correspondence in support of their
plans. It should be remembered that Jefferson never gave up his
lifelong hatred of war. 'But my hope is peace,' he asserted in a let
ter penned before the news of the Treaty of Ghent had reached
America. In mentioning his fear that the defeat of the Monroe
plan would prolong the war another year, Jefferson indicated an
other of the reasons for his support of the measure.[26]

Secretary of War Monroe's plan for enrolling and classifying the
militia reached the floor of the Senate in November 1814 in the
form of a bill to authorize the federal government to draft eight
thousand men from the state militia for a period of two years
This measure was immediately subjected to detailed criticism by
Federalist Senators. A draft was denounced as a violation of in
dividual liberty and as a grant of unconstitutional powers to the
central government. David Daggett of Connecticut declared
'This bill is not only unconstitutional, but it is unequal, unjust
and oppressive.' He found it 'utterly inconsistent' with the princi
ples of free institutions 'to compel any man to become a soldier
for life, during a war, or for any fixed time.' Jeremiah Mason of
New Hampshire argued that if the Constitution intended the
grant of such vast powers, it would have been pointed out in
the course of the debates over its adoption. 'Nor is it believed,'
Mason added, 'that with this construction, the Constitution would

ave been adopted by a single state of the Union.' Christopher
Gore of Massachusetts saw the militia draft as 'the first step on
he odious ground of conscription . . . in a manner presumed
o be the least disgusting. . . . The people readily discern that
he next step will be for a conscription, for any purpose, and by
ny individual designated by the General Government.'[27]

Although passed in the Senate, the draft bill was defeated in
he House of Representatives, where a larger number of Federal-
sts, including Daniel Webster, had been elected as antiwar can-
lidates in the fall of 1812. Webster himself delivered one of the
ey speeches on a motion to postpone the bill indefinitely. Al-
hough written out, this speech was not published and was for a
ong time thought to be lost. Now famous, Webster's speech and
lis role in the defeat of the Monroe conscription plan were always
 source of satisfaction to him in his later life.[28] An equally severe
ndictment of the militia draft plan was delivered on the floor of
he House, the day before Webster's effort, by his colleague Morris
. Miller, also a new member of Congress. Placing himself in di-
ect opposition to the 'whole system of force and coercion,' Miller
ontended that 'under this Constitution you have no right to raise
rmies except by voluntary enlistment; and further, that if you
ad the right it would not be discreet to exercise it.' Ridiculing the
ttempts to cloak the bill under such terms as 'classification and
enalty,' 'classification and draught,' he declared:

> Sir, there is poison in the dish; garnish it as you please, there is
> poison still. . . . The times demand that things should be called
> by their right names — this is conscription, and with features,
> more hideous, than are to be found in the exploded system of our
> unfortunate cousin of Elba.

onvinced that conscription would change the American people
nto a military nation, he predicted: 'If this conscription system is
dopted, farewell to all our claims to personal freedom — farewell
 all our boast of civil liberty. By this system, the people of the
'nited States will be instantly and forcibly transformed into sol-
iers.'[29]

The lack of sympathy with conscription on the part of Congress
as paralleled by the denunciation with which the idea was

greeted by Federalists in New England and New York. The Con
necticut legislature, in session at this time, drafted a resolution
attacking the plan as 'not only intolerably burdensome and oppres
sive, but utterly subversive of the rights and liberties of the people
of this state.' It was pointed out that according to the principles
of the draft 'our sons, brothers and friends, are made liable to be
delivered against their will, and by force, to the marshalls and re
cruiting officers of the United States, to be employed, not for our
own defence, but for the conquest of Canada.' In the event that
the conscription measure passed the United States Congress, the
governor of the state was requested to reconvene the legislature
'to consider what measures may be adopted to secure and preserve
the rights and liberties of the people of this state.' [30] In New York
Chancellor James Kent of the state supreme court devoted his
legal scholarship to the task of arguing the unconstitutionality of
conscription.[31]

Federalist opposition to both the war and the policies of the
Madison administration reached a climax in the meetings of the
Hartford Convention attended by delegates from the legislatures
of Massachusetts, Connecticut, and Rhode Island. Prominent
among the subjects of complaint and apprehension occupying the
attention of the convention was the authority exercised by the
federal government over the state militia. Following the stand
taken separately by the New England states in 1812, the delegates
reported that, except in cases of actual invasion or insurrection, the
states should retain control of their own militia. The convention
strongly denounced the attempts to find constitutional sanction for
a federalized militia or for conscription by resort to the clause
empowering Congress to raise armies. This clause, it was argued,
applied only to volunteers. Citing the recent example of France
under conscription, the final report of the Convention affirmed,
'An iron despotism can impose no harder servitude upon the citi
zen, than to force him from his home and occupation, to wage
offensive wars, undertaken to gratify the pride or passions of his
master.' [32] Theodore Dwight, one of the delegates to the Conven
tion, in his history of the affair published some years later, de
clared of the Monroe plan in retrospect: 'The truth is, the whole
scheme was not only unconstitutional, and oppressive in the most

extravagant degree, and totally at variance with the rights and liberties of the citizens, but it was in an equal degree preposterous and absurd.' [33]

Dwight's strictures were reminiscent of the language used by Jeffersonian Republicans in their attacks on Federalist preparedness policies in 1798. Although the antiwar Federalists of 1812 were also open to the charge of inconsistency, in some cases clamoring for war until it arrived, the Republican break with past tradition was by far the greater. Surely it was one of the paradoxes of the War of 1812 that the opposition to its militaristic implications should have come from conservative Federalists, while the liberal Republicans conjured up schemes for conquest abroad and conscription at home. Neither party's principles, it would seem, were immune to the transformations effected by the burdens of responsibility and the privileges of power.

V

A More Militant Nationalism

and Growing Pacifism

THE CLOSE OF the War of 1812 marked the beginning of a new era in American life. Albert Gallatin, one of the peace commissioners and, as Secretary of the Treasury, an intimate associate of Jefferson and Madison, believed that the war had exerted a beneficent influence in the impetus that it gave to American nationalism and patriotism. On the other hand, Gallatin, perhaps recalling his own earlier efforts for peace and economy, was forced to admit that 'the war has laid the foundation of permanent taxes and military establishments, which the Republicans had deemed unfavorable to the happiness and free institutions of the country.' [1] Looking back upon this period from the vantage point of an American living abroad, Thomas Low Nichols recalled: 'The military spirit and the spirit of patriotism, in my early days were universal.' During the years of intense nationalism that succeeded the War of 1812 Nichols remembered that young people were educated in American patriotism until it became with them a religious faith. [2]

Certainly the wartime experience carried much farther that retreat from Jeffersonian principles which had already begun in the latter half of Jefferson's own administration. And yet, as Henry Adams, the biographer of Gallatin and historian of the Jefferson

nd Madison administrations, has pointed out, the militarist reac-
ion that followed Jeffersonian pacifism was not lasting. Only more
vars and greater strength, Adams felt, could transform the Ameri-
ans from a peace-loving people into a militarist nation.[3]

Despite the occasional alarm raised by American statesmen, as
t the time of the formation of the Quadruple Alliance in Europe,
he United States after 1815 had little reason to fear an attack or
nvasion by some conjunction of foreign powers. More effective in
keeping alive a military spirit was the intense nationalistic senti-
nent that succeeded the War of 1812. This nationalistic temper at
imes led to a demand for a more aggressive foreign policy, supported by military power. It was also evidenced in the popular
ondness for elevating military heroes to public office and in the
nartial atmosphere of many Fourth of July celebrations. The chief
pportunity for a display of arms, as well as for actual fighting
luring these years, came from the recurring warfare against the
ndians. These wars contributed to the decision at the conclusion
f the War of 1812 to retain a permanent standing army of over
en thousand men, while later troubles with the Indian tribes were
esponsible for the Western demand that the army be made even
arger.

Especially stimulating to American nationalistic pride, as well
s an immense boon to the prestige of the United States navy, were
he wartime exploits of American naval commanders. Spectac-
ular oceanic duels with the British and decisive American vic-
ories on Lake Erie and Lake Champlain gave a new-found popularity to the navy which was reflected in the program of naval
onstruction adopted after the Peace of Ghent. In 1816, Federalists
nd Republicans united to pass a bill providing a gradual increase
n the navy over a period of several years. A few months before
his measure, Congress also approved the creation of a Board of
Naval Commissioners to assume control of many of the technical
letails of the establishment. Although the commissioners were to
dvise the Secretary of the Navy, it was carefully stipulated in the
aw, and clearly intended by Congress, that authority in all mat-
ers of policy should remain in civilian hands. This wartime renais-
ance of the navy was comparatively brief. Even the Act of 1816,
ncreasing the establishment, called for the prompt liquidation of

certain naval forces upon the inland lakes. A year later the parti
demilitarization of the maritime frontier between the Unite
States and Canada under the terms of the Rush-Bagot Agreemen
gave further encouragement to this policy and prevented a
Anglo-American naval race for control of the Great Lakes.[4]

Meanwhile, traditional Jeffersonian hostility to a navy was re
viving among Republican members of Congress. Lewis William:
a member of the House of Representatives from North Carolina
expressed in interesting terms the old agrarian arguments agains
a navy. Noting that his nationalist colleagues favored a high tari
on manufactures as well as a large navy, he attacked the logic c
cutting off American foreign trade by a tariff, while at the sam
time developing a navy for its protection. Personally, he coul
'never agree to tax his constituents, in the first place, to suppoi
manufacturing establishments, and then to support an army and
navy, rendered wholly useless and unnecessary by the policy prc
posed to be pursued.' Williams's attitude also derived muc
strength from the general demand for economy that accompanie
the economic setback after the war. Thus, in 1821, measures wer
introduced to cut the outlay for new construction under the 181
building program. Over the next four years, covering Monroe'
second administration, the annual appropriations for the navy de
clined from a previous yearly average of nearly $3,700,000 to a
average of $2,900,000 per year.[5]

The slump in naval appropriations during the 1820s was paral
leled by a strong movement to reduce the size of the military es
tablishment. After the war, the regular army was fixed at ten thou
sand men, a number almost double the prewar figure. Althoug
the war experience had not diminished the general American fait
in a volunteer or militia force, 'the never-ending task of guardin
the frontier weakened the prejudice against a standing army an
caused the nation to tolerate the growth of a policy it never de
liberately adopted. This change is especially noticeable in th
decade after the War of 1812, when a standing army was avowedl
accepted for the first time.'[6] Acceptance of the principle of :
standing army did not of course interfere with increasing Congres
sional sentiment for its reduction in practice. A particular subjec
of criticism by the old group of prewar Jeffersonians, includin

Randolph, Macon, and Eppes, were John C. Calhoun's reports as Secretary of War in the Monroe administration. As a member of Congress and then as Secretary of War, Calhoun favored the enactment of some form of federal militia conscription along the lines of Monroe's own defeated wartime plan. Unable to gain Congressional approval of a conscription scheme, Calhoun then turned to advocating the cause of an increased standing army.[7]

The reason for Calhoun's adherence to the principle of a regular standing army stems from the fact that he realized the distinction between a well-trained militia and the militia as it actually existed in the United States. In the latter sense, the militia was not the equal of a standing army, but to discipline the militia to a point where it would be somewhat comparable to regular troops was contrary to American thinking and experience. A militia fully trained was not a militia at all in the American understanding of the term. It was, rather, a counterpart of a large standing army. Although he did not believe that the danger of such a force stemmed primarily from its size, Calhoun did not attempt to argue that a citizen army or militia, rigorously trained and disciplined, differed in any way from a standing army. 'It is mere deception,' he wrote, 'to place our militia on the footing of regular troops, and the reference to the militia of Rome, or Switzerland to establish the superiority of ours is an unworthy sophism to maintain that deception. In our sense of the word, they were not militia.'[8] Calhoun accordingly relegated the partially trained, unorganized militia to the catagory of a reserve force. In the absence of an American militia of the Roman or Swiss type, which he thought of as synonomous with a standing army, Calhoun avowed a frank preference for the regular army as a peacetime establishment.

Calhoun's reports, which state the militarist point of view after the War of 1812, met with little favor in Congress, where the postwar feeling against the military establishment was growing. Congress refused, for example, to act on proposals for the classification and compulsory training of the militia presented by William Henry Harrison.[9] To the bewilderment and dismay of its more military-minded members, Congress maintained an equal opposition to large standing armies and to any schemes for the classification or conscription of the militia. Alluding to this feeling, Repre-

sentative Eldred Simkins of South Carolina asked: 'How then ca
it be reconciled that those members, so jealous of a standing arm
are not among the first to give us an *efficient* militia?' The answ
Simkins supplied by his own argument linking a well-trained mil
tia to the cultivation of a proper military spirit in the United State
The opponents of a military way of life preferred to see a sma
standing army rather than a disciplined militia. Representati
R. M. Saunders, a Democrat from North Carolina supporting suc
a policy, explained that a comprehensive plan for training th
militia would result in a vast diffusion of the military spirit amoi
the people, diverting them from their peaceful pursuits and fillii
them 'with that martial feeling, "the pride, the pomp, and the ci
cumstance of war," which might lead them in quest "of food,
plunder, and of glory." ' [10]

The Calhoun-Harrison scheme for classifying the militia ar
placing it under federal control was also open to objection (
grounds of state rights. William H. Sumner, the Adjutant Gener
of Massachusetts, in an open letter to John Adams stressed th
traditional function of the state militia as a bulwark against fede
centralization and a standing army. Adams, though a long-stan
ing friend of an improved state militia, agreed completely wi
Sumner's attack on the concept of a federally controlled, sele
militia. Such a force, Adams wrote, 'will soon become a standi
army, or a corps of Manchester yeomanry.' [11]

Congress considered a well-trained and disciplined militia as
different from a standing army. There was accordingly no contr
diction in its opposition to both types of a military establishme
Ignoring the arguments of Monroe, Calhoun, and Harrison, t
majority of the members preferred to rely on a relatively untrain
and unorganized militia supplemented by volunteers. Such a for
together with the small regular army, was deemed a sufficient c
fense against invasion. Preparedness beyond that point would i
volve the danger of militarism.

The growing criticism in Congress directed against the size
the military establishment after the War of 1812 resulted, in 18:
in the reduction of the army from ten to six thousand men. T
leader of this campaign for a smaller army was Lewis Williams
North Carolina, whose long period of Congressional service fr

815 to 1842 earned him the title, 'Father of the House.' Williams, dopting the mantle of John Randolph, introduced in each Conress a resolution to reduce the army to six thousand men. In support of his successful bill of 1821, Williams attacked the argument hat a large army and navy were necessary for national glory. 'Of 'hat avail,' he asked, 'is it to talk about the splendid victories of Decatur, if, in order to obtain those victories, the people had een obliged, by taxation, to give up so much of their own prop-'ty as would compel them to go supperless to bed?' Condemning he moral effects of a standing army, which he termed 'a kind of *cessary evil*,' Williams asserted that 'in our free country persons ibituated to military life become, as officers, on the one hand,)mineering and intolerant, and, as soldiers, on the other, servile id dependent.' Confident that distance from Europe would give te United States two or three years advance notice of any in-sion, Williams asked why the enlarged navy could not protect e country. Instead, he noted a tendency on the part of Congress) think the Army ought to be increased in direct ratio with the in-ease of the Navy.' Finally, Williams struck back at those of his itics who asserted that the army represented no threat to civil in-itutions. What was the function of Congress, he inquired, if it uld not reduce the army when the people were crying for tax re-:f? 'The Army was made for the country, not the country for the :my,' he concluded.[12]

Although the attitude of Congress toward the army was in part fluenced by the need for economy after the Panic of 1819, it was so true that many of the members were strongly opposed in prin-ple to a standing army and conscription. In this stand, they re-ived considerable support from adherents of the newly organ-ed peace movement. Two of the peace leaders, William Ellery ianning and Noah Worcester, who together founded the Mas-chusetts Peace Society, were particularly active in calling atten-n to the militarist implications of war. Channing made an es-cial effort to warn the American people of the danger in pursu-g Napoleon's policy of conquest abroad and conscription at me.[13] Following the conclusion of the War of 1812, he was un-ppy to observe continued evidences of a military spirit in the untry, with public revenues 'exhausted in military establish-

ments,' while internal improvements and the arts of peace wer
neglected. Victory in a future war, he warned, might be at the e
pense of freedom at home. 'In a community, in which precedenc
is given to the military profession, freedom cannot long endur
The encroachments of power at home are expiated by foreign tr
umphs.' [14]

Noah Worcester, Channing's colleague in the New Englan
peace movement, used his magazine *Friend of Peace* to attack co
scription and a standing army. Although Americans were quick †
criticize the British impressment policy and the French conscrip
tion, he pointed out that 'We have our *slave ships* and our regula
army, in which fellow beings are the subjects of military despotis
during the term of their enlistment.' These were a natural ou
growth of the war system which Worcester, citing Tom Paine, d
clared was 'the art of conquering at home.' Urging the America
people 'to forgive but never forget' the step of conscription pr
posed during the War of 1812, Worcester denounced enforce
military service as a violation of the principles of free governme
and of the natural rights of the individual. Worcester's magazi
also made a comparison between conscription and the rights
property. Although, as yet, 'No man is compelled to be a contract
for our armies' or devote his property to war, 'If we allow our rule
the power of raising armies by conscription, the next step may I
to raise money by arbitrary contributions. The latter however
the less evil of the two.' [15]

Peace leaders did not believe they exaggerated the danger
the United States of the European system of conscript standi
armies. By the 1820s, the reduction in the size of the regular arm
and the defeat of the various plans for a compulsory federal milit
made it possible for the antimilitarist spokesmen to exert the
efforts in other areas. Their attention during the 'thirties a
'forties was directed particularly to the issues of service in the sta
militia and West Point's role in creating a military aristocracy.

Until the Civil War, the contact of the average citizen wi
military service was almost entirely through the state militia. /
though brief periods of compulsory militia training and duty ha
been exacted from early colonial times, this service became le
important as the Indian tribes were pushed farther west. In N

ngland after the American Revolution, the militia training day
oon became a gala social occasion and patriotic holiday, useful
hiefly as a kind of democratic get-together. Along the South-
estern frontier in the early nineteenth century militia duty
ended to be a more serious matter. Even when not compulsory,
niversal service was often enforced by the pressure of public
pinion. After the danger from the British, Spanish, and hostile
ndians receded, the militia muster in the Southwest also lost its
martial air and became only a legal form or an excuse for a social
athering.[16]

The earliest instances of opposition to compulsory militia duty
ame from the Quakers, who protested that the payment of a fine
r equivalent as a substitute for militia service forced them to
ompromise their stand against war. Faced after 1812 with the
wartime militia calls and possible federal conscription, the Society
f Friends and the Shakers petitioned state legislatures for exemp-
on. A plea to the legislature of Virginia from the Society of
riends in 1816 defended freedom of conscience as sanctioned, not
nly by Christianity, but also by natural law. The obligation to fight
nd defend one's country, the Quakers believed, was a matter to be
overned by the individual's own conscience.[17] In this same period
umerous memorials from the 'Society of People commonly called
hakers' were presented to the state legislatures of New York and
ew Hampshire. In response to the demand that they should pay
special tax as a substitute for militia service, the Shakers asked:
What is this but indirectly supporting the cause of war?' [18] In New
ork state, the pleas of the Quakers and Shakers were given recog-
ition by Governor De Witt Clinton, who called the attention of
ne legislature to those citizens who 'are conscientiously opposed
o bearing arms, and to the payment of fines imposed for non-
ttendance in the militia.' Advising some mitigation of the penal-
es inflicted against the exercise of freedom of conscience, Clinton
eclared: 'In this enlightened age, when the rights of man are fully
nderstood and practically asserted, it is surely not compatible
ith the tolerant and liberal spirit of the times, to wound the con-
iences of our unoffending fellow men.' [19]

In the late 1820s the campaign against compulsory militia serv-
e was greatly fortified by the protests of workingmen's organiza-

tions, which looked upon the militia system as a discriminator economic burden. While the wealthy were able to escape servic by paying their fines, the poor man lost both time and money i having to attend the drills or muster. In Philadelphia, labor's com plaint was first expressed in the political campaign of 1828. Afte a vigorous program of protest meetings and petitions to the legis lature in the following year, the workingmen were able to secur pledges promising militia reforms from some of the candidates. I an address to their fellow workingmen in 1830, the Philadelph labor party declared that the existing militia, characterized mainl by drunken parades, was inferior to a voluntary system. The Nev York Workingmen's party also demanded the abolition of com pulsory militia duty, adopting a resolution which asserted 'tha our present militia system is highly oppressive to the producin classes of the community, without any beneficial result to indivic uals or the state.' [20]

The workingmen's protests gave impetus to the movement fc reform of the militia system. While some states abolished militar parades, Delaware abandoned her militia entirely.[21] On the othe hand, conservatives and military spokesmen, who regarded th militia as a valuable safeguard aginst lawlessness, regretted th increasing popular hostility. Joseph Story, who had delivered th opinion of the Supreme Court upholding Madison's use of th militia in the War of 1812, in his *Commentaries on the Constitu tion* supported the doctrine that the powers of Congress wer virtually unlimited in time of war. Believing it to be 'agains sound policy for a free people to keep up large military establish ments and standing armies in time of peace,' he saw in the militi an ideal substitute.

> And yet, though this truth would seem so clear, and the im-
> portance of a well regulated militia would seem so undeniable, it
> cannot be disguised, that among the American people there is a
> growing indifference to any system of militia discipline, and a
> strong disposition, to be rid of all regulations.[22]

Thus Story came regretfully to the conclusion, already reached b Congress, that the American people desired neither a large stand ing army nor an organized militia.

At the opposite extreme from the informally trained state militia was the United States Military Academy established at West Point during Jefferson's first administration. Although Jefferson favored the idea of an academy and later supported some sort of military drill at the University of Virginia, his followers in Congress were less enthusiastic, and the Academy languished in a state of disrepair and inefficiency. During its first years it received little attention from Jeffersonian Republicans, and after the War of 1812 it became an object of increasing suspicion as the cultivator of a military aristocracy.[23] In 1818, a group of five cadets, speaking on behalf of 189 of their fellows, complained of conditions at the Military Academy under the despotic administration of Sylvanus Thayer, the new superintendent. The House Committee on Military Affairs reported that they found some basis for the charges by the five cadets and expressed a regret that they had already resigned from the Academy. Nevertheless the committee, though not approving Thayer's conduct as altogether satisfactory, noted 'that *obedience and subordination are the essential principles of the army*, which is not the place for the exercise of liberty.' [24] Two years later, in 1820, Representative Newton Cannon of Tennessee introduced the first of a long series of almost identical resolutions, designed 'to inquire into the expediency of abolishing the Military Academy at West Point.' The basis of Cannon's objections to the Academy was his conviction that it was an aristocratic institution, limited to the select few, from which the country as a whole derived no benefit. A former colonel of the 'Tennessee Rifles,' Cannon wished to see the money expended for West Point devoted to training militia officers.[25]

This dislike of West Point as an aristocratic and militarist institution was illustrated in an interesting way by the attitude of the two Adamses. In the summer of 1821 the cadet corps stopped at Quincy, Massachusetts, to be reviewed by old John Adams before they continued on to Boston. Adams, who never forgot the significance of the Boston Massacre as an argument against military supremacy, told the future officers that, although their profession was identified with national glory, real glory depended on wisdom and benevolence. Contrasting the example of a George Washington with that of a Caesar or an Alexander, he congratulated the cadets on the fact that they too were fitted to pursue the arts o peace as well as of war.[26] Five years later, John Quincy Adams re ceived a similar visit, for which he expressed his appreciation, bu afterwards noted in his diary that he 'felt no inclination to extol th system of military education.' The next day, while observing Columbian College commencement in Washington, he contraste it with the West Point type of education, remarking: 'That was show of bodily exercise, and this of the cultivation of the mind My predilections continue strong in favor of the college.' [27]

During the 1830s the attack upon West Point received new im petus from the ranks of Jacksonian Democrats. The Tennessee an Ohio legislatures called upon Congress to abolish the Academy while Franklin Pierce, in 1836, announced on the floor of th House that he would 'refuse to appropriate the first dollar for it support' until Congress agreed to launch an investigation of con ditions in the institution. The following year, a report to the House from a select committee established to investigate the Academy recommended as an alternative the institution of some system o education for those officers already in the army, which 'in all it grades, should be kept open to the fair, manly, and impartial com petition of all citizens, like every other department of Govern ment.' [28] The hard times following the Panic of 1837 encourage further attacks upon West Point as a useless extravagance. variety of resolutions was again introduced in Congress, and movement against the Academy was started in some of the Nev England states.[29] On the eve of the War with Mexico, Representa tive William Sawyer of Ohio expressed the hope 'that we may cu off this rotten and corrupt institution, that is a drain upon th public treasury; this thing that is demoralizing in its effects; tha has no tendency to good, or to the preservation of liberty an union.' [30] Although democratic hostility to West Point lingered on particularly in the attitude of a staunch Jacksonian like Thoma Hart Benton, who refused to accept appointment as a Congres sional visitor to the Academy,[31] the record of its graduates in th Mexican War seems to have allayed somewhat the force of the op position.

The domestic debate over the relative merits of a standing army military academy, trained or untrained militia, did not escape the notice of the host of European travelers who visited the United States in the decades after 1815. While often prejudiced against the American form of government, the European observers were also curious to see how the republican experiment was working out in practice. From the time of the Revolution, American leaders had made much of the argument that a republic, in contrast to European monarchies, was a government of peace, free of the burdens of tremendous military establishments. The Marquis de Condorcet, the optimistic philosopher of the French eighteenth-century *idéologues,* in his *Influence of the American Revolution on Europe* (1786) commented upon the lack of militarism in the United States. Although zealous in the prosecution of the late war against the mother country, Condorcet believed that Americans lacked any disposition to wage a war of conquest. The example of the New World to the Old was one of peace, and Europe had nothing to fear from the success of the American Revolution.[32]

Despite the expansionist aims of the War Hawks in the War of 1812, Condorcet's picture of the pacific nature of the United States was generally accepted by later European observers of the American scene. The small standing army of some six thousand men furnished the most obvious evidence to support this view and also served as an example to the Old World to reduce the expense of its oversized armies. If the sons of the nobility would go to the United States and see at first hand the good government practiced there, 'they would be convinced,' an English traveler wrote, 'that a large standing army in time of peace is unnecessary.'[33] As the republican alternative to a standing army, the militia attracted especial attention. Although not considered a formidable fighting force, it was viewed as inspiring a sense of civic duty and patriotism. At the same time, it avoided the danger to republican institutions of a standing army or of a military tyrant. Frances Wright, the Scottish freethinker and feminist, believed that when a government was supported by a regular army, the people's liberties 'are no longer held of right, but held as a matter of grace and favour.' In the United States she noted: 'The people keep the sword in their own hands, and leave their rulers without any; they are thus the

guardians of their own rights, and the enforcers of their ow
laws.' [34]

In 1833, when Captain Thomas Hamilton of the royal navy pul
lished his *Men and Manners in America*, he commented on wha
he felt to be the ridiculousness of the American fear of the Pres
dent's becoming a military dictator.[35] Two years later, Alexis d
Tocqueville, who also visited the United States during Andre
Jackson's Presidency, published the first volume of his celebrate
work, *Democracy in America*. In contrast to Captain Hamilton an
many another early observer, Tocqueville believed that, while
free people could rise to meet a threatened danger with more ei
thusiasm than a people under despotic rule, freedom itself wa
not suited to a long-drawn-out struggle of the type lately wage
in Europe. For example, the impressment and conscription ei
gendered by such a war were largely unknown in America, wher
he asserted, 'men are induced to enlist by bounties. The notior
and habits of the people of the United States are so opposed i
compulsory recruiting that I do not think it can ever be sanctione
by the laws.' [36]

In a famous chapter entitled 'Why Democratic Nations Natu
rally Desire Peace, and Democratic Armies, War,' Tocquevil
gave a clear explanation of the American aversion to a large arm
whether a standing force of volunteers or an organized militia
conscripts. While the general population of a democracy desire
peace and the enjoyment of their free institutions, a democrat
army, especially its lower ranks in their search for advancemei
and promotion, might easily lend itself to a movement for war
to the ambitions of a military despot. Since democratic armi
tended to become numerous and since the people were not apt
volunteer, conscription was the eventual result. This would I
borne as long as the burden was distributed equally, but the cit
zen army, due to its short term of service, might become imbue
with ideas of military glory and advancement which, in tur
would make it a danger to the community. In other words, th
very martial enthusiasm that made democratic armies formidab
fighting forces also made them a threat to civil institutions of s
ciety and government. Although Tocqueville believed that th
remedies against such a military usurpation were to be sought

firm civil control of the army and in the maintenance of civil freedom to prevent military domination, he warned his readers that:

> After all, and in spite of all precautions, a large army in the midst of a democratic people will always be a source of great danger. The most effectual means of diminishing that danger would be to reduce the army, but this is a remedy that all nations are not able to apply.[37]

Tocqueville's conjecture that the United States, despite its small standing army, was by no means free of the danger of militarism received support in the observations of James Silk Buckingham. As he traveled about the United States, Buckingham found evidences of the military spirit on all sides. Although he noted that the love of parades and of military titles and uniforms was greatest in the South, Buckingham also found evidences of the same fondness for martial display in the larger cities of the North, where Washington's birthday and the Fourth of July were apt to be celebrated in a militia parade. After spending a day in reviewing the marching of the volunteer militia companies of Boston, he expressed the belief that the event was undesirable because 'it keeps too much alive the warlike dispositions of mankind.' The Presidential campaign of 1840 especially attracted Buckingham's attention, and he saw the Whig choice of Harrison over Clay as an example of the continuing American disposition to honor military heroes in the Andrew Jackson tradition.[38]

Although the travelers, in general, accepted the American view that democratic institutions were a force for peace, they could not refrain from noting the militant nationalism that developed side by side with the tradition of a small military establishment. In the case of Tocqueville, later critics of his *Democracy in America* have ascribed much of his pessimism over the future of democracy and his fears of militarism to the bitter controversies of the Jacksonian era. Contemporary Whig politicians, observing the actions of President Jackson, were even more dismayed than Tocqueville and did not hesitate to denounce the President as a military tyrant.

VI

A Military Hero and Manifes Destiny

THE NEW DEMOCRACY of America, which so impressed Tocquevill and other observers of the American scene, was a curious con pound of idealism and nationalism. The idealism and humanita ianism implicit in this democracy reinforced the antimilitarist tr ditions of the young republic and strengthened American sent ment for peace. But the nationalism associated with United State democracy was a stimulus toward expansionism and war and con tributed heavily toward the development of a military point of view among the people in the decades following the War of 181. Thus, in that period of American history concluded by the ou break of the Civil War, the idealism of the new democracy ushere in an age of progress and universal reform, while at the same tim its nationalism, under the banners of manifest destiny, carried the country into war with Mexico.

The hero and symbol of this democracy, in both its idealist an nationalist sense, was Andrew Jackson, the victor of the battle of New Orleans. The second general elevated to the White Hous Jackson's qualifications for that high office seemed much inferic to those of George Washington, his only military predecessor. Ex ibiting in his sensational career a marked capacity for abrupt, violent, and even illegal action, Jackson's election to the Presidency naturally aroused the fear that he would apply military methods to civil problems.

In Congress, Henry Clay, Jackson's rival for the political support of the West, was one of a number who criticized the general's high-handed method of conducting war along the Florida frontier. Then, in 1824, Clay was able to use his great popularity in the House of Representatives to help secure the choice of John Quincy Adams over Jackson as President. Charged with having entered into a corrupt bargain with the Adams party, Clay defended himself in a public letter to his constituents. While not opposed to a soldier's becoming President, Clay complained that Jackson did not possess the statesmanlike qualities of a Washington and was deficient in an appreciation of a civilian point of view. In private correspondence, Clay asserted that his conscience would not permit him to contribute to the election of a military chieftain, 'of whom I can not believe that killing two thousand five hundred Englishmen at New Orleans, qualifies for the various, difficult, and complicated duties of the chief magistracy.' [1]

Although Clay's decision was commended by many prominent men of his day, there was little doubt that the majority of the people would have preferred to see Jackson rather than Adams in the White House. Assaying the Jackson candidacy in 1827, the Washington *National Intelligencer* expressed the belief that military fervor played the leading part in Jackson's popular support. In the late campaign of 1824, referred to as an example of 'the seductiveness of military force in popular governments,' the *Intelligencer* charged that the militia 'marched almost literally in embattled legions to the polls' to vote for Jackson. While not apprehensive that Jackson would overthrow the Constitution, the *Intelligencer* objected

to placing a military man in the chief authority because, having once tasted of the pleasure of absolute command, as in the field of battle, he may retain the relish for it, and is too likely, in the exercise of public duties, to substitute for the injunctions of law, or the suggestions of policy, his own sovereign will and pleasure. He cannot endanger the existence of the Government, but he may endanger the public peace, at home as well as abroad. We object to such an elevation of a military man, especially, when his military fame is the only argument in favor of it, and when his civil qualifications are either not inquired into, or not established.[2]

As President, Jackson hardly justified the exaggerated fears o his political enemies, although his willingness to use military force against Indians, nullificationists, Frenchmen, or Mexicans wa hardly calculated to allay the alarm of his less militant opponents In his inaugural address, Jackson recommended no increase in th army or navy, and in his later messages to Congress, he confined himself mostly to the traditional and perfunctory advice to im prove the militia as a substitute for the unrepublican policy of large standing army. Meanwhile, the new Democracy in Congres introduced resolutions to eliminate the superfluous officers in both the military and naval establishments. Secretary of the Navy, John Branch, in his first annual report, stated that 'The present nava corps of the United States is believed to be more numerous than is required for the wants of the service.' He also pointed out tha 'It is now twenty-eight years since a judicious pruning was given to the navy.'[3]

Jackson's political opponents were much worried over the popu lar appeal of many of the President's policies. Equally upset by the personal and often arbitrary methods that Jackson used to accom plish his ends, his critics likened the President to a despotic mon arch, calling him King Andrew the First. Jackson's request for 'force bill' to enable him to use troops against the South Carolina nullificationists especially rallied the opposition. Daniel Webster although by now no friend of nullification doctrines, asserted be fore a Whig gathering in Massachusetts that he was 'against the unauthorized employment of military power, and against super seding the authority of the laws, by an armed force, under pre tence of putting down nullification.'[4] John Tyler, the advocate o state rights, complained that it was 'idle to talk of preserving republic for any length of time with an uncontrolled power over the military, exercised at pleasure by the President.'[5] In the United States Senate, George Poindexter of Mississippi, a bitter personal enemy of Jackson, introduced a resolution requesting the President to submit copies of his order to United States troop

South Carolina. Alleging 'that there is something rotten in the state of Denmark,' Poindexter charged that 'the Executive is disposed to excite discord and civil war in the South, in order to have pretext to march an army to overrun the country.' Condy Raguet's *Examiner and Journal* in commenting upon Jackson's other great controversial measure, the 'war' against the Bank of the United States, observed that those thousands who had clamored to give Jackson the power of the sword against South Carolina now proposed to give him the power of the purse and so render the despotism complete.[6]

Jackson's interpretation of the powers of the President, although it gave offense to his political enemies, was on the whole circumspect in the realm of military affairs. Until the close of his second administration there was no executive interference or pressure to strengthen the military power. Because of this, later opponents of militarism sometimes coupled Jackson with Jefferson as exemplifying the small army and navy tradition of the Democratic party. The chief exception to this antimilitarism came in 1835 when Congress faced the possibility of Jackson's involving the country in a war against France in retaliation for the latter's refusal to pay spoliation claims due American citizens. At the same time, there was the ever-present danger of conflict with the Indians and the possibility of a break with Mexico over the Texas question. Despite a bellicose message from the President at this juncture, Congress refused to go along with Jackson's suggested preparedness program. In the last moments of the Twenty-third Congress, an amendment to an appropriations bill authorizing the President to spend, if needed, three million dollars for the army and navy during the period of the Congressional recess passed the House. The Senate, led by Clay, Calhoun, and Webster, defeated the amendment and refused any compromise with the House version of the bill. Although the action of the Senate was denounced by Jackson and by some later historians as an example of unpatriotic factionalism, the unpreparedness of the United States may have persuaded the President to settle the dispute with France by diplomatic instead of military means.[7]

The threatened use of force, implicit in the Jacksonian preparedness legislation of 1835 and 1836, foreshadowed the bellicose at-

mosphere of the expansionist 'forties. Although attacked at ever
turn by peace leaders and by some of the Whig opposition, Jacl
son's successors were to carry an aggressive military and foreig
policy to its logical conclusion in the War with Mexico. A state:
man who played a leading role in drafting the more militant polic
of the decade preceding the Mexican War was Joel R. Poinset
President Van Buren's Secretary of War. Poinsett, a native Sout
Carolinian, had served the Jackson cause as an opponent of nullif
cation in his own state and as Minister to Mexico during the wa
for Texan independence. The author of a learned treatise forecas
ing the decline of the Indian races, Poinsett was a scholarly advc
cate of manifest destiny. As Secretary of War, he attempted t
revive interest in the old Calhoun-Harrison scheme for the classif
cation and training of the militia, and he enthusiastically recom
mended that the army be increased to fifteen thousand men. R(
sponding to this request, Congress in alarm over the Seminol
Indian War and border raids along the Canadian frontier voted i
July 1838 to expand the regular army to twelve thousand men.[8]

Along with his suggestions for augmenting the regular arm)
Poinsett tried with much less success to persuade Congress to r(
organize the militia. According to Poinsett's scheme, the countr
was to be divided into eight districts with 12,500 men in activ
service and an equal number in reserve. In all, 200,000 men b(
tween the ages of 21 and 37 would be enrolled at one time, the in
dividual's length of service amounting to eight years, half on activ
duty and half in the reserve.[9] This elaborate plan was immediatel
denounced by members of both political parties. Whigs attacke
it as a militaristic scheme to fasten conscription and a vast stand
ing army upon the people through the device of training th
militia. A general convention of the Whig party of New Englan
adopted a resolution drafted by Daniel Webster, the president c
the convention, protesting against the Poinsett plan as an uncor
stitutional interference with state control of the militia. The resc
lution concluded with satisfaction that the project 'has been s
scorched by public rebuke and reprobation, that no man raises h
hand or opens his mouth in its favor.'[10] Democrats, alarmed at th
public outcry, hastened to disavow any party support for Poinsett'
report. James Buchanan, in a speech before the Pennsylvania stat

emocratic convention, recalled that Harrison, the Whig President, had recommended a similar plan in the 1820s, which would ave gone so far as to include military instruction in the schools. laiming that President Van Buren, and the Democrats generally, d repudiated Poinsett's ideas, Buchanan went on to attack the inciple of conscription and of military drill in the schools. 'Such system,' he declared, 'would soon convert this country into a ilitary despotism.'[11]

Poinsett's conscription plan was the most systematic and exeme expression of the militarist point of view at this time. Yet, the country were going to pursue the aggressive expansionist licies envisaged by Poinsett and other advocates of manifest stiny, his preparedness schemes were not, perhaps, too drastic unrealistic. A militarist philosophy, despite the encouragement rnished by the later Jacksonian years, was still to have difficulty gaining the backing of either Congress or the country. Influenl citizens, particularly those from the ranks of the intellectuals, ormers, and clergy, were highly critical of military preparedss. George Bancroft, historian and Democratic politician, argued it the accomplishments of modern civilization were not due to nies or conquests, but rather to the efficacy of popular efforts at l improvement. Francis Wayland, President of Brown University, in his popular text on political economy pointed out that the eapest defense of nations' was in 'the exercise of justice and evolence.' And Laurens P. Hickok, a fellow educator and rgyman, included among 'the sources of military delusion' the ion that preparedness for war secures peace. Horace Mann, the ous Secretary of the Massachusetts Board of Education, comined that the children's school books gave exaggerated emphato war and martial glory. He also denounced a government and iety that neglected public education in favor of expenditures military academies, militia musters, and the manufacture of aments.[12]

uring the early 1840s a decline in Indian fighting, lull in the tation for annexation of Texas, and improvement in relations Great Britain, together with demands for economy after the ic of 1837, all helped to bring about a reduction in the size of army establishment and a partial rejection by Congress of the

Tyler administration's plans for substantial naval increases. The
victories could only delay the surge of expansionist sentime:
coursing through the western part of the United States. We
aware of the militant feeling of the country, John Quincy Adam
who had supported the army reduction bill, lamented the declir
of the old Revolutionary opposition to standing armies. Althoug
he believed that the danger of war was becoming less, he w
alarmed to see projects, 'full of a military mind,' that embrace
the construction of railroads and a chain of forts in the We
Adams also attacked the creation by the navy of a home squadre
as a useless expense, and he announced that he 'saw no necessi
for a large navy, unless it was to insult other nations, by takir
possession of their territory in time of peace.' [13]

The possibility of United States territorial aggression was e
pecially alarming to spokesmen of peace. War for such a purpo
would compromise democracy and the ideals of the republic. A
ticipating later abolitionist attacks on the Mexican War, Willia
Ellery Channing gave voice to this argument in his criticism
American policy regarding Canada and Texas during the 1830s
Also fearful of the possibility of war by the action of the Americ
government, William Jay, the son of the John Jay whose unpopul
treaty had helped prevent war with Great Britain in 1794, pointe
out that the evils of war were not confined to the period of he
tilities. In the United States the war spirit was apparent in t
militia system, the frequent parades and displays of arms, t
permanent garrisons and navy, and the military schools. Skeptic
of the frequently asserted claim that free institutions were a gua
antee of peace, Jay showed how the greater part of the feder
budget was devoted to paying for past wars and to preparati
for future conflicts.[15]

As the United States approached an open conflict with Mexi
over the question of the Texas boundary, Charles Sumner, a risi
young Massachusetts attorney, made a sensational attack up
the war spirit and the military establishment which served to e
courage it. Invited by the city of Boston to deliver the annu
Fourth of July oration commemorating American independen
Sumner, in place of the traditional holiday ode to the patrioti
of the founding fathers, asked the provocative question: 'what,

ur age, are the true objects of national ambition — what is truly ational glory — national honor — WHAT IS THE TRUE GRANDEUR F NATIONS?' In the face of impending hostilities with Mexico and ngland, he attacked the customary identification of the pursuit f war with national glory. Among the institutions and influences erpetuating war, Sumner included the 'Christian Church,' 'love f country,' and 'preparations for war, in time of peace.' Then, omparing the costs of war preparation in Europe and Amer- a, Sumner charged that United States expenditures were rela- vely much greater and, in addition, far exceeded the amount ent on education in America. Finally, to the great indignation f the military guests seated in uniform among the front rows, he ked: 'What is the use of the Standing Army of the United States?' cluding the navy in his denunciation, Sumner pointed out that s costs were greater than the value of our annual overseas mer- ant trade. The militia was likewise useless and should be sup- anted, he asserted, by a local police force.[16]

Although Sumner, who later gave his support reluctantly to e Civil War, was not a complete nonresistant pacifist, he attacked ore eloquently than any of his contemporaries the growing reparations for war and the rising military spirit. Opposing the hristian spirit of love to the doctrine of force, he pointed out that med nations had also been the most belligerent nations in world story. Touching off a wave of both protest and approval, Sum- r's oration was particularly significant because of the time and rcumstances surrounding its delivery and because of the un- ompromising nature of its arguments. Unable to forestall the ming war with Mexico, the address nevertheless was a rallying int for the New England opposition.[17]

The formal declaration of war against Mexico in May 1846 osed a long era of peace. Except for frontier Indian conflict in e United States and revolutionary strife in Europe, the Western orld had not been so generally free of war since the time of the ugustan Age of the Roman Empire. Although the Mexican War me as a bitter blow to those Americans who were convinced that e progress of civilization and establishment of a democratic rm of government precluded an appeal to arms, the outbreak hostilities was not unexpected in view of the militant temper

of much of the country. The prediction that continued expansic
by the United States would lead to war with Mexico or Grea
Britain had often been stated by peace leaders and by Whig oj
ponents of the aggressive policies of Presidents Jackson, Tyler, an
Polk.

The Democrats themselves were hardly consistent in the
war policies. Members of the party in Congress clamored for tl
occupation of Oregon and the annexation of Texas at the sam
time that they voted down any increase in the army or navy. A
though the Naval Academy at Annapolis was established durir
the Polk administration, the President and his followers in Co:
gress remained loyal to the antinavy policies of the Democrat
party. In his first message to Congress, the President, despite
reference to the changing economic interests of the United Stat.
which seemed to require a stronger navy, reaffirmed the trac
tional view that 'Our reliance for protection and defense on tl
land must be mainly on our citizen soldiers.' [18]

The United States in 1846, as in 1812, entered upon a war
its own choosing without having made any particular efforts
military preparation. This unreadiness from a military standpoi
is partly explained by the general confidence of the America
people that the war could easily be won by an army of voluntee
and militia. The lack of preparedness was also traceable to tl
fact that widespread opposition to Polk's Mexican policy, ar
Whig charges of military despotism, prevented the passage
more militant measures and made it politically necessary for tl
President to adopt the stratagem of American defense in a w
which, he alleged, was 'begun by the act of Mexico.' Milita
historians have laid the blame for the unpreparedness of tl
country upon those peaceable Americans who opposed a larg
standing army, stronger navy, and well-disciplined militia. It
however, open to some question as to whether the fault did n
rest with the Polk expansionists, who, like the War Hawks of 181
seemed determined upon a conflict despite the opposition of
considerable proportion of the American people.

Opponents of the Mexican War included Whig politiciar
abolitionists, pacifists, reformers, and anti-expansionists. The:
groups were concentrated for the most part in New England, b

ie war was far from popular in some areas of the Old South. Al-
hough all sorts of arguments were naturally invoked by an opposi-
on so diverse and widespread, a common element of their attack
pon the war was that it would foster a spirit of militarism at
ariance with past American traditions and policy. Reluctant to
o as far in their criticism of the war as did the abolitionists and
acifists, Whig statesmen instead devoted themselves to showing
ow a war of conquest conflicted with American constitutional
overnment. Daniel Webster, leader of the New England and
onservative Whigs, accused President Polk of usurping the pro-
ision of the Constitution reserving to Congress the power to
eclare war. Webster asked

> what is the value of this constitutional provision, if the President
> of his own authority may make such military movements as must
> bring on war? If the war power be in Congress, then every thing
> tending directly or naturally to bring on war should be referred to
> the discretion of Congress? [19]

he Massachusetts legislature resolved that the war had been
inconstitutionally commenced by the order of the President, to
eneral Taylor, to take military possession of territory in dispute
etween the United States and Mexico.' Attacking the position of
ie United States as that of an aggressor and conqueror, the
egislature termed it a Christian and patriotic duty 'for all good
tizens to join in efforts to arrest this war.' [20]

In Congress, the war was subjected to a steady undercurrent of
riticism although the Whig opposition, which included Daniel
/ebster and Abraham Lincoln, was careful to vote the appropria-
ons necessary for its successful prosecution. On the other hand,
shua Giddings, a prominent antislavery Whig Congressman
om Ohio, denounced the concept that every American must
ipport a war, even if unjust; and he called for the withdrawal
f all American troops from Mexico. In the Senate, Thomas Cor-
in delivered one of the most famous indictments of the war,
uestioning the whole philosophy of manifest destiny and the
elief that a nation must advance at the expense of its neighbors.
trust,' he declared, in recalling the old opposition to a standing
rmy, 'we shall abandon the idea, the heathen, barbarian notion,

that our true national glory is to be won, or retained, by militar
prowess or skill, in the art of destroying life.' John Bell of Ten
nessee predicted that the continuance of the war and the triump
of so-called 'progressive Democracy' would lead to a standin
army of fifty thousand men. 'But,' he added sarcastically, 'we ma
console ourselves with the reflection that the forms of the republi
will still be preserved. The republic in ruin will still flourish i
name. . . .' [21]

The purpose and conduct of the war were also attacked in th
press. The New York *Evening Post,* Washington *National Intell*
gencer, and various New England Whig newspapers denounce
the war on grounds that it would establish a military aristocrac
and demoralize the country.[22] A most detailed contemporar
critique of the war in the public press was embraced in a series c
articles written for the *American Review,* a semiofficial Whig o
gan, by Daniel Dewey Barnard, a former Congressman from Ne
York. The war was especially a matter of regret, Barnard wrot
because it violated over thirty years of peace and because it ca
doubt on the tradition that a republican form of government wa
immune to military ambitions. Echoing Daniel Webster's positio
concerning the origins of the war, Barnard stigmatized the whol
affair as President Polk's 'unhappy war, in which, by his ow
deliberate, unauthorized and criminal act, he has involved th
country.' [23]

Whig criticism of the militarism engendered by War with Me
ico was, of course, partly motivated by political jealousy. Mo
extreme, and probably more sincere, was the denunciation of th
Mexican War voiced by a number of abolitionists and peac
leaders in the North. In their writings and speeches they que
tioned not only the justice of the war but also the doctrine c
the citizen's obedience to the state and his duty to perform mil
tary service. In his *Biglow Papers,* James Russell Lowell wrote
celebrated popular satire of the Mexican War as well as a stron
indictment of all war and military display. Lowell's interpretatio
of the conflict as a war of conquest and slaveholders' plot wa
shared by Henry David Thoreau whose *Essay on Civil Disobed*
ence was destined to become an important classic in the liter:
ture of pacifism. His objections to a standing army and the profe

on of the soldier were extended to include the political state
nd government as well. Appealing for the right of individual
onscience, Thoreau labeled the mass of men who served the state
s machines.

> They have the same sort of worth only as horses and dogs. . . .
> I say, let us not have such a machine any longer. In other words,
> when a sixth of the population of a nation which has undertaken
> to be the refuge of liberty are slaves, and a whole country is un-
> justly overrun and conquered by a foreign army, and subjected to
> military law, I think that it is not too soon for honest men to rebel
> and revolutionize. What makes this duty the more urgent is the
> fact, that the country so overrun is not our own, but ours is the
> invading army.[24]

'horeau called for individual resistance to the point of going to
rison and refusing to pay war taxes, and he himself spent a brief,
ut famous, night in the Concord jail.

Much denounced in the North, the War with Mexico was not
opular with all groups even in the South. To many Southern
aders, the war seemed certain to result in demands for higher
riffs to pay the costs of an army and an increasing horde of
deral officeholders. Alexander H. Stephens of Georgia, a leader
f the Southern Whigs, vied with his Northern colleagues in Conress in his denunciation of the war. Robert Toombs, another
eorgia Representative, criticized President Polk's attempts to
ifle all opposition. Toombs also opposed any increase of the
gular army and, as early as January 1847, called for a peace offer
Mexico.[25] In South Carolina, the Calhounite organ, the *Charles-
n Mercury*, was hostile to the war, while Calhoun himself was
nsparing in his criticism. Speaking on his resolution, which
ffirmed that the War with Mexico 'is not and should not be one
f conquest,' he called for a purely defensive war and the return
f all United States troops to the Rio Grande. The alternative of
ggressive war would result, he feared, in an army greatly in-
reased in size and cost. The Mexican conflict, he felt, cast doubt
pon the United States reputation 'for justice, moderation, or
isdom'; and, in the increasing powers which it gave to the
overnment, the war violated traditional American liberty. 'In
ie early stages of our Government,' Calhoun pointed out, 'the

great anxiety was how to preserve liberty; the great anxiety nov
is for the attainment of mere military glory. In the one, we ar
forgetting the other.' [26]

Objection to the Mexican War as a militarist enterprise woul
have been far stronger if the Polk administration had attempte
to raise an army by levies upon the state militia or by the threa
of conscription. The use of the volunteer system allayed somewha
hostility to the war and, at the same time, afforded an outlet fc
the martial enthusiasm of the younger devotees of manifest de:
tiny. Volunteers were also preferred because it was thought tha
they were cheaper, and because of a long-standing opposition t
the idea of a large regular army. Desertion and disaffection amon
the regulars had always been great, and the profession of a soldie
was held in no great esteem in the United States. At the time c
the War with Mexico, for example, from a fourth to a third of th
American army was composed of aliens. Often the men had er
listed to save themselves from starvation. As a result, Mexicans a
first did not fear the United States army and, indeed, one battalio
of their forces was made up of deserters from the United States.[?]

Although American troops, contrary to Mexican expectation:
fought well, there was a certain distrust between volunteers an
regulars, and an equal lack of confidence between ranking Whi
generals and the Polk administration. The very success of Amer
can arms seemed to arouse the fears of opponents of the war a
home. Thus the war for the defense of Texas had led America
armies into the heart of Mexico and across the mountains to Cal
fornia, while the growing popularity of Generals Winfield Scot
and Zachary Taylor threatened the political hopes of civil aspirant
to the Presidency.[28] At the same time, Northern hostility to th
probable expansion of slave territory increased as the war cor
tinued.

The question of how the newly conquered territories would b
governed also provoked a spirited controversy, occasioning alarr
in Congress as early as 1846. Garrett Davis of Kentucky, electe
to the House as a Henry Clay Whig, likened the President to a
emperor for permitting the United States army and navy to inst:
tute territorial governments without prior legislation by Congres:
Preferring the customary military government of the conquerc

) the establishment of civil government by the President and the
ıilitary office without the consent of Congress, Representative
ʲornelius Darragh of Pennsylvania declared: 'The moment you
ıvested him with a power like that, you made him at once a
ictator.' [29] After the war, the Supreme Court, called upon to
ıle in a case involving United States jurisdiction in the Mexican
ort of Tampico, decided that conquest, without the ratification
f a peace treaty, did not automatically extend the authority of
merican civil law. Chief Justice Taney, in delivering the opinion
f the Court, pointed out that 'the power to declare war was not
onferred upon Congress for the purpose of aggression or ag-
ʳandizement.' [30] In various ways the War with Mexico seemed
» be in conflict with American traditions, making an early peace
ll the more desirable.

Although the victorious troops of the Mexican War were speed-
y demobilized, the restoration of civil attitudes came more
owly. A war so easily won could not fail to create a certain mar-
al spirit. This was quickly demonstrated in the bellicose tone of
merican foreign policy in the 1850s. It was not surprising, as a
ʳominent historian has pointed out, that John A. Quitman, a
ader in the assault on Mexico City, was also during the next
ecade an organizer of filibustering raids against Cuba.[31] The
ʲ50s was also characterized by a new-found interest in naval ex-
ınsion paralleling the growing American commercial contacts
ith Central America and the Far East. The Democratic party,
ꞏw no longer representing the old agrarian views of Thomas
fferson and Andrew Jackson, pursued a vigorous policy of ex-
ınsionism which included the attempted acquisition of new terri-
ʳry, the spread of overseas commerce, and the support of republi-
ınism in Europe. At the same time, President Pierce, candidate
ꞏ the Democrats in 1852, despite his own private misgivings over
ıe Mexican War, brought into the White House the spirit of
ilitarism that the war had fostered.[32]

When Congress met in December 1853, the administration was
ady with a program calling for sweeping naval reforms and the
ꞏnstruction of new ships designed to protect not only the United
ates coastline but also American commerce overseas. Thomas
ʲart Benton, an old Jacksonian Democrat of Jeffersonian per-

suasions regarding a navy, declared at once that he would approve a navy only as a defensive force. Opposed to a policy of
conquest or of competition for supremacy of the seas, Benton
asserted that just as 'A standing army was always condemned by
the American people,' so 'A standing navy, a navy in time of peace
was always rejected by the American people.' [33] The opposition to
the Pierce naval measures, expressed by Benton and others, was
in large part overridden as the need for greater naval preparedness was dramatized by such events as Commodore Matthew
Perry's show of force against Japan. Even though Benton in his
hostility to the navy no longer spoke for the majority of the
Democratic party, still the Pierce administration was unable to
accomplish all that it desired in the way of constructing new
ships. In the succeeding Buchanan administration the ambitious
naval program of the 'fifties encountered still further difficulties in
Congress.

One source of bitter complaint in regard to the navy that was
finally removed during the 1850s was the use of flogging as
means of punishment for the enlisted personnel. Although abolished by act of Congress in 1850, agitation for a return to the
discipline of the whip and lash was slow to die out. The brutality
of flogging, and its connection with the undemocratic caste system dividing officers and men in the navy were effectively set
forth in Herman Melville's *White Jacket* and in Charles Nordhoff's
Man of War Life. These popular novels, giving realistic accounts
of navy life by former American sailors, stirred popular indignation and contributed to the defeat of schemes to revive flogging
on American naval vessels.[34]

By the close of the 1850s, naval expansion as well as all other
issues were yielding their claims for public attention to the slavery
question. Antislavery Congressmen were reluctant to vote increases for the army if federal troops were to be used to protect
slavery in the territories or to recapture fugitive slaves. With many
of the abolitionists also devoted followers of the peace movement
an antislavery and antiarmy point of view were often in conjunction. On the other hand, the South accused antislavery but big
navy Senators in the North of using the suppression of the African
slave trade as a pretext to build up an expensive naval establish-

ment. More and more in the 'fifties the bitter antagonism generated between North and South by the slavery controversy prevented any unified policy of strengthening either the army or the navy.

By the 1860s, the open conflict between North and South was to exert a profound and adverse effect upon the American antimilitarist tradition. Because of the easy success achieved by American arms in the War with Mexico, many a Northern or Southern extremist was all the more ready to carry his views to the point of war in 1861. Yet, in the years from Jackson to Lincoln, antimilitarism, despite the setback of Mexican War, remained strong. Though fond of martial display and military heroes, the American people continued to resent the militarism implied by a standing army or disciplined militia. Even Andrew Jackson, soldier President and hero of the age, was in many ways not a typical military figure. Thus the American people entered upon the crisis of 1861 imbued with a firm belief in their own nonmilitary character.

VII

The Menace of Civil War

THE CIVIL WAR was the most important American conflict between the Revolution and World War II. Casualties of one million men killed or wounded on both sides and economic losses running into billions of dollars illustrate the more direct impact of the war. Termed 'a Second American Revolution' by the Beards in reference to its effect upon the American economy, the war also helped to bring about changes of far-reaching importance in other aspects of American life and thought.

At the outset of the Civil War the United States, despite a certain martial enthusiasm displayed at various times in its history, was not a militarist nation. But in the course of four long years of fighting between North and South, democracy was often compromised and the American antimilitarist tradition was at times severely scarred. The Anglo-Saxon tendency to emphasize the rule of law and to hold the military subservient to the civil power was challenged by arguments that the Constitution no longer operated in wartime and that 'military necessity knows no law'. Over the bitter protests of a minority, who held that the government should adhere to the Constitution even in so grave a crisis as a civil war, the United States was placed under what, for all practical purposes, amounted to a military dictatorship. Although President Lincoln was generally modest and circumspect in his exercise of extraordinary war powers, in a democracy even a benevolent and temporary dictatorship is open to question.

In the early months of 1861, the prospect of a civil war was looked upon with dismay by most thoughtful Americans. In his inaugural address, Abraham Lincoln was careful to avoid the suggestion of force to coerce the South, preferring to use the less bellicose concept of a war for defense. Leaders of the vigorous peace movement of the 'forties and 'fifties realized especially well the threat that a war held for American free institutions. At the same time, because the pacifists were usually also staunch abolitionists, they were faced by a conflict of loyalties. After the Sumter incident many of the peace leaders went along with the majority of the American people in their acceptance of the Civil War as a necessary struggle. The abolitionists, at least, hoped that with the emancipation of the Negro slaves some good would come out of the military experience. Wendell Phillips, the radical antislavery leader, told a lecture audience in December 1861:

> The war is better than the past, but there is not an element of good in it. I mean, there is nothing in it which we might not have gotten better, fuller, or more perfectly in other ways. . . . Neither will I remind you that, when we go out of this war, we go out with an immense disbanded army, an intense military spirit embodied in two thirds of a million of soldiers, the fruitful, the inevitable source of fresh debts and new wars.[1]

Charles Sumner, a former pacifist sympathizer, and a loyal abolitionist and Republican as well, reluctantly prepared 'to give up early visions, and to see my country filled with armies, while the military spirit prevails everywhere.' [2]

Although united behind the idea of war after the outbreak of hostilities, neither North nor South was prepared in a military way for a long and costly struggle. This lack of preparedness was, of course, understandable. Before 1861, any sudden attempt on the part of the federal government to recruit a large army would have conflicted with the popular aversion to coercion of the South. In view of the sectional strife of the 1850s, Congress could hardly have passed a large army or navy bill without arousing the suspicions of both sections, and perhaps precipitating the war. No matter how large or efficient the army, it would have included its

proportion of loyal Southerners, thereby strengthening the force
of resistance as well as of coercion. The fact that so many Wes
Pointers became famous as Confederate officers exerted a pro
found psychological effect upon both sections. Although the nav
and the great majority of the army's enlisted men remained loya
to the Union, the Secretary of War in his report of July 1861 asserte
with regard to those officers who had joined the South that, 'Bu
for this startling defection, the rebellion would never have as
sumed formidable proportions.' [3]

With little advance preparation, but buoyed by a wave o
popular excitement, the Union and Confederate government
undertook the complex task of raising an army. President Lincol
without summoning Congress issued an executive proclamatio
on 3 May 1861 calling for volunteers to serve three years, thes
volunteers being in addition to the seventy-five thousand militi
already assembled. At the same time, in direct violation of th
constitutional provision leaving the size of the military establish
ment to be determined by Congress, Lincoln directed an increas
of ten regiments for the regular army. When Congress was finall
called into special session in July 1861, it had almost no alternativ
to ratifying Lincoln's proclamations and giving belated legislativ
sanction to measures that the President himself admitted migh
not have been strictly legal. Objection to Congressional approva
of the Lincoln emergency acts came chiefly from representative
of the border states who resented the use of force against th
South and the dictatorial military powers assumed by the Pres
dent. [4]

Outside the halls of Congress and further removed from th
war-charged atmosphere of Washington, a significant minorit
questioned the Lincoln emergency measures. Many of the north
ern newspapers that had supported Douglas, Breckinridge, o
Bell in the campaign of 1860 continued, even after Sumter, t
oppose the use of force to coerce the South. Apprehensive of th
effects of a war, they were highly critical of the methods used b
the Lincoln administration to suppress dissent and carry out it
policies. On 27 June 1861 in New York City at a meeting of editor
representing thirteen papers opposed to the war, a resolution wa
passed denouncing the militaristic policies of the federal govern

ment. The Newark, New Jersey, *Evening Journal,* a Breckinridge supporter, predicted that a civil war might continue 'until perchance, confusion and anarchy pave the way for a military dictator to ride rough shod over the people, and establish a grinding despotism at the expense of justice, constitutional liberty and right.'[5]

The presence of a strong and vocal opposition, which often included active proponents of the cause of the Confederacy, posed a grave problem for the Lincoln administration. Anxious to curb dissenting opinion as well as disloyalty, Republican party leaders frequently went beyond the lawful prosecution in the courts of actual cases of treasonable activities. Through a policy of arbitrary arrests, made possible by Lincoln's suspension of the writ of habeas corpus, persons were seized and confined on the suspicion of disloyalty or of sympathy with the Southern cause. In the course of the Civil War, a total of thirteen thousand civilians was estimated to have been held as political prisoners, often without any sort of trial or after only cursory hearings before a military tribunal.[6]

One of the earliest and most important criticisms of the practice of arbitrary arrest was made by Chief Justice Roger B. Taney in the case of John Merryman. Merryman, an officer in a secessionist drill company, was arrested and placed in military confinement on orders of the Union general commanding the Maryland district. A petition for a writ of habeas corpus was then presented to Taney, who directed that Merryman be brought to court for a judicial examination into the cause of his imprisonment. Acting under orders and citing as authority the President's suspension of the writ of habeas corpus, the army refused to produce the prisoner. Rebuffed in an attempt to serve a writ of contempt upon the general holding Merryman, Taney, deprived of any further recourse, filed a written opinion for the record and sent a copy to the President. Strongly denying the latter's right to suspend the writ of habeas corpus, the Chief Justice also charged that the military had gone beyond a proper interpretation of the President's decree.

It has, by force of arms, thrust aside the judicial authorities and officers to whom the Constitution has confided the power and duty of interpreting and administering the laws, and substituted a military government in its place, to be administered and executed by military officers.

Pointing out that the civil authority was still in office and carrying out its functions, Taney further asserted: 'There was no danger of any obstruction or resistance to the action of the civil authorities, and therefore no reason whatever for the interposition of the military.' [7]

Contemporary reaction to the Merryman case varied, but it included some forthright and uncompromising praise of Taney's action. Former President Franklin Pierce, who shared Taney's dislike of the war and denounced all of Lincoln's arbitrary measures, congratulated the Chief Justice upon his opinion.[8] A committee of the Maryland legislature, a body that contained many Confederate sympathizers who were also later placed under arrest, cited the Merryman case as proof that the Unionist governor of the state had not properly protected Maryland citizens against the federal government. The committee recommended that the legislature pass a resolution of 'protest against the oppressive and tyrannical assertion and exercise of military jurisdiction, within the limits of Maryland, over the persons and property of her citizens by the Government of the United States.' [9] In Congress, Senators Lyman Trumbull and John P. Hale, both strong abolitionists, denounced the military arrests; and it is probable that Lincoln himself disliked the illegal and unconstitutional methods that he allowed to be used. In his message to Congress in December 186 the President made no mention of the Merryman case or his own exercise of extraordinary powers, perhaps because 'he himself had misgivings about the necessity of many things that had been done by his agents.' [10]

Criticism of Lincoln's arbitrary measures increased as the war continued on beyond the few months originally thought necessary to suppress the rebel South. English opinion of the Unionist cause already rendered bitter because of the *Trent* affair, became ever more hostile as news of the Lincoln policies reached Europe. There was an outcry among all classes of the English people against the arbitrary arrests, coercion of the press, and suppression of dissent in the North. Charges of a Lincoln military despotism

ere made by British newspapers, and his administration was
ompared to Milan under Austria and Naples under the Bour-
ons. Some fear was expressed lest American democracy degen-
ate into a military despotism and become a threat to Europe.[11]
An attack on Lincoln's policies, which attracted the attention of
rists in England as well as in the United States, was made by
enjamin R. Curtis, a well-known lawyer and co-author of the
mous dissenting opinion in the Dred Scott case. His pamphlet
xecutive Power, published in 1862 after the announcement of
e Emancipation Proclamation, impressed both Lincoln and
cretary of War Edwin M. Stanton, although it seemingly had
tle effect upon public opinion at the time. Curtis belabored the
olicy under which, he asserted,

my neighbors and myself, residing remote from armies and their
operations, and where all the laws of the land may be enforced by
constitutional means, should be subjected to the possibility of military arrest and imprisonment, and trial before a military commission, and punishment at its discretion for offences unknown to the
law.

irtis also severely denounced the argument that such powers
re justified by the President's role as commander in chief of
e armies. Because the framers of the Constitution desired to
ace the military under a civil commander did not mean, he
inted out, that they wished to enhance the President's power
 the extent that he could disobey the Constitution and laws of
 own country and exercise complete authority over all its citi-
ns.[12]
Opposition to the Lincoln policies was also reflected in the
ectoral victories scored by the Democratic party in 1862. On
e eve of these elections Joel Parker, a professor in the Harvard
w School, publicly charged that 'the President is not only
monarch, but that his is an absolute, irresponsible, uncontrol-
le government; a perfect military despotism.' Although the
cline of the Republican majorities in Congress was primarily a
ult of the military reverses suffered by the Union armies, it
licated too the growing protest against the administration's
r powers. Newly chosen Democratic governors, including Hora-
Seymour in New York and Joel Parker in New Jersey, were

antagonistic to much of the Lincoln program. In his first annua message to the state legislature, Seymour attacked the militi draft and the vast powers exercised by the President and the Wa Department through their use of martial law and arbitrary arrest Believing that the war itself should have been averted, he pointe out that its continuance served to strengthen extremist thinkin in both the North and the South, while the compromise sentimer of the Central and Western states was ignored. Although not goin as far as Seymour, Governor Andrew G. Curtin of Pennsylvania, Republican and friend of the Lincoln administration, made strong criticism of the system of arbitrary arrests in a speci message to the state legislature.[13]

The attack on wartime militarism and the development of peac sentiment were especially prevalent in the Middle West, Oh Valley region. Here the label Copperhead was fastened upon th defeatist and pacifist wing of the Democratic party and its lead Clement L. Vallandigham. As a member of Congress from 18 to 1863, Vallandigham had been a consistent foe of militarism ar war. An opponent of a standing army before the war, he continue to vote against all military bills including the Conscription Ac In a famous address before the Democratic Union Association New York on 7 March 1863, Vallandigham censured the gover ment for usurping the powers of the purse and sword in ord to establish a dictatorship. Protesting against the effort to coerc people to accept a war against slavery, he called for a 'VIGORO PROSECUTION OF PEACE FOR THE UNION.' [14]

These same sentiments were repeated by Vallandigham a fe weeks later in the course of a political speech in Ohio, in whic he charged the administration with needlessly prolonging the wa On the basis of this address, Vallandigham was accused of viola ing the orders forbidding the expression of sympathy with th South that had been issued by General Ambrose E. Burnside, cor manding in the Ohio area, and on the night of 5 May he was su denly seized by Burnside's soldiers. This capture stirred th country and provided a dramatic example of the encroachment the military upon civil authority. Governor Seymour, in a lett addressed to the chairman of a mass meeting assembled to prote Burnside's action, asserted: 'If this proceeding is approved

ne government, and sanctioned by the people, it is not merely a
tep toward revolution, it is revolution; it will not only lead to
uilitary despotism, it establishes military despotism.' [15]

Although Vallandigham's numerous speeches attacking the Lin-
oln administration and his popularity with antiwar Democrats
uade him a natural target of suspicion, General Burnside's pre-
ipitate action took Washington by surprise and posed a difficult
roblem for the government. Lincoln and his Cabinet, while they
egretted the arrest and doubted its legality, felt that the general
ad to be supported. The solution to the dilemma was found in
incoln's order commuting Vallandigham's sentence to prison by
military commission into exile to the Confederate States. At the
ume time, Burnside was warned by his superior, General Halleck,
aat in the loyal states 'it is best to interfere with the ordinary
vil tribunals as little as possible. Treasonable acts, in those
ates, unless of immediate and pressing danger, should be left
r trial by the courts, as provided in the Act of Congress.' Cau-
oning Burnside 'against inciting opposition to the Government by
nnecessary arrests and military trials,' Halleck complained: 'It
ems difficult to find military commanders of sufficient judgment
ad discretion to avoid conflict with civil authorities "in the loyal
ates." In many of these conflicts the officers have been entirely
. the wrong, assuming powers which do not belong to them.' [16]
urnside, however, continued to interpose his military authority
ad committed the 'further folly' of suspending the New York
'orld and the Chicago Times.

These difficulties with Burnside were paralleled by other no-
ble clashes between the civil and military authorities. For ex-
nple, General John C. Frémont, the Republican standard bearer
1856, and General Benjamin F. Butler both incurred Lincoln's
rly displeasure when, at the very start of the war, they used
eir military powers to free Negro slaves coming within their
nes. The most famous instance of a dispute between Lincoln and
s generals occurred in the case of George B. McClellan, who in
662 was relieved of his command of the Army of the Potomac.
nere is little doubt that McClellan had political ambitions of his
vn and that he was out of sympathy with the Lincoln administra-
on. Yet, his youthful egotism in all probability offered less of a

threat to civil authority than the army practice of arbitrary arrest and trial before military commissions of private citizens like Vallandigham.

During the war, the effort of Vallandigham and others to secure Supreme Court protection and redress from the decisions of the military commissions was unsuccessful. In 1866, after the war was over, the Supreme Court in the somewhat similar Milligan case passed upon the power of military commissions to try civilians in areas, not in the immediate vicinity of the war, where the civil courts were still functioning. In its decision, the Court ruled that 'Martial rule can never exist where the courts are open and in the proper and unobstructed exercise of their jurisdiction.' Nor could martial law be invoked in the case of threatened invasion, but 'The necessity must be actual and present; the invasion real, such as effectually closes the courts and deposes the civil administration.' [17] Judicial retribution for the usurpation of power by the military commissions had to await the close of the war. Even then, in the midst of Radical Reconstruction, the Milligan case 'was greeted with a virulence reminiscent of that produced by the Dred Scott decision.' Over the years, though, it has stood as a landmark in the cause of civil supremacy, with the judgment of the future well expressed in the contemporary comment that:

> It is not the crime of treason which is shielded by this memorable decision, but the sacred rights of the citizen that are vindicated against the arbitrary decisions of military authority. Above the might of the sword the majesty of law is thus raised supreme.[18]

The American antimilitarist tradition, already seriously endangered by the Civil War policy of arbitrary arrest and imprisonment, was still further threatened by the passage of a federal conscription law. The resort to a draft came, in part, as a natural result of the wartime tendency to concentrate power in the executive branch of the federal government. With Lincoln as a symbol of unity, and by a thorough use of propaganda and of curbs of liberty, the Northern people were gradually won over to an acceptance of a heightened nationalism. *Harper's Weekly*, for example, believed the draft would demonstrate to Europe and the South like the moral solidarity of the Union cause.[19] Conscription was also regarded as necessary to counteract a growing war-weariness, which, along with the realization of the costs of the war in terms of human life, was responsible for an increase in soldier desertions and for a decline of volunteering.

On 2 July 1862, Lincoln issued a call for three hundred thousand volunteers to serve for three years. This proclamation met with immediate objections on the part of state governors, who especially questioned the three-year term of enlistment. The collapse of state recruiting efforts, the example of the Confederate Draft Act, and the trend toward nationalism at the expense of state rights all contributed to the drive for drastic federal legislation. Since Congress was reluctant to pass a national conscription law, the members voted instead for a militia draft, utilizing the nominal principle of universal service in the militia, but leaving the actual method of choice to the individual states. In its final form, the Draft Act of 17 July 1862 authorized the President to summon the militia for nine months and to apportion quotas among the states. The states, in turn, might draft men to fill the ranks of their militia regiments and thus meet the federal quota, but they were under no compulsion to do so. State exemptions from the militia draft were liberal on the whole, New York, for example, excusing ministers, Quakers, Shakers, college and public-school teachers and students. Despite its mildness, this early militia draft met with organized resistance in some of the states, with hostility particularly strong among the foreign element of the population.[20]

A much more extreme measure than the 1862 militia bill was the Enrollment Act of 3 March 1863, which made no use of the militia system but bluntly called for universal compulsory service by means of federal conscription. Introduced in its first form by Senator Henry Wilson of Massachusetts, never a real friend of conscription, the bill was designed more as a whip of the federal government over the states or 'a threat of national force.' [21] Wilson also alluded to the drying-up of pools of volunteers and to the need of a draft in order to preserve the Union. Senator James W. Nesmith of Oregon, who believed the draft should have been in use from the outset of hostilities, announced that conscription was

necessary to impart the iron discipline needed to win the wa
'Without that sort of discipline,' he declared after criticizing th
equality of officers and men in the militia, 'no Government i
the world can succeed with its armies. Your armies controlled b
Democratic sentiment are nothing but a mob, and never can b
otherwise.' [22]

Friends of the bill, avoiding the use of the term conscription an
leaving the opposition little time for debate, attempted to rus
the draft legislation through Congress. Despite this haste, a sma
group of Democrats was able to launch an attack on the measur
terming it an unconstitutional expansion of the powers of th
federal government, which continued the trend already begu
with the suspension of the writ of habeas corpus and the arb
trary arrests. Robert Mallory of Kentucky and George Pendleto
of Ohio saw in the draft bill a reflection of the changing purpos
of the war from one to preserve the Union to an aggressive stru
gle to free the slaves. The draft bill, it was charged, was a subtl
way of enlarging the regular army and of covering the countr
with a huge network of federal marshals.[23]

The Conscription Act of 1863 furnished an additional bas
upon which the opposition could denounce the Lincoln admini
tration and its conduct of the war. In contrast to the arbitrar
arrests or the censorship and suppression of news, the draft la
affected virtually every American household. Going far beyon
the degree of compulsion exacted in theory by the state militi
laws, the national conscription law was without precedent in th
annals of either the United States or Great Britain. The historia
James Ford Rhodes in his account of the Civil War draft oppos
tion expressed a doubt that so untraditional a course enjoyed th
support of American public opinion.[24] Horace Greeley, the fa
mous editor of the *New York Tribune,* warned Secretary of Wa
Stanton that in a free state drafting was an anomaly which th
mass of the people would not accept.[25] Something of the shoc
that the draft occasioned among believers in the old Anglo-Saxo
tradition of personal liberty was indicated by Anthony Trollop
the English novelist, who came to America on a visit early in th
Civil War. Friendly to the North but aghast at the wartime co
ruption and military dominance that prevailed on all sides, Tro

ope on his return home was even more dismayed to learn of the
passage of the 1862 militia conscription act. To an American friend
he wrote:

> This conscription is very bad. Was it absolutely necessary? My
> feeling is that a man should die rather than be made a soldier
> against his will. One's country has no right to demand everything.
> There is much that is higher and better and greater than one's
> country. One is patriotic only because one is too small and too
> weak to be cosmopolitan. If a country cannot get along without
> a military conscription, it had better give up and let its children
> seek other ties.[26]

The question of the constitutionality of the Civil War conscription law did not come before the Supreme Court although
Chief Justice Taney wrote out an opinion, later found among his
papers, which indicates that he would have held it an unconstitutional violation of the states' authority over their militia. In the
well-known Pennsylvania Supreme Court decision of *Kneedler*
v. Lane, the federal Draft Act was at first held unconstitutional on
this basis, but in the reargument of the case the earlier decision
was reversed.[27]

Opposed as an unconstitutional violation of American traditions,
the draft was also criticized as a loosely drawn and unfair measure
that enabled wealthier individuals to hire a substitute or pay a
commutation fee of three hundred dollars. The Civil War law also
failed to make any provision recognizing the conscientious objection to war of Quakers and other pacifist groups or individuals.
Most states in the North traditionally exempted such persons or
required some equivalent in place of militia service. The compromise with conscience involved in a commutation fee or in the
hiring of a substitute was extremely distasteful to the Quakers,
who brought pressure to bear on Secretary of War Stanton to
provide some form of alternate service. Although Stanton and
Lincoln were not unfriendly to the Quaker position, they were
fearful of encouraging draft resistance and accordingly were reluctant to recommend measures to Congress for the relief of conscientious objectors drafted into the army against their will.[28]
Finally Congress, in response to the pleas of Charles Sumner,
Henry Wilson, Thaddeus Stevens, and others, made provision for

conscientious objectors to engage in hospital work. Before thi
was done, many Quakers and other pacifists had suffered sever
hardships and in some cases were sentenced to death, althoug
that extreme penalty was not carried out.[29]

The struggle of the conscientious objector for political recogni
tion proved more difficult in the South. Most of the state law
there contained no provision for exemption from militia servic
and Jefferson Davis was not as sympathetic as Lincoln to th
pacifist cause. The greater problems of the South in raising troop
also militated against consideration of the conscientious objecto
although Assistant Secretary of War John A. Campbell tried t
be of some help. Few, of course, went so far as the Quaker con
scientious objectors in their opposition to the Civil War, but 'In
nate aversion to military service . . . was undoubtedly as stron
a trait of the American people from 1861 to 1865 as ever befor
or after.' [30]

This dislike of military service became readily apparent as th
federal government began to enroll the men necessary to fill th
quotas of the various states. The most serious violent resistanc
to the draft occurred in New York City, but hostility was wide
spread and included the larger cities and industrial areas of th
East as well as the agricultural states of the Middle West. In Ne
York, Governor Horatio Seymour, an avowed opponent of con
scription, carried on a bitter correspondence with President Lir
coln and the War Department, protesting both the constitutionalit
of the draft and the fairness of the quota meted out to New Yor
City. Speaking in that city on 4 July 1863, Seymour attacked th
administration argument that 'public necessity' justified the war
time suppression of the Constitution and laws. Such a doctrine
he warned, could be invoked by the mass of the people as we
as by the government.[31]

Seymour's prediction came true when less than two weeks late
a crowd of people sought to prevent the federal marshals fror
making up their enrollment lists. Degenerating into an angry mob
the populace directed its wrath against abolitionists and Negroe
attacking Greeley's *Tribune* office and burning a colored orpha
asylum. Despite accusations that his own legalistic opposition t
the draft had encouraged the riots, Governor Seymour did no

give up his efforts to gain a postponement of the Draft Act in New York. Rebuffed in this regard, Seymour also incurred the displeasure of General John A. Dix, commanding officer in the Department of the East, for calling the draft 'the conscription act.' This term, Dix wrote the governor, was 'a phrase borrowed from a foreign system of enrollment, with odious features, from which ours is wholly free, and originally applied to the law in question by those who desire to bring it into reproach, and defeat its execution.' [32] In his annual message to the legislature at the close of the year, Governor Seymour explained again his stand on the draft issue. Calling attention to the danger that conscription and coercion would cause further disaffection between the army and the citizenry, he accused the President of having already subordinated the civil power to military authority.[33]

The events in New York were paralleled by similar outbreaks of popular resentment in neighboring states and in the Middle West, although the loss of life and destruction of property were not so great as in New York City. As a way of securing men for the Union army, conscription was far inferior to the more traditional means although it may have acted as a stimulus or goad to volunteering. In all, 46,000 conscripts and 118,000 substitutes, only 6 per cent of the Union forces, were secured through the operation of the conscription laws,[34] and this number hardly compensated for the scandal and violence accompanying the administration and enforcement of so unpopular a device. Regarded as an unfair discrimination against the poorer people, the draft laws were also resented as a break with American traditions of individual freedom. Nothing in past American history had prepared the Civil War generation to accept without protest the degree of nationalism and militarism implied in the practice of conscription.

Within the Union armies there was also increasing dissatisfaction. General war-weariness and mounting casualty lists diminished the flow of volunteers and stimulated desertion. Despite the possibility of the death penalty, over two hundred thousand Union soldiers are estimated to have fled the ranks. The large sums offered for enlistments by the federal and local governments encouraged the practice of bounty jumping and thus contributed to a further decline of soldier morale. Desertion was, of course,

due to various causes, often of a purely personal or material sor
At the same time, the soldier who took such a course was certainl
not imbued with love for a military way of life. Many a soldie
who remained loyal to the uniform nevertheless betrayed in h
letters home an extreme distaste for the army. Even in the highe
ranks, volunteer officers were embittered at the disdainful trea
ment they received from West Pointers and at the inefficiency c
the army.[35]

All of the North's wartime problems involving civil-militar
relations were paralleled or, in some cases, anticipated by th
experience of the South. Although the South as well as the Nort
shared the Anglo-Saxon tradition against a standing army or mil
tary domination of the civil society, yet the South since coloni
times had displayed a greater fondness for arms. Thus the care
of an army officer had long enjoyed a notable popularity wit
Southern gentlemen. The celebrated Virginia Military Institut
became a mother of similar schools below the Potomac, and b
1854 South Carolina, for example, was subsidizing a fourth c
the students attending the Citadel or the Arsenal, the two leadin
military institutions in that state. Militia companies grew t
amazing numbers between the Mexican and Civil Wars. In th
1840s and 1850s this indisputable martial spirit was becomin
connected with the rising tide of Southern nationalism. 'The mil
tary cult fed the feeling of nationalism and nationalism gave im
petus to the military cult.' [36]

At the same time, the Southern nationalists and militarists, wh
achieved a temporary dominance in the initial flush of secessioni
and post-Sumter enthusiasm, were not able to overcome th
equally strong Southern tradition of state rights. Like many a
American in the days of 1776, Southerners, rebelling against wha
they felt was the tyranny of the North, were not disposed to be
come, in turn, the slaves of their own government. Nor was marti
spirit able to forestall the decline in soldier and civilian moral
that accompanied the dragging-out of the war. By April 186
the Confederacy deemed it necessary to pass its first conscriptio
act. Subject to widespread evasion and resistance, this measure, a
President Davis admitted, 'has not been popular anywhere out c
the army.' A recent historian of 'Johnny Reb' has noted that all th

coercive acts of the Confederate Congress were subjected to widespread sabotage by the states, and this was certainly true in the
case of the conscription law, which was bitterly opposed by no
less a figure than Alexander H. Stephens, Vice President of the
Confederacy.[37]

In contrast to the North, the South very early in the war faced
the menace of invading armies and permanent military occupation
of its territory. Backed up by federal confiscation acts, General
Butler's army of occupation kept the city of New Orleans in tur-
moil and illustrated 'the excesses of a military regime in which civil
government is subordinated to the whim of military officers.' Conquests by the North intensified opposition to Jefferson Davis's policies and led to demands for a compromise peace. This was especially true in those areas where the individualist philosophy of men
like Vice President Stephens was a strong factor. On the other
hand, the impending collapse of the Confederacy also led to a
movement to increase the powers of the government and to grant
greater authority and independence to the army. Late in the war
there was talk that Lee be made a dictator. Finally, the Confederate Congress, following the precedent of the North, created the
office of general in chief of the armies, and in February 1865 Lee
was appointed to the unified command.[38]

In the North, the concluding days of the war also witnessed a
clash between the sentiment for peace and the demand for complete military victory. On both sides, the lengthy and costly struggle heightened the two extremes of defeatism and militarism. The
longing for peace, desire for victory, and fear of militarism thus
provoked a conflict of loyalties that was inherent in the whole war
process. This paradox was seen clearly by the youthful Adams
brothers as early as 1862. From London in May of that year, Henry
wrote to his brother Charles: 'I dread the continuance of this war
and its demoralizing effects more than anything else, and happy
would be the day when we could see the first sign of returning
peace.' Yet, in another letter composed a few months later, Henry
announced that he could see no peace as long as the Southern
people continued to exist. 'We must ruin them before we let them
go or it will all have to be done over again. And we must extermi-
nate them in the end, be it long or be it short, for it is a battle be-

tween us and slavery.' Charles accepted his brother's point of view
but, at the same time, he predicted that the difficulty of subjectin
the South would strengthen the hand of radicals and extremists i
the North.

> These men, and they will always in troublous times obtain tem-
> porary supreme control, will bankrupt the nation, jeopard all lib-
> erty by immense standing armies, debauch the morality of the
> nation by war, and undermine all republican foundations to effect
> the immediate destruction of the one institution of slavery.[39]

Such gloomy forebodings over the fate of the nation were swiftl
drowned out as the Northern armies achieved their final victorie
in the spring of 1865. The Union had been preserved and slaver
abolished, although only after resort to force and coercion. In th
moment of triumph, few complained of the enormous price c
victory — the loss of lives and destruction of property, the wai
time subversion of traditional civil liberties and constitutional gov
ernment. To the task of binding up these battle wounds and c
reconciling older American beliefs with the newer wartime ph
losophy, the people of the North and South turned with feeling
of enthusiasm and bitterness.

VIII

The Reconstruction of Civil Society

THE SURRENDER of the Confederate armies in the spring of 1865 terminated the Civil War. Although issues raised to prominence during that conflict would continue to arouse controversy, four long years of fighting had brought a reaction in favor of peace. In an atmosphere of conciliation exemplified by Lincoln's plea: 'With malice toward none, with charity for all,' and by Grant's generous terms at Appomattox, the nation turned from war to the task of reconstructing the Union.

The soldiers had had enough of fighting. Anxious to go back home and impatient of any delay in demobilization, officers and men alike revealed a strong distaste for professional army life. Though received as heroes, many Civil War veterans soon found difficulty in getting jobs or in adjusting to civil life. Now that the fighting was over, civilians were suspicious of the training provided by the army and distrusted the abilities of the returning soldier. Looking back upon this period from the vantage point of another great war, an American historian writing in 1919 noted that, although the Civil War veterans did learn to wear ready-made clothes; they did not become militaristic in their ideas. No generation has existed in the United States so fundamentally opposed to war and to territorial expansion; never before was the army brought down to so small a percentage of the population, so little attention given to the militia, and the navy allowed so rapidly to dwindle away; the military training so toilfully acquired was used chiefly to make political processions gay.[1]

As a comment on formal demobilization after 1865 this state ment is accurate, but it is also true that so tremendous a struggl as the Civil War inevitably left deep scars upon the traditiona American way of life. In addition to the staggering toll of live and vast destruction of property, there was the less tangible, bu no less important, impact of the war upon the American mind Important evidence of the militaristic effect of the Civil War ca be seen in the repeated emphasis upon the country's debt to it ex-soldiers. Capitalizing on this sentiment, veterans, disillusione with the discipline but not the glory of war, organized the Gran Army of the Republic and pressed their claims for pensions an preference in federal appointments. It was even feared that th G.A.R. might serve as the spearhead for a joint Radical Republi can military coup aimed at seizing the government from Presiden Johnson or at taking over Washington in the event that Presiden Hayes was not safely inaugurated in 1877. However remote thi threat, it is still true that membership in the G.A.R. was for year a virtual prerequisite for an ambitious politician, and the organi zation was accused with good reason of being an adjunct of th Republican party.[2]

Other evidence of the continued effect of the late war was th tendency of former army officers to assume important politica positions. At the same time, the professional soldier was still some what suspect, and although General Ulysses S. Grant succeede Andrew Johnson as President, it was to his political advantag that he had never been typical of the regular army man. Some thing of a pacifist in his dislike of military display, it has bee suggested that Grant stayed in the army more from habit tha from inclination.[3] The other Civil War generals elevated to th Presidency — Hayes, Garfield, and Harrison — had seen servic

ıly as volunteer officers, and in the 1880 campaign the Republi-
ıns were able to contrast James A. Garfield, the citizen soldier
: the Civil War, with Winfield Scott Hancock, the Democratic
ɔminee, who had been educated at West Point and was still
ı officer in the regular army. 'Hancock is not a soldier in the
ınse that Grant was a soldier,' the *New York Tribune* argued.
Ie represents the regular army and West Point alone. Grant was
f the people, for he entered the Army at the beginning of the
·ar from civil life.' [4] As if to apologize for Hancock, the Demo-
:atic party platform in 1880 included a provision favoring the
ıbordination of the military to the civil power.' [5]

The belief that a military man should not fill an important civil
ffice was best expressed by General William T. Sherman, who
ad himself been criticized for harboring dictatorial aspirations.
herman in 1888, in a public letter disqualifying himself as a pos-
ble Republican nominee for the Presidency, asserted:

> Any Senator can step from his chair at the Capitol into the
> White House and fulfil the office of President with more skill and
> success than a Grant, Sherman or Sheridan, who were soldiers by
> education and nature, who filled well their office when the coun-
> try was in danger, but were not schooled in the practice by which
> civil communities are and should be governed.[6]

While Grant was the only regular army man to reach the White
Iouse, the army itself was entrusted with new responsibilities in
ıe period after 1865. The assumption of these tasks was an indi-
ation of the growing power of the military after the Civil War.
.t the same time use of the army to garrison the South, fight
ıdians, and break strikes aroused opposition to the military es-
ıblishment.

The whole question of civil or military rule, which had been a
ital issue during the Civil War, was projected into the postwar
·eriod by the Radical Republican policy of reconstruction and
he attendant military occupation of the South. Critics of the Civil
Var resort to arbitrary arrest and military trial saw an equal dan-
·er to the country in rule of the South by detachments of the
Jnion army. Although it was believed necessary to keep a portion
f the army in the South as a temporary measure, there was wide-

spread opposition to any policy based on continued militar
coercion of the former Confederate states. President Johnsor
who held to this view, justified his amnesty proclamations on th
basis that there was no longer any threat of resistance from th
South. As he pointed out, 'large standing armies, military occupa
tion, martial law, military tribunals, and the suspension of th
privilege of the writ of *habeas corpus* and the right of trial b
jury are in time of peace dangerous to public liberty.'[7]

In Congress, the attack on Radical Republican policies was le
by Democratic members, largely from the border states, wh
strenuously denounced the use of federal troops in the South
Two Senators from Maryland and Delaware, Reverdy Johnso
and Willard Saulsbury, charged that the Reconstruction Act o
1867, dividing the South into five military districts, prepared th
way for a military despotism under a standing army. 'It is a cor
fession to the world,' Senator Johnson declared, 'that our institu
tions are a failure.' Garrett Davis, Senator from Kentucky, attacke
the Reconstruction Act as an unconstitutional attempt to coerc
the entire body of the states, going beyond the scope of the Civ
War which, in theory at least, was fought against the rebel ele
ment only. Protesting that the measure would enfranchise an
protect the Negro while it made the white population prisonei
of war under five military satraps, Davis warned: 'To give ove
the constitutional and legal rights and liberties of any people int
the protection of a standing army is to give the lamb into th
keeping of the wolf.' In replying to this Democratic criticisn
Senator Jacob M. Howard of Michigan professed to have 'no fea
from the establishment of military governments in the rebe
states. It is not in the nature of the American people,' he asserted
'to tolerate a military government anywhere longer than the actua
necessity exists which calls for it.'[8]

In the spirit of the legislation establishing military rule in th
South, the Radical group in Congress also passed a measure whicl
provided that the President or the Secretary of War must issue al
military orders through the General of the Armies, who was pro
tected against removal or reassignment except with the consent o
Congress. By this law, the President was denied his constitutiona
power as commander in chief of the army, and the South wa

prived of any executive check upon rule by the army. Earlier,
epresentative Andrew J. Rogers of New Jersey attacked the bill
'an attempt for the first time in the history of our Government
inaugurate within this Union a government founded on mili-
ry power. . . . Why,' he asked, 'should we now impose upon
e mass of them a military despotism of such a character as to
·serve the forcible opposition of every American citizen?' The
ilitary features of the reconstruction legislation were also de-
ıunced by Representative George S. Shanklin of Kentucky, who
serted that 'any upstart with brass buttons and shoulder-straps,
ith or without brains or heart may control the courts of law.' ⁹
With the Reconstruction Act of 1867 as a basis, a decade of
ilitary rule followed in the South. Although a semblance of civil
·vernment was gradually restored either through 'carpetbag'
·vernments or by return of the southern states to home rule, the
st federal troops were not recalled until 1877. Meanwhile, the
ovocation offered by the army varied according to the policies
individual commanders. Particular complaint was made of
:neral Philip Sheridan, who ruled New Orleans and Louisiana
a manner reminiscent of General Butler's wartime command in
at same area. Finally, Sheridan's policies, including the arbitrary
·moval of state and city officials, aroused so much agitation and
sorder that he was transferred to another post.¹⁰
One of the functions of the troops in the South was the super-
sion of federal and state elections. By this means, the Negroes'
ght to vote was protected, and disfranchised Southern whites
:re kept from the polls. During the Civil War, Union armies had
·liced elections, and the continuance of this practice after the
ar, in the North as well as in the South, occasioned a growing
·lume of bitter criticism. When troops were brought to New
·rk City in 1870 to insure the enforcement of the Fifteenth
nendment, Governor John T. Hoffman was able to prevent their
·rvice although he noted that two thousand deputy marshals
·re armed and employed in their stead. Registering an official
·otest against such federal interference, Governor Hoffman told
e state legislature that the use of military force at elections
·uld only perpetuate the very frauds it was designed to prevent.
> subject 'elections to the control of the President, supported by

armed forces, is to surrender liberty and to abandon a republic he concluded.[11]

Although a federal election law was a subject of debate for number of years, the use of the army to reinforce federal supe vision in elections was stopped after the Presidential canvass o 1876. The very next year, Congress was the scene of a spirite battle between the Democratic House and the Republican Senat when the latter refused to accept an amendment to the militar appropriations bill stipulating that no army funds or troops involved in any federal election within a state. As a result of th deadlock between the two Houses, no appropriation for the arm was approved. Later, at a special session of Congress called t meet the emergency, the House of Representatives yielded an passed a bill without the limiting amendment. Abram S. Hewit chairman of the Appropriations Committee, however, served n tice that at the next regular session of Congress the House wou take the necessary steps to repeal all federal election laws, an in 1878 the Democrats under his leadership were able to secur the reluctant acquiescence of the Senate and of President Hay to a law prohibiting the use of the army for civil purposes.[12]

Opposition to a federal army in the South served to strengthe the movement in Congress to lower the size of the army to a figu more nearly resembling that of the prewar establishment. A fe months after the cessation of hostilities, the Secretary of War, calling attention to the presence of vast numbers of battle-traine veterans in the North, suggested that the standing army of t United States could be reduced 'to a lower degree than any oth nation.' [13] Although hundreds of thousands of Union soldiers we mustered out of the service in a comparatively short time, Co gress at first did not scale down the regular army. Instead, on July 1866, it authorized a force of over eighty thousand men. Th number far exceeded the pre-Civil War establishment of less tha twenty thousand men and resulted almost immediately in agit tion by Congress for an investigation into the necessity of mai taining such a large body of troops in peacetime. On 12 Decer ber 1867 Lewis W. Ross, a Democrat from Illinois, was able secure the temporary approval by the House of his resolution i structing the Committee on Military Affairs 'to inquire into tl

xpediency of reducing the Army to a peace establishment, and
lereby relieve the taxpayers of the useless and unnecessary
harges of a large standing Army in time of peace.' Ross's resolu-
on, which contrasted the cost of the army with that of the gov-
rnment as a whole 'in its earlier and better days,' was deemed
n insult to the Republican administration, and a more politely
hrased measure embracing the same principle was substituted
nd passed unanimously.[14]

A gradual pruning of the army by prohibiting new enlistments
nd by eliminating unfit officers did not completely satisfy Conress, and bills providing a more drastic and immediate reduction
) thirty or even twenty thousand men were introduced. In 1869,
ernando Wood of New York declared his belief that 'the country,
ke myself, is tired of hearing of a reduction of the Army when
1ere is no practical proposition to reduce the Army. Our avenues
1d streets,' he complained, 'are filled with generals and major
enerals and captains and colonels drawing full pay, while the
)or tax-payer is overburdened with unnecessary taxation, wrung
om him for the purpose of supporting these idle vagabonds who
'e so well paid and do nothing.'[15] Benjamin F. Butler, who
1ared Wood's dislike of the regular army, introduced a detailed
lan of reduction in which he criticized the army's waste and
xtravagance, and its policy of allowing superannuated officers
) draw full pay while performing no actual work. Citing the case
f General Lorenzo Thomas, who after forty-six years in the army
rew a salary, including all emoluments, of from twelve to thir-
een thousand dollars a year, Butler asserted: 'His duty has been
>r more than two years past inspecting grave-yards all over the
)untry — nothing else — except when he was Secretary of War
d interim. . . . He has made more profits than any other under-
ker in the whole country.'[16]

A bill fixing the size of the army establishment at thirty thou-
nd men received the approval of Congress in 1870. It was
1ampioned in the lower House by John A. Logan, Illinois Re-
iblican, a leader of the G.A.R., and one of the ablest of the
)lunteer generals in the Civil War. In his speech, Logan de-
nded the principles 'that the military arm should never be
ronger than absolute necessity requires,' and 'that the Govern-

ment has the right to dispose of its military officers or the militar
appointments the same as with civil officers and civil appoin
ments.' Charging that the army was over-officered and inefficien
as compared with European armies, he alleged that this surplu
of officers was disguised by the army custom of using high-rankin
officers for menial tasks that could be much better performed b
a civilian clerk. Thus, he said, 'if you put a man in charge of th
commissary department you have to make him a brigadier gen
eral. Brigadier general of what? Of beef and molasses and por
and beans.' When a fellow Congressman interrupted with th
remark, 'Brigadier general of bean soup,' Logan replied: 'Yes, si
the gentleman is right, a brigadier general of bean soup.' Logan
speech drew a hot letter of protest from General Sherman, h
former commanding officer in the Army of Tennessee, whi
Logan, in rejoinder, accused Sherman of attempting to use h
office as General of the Army to dictate legislation.[17]

Pressure for a further slash in the size of the army was strengtl
ened by the Panic of 1873 and the hard times that followe
Against the opposition of Sherman and other high-ranking arn
officers, Congress provided in 1874 that no money should be use
to enlist troops beyond the number of twenty-five thousar
men.[18] It thus effected a reduction in the army from the form
authorized strength of thirty thousand men and came closer to r
gaining the old prewar figure of around sixteen thousand regular

In the generation following the Civil War, a large part of th
regular army was stationed in the Far West, where it performe
one of its oldest responsibilities, that of guarding the fronti
against the Indians. In these years, increasing white migration
the trans-Mississippi West touched off a series of bitter conflic
and aroused agitation for a reform in United States policy towar
the Red Man. Since 1849, Indian administration had been handle
by the Bureau of Indian Affairs in the Department of the Interic
but the army, never reconciled to civil control, saw an opport
nity in the post-Civil War era to regain authority over the Re
Man. After the war, Indian affairs also became entangled in th
partisan politics of the Reconstruction era, and by the time
Grant's Presidency the issue of military or civil control of th
Indians had reached a climax. Grant, who was interested in peac

ıl methods of dealing with the Red Man, opposed the army's de-
nands. In Congress Radical Republicans, who defended the use of
ıe army in the South, also sympathized with the army's view that
ı order to subdue the warlike tribes it should be entrusted with
ivil as well as military responsibility. In support of its claims, the
rmy criticized the Bureau of Indian Affairs as ridden with cor-
ıption and inefficiency.[19]

Public opinion was divided on the question of transferring
ndian affairs to the army. Opponents maintained that the army's
ggressive policy against the tribes only provoked their further
esistance while, at the same time, serving as a pretext to prevent
reduction in the peacetime military establishment. Citing an in-
:ance when fifteen hundred troops were used to escort a Northern
acific Railroad survey party seven hundred miles into Indian ter-
tory, Representative William A. Wheeler of New York declared:

> . . . it is really a debatable question how far the Government
> ought to go in protecting adventurous men, who push out beyond
> the bounds of civilization, often for the very purpose of inciting
> Indian outrages, in order that they may invoke the military arm of
> the Government, and then profit by the attendant pecuniary ex-
> penditures.[20]

Vhile the West favored army control of the Indian as a means to
is more rapid extinction, the East, in response to religious and
umanitarian sentiment, espoused a policy of fair dealing with the
ed Man and the continued administration of Indian affairs by
ıe Department of the Interior. Friends of the Indian, making full
se of the American antimilitarist tradition, waged a bitter lit-
:ary attack on the army. The conduct of American troops in the
Vest was cited as an indication of their unfitness for civil re-
ıonsibility, and the army was charged with pursuing a deliberate
olicy of extermination.[21]

In *Council Fire*, a journal edited by Alfred B. Meacham, former
nployee in the Indian service, Theodore A. Bland published a
:ries of articles entitled 'Abolish the Army.' Charging that 'the
anding army, has become as aristocratic and arrogant as were
ıe slave-drivers of the cotton States,' Bland proposed that it be
isbanded and that West Point be turned into an industrial col-
·ge. Bland and other friends of the Red Man believed that the

army, instead of protecting the frontier, was responsible for nearl
all the Indian trouble. The whites were the aggressors, and whe
the Indians retaliated, they were massacred. 'The soldiers de
moralize the Indian men by whiskey and cards, and debauch th
women, and the officers insult the chiefs by their arrogant a
sumptions of superior power and authority.' Bland further de
clared 'that the sole object of the War Department in urging tha
the Indians be turned over to the army is, that said army ma
have some pretense for continued existence. . . . Profession
soldiers do not want peace. War is their opportunity, fightin
their only business.' [22]

An important factor in the final defeat of the army plans wa
the reform of the Indian Bureau undertaken by Carl Schur
Secretary of the Interior under President Hayes. In other respect
too, the administration of President Hayes, beginning in 187
marked an important period in civil-military relations. Despite
decade of agitation, the army had not been successful in the a
tempt to expand its authority over the western Indians. Also
this time the regular army was reduced in size and withdraw
from the South. Meanwhile debate over the proper functions c
the military establishment revived in connection with calling ot
federal troops to quell the great railroad strikes of 1877.

Originally suspicious of the Civil War and opposed to the dra
laws, American labor after the war was faced by a decline in re
wages that accompanied the inflationary trend of the period. I
addition, labor leaders remembered that during the war the Unio
army had been used to aid employers and to prevent strike
while scores of businessmen had reaped tremendous profits fro
government contracts. William H. Sylvis, an important labc
leader of the period, alluded to this in a speech at Chicago i
January 1865, and the 'Platform of Principles' of his Nation
Labor Union included the statement:

> That we view with apprehension the tendency to military dom-
> ination in the Federal government; that standing armies are dan-
> gerous to the liberties of the people; that they entail heavy and
> unnecessary burdens on the productive industries, and should be
> reduced to the lowest standard.[23]

'he platform also attacked the Civil War pension system for its iscrimination against enlisted men in favor of the officers. It oncluded 'that all this shows that patriotism is in the people, mbition and plunder in the officers, injustice and ingratitude in 1e government.'

This hostility toward the military establishment on the part of rganized labor received ample basis for expression as the regular rmy was called out for police duty in a succession of postwar 1dustrial conflicts. Previously, the regular army had been little sed in the case of civil disorder, but after 1877 federal troops 'ere marshalled on numerous occasions to supplement state 1ilitia.[24] While federal intervention intensified labor's hatred of 1e army, the military office won support from conservatives, some f whom had previously distrusted the program of military re-onstruction of the South. Godkin's *Nation*, for example, praised 1e efficiency of the army and questioned the wisdom of labor's pposition to its increase. Other journalists called attention to the eed for effecting an improvement in the militia, while in the *orth American Review* of 1878 James A. Garfield, long a staunch :ongressional advocate of the military's cause, published a :ngthy defense of the army, in which he also accused the Demo-ratic party of undue hostility to the military establishment.[25]

In Congress, the railroad labor disturbances of 1877 led to a emand for an increase in the size of the army. Against this view, .bram S. Hewitt, the Democratic leader, delivered a long speech efending his party from Garfield's criticism and supporting the eed for a reduction of the army on the basis of economy. Hewitt specially attacked the position of those who advocated a large rmy for use in strikes. 'The right to strike is a just right,' he de-lared, going on to point out that the duty of checking civil dis-rder belonged to the local and state police. Hewitt also denied 1e argument that the army was an ideal instrument to suppress .dicalism and social discontent. 'If you have a great standing rmy in this country,' he warned, 'you have got to pay for it; the 'orking industry of the country has got to pay for it. Their suf-:rings will go on increasing from day to day until they will break ut into revolution. . . . Now if you want to fan communism,'

he concluded, 'increase your standing Army and you will hav
enough of it.' [26]

The climax in the mobilization of the army against labor cam
in 1894 as a result of the Pullman strike. Grover Cleveland, it wa
charged, sent federal troops to Chicago, not to preserve order an
insure delivery of the mails, but to break the strike. At a ma
meeting of ten thousand workingmen in New York City, Henr
George declared that, while he yielded to no one in his respect fc
law and order and the rights of property, 'yet I would rather se
every locomotive in this land ditched, every car and every depc
burned and every rail torn up, than to have them preserved b
means of a Federal standing army.' [27] Governor John P. Altgel
of Illinois, who had maintained that the local police and stat
militia were able to cope with the Chicago disturbances, pointe
out that, if the President could send troops to any part of th
country by the exercise of his own judgment, he was no differer
than a czar or emperor and could destroy at will the local sel
government which was the basis of American freedom. Becaus
'the American people, as all other free and intelligent people, ar
jealous of a central military power' was the reason, Altgeld be
lieved, why 'great precautions have been taken to limit the use c
such power. . . .' [28] Although Cleveland's use of the army wa
acceptable to conservatives and would probably have been ap
proved by most people at the time, there was an ingrained Amer
ican dislike of seeing the army serve as a police force. The meri
of Altgeld's position, therefore, eventually was to win acceptance
even though the use of federal troops in labor difficulties was b
no means ended.

Another example of the army's expanding functions after th
Civil War was in the field of higher education. During the wai
for the first time in the United States, public education to enabl
an individual to improve his capacities was forced to compet
with education as a system of training for the army or the state
Henry Barnard, later to become the first United States Com
missioner of Education, argued the need for military education i
the schools as a preparation for service to the country. Through
out the war years, a lengthy series of articles in Barnard's *Amer
ican Journal of Education* was devoted to a review of the type

f military education prevailing in the various countries of Eu-
ope and at West Point.[29] In Massachusetts, Governor John A.
Andrew, a former pacifist, with the support of James Freeman
Clarke, the Unitarian clergyman, advocated military drill in the
public schools. Often linked with ambitious plans for an improved
militia, the idea of universal military training in the schools was
also favored by some as a possible alternative scheme in the event
that the returning Civil War veterans showed no taste for further
drill or marching.[30]

The most fateful change in American education coming out of
the Civil War was a result of the passage of the Morrill Land
Grant Act. This act laid the foundation for the inclusion of
military instruction in American institutions of higher learning.
The original land-grant bill, introduced in Congress in 1857 by
Representative Justin S. Morrill, provided an appropriation of land
to the states to enable them to establish and maintain colleges
that would devote especial attention to the study of agriculture.
At that time, no provision was made for military training, and
the question did not arise in the discussion of the bill in Congress.
Five years later, in the midst of the Civil War, a new version of
the bill included military tactics among the subjects to be taught,
along with agriculture and the mechanic arts. While it is not clear
from the history of the measure whether the instruction in military tactics was to be compulsory or optional, the Morrill Act, by
serving as the basis for the inclusion of military education in the
land-grant colleges of the United States, broke a precedent in
American higher education, introducing military training where
it had hitherto been comparatively unknown.[31]

The full significance of the military education features of the
Morrill Act was not immediately realized. In the period following
the Civil War, there was a reaction against the whole concept of
military training, while personnel to teach the appropriate military courses in the colleges was difficult to obtain until Congress
in 1893 authorized the special detail of regular army officers as
instructors. Previous attempts by Congress to approve this type
of measure had aroused strenuous opposition. John Sherman, for
example, as early as 1866 introduced a bill providing that not
more than twenty army officers be made available to schools or

colleges that requested their services as presidents or superin-
tendents of the institutions. When the objection was raised that
few colleges would accept an officer as president, although they
might be willing to hire him as a professor, Sherman explained
that he 'did not think the United States ought to contribute in
this way to the support of a military school unless the officer detailed should have sufficient power over it to give it a *quasi*
military character. A mere professor would have no control over
the institution.' [32] Sherman's bill was more extreme than other,
but also unsuccessful, measures offered in the 1860s. As Senator
Thomas A. Hendricks of Indiana pointed out in 1868, the enthusiasm for military education had passed and 'after a little it will
not be so popular to fill our colleges with military men.' [33]

The postwar feeling against military schooling extended also
to the Military Academy at West Point. The old prejudice against
the Academy as an aristocratic institution was now reinforced
by the charge that a disproportionate number of its graduates had
enrolled in the cause of the Confederacy. Resolutions were accordingly introduced in Congress to abolish West Point and dis-
tribute the cadets among a group of selected colleges or military
academies scattered throughout the country. Gradually these
postwar attacks on West Point subsided, although there were
again brief flurries of strenuous criticism in the midst of the depression periods of the 'seventies and 'nineties.[34]

During the Franco-Prussian War, which broke out in 1870,
considerable American interest was exhibited over the various
European systems of military education. The long-standing American admiration for the Prussian plan of state education was carried over to her citizen army, which the American press praised as
an educated, thinking army. Many Americans believed the Prussian military system, based on compulsory service, was both
democratic and non-aggressive.[35] Such a favorable view of Prussian militarism, identifying compulsory military training with
democracy, was not, however, generally accepted in the United
States. The American people were familiar with the numerous
instances of European youths emigrating to the New World to
escape conscription. Noting that these young men sometimes
even went to the length of committing petty crimes in order to

void being drafted, a Philadelphia newspaper observed: 'That must be a cruel system which makes men either thieves or exiles.'[36] Karl Heinzen, one of the ''forty-eighters' who had been embittered by a year of Prussian military service, devoted a large part of his life in the United States to writing against war and militarism. Not favorably impressed or optimistic over Bismarck's unification of Germany, Heinzen vigorously attacked Prussian militarism during the 1860s and 1870s.[37]

In the midst of the Franco-Prussian War, some American newspapers lost their initial enthusiasm for the cause of the German states and voiced their dislike of both the Napoleonic and Prussian varieties of militarism. Feeling that the latter had become the greater menace, certain New York City journals, for example, strongly denounced all evidences of Prussian statism. Much the same attitude toward the Franco-Prussian War was expressed by Charles Sumner in his lecture 'The Duel Between France and Germany.' Prussia, Sumner declared, was a military despotism enforcing universal military service or 'bondage.' Unless the war system were abolished, Sumner warned his American audiences that all nations would eventually have to follow the Prussian example and adopt its hated conscription.[38]

Despite the flurry of interest in military training fostered by the Civil War and the conflict of 1870 in Europe, it is worthy of note that the movement made little headway in the United States until encouraged by the world-wide resurgence of navalism and militarism in the late 1880s and 1890s. Even Germany, increasingly regarded in the United States as the most militaristic nation of Europe, was careful to keep its system of military training out of the schools, and most American educators favored the same separation. A celebrated instance of this feeling in the period after the Civil War was provided by General Robert E. Lee's conduct as the newly installed President of Washington College. There was some expectation that Lee would attempt to introduce the West Point system of discipline at the college, but he turned away from it altogether, placing emphasis upon the students' own voluntary action. His private misgivings about war and a military career were confirmed by his five years at Washington College, and he is reported to have declared, 'The great mistake of my life

was taking a military education.' Lee distinguished sharply be
tween the sort of education desirable for a military career and
that needed for entrance into civil life. 'For many years,' he said
'I have observed the failure in business pursuits of men who have
resigned from the army. It is very rare that any one of them ha
achieved success.' As a college president, Lee purposely de
emphasized his past connections with the army, and in academic
processions he seemed always to walk out of step with his com
panion or out of time with the music.[39]

The sentiment for military education was, of course, stronges
in those agricultural and technical colleges which were receiving
federal funds according to the Morrill Act. Senator John T
Morgan of Alabama, for instance, complained that he did no
'know one of these agricultural colleges which is not a regular
barrack, a camp of soldiery, where the youths of the country are
made to step about and strut about in uniforms, wearing sword
and carrying guns.' Although in favor of military education, the
land-grant colleges resented attempts on the part of the War De
partment to control their policies and curricula, and in 1889 they
forced the army to withdraw its plan to share in the interna
management of the colleges.[40]

In 1894, former President Harrison's espousal of military in
struction in schools and colleges provoked a strong rejoinde
from pacifists and educators. Denying that any physical or dis
ciplinary advantages were derived from such training, Benjamin
F. Trueblood, a leader of the American Peace Society, declared
'We ought to educate for peace and the future, and not for the
past and war.' [41] Alfred H. Love, President of the Universal Peace
Union, asserted: 'Military life is a phase of slavery. Militarism i
not republicanism. The individual is not allowed to think fo
himself; it is stolid obedience; it is one-man power; it is surrende
of individuality; it is anti-American.' [42] Benjamin O. Flower, edito
of the liberal magazine *Arena,* saw the era following the Civi
War as a period of corruption and militarism in America. Con
fident that if Jesus returned to the world his first command woul
be to 'ground arms,' Flower observed: 'The introduction of mil
itary training into the common schools of America marked th
triumph of the military spirit of despotic Europe over the long

herished traditions of the Republic.' [43] Although the agitation
or military drill in the schools was destined to grow stronger after
he War with Spain, the opposition to its introduction in the
890s was reflected in the governor's veto of such a measure in
New York state in 1895.[44]

Ever since the Civil War an uneasy equilibrium had been main-
ained between the civil and military power. Although the army
was raised to new importance as a result of that conflict, the
American people also experienced a strong reaction against the
wartime ascendancy of the military office. Reduced in size and
under attack for its role in Indian affairs and in labor disputes,
he regular army was not popular in the postwar years. At the
same time the Civil War had familiarized a whole generation with
a philosophy of war and force and provided a foundation for the
military approach to national problems. By the 1890s, there were
indications that the feeling against the military was diminishing.
Symbolized by the increasing interest in military education, the
change in American sentiment was even more dramatically exemplified in the rising tide of navalism and imperialism that preceded the War with Spain.

IX

The New Threat of
Imperialism and Navalism

EDWIN L. GODKIN in an editorial retrospect in the *Nation* of 189
recalled that in 1865, when his magazine was founded, it had ap
peared as though the Civil War military spirit would continu
indefinitely.[1] This fear, though not without basis, had gone un
realized as the reaction from the war served at first to strengthe
the American antimilitarist tradition. Nevertheless, by the decad
of the 1890s, the tradition was again seriously threatened a
economic nationalism, imperialism, and navalism spread ove
Europe and the United States. In the search for world market
and colonies, and in the development of a large navy to protect it
overseas commerce, the United States was following the cours
set by the leading industrial states of Europe. As a result, th
American people seemed to be confronted with the dilemma c
trying to reconcile a new ideology of militarism and imperialisr
with the older values of liberalism and democracy.

Imperialism and militarism, clearly foreshadowed by the event
of the 1890s, marked a sharp break with the American past. Dui
ing the greater part of the nineteenth century the United State
with a continent to develop and separated from Europe by thre

124

housand miles of ocean, had remained relatively free of the con-
licting rivalries of the great powers. Serene in the contemplation
f their economic and geographic security, the American people
n the thirty years that succeeded the Civil War looked with little
nthusiasm upon the idea of annexing overseas territory. The
urchase of Alaska was accomplished before postwar antiex-
ansionist sentiment had fully crystallized. Even then, Congres-
ional approval was secured only after extensive lobbying ac-
ivities by proponents of the treaty. Greeley's *New York Tribune*
rotested the purchase on the grounds that it would be a step
oward war and militarism, but others reasoned that the new ter-
itory, while not contiguous to the United States, was still a part
f the North American continent.[2] Further plans for territorial
cquisition or commercial advantage embracing Cuba, Santo
Domingo, the Danish West Indies, a Nicaraguan canal, Samoa,
nd Hawaii met with little or no success. With their own civil
onflict a fresh memory, the American people and Congress were
eluctant to add to the Union overseas possessions that might in-
olve expensive naval building, imperialism, and perhaps foreign
var.

The antiexpansionist point of view was ably expressed by
Charles Sumner, chairman of the Senate Committee on Foreign
Relations. Sumner, who had been a pacifist sympathizer before
he Civil War, again became a severe critic of the tendency to-
vard militarism and navalism, which he discerned both in Europe
nd America. In 1871, in an important speech on the 'Employ-
nent of the Navy at San Domingo,' he attacked the whole Seward
nd Grant foreign policy. A year later, he presented a much de-
ated resolution to investigate the sale of munitions to France
uring her war with Prussia.[3]

Congressional criticism of the navy during the 'seventies and
ighties duplicated in many ways the attacks that were made
pon the regular army in these decades. With no colonies to pro-
ct, and with the American people consuming the products of
heir own factories, a large navy was viewed as a useless luxury
nd provocation to war. The expense of a naval establishment,
orruption in connection with building contracts, lack of tech-
ological development, excessive number of officers, and a rigid

caste system were focal points of much complaint in both Hous
and Senate. Underlying some of the hostility to the navy voice
in Congress was the fear that a larger force would become
spearhead for United States imperialism. Proponents of nav
building were accused of harboring expansionist intentions, an
of advocating the abandonment of the traditional concept of th
navy as a defensive force designed to prevent an invasion of th
United States.

The strength of this concept of a navy solely for defense
evidenced in its acceptance by all American Presidents during th
nineteenth century, except perhaps Andrew Jackson. In 187(
Secretary of the Navy, George M. Robeson, refuted the notio
that the United States required a large offensive fleet. Favorin
the construction of fast wooden cruisers and monitors, he wrote i
his annual report: 'With such a force and with no colonies to d
fend, I think we may well dispense, for the present at least, wit
the heavy-armored and unwieldy iron-clads of European nation
and, also, with the monster cannon necessary to penetrate them.'
A year later, however, Robeson's successor, Richard W. Thom
son, suggested the advisability of revising traditional Unite
States naval policy. Although it had not reached the overpopu
lated conditions and conflicting economic rivalries which require
the European powers to maintain large armies and navie
Thompson felt that the time had come for the United States t
adopt a policy adapted to its own changing economic interest
'Without foreign commerce,' he wrote, 'we must sink into i
feriority; and without a Navy amply sufficient for this purpos
all the profits of our surplus productions will be transferred fro
the coffers of our own to those of foreign capitalists.' [5]

Congress, as early as the 'eighties and 'nineties, devoted seriou
attention to this question of whether the United States shoul
build up a large navy to defend American overseas commerc
During the Presidential administration of Chester A. Arthur, th
period of the beginnings of the modern navy, another argumer
for the construction of ironclads was that they would reinforc
the conduct of United States foreign relations. Congressma
George M. Robeson of New Jersey, who as Secretary of the Nav
under Grant had opposed the construction of iron or steel ship

ow declared that one United States ironclad in the harbor of
allao would have prevented the dismemberment of Peru in her
ar with Chile and Bolivia. If Robeson's contention were correct,
len, as Perry Belmont, a Democratic Congressman from New
ork, pointed out: 'It is not difficult, therefore, to conceive the
ircumstances in which a necessity might be created for building
 large navy.' All this Belmont refused to accept and, accusing
le State Department of unnecessary meddling in South America,
e concluded: 'A hundred iron-clads in the harbor of Callao could
ot prevent the unfortunate position in which this Government
as placed by its State Department.' [6]

The building of a new navy of ironclads in the Arthur ad-
linistration inaugurated a period of expansion that continued
ntil the United States took first rank among the world's naval
owers. This development of United States naval power was not,
f course, without significance in American domestic affairs. With
le shift from wooden to steel vessels, American industry achieved
 vested interest in the navy and became the active lobbyist and
ropagandist for naval expansion.[7] The alluring prospects of naval
ontracts came at a time when American businessmen were be-
inning to feel the serious need of cultivating foreign markets.
'hen, by the 1890s, the passing of the frontier and economic dis-
ontent at home among farmers and factory workers gave further
mphasis to the desirability of securing additional outlets for
merican manufactures.

With this background of events and conditions, a school of
lought emerged in the United States urging the frank adoption
f a policy of imperialism. Led by Captain Alfred Thayer Mahan,
hose book *The Influence of Sea Power upon History* (1890)
xerted a profound effect in civil as well as naval circles, a sizable
roup of American statesmen, including Henry Cabot Lodge and
heodore Roosevelt, became the staunch advocates of an expan-
onist policy. Utilizing an expanded version of American manifest
estiny, it was argued that the United States should acquire over-
eas colonies as sources of raw materials and as naval bases. The
avy, in turn, would have to be enlarged to protect the new colo-
ies and resulting increase in American trade. According to this
:heme of things, the navy would no longer be confined to a

purely defensive role but would be composed of capital ships abl
to control the high seas.

The Mahan formula for seapower thus neatly linked togethe
the interests of navalism and imperialism, each serving as bot
cause and effect. Coming at a time when American business wa
eager for new trade outlets, Mahan's views received a ready aud
ence. The able popularizer of a trend already developing, Mahar
who had once been an anti-imperialist critical of James G. Blaine'
aggressive foreign policy, now became the leading apostle of ex
pansionism and preparedness. Merchants, shipbuilders, big-nav
men, armaments manufacturers, naval personnel, expansionis
statesmen, and publicists all used the Mahan theories for their ow
ends. Mahan himself was primarily interested in indoctrinating hi
own countrymen, but his influence extended abroad and served a
an ideological stimulus for naval building in Great Britain, Franc
Germany, and Japan. Mahan, in his defense of militarism and wa
as a moral system, stood as the leading American example of th
Prussian deification of war. Both the product and the spokesma
of an age of ruthless militarism and imperialism, Mahan whole
heartedly espoused the doctrines of force and power politics.[8]

The views of Mahan and his fellow imperialists were destine
to achieve a triumph in the War with Spain, although many Amer
icans refused to accept without protest so fundamental a brea
with past traditions of peace and antimilitarism. This oppositior
though powerless to halt the trend toward imperialism and wa
was able to modify the more extreme demands of big-navy advo
cates and at the same time call attention to the desirability c
arbitration and disarmament. The basic conflict between thes
two points of view regarding American foreign policy was brougl
out clearly with the presentation to Congress of the naval est
mates for 1890.

Although Presidents Arthur and Cleveland had been sympa
thetic to the requirements of the new navy, Benjamin Harriso
who became President on 4 March 1889, may be regarded as th
first outspoken advocate of a big navy. At the same time, Jam
G. Blaine's return to office as Harrison's Secretary of State ind
cated the pursuit of an aggressive foreign policy, while the Re
publicans, generally regarded as more favorable to expansionis

nd a large navy, controlled both houses of Congress. In this
uspicious setting, the new Secretary of the Navy, Benjamin F.
'racy of New York, expressing ideas that 'were indubitably
Mahan's,' advocated in his first annual report a building program
hat included twenty battleships and sixty fast cruisers. Still
nore revolutionary than Tracy's report were the recommendations
f a Policy Board of six naval officers, whom he had appointed to
tudy the naval requirements of the United States. This board
alled for the adoption of the type of naval program delineated in
Mahan's imperialist conception of seapower.[9]

The reports of the Secretary of the Navy and the Naval Policy
Board, advising the creation of a fleet of long-range battleships,
roused a storm of protest. Scores of petitions from pacifists and
ther groups protesting the large appropriations for the navy were
eceived in Congress.[10] Quoting from these petitions, Senator
'rancis M. Cockrell of Missouri, a former Confederate army offi-
er destined to serve thirty years in the Senate, asked why, in
ime of peace and with no threatened invasion, the United States
vas preparing for war? William E. Chandler, a Senator from New
Hampshire, who as Secretary of the Navy in the early 1880s had
played an important role in modernizing the navy, explained why
e, nevertheless, adhered to the tradition of a navy for coastal
efense. The reversal of 'true American policy' forecast in the
roposed construction of a fleet of long-range battleships would,
e informed the Senate,

> go far toward bringing the United States into the lamentable con-
> ditions of the nations of Central Europe. They are burdened with
> great navies and enormous standing armies which are draining the
> life-blood of the people and imposing burdens of debt and taxation
> so grievous that before many years relief from them, if not afforded
> in any other way, will be accomplished by revolutions.[11]

'o meet these objections, friends of the battleship bill argued that
he best coast defense was a fighting fleet able to keep an enemy
ffshore. Congress accordingly approved the far-reaching naval
neasure, its opposition coming chiefly from the Democratic mi-
ority and from members representing interior districts.

Two years later, in 1892, with the country on the brink of an
conomic depression and the Democrats now in control of the

lower House, a bitter attack was launched on the annual nava
appropriation bill, which again called for more new ships. Demo
cratic Congressmen, with the aid of their newly elected Populis
colleagues, contrasted the costs of a large navy with the country'
need for economy and retrenchment. William S. Holman of Indi
ana questioned the sincerity of those who advocated a sizabl
navy as a means of defense against attack from Europe. Believin,
that the demand for a large navy came from the capitalist clas
which benefitted by the legislation, he warned that the America
people would not stand for 'a "splendid" government, supporte
by a great army and navy, under which the enormous corporat
wealth and imperial private estates which by law you are creatin;
will take shelter.' Samuel W. Peel of Arkansas was aroused be
cause the naval bill was given precedence over his measure t
open up six million acres of land to needy homesteaders.[12] Fred
erick E. White of Iowa, referring to the Harrison administration'
policy in Chile and the indiscreet conduct of the navy in tha
country, declared: 'To prepare for war is in many instances t
invite it.' Decrying all talk of war and the possible destruction o
Eastern seaboard cities, William Baker, a Populist Congressma
from Kansas, asserted that the development of the military an
naval power of the country was incompatible with the preserva
tion of civil liberty and republican institutions.

> Has not the experience of the past demonstrated that just as
> you increase the army and navy of a country you deprive a peo-
> ple to that extent of their liberties? You can not point to a nation
> today which has a large army and which has a free people. It is
> impossible.[13]

Friends of the navy hastened to its defense, and the necessit
for a large force was most frankly presented by Henry Cabc
Lodge, a member of the House Naval Affairs Committee. In
speech replying to Tom Watson's Jeffersonian attack on the navy
Lodge, the biographer of Alexander Hamilton, declared that 'fo
the protection of American business interests, and American citi
zens in all parts of the world wherever they may go, we want t
have the American flag on American men-of-war.' [14]

The criticism of the naval increases voiced in Congress receive widespread support as the hard times after the Panic of 1893 seemed to underscore the need for economy. Among the most prominent opponents of navalism and militarism during this period was Carl Schurz, who had come to the United States after the failure of the revolutions of 1848 to begin a successful career as a Civil War general and Republican party leader. 'In spite of his war record,' Schurz, in the words of his most recent biographer, 'was a pacifist at heart, with a deep distrust of militarism, especially when it was connected with "expansionist" ambitions.' [15] Under the title 'Manifest Destiny,' Schurz published in *Harper's* in 1893 an attack on the reviving American sentiment for imperialist expansion. Pointing out that the pursuit of such a course would involve the United States in war and jeopardize American freedom, Schurz added:

> Nothing could be more foolish than the notion we hear frequently expressed that so big a country should have a big navy. Instead of taking pride in the possession of a big navy, the American people ought to be proud of not needing one. This is their distinguishing privilege, and it is their true glory.[16]

This same point of view, still widely supported in the 1890s, was well expressed by the *Scientific American*, which favored building up coast defenses instead of a large navy. 'Our naval programme,' the editor wrote, 'should be laid down with strict regard to a home, as distinct from a foreign — a Republican as distinct from an Imperial policy.' [17]

Schurz and other opponents of a strong navy believed that such a force would only encourage the United States to carry out a policy of imperialism, leading inevitably to war and militarism. American anti-imperialists and small-navy men, in support of their position, called attention again to the folly of the United States adopting European ways. They repeated Herbert Spencer's warning that a civilization based on war and militarism was incompatible with one devoted to industrial progress. As one writer expressed it, 'America cannot serve the two masters militarism and industrialism.' [18] Advice on the subject of American foreign policy was also extended by James Bryce. Already famous as an exceptionally keen observer of the American political scene, Bryce

stated that in his opinion American institutions of self-rule an
representative government were unsuitable to imperialism. 'Th
policy of creating great armaments and of annexing territory be
yond the seas would be,' he told his American readers in Decem
ber 1897, 'an un-American policy, and a complete departure fror
the maxims — approved by long experience — of the illustriou
founders of the Republic.' [19]

Bryce penned his criticism of imperialism at a moment whe
the American people were being prepared for war with Spair
Despite its own long tradition of opposition to overseas expansior
the United States by the 1890s had reached that point in its indus
trial development which inclined many of its leading statesme
to advocate an adventure in imperialism. Such navalists and im
perialists as Mahan and Theodore Roosevelt were quick to seiz
the opportunity presented by the War with Spain. As Roosevel
remarked some years later, 'It wasn't much of a war, but it wa
the best war we had.' [20] Businessmen, though at first lukewarm t
the notion of hostilities, readily perceived the commercial advar
tages opened up by Dewey's victory at Manila Bay. Conservative
were also pleased by the wartime patriotic unity that succeede
the bitter labor strife and Populism of the 1890s. In the word
of Tom Watson, Populist candidate for Vice President in 189(
'The blare of the bugle drowned the voice of the Reformer.' [21]

On the other side of the ocean European observers, thoug
divided in their sympathies between the United States and Spair
tended to agree that the war marked the entrance of the Unite
States into world affairs, and her eventual adoption of Europea
policies of imperialism, militarism, and navalism.[22] In some Britis
circles, disappointment was expressed at the United States subst
tution of the methods of militarism for those of peace and demo(
racy. The official attitude, however, was one of rejoicing ove
American emergence from traditional isolationism. In Englan
and the United States alike, navalists, imperialists, business lead
ers, and advocates of Anglo-American co-operation were agree
in welcoming the War with Spain as a symbolic expression of
new American foreign policy.

An expansionist point of view naturally received powerful sup
port from the circumstances surrounding the war, but it did n(

go unchallenged. In the midst of the fighting, an Anti-Imperialist League was formed, attracting to its membership many of the most prominent statesmen and intellectual leaders of the day. Stressing the effect of imperialism upon American democracy, the first meeting of the League in June 1898 set forth the principle that a policy of annexation would mean a larger army and navy and higher taxes. At a meeting in Chicago the following year, a resolution was adopted stating 'that the policy known as imperialism is hostile to liberty and tends toward militarism, an evil from which it is our glory to be free.' [23]

Although the Anti-Imperialist League was a rather vague body, strongest in New England and the Middle West, its emphasis upon the danger of imperialism and militarism to American democracy formed the central theme of much of the individual anti-imperialist argument. Militarism was viewed as the inseparable ally and inevitable result of imperialism. At a convocation address delivered to students at the University of Chicago, Carl Schurz warned that under the policy of imperialism, which could be expected to accompany the annexation of the Philippines, 'every American farmer and workingman, when going to his toil, will, like his European brother, have "to carry a fully armed soldier on his back."' [24] Before similar academic audiences, President David Starr Jordan of Stanford University depicted imperialism as entailing an aggressive, militant foreign policy incompatible with the preservation of American democracy and individualism. 'As militarism grows democracy must die,' he declared. In the fate of Rome, which declined after its overexpansion, Jordan saw an instructive example for the United States. [25]

According to William Graham Sumner's famous essay, *The Conquest of the United States by Spain,* the decay of American democracy had already set in. Writing in the year when American arms had seemingly won an easy victory, Sumner maintained that the United States had, rather, been conquered by the European philosophy of militarism. He also pointed out that the plutocracy and imperialists now attacked the very American traditions he himself had once been accused of violating, and he predicted that the United States would eventually lose its freedom and democracy. 'The answer is: war, debt, taxation, diplomacy, a grand governmental system, pomp, glory, a big army and navy, lavish expenditures, political jobbery — in a word, imperialism.' 'McKinley will not wear the crown, and Congress will not introduce military service, next winter,' he wrote in 1900 in the midst of the Presidential campaign, but the danger of militarism, however slight at first, would grow with time. When presented with the refutation that it was necessary for the United States to accept the privileges and responsibilities of being a world power, Sumner and the other anti-imperialists pointed to the high cost the American people would have to pay for the dubious advantages of world prestige or international trade.[26]

The academic opponents of the new imperialism and militarism were joined by an impressive array of statesmen, especially those high in the counsels of the Democratic party. Former Secretary of State Richard Olney, enrolled in the anti-imperialist ranks along with former President Cleveland, wrote in the *Atlantic Monthly* that the United States could not pursue an aggressive foreign policy without paying the costs in terms of a greater army and navy.[27] In a political address entitled 'America's Mission,' William Jennings Bryan, McKinley's opponent in the campaign of 1900, denied that annexation was necessary to make the United States a world power. The growth of democracy, he asserted, 'would be weighted down rather than aided by the armor and weapons proffered by imperialism.'[28]

Despite his opposition to the provision of the peace treaty calling for the annexation of the Philippine Islands, Bryan as party leader finally advised the Democratic Senators to vote for ratification. Bryan seems to have believed that the proper course was to accept the treaty and demand that the Philippines be set free. Imperialism would then become the paramount issue in the Presidential elections of 1900. Bryan's strange tactics, which really made it possible for the McKinley administration to secure approval of the treaty by the narrowest possible margin of one vote above the necessary two-thirds, were based in part on his desire to bring to a close the war and the militarism he associated with it. The Democratic platform of 1900 reflected his stand, condemning a war for the Philippines as unnecessary and unjust. The imperialist policy of the administration was viewed as placing the United States 'previously known and applauded throughout the world as the champion of freedom, in the false and un-American position of crushing with military force the efforts of our former allies to achieve liberty and self-government.' [29]

Following President McKinley's victory, Bryan accused the Republicans of waiting until after the election to attempt to increase the standing army.[30] This drive for a larger army to suppress the Filipinos' insurrection provided a new issue for the anti-imperialists. Denounced by Secretary of War Elihu Root for giving indirect aid and comfort to the Filipino cause, the anti-imperialists in turn charged the War Department with using the insurrection as a pretext for their own militarist purposes. Then, when the outbreak in the Philippine Islands degenerated into a struggle more costly in terms of American lives than the late, brief War with Spain, it seemed to furnish a basis for the opposition's contention that American imperialism could only be enforced by the power of the sword. The Anti-Imperialist League made effective use of reports of brutality on the part of United States troops. Although the War Department tried to suppress or minimize these revelations, the charges led to a Congressional investigation and indicated also the desirability of placing the islands under some permanent system of civil government.[31]

As the anti-imperialists had feared, the new responsibilities of the United States army in the Pacific gave Secretary Root an opportunity to press for an increase in the size of the military establishment. In the War with Spain, regulars had been supplemented with volunteers and contingents of the organized state militia, taken into service as a part of the Volunteer Army of the United States. Although the subsequent fighting in the Philippines forestalled the customary postwar reaction in favor of cutting the army, Congress, mindful of tradition, refused at first to accede to the War Department request for a regular army of one hundred thousand men, preferring instead to pass a measure that provided for sixty-five thousand regulars and thirty-five thousand volunteers. The bill contained an amendment calling for a reduction of the army to its prewar figure by 1 July 1901, but before this time

the President and the Secretary of War had secured Congressiona
approval for a permanent standing army of between sixty an
one hundred thousand men.[32]

Although symptomatic of further breaks with past militar
policy that were to come in the 1900s, these bills increasing th
army were not passed until after members of both parties in Con
gress had severely attacked American Philippine policy. Th
idealism of the war to free Cuba was contrasted with the postwa
imperialism in the Pacific. In Congress, a strong argument agains
both the peace treaty and the proposed assimilation of the Fili
pinos was that the acquisition of an empire would inevitably mea
heavier taxes to support a larger army and navy. Anti-imperialis
Congressmen attempted to force the issue of Philippine inde
pendence by refusing to vote the new military budget. As Nicho
las N. Cox of Tennessee expressed it, 'Imperialism and militarisr
are always twin sisters. No imperialism will be inaugurated if i
has no military force to back it.' [33]

Another problem, particularly alarming to Congressmen fror
rural districts, was the threatened competition of Philippine agri
cultural products with certain American crops. John Sharp Wil
liams of Mississippi raised this question in an anti-imperialis
speech delivered in connection with an agricultural appropriation
bill in December 1898. Pointing out that the islands would hav
to be included in the American tariff system, he asked how w
could open the door in China and close it in the Philippine:
Furthermore, he noted that annexation would entail an occupatio
force of fifty thousand and a standing army of one hundred thou
sand men, as well as costs of at least one hundred million dollar
annually. Echoing Williams's position, Senator H. D. Money c
Mississippi, in the debate on the army bill of 1901, also denounce
the missionary argument of the white man's burden to civilize an
Christianize the Filipino. Calling attention to the fact that th
Philippine Congress included a higher percentage of college
trained men than did its American counterpart, Money declared
'I do not believe when Jesus Christ said to His disciples "Go y
into all the world and preach the gospel to every creature" tha
He meant to say, "Go ye into all the world and shoot the gospe
into every creature." He was the Prince of Peace.' [34]

Despite all their efforts, the anti-imperialists in Congress were no more successful in resisting the increase in the army than they had been in preventing the war and imperialism that occasioned such expansion. These growing military expenditures by the United States came at just the time when some of the European states were beginning to realize the tremendous costs and possible dangers of a world-wide armaments race. Soon after the conclusion of the hostilities between the United States and Spain in 1898, Czar Nicholas II of Russia invited the major world powers to meet at the Hague to discuss the problem of armaments. Although sympathetic with the Czar's idea, the United States military forces in relation to population, wealth, and territory were, as President McKinley told Congress, 'so conspicuously less than that of the armed powers to whom the Czar's appeal is especially addressed that the question can have for us no practical importance.' [35]

McKinley's virtuous assumption, though a substantially correct description of the American past, paid scant attention to the changes taking place in United States army and navy policy as a result of the War with Spain. Having assumed the position of a world power, the United States was preparing to build up its own armed strength in preference to a policy of international co-operation. Thus at the Hague Conference the United States, like the other powers, was dominated by a nationalistic, military point of view which prevented it from assuming leadership in the movement for disarmament. Admiral Mahan, who was a member of the American delegation, made it clear that the United States intended to augment its military resources and would refuse to consider the question of naval disarmament.[36] He was able to persuade his American colleagues to oppose any plans that involved a compromise with national interests. This attitude, by no means unique among the delegates, helped to bring about the failure of the conference. It also provided an illustration of the militaristic thinking of the great powers at the turn of the century.

Those Americans who had not enrolled in the Mahan school of power politics bitterly criticized the United States for its failure to lead the world toward disarmament and peace. Since the beginnings of the republic, Americans had prided themselves on

their historic mission to advance the cause of world peace. Th
wars and militarism of the Old World had long been viewed as a
unpleasant contrast to the peace and progress enjoyed in the Nev
To many observers it now seemed as though the United State
as a result of the War with Spain was about to abandon its hi
toric ideal of peace and accept instead the inevitability of futur
war. A member of Congress, in commenting upon the irony of th
Hague Conference being held in the midst of world-wide navalisr
and imperialism, declared that he was 'forced to conclude tha
what is called "Christian civilization," when put in the scale an
weighed against the interests of commercialism, the interest o
trade and traffic, has but little influence in controlling the affair
of this world.' [37] David J. Brewer, Associate Justice of the St
preme Court, expressed the disillusionment of the anti-imperiali
forces. 'It is a strange commentary,' he said in an address at Bu
falo,

> that at the close of the nineteenth century the head of the most
> arbitrary government in the civilized world, the Czar of the Rus-
> sias, is inviting the nations of the world to a decrease in their
> arms, while this, the freest land, is proposing the increase in its.
> Yet such seems the imperative need, if we enter upon the system
> of colonial expansion. [38]

Other anti-imperialist spokesmen, led by Carl Schurz, pointe
to the paradox of world rearmament in the midst of the vaunte
progress of the nineteenth century. The policy of war and mil
tarism was viewed as incompatible with American democrac
and dangerous to the future welfare of all nations. Schurz fel
whatever the Czar's ulterior motives, the correctness of his opinio
that armaments were leading the world to cultural and econom
ruin could not be denied. [39] Following the Czar's invitation, th
American Federation of Labor took a strong stand against a
increase in the United States army. Pointing out that 'Large stanc
ing armies have always been, are now, and can never be othe
than a menace to liberty, a challenge to the people, a defiance an
denial of their rights,' the Federation denounced attempts to spu
the people into an acceptance of imperialism. [40] While advocate
of army and navy increases depicted the advantages of America
entrance into world politics, labor spokesmen recalled the histor

nited States mission to serve as an asylum of the oppressed.

The *Nation,* perhaps the foremost liberal organ in the United tates at the turn of the century, used the Hague Conference as a asis for criticizing the navalism and imperialism advocated by dmiral Mahan. E. L. Godkin, the editor and founder, had been ne of the early and conspicuous exceptions to the praise ac-rded Mahan's writings, attacking the admiral's glorification of ar and large armaments.[41] The *Nation* also contrasted the spirit f the Czar's proposal with the increasing militarism of the nited States. Despite the failure of the First Hague Conference, found encouraging the report that the Czar's peace efforts were eing continued. It was, the *Nation* believed, tragic to have to oint out that, while Europe sought to free itself from the arma-ents burden, the United States, under the spell of army and avy protagonists, was preparing to assume the crushing expense f preparedness. The free-trade *Nation,* citing the historic opposi-on of Peel and Cobden to English militarism in the nineteenth ntury, also pointed out that there was a more than incidental nnection between militarism and the higher taxes that were urting normal business and industry in the United States. View-g the United States as about to give up the traditional bases of s prosperity for the delusions of world power, it noted that Amer-ans who formerly criticized Europe for strapping soldiers on e backs of the people were now inflicting upon themselves the me burden.[42]

This American dislike of a large army was, of course, traditional. hus Theodore Roosevelt, for example, was able to recommend ductions in army appropriations at the same time that he called r increases in naval expenditures. Such a distinction, however, und no favor among anti-imperialists and antimilitarists. They greed with the *Nation's* comment that the United States was ly 'strapping on a sailor instead.'[43] By the early 1900s the oosevelt-Mahan imperialist point of view was exercising increas-g influence upon military and naval legislation passed by Con-ess. At this important juncture, the whole philosophy of pre-aredness gained new and dramatic support with the elevation of heodore Roosevelt to the White House.

Theodore Roosevelt and

Modern American Militarism

THE ROOSEVELT YEARS following the War with Spain were a pe riod in which for the first time the antimilitarist traditions of th republic seemed to be seriously and continuously threatene Previous American wars, including even so severe a conflict as th Civil War, had been succeeded by a strong hostility to all thing military.

In 1898, the arguments of the anti-imperialists were rejecte and the United States turned toward a policy of expansion backe up by military and naval preparedness. Swept along in a worle wide current of exaggerated nationalism and imperialism, th United States after the War with Spain did not experience an intense aversion to military activity. The call of manifest destin and of markets across the seas was perhaps too strong to resis and it was also true that United States victory in 1898 had bee achieved so swiftly and cheaply that it left no deep or lastin resentment. At the same time, disillusionment over America Philippine policy was not strong enough, or sufficiently wide spread, to counterbalance the economic forces that were helpir to push the nation into world politics.

The departure from long-standing American antimilitarist tradi-
ons was reflected in the program pursued by the new political
nd military leadership that came into power in the United States
t the turn of the century. In September 1901 Theodore Roose-
elt, characterized in a recent interpretation of his career as a
ierald of modern American militarism and imperialism,' [1] suc-
eeded the much less bellicose McKinley as President. Although
oosevelt was to perform some genuine services for the cause of
orld peace, receiving the Nobel Prize for his efforts, he never
ally outgrew his adolescent love of war. As Governor of New
ork his 'trigger-like willingness to use troops in labor disturb-
nces antagonized organized labor.' [2] All his life he continued to
orship military efficiency and to long for active service in the
eld. It is not surprising, therefore, that the entrance of Roosevelt
ito the White House gave added prestige to the ideas of men
ho, like himself, favored an aggressive national policy reinforced
y a strong army and navy. Roosevelt's close friend, Henry Cabot
odge, now found in the executive branch of the government
mple support for his own imperialist views. The naval philosophy
f Alfred Thayer Mahan also secured a ready hearing, and Mahan,
n old confidant of the President, was given every encouragement
) continue his writing and to publicize his thesis of the influence
f sea power upon history.

These years after the Spanish-American War were also a period
eculiarly favorable to the reorganization and building up of the
nited States army. In response to public pressure aroused by
ports of the extreme inefficiency of the army in the late war,
ecretary Russell A. Alger was replaced in the War Department
y Elihu Root, a New York lawyer. Root was expected to make it
ossible for the army to become an effective fighting force, and in
is first annual reports he frankly advanced the propositions:

> That the real object of having an Army is to provide for war. . . .
> The restoration of the normal conditions of peace, and the re-
> turn of the greater part of the Army to the United States, have
> made it possible to resume with increased activity the work of
> preparing for future wars.[3]

apitalizing on demands for revamping the army, which had been
imulated by the recent unhappy wartime experiences, Root sug-

gested, and in large part secured, the adoption of a program tha
went far to change the traditionally minor role assigned to th
standing army in the United States. President Roosevelt, althoug
personally more interested in naval affairs, gave his full backing t
Root's plans for the army, continuing him in office as Secretar
of War until February 1904, and then a year later appointing hir
as Secretary of State to succeed John Hay.

Root's successive secretaryships illustrated the growing ties be
tween American foreign and military policies. Root himself wa
one of the chief architects of United States colonialism and th
author of the Platt amendment governing our relations with Cub;
As Secretary of War, it was Root who played an important role i
securing legislation which provided for an increase in the size c
the regular army, the creation of a general staff, and the federaliz;
tion of the state militia. When the General Staff bill was befor
the Senate, Root organized the Senators in its behalf and prompte
them in their questioning of witnesses. One strong objection to th
measure was that it reversed American traditions and created a
organization based on European models. Thus the prescribed li
of duties for the General Staff in 1903 was taken directly from
German treatise on the subject, and French and English concep
also found their way into the American organization.[4]

Root himself referred to the creation of the General Staff ;
'civilian control of the military arm.' It is true that it was Roo
a civilian, and not army personnel who initiated the legislatio:
Also many army officers, led by General Nelson A. Miles, wer
opposed to the idea of a general staff. Ultimately, however, th
General Staff won the army's enthusiastic acceptance and becam
the vital center of army power and propaganda, often overshad
owing the civilian Secretary of War, and able on numerous o
casions to impose its point of view upon Congress. When Gener
Leonard Wood, Roosevelt's old Rough Rider friend, becam
Chief of Staff in the Taft administration, he carried his lobbyir
and propaganda efforts to such an extreme that he received th
rebuke of the President and aroused the suspicions of Congress
United States experience with a general staff thus seemed 1
duplicate that of Europe. Wherever created, a general staff fu

shed a means of militarist intervention in civil affairs that was compatible with American traditions.

Almost as revolutionary as the law setting up the General Staff as the Root militia bill, or Dick Act of 1903, which provided for lling up a portion of the state militia to serve as a National uard under federal authority and pay. Later, in 1908, the Dick ct was amended to enable the National Guard to serve 'either ithin or without the territory of the United States.'[6] Although milar attempts to provide greater federal control over the state ilitia had often been defeated in the past, the Dick Act like the eneral staff legislation was passed by an almost unanimous Conress. The possible militarist implications of the militia reorgani-tion measure were indicated by Root himself in an address on May 1903 before the National Guard Association. Looking into e future, Root told his listeners that the regular army would ntinue to perform the work of a central organization, embracing lartermaster duties and similar functions. But, he added, 'when u come to the creation of the military spirit among the youth the country, to the education and training of that military irit, there you step in; that is your function of preparation, for at cannot be done at the center — that must be done all over is country.'[7]

Although Congress voiced little opposition to the Root bills at e time of their passage, the aggressive military spirit of the osevelt period provoked some reaction among the general pub-. Organized labor was hostile to all Root's military measures and Roosevelt's imperialism. Mindful of the way in which federal ops had been used against strikers, labor could not be expected show enthusiasm over legislation strengthening the regular my. While the Root projects were pending, anti-imperialists d peace leaders published severe criticisms of the regular army d of the professional soldier. The blind obedience exacted by e army was attacked as a threat to American individualism and mocracy.[8] Articles by European writers warned the American ople of the pitfalls of militarism.[9] A popular novel of the time, *iptain Jinks Hero*, written by Ernest H. Crosby, told the story a boy who, after achieving his dream of becoming a military

hero, lapsed into insanity because his efforts to militarize th
country went unheeded. Crosby, a disciple of Tolstoy, wrote h
book with a serious purpose, although readers were probabl
more amused by the satire than aroused over the danger of mil
tarism in the United States.

Despite the far-reaching implications of Secretary Root's pro
gram, the American people could see little concrete evidence o
increasing army power or influence. For example, the general sta
idea was put into practice very gradually, and a veteran Republi
can Senator complained that he had not realized the extent t
which it could make the Secretary of War a figurehead, forced t
yield to 'the desire of the professional men in the Army and Nav
to reduce and at last eliminate the civilian power.' [10] Democrat
members of Congress, though they found it difficult to resist th
Roosevelt pressure for preparedness, occasionally expressed the
resentment. Speaking on the subject of the army appropriatic
bill in 1902, Representative James A. Norton of Ohio, a Civil Wa
veteran, asserted: 'The course of the Administration can not l
defended upon any moral or religious ground. It is only upon th
assumption that "might makes right," and that the "almight
dollar" is in it, that the advocates of the continuance of the prese
policy can stand.' In the House debate over the army appropri
tion bill for 1904, Robert Baker of Brooklyn, New York, charge
his colleagues with ignoring the implications of an aggressi
United States policy contained in the bill. 'It should,' he mai
tained, 'be designated "A bill to appropriate $75,000,000 to i
crease the power of one strenuous man to get this country in
possible conflict with one or more civilized nations." ' [11]

In the Presidential campaign of 1904, the Democrats mad
some effort to arouse opposition to the Roosevelt-Root milita
program. Judge Alton B. Parker, in his address accepting th
party's nomination for President, declared that Americans were
peace-loving and not a military people. 'The display of great mi
tary armaments may please the eye, and, for the moment, exci
the pride of the citizen, but it cannot bring to the country th
brains, brawn and muscle of a single immigrant, nor induce th
investment here of a dollar of capital.' After Parker's overwhel
ing defeat, William Jennings Bryan admitted the difficulties face

y the Democrats in attempting to win election on the issues of ilitarism and imperialism. Despite the unfavorable verdict, ryan believed that the Democrats 'must continue to protest gainst a large army and against a large navy.' [12]

President Roosevelt, aware of the criticism of the army and of is own role in its development, told Congress with some indignaon that 'Declamation against militarism has no more serious lace in an earnest and intelligent movement for righteousness in is country than declamation against the worship of Baal or staroth.' [13] Roosevelt believed that militarism was a nonexistent vil in the United States and that no country in the world, including even China, had been so free of militarism as the United tates. Considering only the regular army and excluding American aval power, the President's defense was not extravagant. On the her hand, it should be noted that during his administration the reater threat to American traditions came not from the army, but om the large building program inaugurated for the navy.

President Roosevelt had been an enthusiastic and influential lvocate of naval preparedness ever since the days when, as ssistant Secretary of the Navy and an 'avowed opponent of eace,' he had played a large part in readying the American fleet r war with Spain.[14] After the war, Roosevelt became obsessed ith the idea that Germany intended some sort of aggressive ction in South or Central America. At the same time, the Open oor policy in regard to China and the acquisition of the Philipines brought the United States into rivalry in the Far East with nportant European naval powers, and more especially with the sing sun of Japan. However warranted or belied by the facts of le situation, Roosevelt's fear of possible German or Japanese aval aggression against the United States was accepted with the reatest seriousness by the general public. This popular alarm, toether with the gradual realization that United States commitents in the Far East would be difficult to defend without a sizole navy, helped to influence opinion in behalf of the naval proram that Roosevelt presented to Congress.

In his attempt to arouse public sentiment in favor of a larger merican navy, Roosevelt did not lack outside support. The books n naval history written by his friend Mahan stirred popular im-

agination. Then, in 1903, the cause of a big navy received tl
backing of a newly founded propaganda organization, the Na\
League of the United States. Modeled after similar societies
Europe, the League united the groups in the United States wor
ing to encourage effective naval legislation. Along with retir
naval officers, it included among its members businessmen ar
industrialists, at least some of whom had a direct pecuniary inte
est in naval expansion. Also numbering former statesmen and to
ranking munitions manufacturers as its honorary officials, tl
League's influence upon Congress and upon the public was sizab
and 'was unquestionably a factor of no small importance in tl
remarkable success with which President Roosevelt brought abo
an increase of naval power, unapproached in any previous cor
parable period in American history.' [15]

Spurred on by 'an almost fanatical desire for a big navy,' The
dore Roosevelt exercised a pressure upon Congress which fe
members, in spite of personal misgivings, were able to resi:
Accordingly, within the four years down to 1905, Congress a
thorized ten battleships as well as numerous smaller vessels, whi
naval appropriations soared from eighty-five to one hundred ar
eighteen million dollars per year, an increase without peacetin
precedent. These results, as has been pointed out, 'were eve
more impressive, because achieved in the face of formidable ar
growing opposition, both inside and outside the halls of Co
gress.' [16] Congressional opponents of the naval building progra
accused the President and the Navy League of fomenting
world-wide naval race that would lead to war. Representativ
Theodore E. Burton of Ohio, a member of the President's ov
party, dismissed the Roosevelt idea of a German attack on tl
United States as a 'hobgoblin.' Burton also criticized the Dem
crats for their failure to present a minority report in 1904 to su
stantiate their traditional opposition to navalism. 'Is not the desi
to be second in the nations of the earth with your Navy an u
building of militarism?' he asked.[17]

The following year the Democratic minority launched a tho
ough attack upon the 1905 naval appropriation bill, which calle
for the expenditure of over one hundred million dollars. Hou
Democrats contrasted Roosevelt's program with the Jeffersoni:

eal of simplicity and economy in government. The United
ates, with a navy inferior only to that of the British, was pic-
red as exceeding the despotism of Russia and militarism of
ermany in its rate of expenditures. With two dollars out of every
ve in United States taxes spent for military purposes, it was
ointed out that the army and navy received 'more money than
le 450,000 public school teachers of this land draw in salaries
or teaching 11,000,000 children who attend the public schools.'
ongressman Morris Sheppard of Texas, indignant at the neglect
f internal improvements and of government buildings, sarcasti-
ally compared the relative needs of the American people for
ourt houses, and for battleships 'or a naval demonstration at
)yster Bay,' near the President's home.[18]

Some Congressmen singled out the Navy League and the steel
rust as the chief offenders in diverting the American people from
ormal peacetime pursuits. These same interests, it was charged,
vere leading the country into war as a part of their selfish zeal
or preparedness. 'Were it not for the Krupps et al. in Germany;
he Armstrongs, Whitworths, Vickers-Maxims of Great Britain,
nd the Cramps, Carnegies and Schwabs of this country,' Con-
ressman Robert Baker of Brooklyn, New York, declared, 'the
ossibilities of war would be almost nil.' In their opposition to the
aval bill, Democratic members of Congress charged that the
vhole Roosevelt concept of preparedness was a cloak for milita-
ism and imperialism. Representative Jack Beall of Texas recalled
hat 'It was said that God had given us the islands of the sea; and
et we were not willing to trust Him in their defense. Battle ships
vere preferable, and the patriotism of all who opposed this policy
vas assailed.' American preparedness, it was asserted, antagonized the European nations and encouraged their further prepa-
ations for war. In the Senate, Edward W. Carmack of Tennessee,
vho believed that it was not the Monroe Doctrine but 'imperial-
sm, that calls for this great and growing Navy,' further declared:

. . . the nations of Europe have a right to suspect that we are
arming not for defensive but for offensive operations. They have
seen the people of the United States by an unprecedented majority elect as Chief Executive of this country the most militant and
strenuous gentleman that ever stunned the sure and firm set earth

with his armed heel, and whose voice, even when he speaks softly, is a terror to the world. They know as we know that he has inculcated the love of war for its own sake as the most indispensable virtue of the soldier. They know that he has tried to inculcate the doctrine that peace is destructive of all the manly virtues. They know that he is inflicted with an incurable propensity for meddling with the affairs of other nations.[19]

The naval appropriation bill for 1905 marked the completio of the first Roosevelt building program and placed the Unite States in the first rank of naval powers, second only to Great Bri ain and, perhaps, France. Two years later, rising anti-Japanes agitation in California and the general situation in the Pacifi plunged the United States into a grave international crisis. A the same time, the British development of the all big-gun battle ship of the *Dreadnought* type led to a demand for adding simila ships to the American navy. While both Congress and the nav were divided on the dreadnought issue, President Roosevelt gav his enthusiastic backing to the new type vessel and in Decembe 1907 astonished the country with a message calling upon Congres to appropriate money for four new battleships, all of the big-gu class.[20]

The President's request for an additional naval program agai met with strong opposition in Congress, and also aroused th hostility of influential groups in the country at large. Peace lead ers, reinforced by clergymen and educators, petitioned Congres to vote down the Roosevelt four-battleship bill.[21] Andrew Car negie's name headed a list of prominent citizens in New Yor City, who protested the policy of spending 65 per cent of the na tional income on wars, past, present, and future.[22] Despite th hysteria aroused by recurrent Japanese war scares, important sec tions of the press held out against the Roosevelt naval program Business and financial elements stressed the need for economy while pacifist spokesmen urged a policy of arbitration and charge that the big-navy policy was leading the United States into war.[2] Sympathetic to this criticism, the *Commercial and Financia Chronicle* affirmed:

Invasion of the United States is so remote a possibility that it may reasonably be dismissed as a dream. The overwhelmingly large navy for which Senator Lodge and his sympathizers argue is more likely to be used for purposes of provocation on the part of an ambitious American government than of protection of the sea-coast by a Government which has in view only the interests of the American people.[24]

The National Association of Manufacturers, in denouncing the Roosevelt policies, declared that in the long run commerce was a better agent of world peace than armaments. At home, in the United States, it pointed out that Roosevelt's conservation pro-gram was impossible 'if our money is to be squandered in so lavish measure upon battleships and militarism.'[25]

In the midst of the controversy over the four-battleship bill, Roosevelt carried through his already announced plan to send an American fleet around the world. From the President's standpoint the cruise had the great advantage, in addition to impressing Japan, of spreading propaganda for naval increases and of coun-teracting the considerable amount of hostility revealed in Con-gress and among the public. Although Congress subsequently refused to approve the Roosevelt proposal for four battleships, the two actually voted exceeded the normal replacement policy of building one new ship each year and thus represented at least a partial victory for the President.

It is interesting to note that in many ways Roosevelt's drive for a big navy, like the writings of Mahan, won a more enthusiastic reception in Europe than in the United States. Following the bat-tleship cruise of 1908, the European press, and especially German newspapers, paid tribute to the President of the United States for having called attention to the importance of the battleship in modern civilization. The United States was regarded as the fore-most exponent of new naval tactics, and the policies of the Ameri-can President were viewed as having stimulated naval building all over the world.[26] At home, meanwhile, the revolt against Roosevelt navalism continued over into the succeeding Taft ad-ministration.

William Howard Taft, who had been Secretary of War during Roosevelt's second term, was expected to carry on the policies of his predecessor. Although much less martial in spirit than T.R., Taft opposed any decline in United States naval construction.

Despite his strong belief in the limitation of armaments and in the arbitration of international disputes, even when questions of national honor were involved, the President felt that the United States must keep pace with contemporary European rearmament.[27] In its public utterances, the new administration urged the necessity of a large navy in order to meet the threat of invasion. In view of the unlikelihood of such an attack, it has been suggested that the real reasons behind Taft's demands were related to his intention to continue the aggressive foreign policy of his predecessor.[28]

Taft's recommendations on naval policy were presented to a Congress that had already shown its hostility to the Roosevelt battleship program. Strengthened by the public outcry over Roosevelt's navalism and by Taft's own political difficulties, members of both parties, and particularly those from districts in the interior of the country, united to attack the Chief Executive's call for naval increases. Republican Congressmen Richard Bartholdt of Missouri and Theodore E. Burton of Ohio were tireless in urging the United States to take the lead in fostering a policy of arbitration as a substitute for naval building. 'If armaments were a guaranty for peace,' Bartholdt asked, 'why is it that the nations of Europe, though armed to their teeth, have been forced to wage so many wars?' Representative Isaac R. Sherwood of Ohio, who became a Quaker after participating actively in forty battles in the Civil War, declared in the midst of debate on the 1910 naval bill that what the country needed 'more than anything else . . . is that we should have more Quakers and fewer battleships.'[29]

Many members of Congress were especially critical of the attempt to influence legislation by arousing the public with war scares. In a typical complaint, Senator Alexander S. Clay of Georgia asserted: 'International peace and good will always prevail until the naval appropriation bill comes up for our consideration, then war looms up with Japan, Germany, or some other country.' Other Congressmen attacked the private shipyards and armor plate manufacturers as the chief forces behind the demand for more battleships.[30] This growing disillusionment over the self-interest of politicians, naval officers, and industrialists was given dramatic force in the remarks of Senator Eugene Hale, veteran

Republican legislator from Maine and chairman of the Senate Naval Affairs Committee. Hale, in looking back over the last twenty-five years, recalled 'that the more we have done for the military the more they have claimed. It is the theory of the army and navy that the Government is run for the benefit of those establishments.' Declining to accept any longer the widespread assumption 'that you can not appropriate too much for military purposes and that the preparation for peace is a war establishment,' Hale concluded: 'Every immense appropriation for a war establishment increases the chances for war.' [31]

The increasing opposition to the Roosevelt and Taft naval program was an indication that a significant portion of the American people was not yet ready to back up the dollar diplomacy of the Republican party with an enlarged military and naval machine. The emphasis upon battleship construction, encouraged by both Roosevelt and Taft, conflicted with the long-standing American tradition of the navy as a primarily defensive force. Despite the discouragement engendered by the failure of the Second Hague Conference on disarmament, and by the unsuccessful attempt of the Taft administration to secure Senate approval of a series of bilateral arbitration treaties, the American people were not willing to accept a military and naval policy based on the premise that another war was inevitable. This strong peace sentiment, reinforced by the demands of liberals and progressives for domestic reform, helped to postpone the realization of the navy's elaborate expansion program until the eve of America's entrance into the First World War. It also resulted, by the closing months of the Taft term, in a full-scale revolt by the Democratic House, which refused to vote any of the battleships recommended by the President. The House eventually agreed to a compromise, but only after the Democratic party at its Baltimore convention nominated Woodrow Wilson, reputedly a strong navy man, and adopted a platform embracing his views.[32]

The debate over naval expansion, which took place during the period between the War with Spain and the First World War, was in part a reflection of the contradictory trends of that era. Despite the increasing emphasis on military preparedness in the United States, the American peace movement revived and added new

strength to the country's antimilitarist tradition. The variou
peace leaders and their allies, who included conservatives as wel
as liberals and radicals, labored diligently to call to the attentio
of the American people the dangers of European militarism. Jan
Addams, founder of Hull House and an outstanding pacifist, de
nounced the conception of 'patriotism founded upon militar
prowess and defence,' and criticized militarists for their inabilit
to foster the constructive side of civilization.[33] Although no paci
fist, William Graham Sumner, the famous Yale professor of sociol
ogy, attacked the notion of preparedness for war as a fallacy an
technological impossibility, entailing never-ending sacrifice
Havelock Ellis and Vernon L. Kellogg, an American zoologis
saw the struggle against militarism as a task for social hygien
and eugenics.[34]

In the early part of the twentieth century, there was conside
able American support for the socialist and radical view of mil
tarism. In contrast to the hopeful faith in state action shared b
most American progressives, socialists and anarchists brought t
the United States Marxian assumptions as to the nature of th
capitalist state and its coercive force upon the working class.
new basis of antimilitarism was added in the socialist argume
that capitalism leads inevitably to militarism and war.[35] The rac
ical Industrial Workers of the World, or I.W.W., at its first co
vention in 1905 passed a resolution condemning 'militarism in a
its forms and functions' and blaming it for 'jeopardizing our co
stitutional rights and privileges in the struggle between capit
and labor.' [36] As an indication of its attitude, the I.W.W. deni
membership to any person who joined the state militia. Th
anarchist magazine *Mother Earth* cited the Surgeon Genera
report on the incidence of alcoholism and venereal disease amor
soldiers as proof of the brutalizing effects of militarism a
warned American youth against being enticed into the Unit
States army. Comparing the job of the soldier to 'that of the pr
fessional cutthroat who kills a man to order,' it argued: 'The mi
tary uniform that seems so gay hides nothing but subjection a
humiliation for the common soldier, and provides only a ve
meagre existence.' [37] Although not always accepting their inte
pretation, antimilitarists in the United States were heartened l

bor and socialist opposition to militarism in Europe. Again and
again they warned the American nation of the tremendous burden
hat militarism placed on the peoples of the Old World.

A special phase of United States militarism, even more alarm-
ng to the pacifist than the navalism of the Roosevelt and Taft
ra, was the growing movement for the military training of youth.
'he indifference to this development on the part of so many
arents and citizens was an illustration of the prevailing Ameri-
an tendency to denounce militarism in Europe while overlooking
imilar trends at home. In the midst of the reviving militarism
nd navalism of the 1890s, the campaign for military training in
ne schools, quiescent since the post-Civil War era, started up
gain. After the Spanish-American War, the new mood was re-
ected in the writings of those army officers and educators who
poke of the inevitability of war and of the necessity of military
raining to inculcate discipline and patriotism in American
outh.[38]

Exponents of military drill wished to see the federal govern-
nent provide funds for such training in schools and colleges that
'ere not already subsidized by the Morrill Act. In 1908, such a
ill was warmly recommended by President Roosevelt. Although
staunch advocate of military training, it is interesting to note
nat Roosevelt did not suggest an army or navy career for his own
on, to whom he quoted the advice of Admiral Mahan: 'I have too
nuch confidence in him to make me feel that it is desirable for
im to enter either branch of the service.' [39] At the Congressional
earings on the 1908 bill, Archbishop John Ireland of Minnesota
tated very frankly the underlying assumption which often moti-
ated protagonists of military training in the schools. Bishop Ire-
and, who believed that 'it is very important in this country to
evelop reverence for the military spirit,' told Congress: 'A great
eal is said nowadays, perhaps too much, against the Army and
gainst the spirit of war. This idea of universal peace is very
ood, but to make it a gospel is a mistake.' [40] A similar point of
iew was expressed by contributors to a prize contest, conducted
y the Military Service Institution, on the subject of military
raining in the schools. In commenting upon these essays, the
Educational Review, edited by Nicholas Murray Butler, observed

with pleasure that at least the authors 'are not in favor of trying to crowd military instruction in any form into the primary schools.' [41]

Despite the increasing sentiment for military training in the schools in the period before the First World War, educators, for the most part, remained hostile to the idea. On the basis of their own experience, they were dubious of the educational value of military drill. Dudley Allen Sargent, Director of the Hemenway Gymnasium at Harvard and a leader in the movement for physical education, devoted almost a lifetime to refuting the claims made for military drill.[42] Sargent's point of view was in general supported by the National Education Association. At a time when the peace movement seemed to be moving toward victory, teachers also showed an increasing interest in the possibility of arbitration and disarmament. Although little headway was made in deemphasizing war in textbooks, peace leaders were invited to address educational meetings and were given a sympathetic hearing.[43]

Outside the schools, there was also some protest against the growing militarization of American youth. Members of Congress lamented the fact that the schools taught war and not peace.[44] Pacifists compared the costs of battleships and school buildings. Even the Boy Scouts and the Sunday School movement were examined for evidences of militaristic thinking. In the case of the former, at least, some substance was lent to the charge of militarism when Ernest Thompson Seton, a pioneer leader of the Scouts, resigned in 1915 because 'you cannot study nature marching by fours. The interest in trees, flowers, woodcraft has given place to military drill and thus has robbed it of its ideals. They have lost touch with the boy and the big outdoor conservation movement.' [45]

Looking back over the period since the Spanish-American War Justice Brewer of the Supreme Court, in a reminiscent address before the New Jersey State Bar Association, observed that the American people, despite the security of their position, were being driven by a series of irrational fears into the delusive security of militarism. The city of Washington, he declared, 'has a different aspect from that which it had a few years ago. Brass buttons and epaulets are filling the eyes.' While the evil of war was generally admitted, Brewer warned that the danger of preparedness was overlooked, and he added:

> There never yet was a nation which built up a maximum of army and navy that did not get into war, and the pretense current in certain circles that the best way to preserve peace is to build up an enormous navy shows an ignorance of the lessons of history and the conditions of genuine and enduring peace.[46]

Parallel in point of time, but the direct antithesis of the point of view of the growing peace movement, was the increasing acceptance of the type of militaristic thinking referred to by Justice Brewer. Owing more to European developments than to any aspect of the American past, militarism in the United States was related to the abandonment of the historic national tradition of isolation. The transition from isolation to imperialism and world politics, which marked the turn of the century, brought in its wake a new attitude toward military affairs. If the United States was to compete with the other great powers for its share of colonies and trade, it would be difficult to avoid the ensuing demand for a strong army and navy. Spurred on by the accumulating pressures of an expanding industrial economy at home and of economic rivalry abroad, and enjoying the enthusiastic encouragement of men like Theodore Roosevelt, Elihu Root, Henry Cabot Lodge, Alfred Thayer Mahan, and Leonard Wood, the philosophy of militarism and navalism exercised an influence on American life in the first years of the twentieth century that was without precedent in American history.

At the same time, a large part of the American people was reluctant to accept the possible resort to military force and war indicated by the new American circumstances and policy. Their attitude was reflected in the support given to the drive for peace and disarmament in the early years of the new century. But before the world peace movement could attain its goal, the period of feverish rearming and of empire-building by the great powers achieved its tragic climax in the beginnings of the First World War.

XI

European Militarism and

American Preparedness

THE AMERICAN ANTIMILITARIST tradition, already severely strained
by the imperialism and world rearmament of the first years of the
twentieth century, was confronted after August 1914 with the
new problems arising from the European war. Long before full
United States participation in that struggle, the American people
were already deeply involved in a discussion of the issues of
neutrality, preparedness, conscription, and general military policy. Despite the nearly unanimous initial American desire to stay
out of the war, United States military expenditures soon climbed
to unprecedented levels. At the same time, agitation increased for
military training in schools and colleges and for some system of
peacetime conscription or universal service. Preparedness on such
a scale, whether designed for defense or for eventual intervention, was out of keeping with historic American policy.

Imbued with a strong belief in the unmilitaristic character of
their own country, the American people were quick to view the
coming of war in Europe as an inevitable result of Old World
decadence and militarism.[1] In the first weeks of the war, important segments of the American public placed a considerable part

of the blame for the debacle upon the armaments race in which all the European powers had participated. This was the interpretation of the coming of the war offered by historian Albert Bushnell Hart, whose *The War in Europe Its Causes and Results* was published in the fall of 1914. Sharing this opinion, the *Nation* pointed out that the cult of militarism was not confined to Germany but pervaded all Europe. A writer in the *Century* saw the war as a natural result of the preparedness efforts of all nations, while the *Forum,* in an editorial entitled 'More Militarism?,' asserted: 'The war broke out, in spite of the pacifists, and because of the militarists.' [2] President Charles W. Eliot of Harvard, in a series of letters to the *New York Times,* blamed large armaments and conscript armies as the twin evils that had made the European war possible.[3] This feeling that the war was an aftermath of European militarism was also a popular belief among American clergymen. While their efforts to prevent war came too late, the sermons and writings of some of the church leaders show that they had not been unaware of the dangers implicit in European militarism.[4]

Although profoundly suspicious of all militarism in 1914, the weight of American sentiment was soon directed more particularly against the militarism and autocracy of the Central Powers. For at least a generation, American statesmen had encouraged the belief that Germany was the outstanding rival of the United States in world politics. This attitude of hostility toward the militaristic and autocratic government of the Kaiser naturally exerted an appeal among the democratically minded people of the United States. But those Americans who confined their criticisms of militarism to the German variety overlooked the parallel militarism of France as well as the navalism of England.[5] Thus, when the *Army and Navy Journal* defended German militarism on grounds that it was not unique, it went too far for American taste and provoked a series of angry retorts from leading newspapers.[6] By the fall of 1914, without realizing it, the American people had begun to take sides and to accept the Allied Powers' thesis of a war to stamp out Prussian militarism. But, as the *Army and Navy Journal* pointed out, it would take militarism to defeat militarism. Rising to the occasion, a small but rapidly growing group of nationalists and militarists renewed their agitation for greater military and naval preparedness by the United States.

The foundations of the preparedness campaign had been laid even before the outbreak of the European war, when, in the preceding Roosevelt and Taft administrations, Admiral Mahan, Homer Lea, Leonard Wood, and other champions of preparedness carried their gospel to the people. As Chief of Staff, Wood in the summer of 1913 set up the voluntary citizens' training camps, called by a later writer 'the most subtle of all the engines with which he was finally to convert the United States to militarism.' The forerunners of what subsequently became known as the 'Plattsburg idea,' the camps were recruited mostly from college students and served as an ideal training ground, not so much to teach military tactics, as 'to develop missionaries in the cause of patriotic service.' [7] Secretary of War Lindley M. Garrison, despite his irritation over what he justly regarded as Wood's insubordination, supported the training camps because 'they foster a patriotic spirit' and 'spread among the citizens of the country a more thorough knowledge of military history.' With the outbreak of the European war, Wood and others had a golden opportunity to advance their ideas. Under the aegis of John Grier Hibben of Princeton and a committee of fellow college presidents, a number of universities were persuaded to offer military training to their students.[8]

The indoctrination of college students, although highly important, was only one aspect of the preparedness campaign. While war in Europe seemed to make an invasion of the United States all the more unlikely, the continued agitation for preparedness created tension and aroused American concern over the issue of national defense. Making political capital of these fears, Republican Congressman Augustus P. Gardner and his father-in-law, Senator Henry Cabot Lodge, introduced resolutions to establish a National Security Commission which would have the duty of investigating the state of United States preparedness for war.[9] Theodore Roosevelt, departing from his original justification of the German invasion of Belgium, published a stream of bellicose, pro-Allied articles in the *Outlook*. Early in December 1914 the National Security League was founded with a membership drawn largely from prominent New York lawyers, businessmen, industrialists, and financiers. Along with the Navy League and other super-patriotic organizations, the Security League helped to develop a far-flung and intensive propaganda drive for increased American preparedness.[10] Strong support for this preparedness agitation came from army and navy officers, who saw an opportunity to secure an expanded military establishment, as well as from business leaders, who envisaged a steady stream of government spending for defense. Even more potent than the propaganda of those who stood to profit from preparedness was the work of superpatriots who sincerely believed the country defenseless or who felt that preparedness was an ideal means of encouraging direct American entry into the war on the side of the Allies.

During the first year of the European war these advocates of preparedness were handicapped by the hostility of Congress and President Wilson. In his annual message to Congress in December 1914, the President made a strong answer to Theodore Roosevelt and those other critics of neutrality who were already calling for greater rearmament by the United States. Preparedness, the President pointed out, was a relative term, and he recalled that the traditional American policy was one of peace and hostility to standing armies. Under his administration, he declared, we will prepare 'to the utmost; and yet we shall not turn America into a military camp. We will not ask our young men to spend the best years of their lives making soldiers of themselves.' In his criticism of the preparedness agitation, the President seemed to represent the point of view of the country, and he was pleased at the generally favorable reception accorded his message to Congress.[11]

Through the spring of 1915, a large proportion of the members of Congress continued to share the President's distrust of the budding preparedness movement. James Hay, chairman of the House Committee on Military Affairs, denounced 'The War Terror' being raised in the United States by the advocates of a large army and navy. A vast army was impossible, he pointed out, unless the country was ready to adopt the European system of conscription and pay the drastically higher taxes involved. Other Congressmen asked for what, or against whom, the United States was being urged to prepare. In preparedness they saw an analogy

to the militarism and wars of Europe.[12] Although many member
of Congress felt certain that the preparedness of the Unite
States, like the rearmament of Europe, would lead eventually t
war, they recognized the popularity of the concept of nation;
defense. To weaken the drive for an increased military establish
ment they attempted to expose the selfish economic motives c
some of the leading preparedness advocates. In an effort to tak
the profits out of preparedness, the prewar agitation for goverr
ment ownership of the munitions and armor plate industries wa
revived. Congress, at the same time, revealed much support fc
placing an embargo on the export of munitions to the belligerent
in Europe. Senator Robert M. La Follette, a staunch proponer
of an embargo, introduced in February 1915 a proposal for a
international peace conference. Unless the war ceased or unles
the United States discontinued its sale of munitions, he feare
America would be drawn into the struggle. La Follette attacke
the whole munitions trade as an industry with but one purpose
'to sacrifice human life for private gain.' [13]

The selfish aspects of the preparedness movement were als
censured by Nicholas Murray Butler who, together with Charle
Eliot of Harvard and David Starr Jordan of Stanford, was one c
the prominent university presidents defending Wilson's peac
policy. In December 1914, President Butler created a stir by giv
ing a press interview in which he criticized the preparednes
organizations in Washington as insincere and not really cor
cerned with so-called national defense. He declared his belief tha
Europe's large-scale armaments had led directly to war, and h
rejoiced that the country had in the White House a President abl
to withstand the preparedness pressure. 'In modern democracie
the functions of the army and navy are police, philanthropic, an
sanitary,' Butler asserted, and he urged the American people t
'put behind us forever the notion that we must arm in peace as
preventive of war, and that we must be perpetually defendin
ourselves or getting ready to defend ourselves against new er
emies. No people will be hostile to us unless we, by our conduc
make them so.' Reaffirming his opposition to preparedness in
letter to the *New York Times,* Butler wrote: 'It must not be fo]

otten that militarism has its origin in a state of mind and that in reality it is a state of mind.' [14]

On the Columbia University campus, President Butler's anti-preparedness position was given enthusiastic support at a meeting of five hundred students. A resolution opposing 'militarism in general and an increase in our army and navy in particular,' offered by Wayne Wellman and seconded by Paul Douglas, was adopted. Faculty members present, including George W. Kirchwey, professor and former dean of the Law School, and two of the younger instructors, Leon Fraser and Carlton Hayes, denounced militarism and pleaded for sanity in American thinking on the war.[15]

By 1915, sanity was beginning to yield to hysteria. Already, most of the large metropolitan newspapers had given their backing to preparedness. Although Atlantic Coast journals stressed the desirability of avoiding any militarism in the American preparedness effort, a strong antimilitarist point of view was being limited more and more to the papers of the Middle West. A nationwide poll of some four hundred editors, made soon after the President's December message to Congress, showed a majority along both coasts favoring a stronger army and navy, while in the interior of the country opinion was more equally divided on the question of any increases in the military establishments. A Missouri editor declared 'that the possession of the finest arms and equipment is always a temptation to use them under very slight provocation.' In optimistic fashion, the St. Louis *Post Dispatch* opposed preparedness because it felt the war might bring an end to all militarism and thus make armaments unnecessary.[16] The Waco *Times Herald* in Texas wanted a proper defense 'without turning the whole country into a vast military camp. . . . A wholesale military establishment is no guaranty of peace, but has been shown to be provocative of war.' In South Dakota, the editor of the Yanktown *Press* expressed the opinion that 'militarism is as great or a greater menace than invasion and the constant burden of a tremendous wasteful war establishment as serious as unpreparedness for a war that is not likely to come at all.' [17]

In 1914, a large proportion of American thought and comment

had been devoted to a detached but highly critical interpreta
tion of the European war. A year later the economic needs of the
Allies, the German submarine campaign, and the propaganda em
anating from both sides made the war much more of a reality to
the American people. Not yet ready to exchange the status of a
neutral for that of a belligerent, the United States plunged instead
into the compromise of preparedness. Popular with militarists,
businessmen, and politicians, preparedness also appealed to ex
treme nationalists and isolationists. At the same time, the pre
paredness movement gradually found favor with many interna
tionalists and idealists, who went along with President Wilson and
urged a peace enforced, if necessary, by American arms. William
Allen White, the famous editor of the *Emporia Gazette,* was a
good example of an early convert to this view. Although he had
a typical Middle Westerner's dislike of the Navy League and
big-business type of preparedness, by 1915 he had come to believe
that it was a war against German militarism, and he accepted
the arguments for an armed peace.[18] This idea, now suddenly
rendered attractive in the excitement of the war, was further
publicized by the formal launching in June 1915 of the League
To Enforce Peace. The League, in offering a formula by which
pacifists could also support the preparedness movement, helped
to disrupt the peace cause and the campaign against militarism.

The sinking of the *Lusitania* and the disturbing international
events of the summer of 1915 gave additional popular incentives
for preparedness. When William Jennings Bryan took this oc
casion to resign as Secretary of State, the antipreparedness forces
lost the advantage of his presence and influence within the Wil
son administration. Although perhaps unskilled in the subtle arts
of diplomacy, Bryan had sincerely endeavored to maintain the
true and impartial neutrality which the President himself had a
first espoused. Moreover, he had exerted his influence against the
military interventionist point of view expressed by such Presi
dential advisers as Colonel Edward M. House, who had been
aggressively pro-Ally from the early days of the war.[19]

With the new freedom permitted by his resignation, Bryan
entered actively into the fight against preparedness. In an address
at Carnegie Hall on 20 June, he appealed to labor to oppose the

ig-business type of preparedness advocated by Theodore Roosevelt, the National Security League, and the League To Enforce Peace. At Madison Square Garden, a few days later, he spoke at a peace meeting attended by twelve thousand persons, while twenty-five thousand more overflowed into the streets.²⁰ Bryan undoubtedly hoped to use his following among the people to rouse antipreparedness sentiment and stiffen the resistance of the Wilson administration to any sort of militarism. This seemed all the more necessary because of recurrent rumors that Wilson was yielding to the agitation of the preparedness advocates.

Several factors probably determined the President's about-face on this issue. Some students of his career emphasize the formidable political pressure exerted by the protagonists of preparedness.²¹ National defense had always been an issue capable of proving attractive to a great variety of both selfish and patriotic interests. Not the least of those so affected in 1915 was Theodore Roosevelt, to whom the war and preparedness were, as one student of his career has written, 'heaven-sent.' ²² Thus Wilson, it is asserted, had to take the leadership of the preparedness movement or yield the White House to Roosevelt and the Republicans in 1916. On the other hand, it was also likely that Wilson himself, by the summer and fall of 1915, had given up the pretense of neutrality in favor of the concept of an enforced peace. Reconciling himself to the likelihood of American intervention in the war, he used preparedness as politically the most acceptable means to that end, although he, of course, continued to stress the motive of national defense in his public utterances on the subject. It has also been pointed out that Wilson contributed heavily to the idea of a defenseless America and the accompanying need for preparedness, by his failure to protest more energetically the British violations of American neutral rights. In this way, the President gave the misleading impression that the United States was powerless on the high seas.²³ Whatever the President's reasons, in July 1915 he told Secretaries Garrison and Daniels to go ahead and draw up preparedness programs for the army and the navy. Then on 4 November, in an address delivered at a dinner of the Manhattan Club in New York, the President formally announced his conversion to the cause of greater preparedness. 'We have it in mind,' he said, 'to be prepared, not for war, but only for defense.' He went on to outline the administration program for half a million trained troops and the second most powerful navy in the world.[24]

Wilson's speech was immediately attacked by former Secretary of State Bryan and others who questioned the existence of any threat to the security of the United States. Across the Atlantic Lord Roseberry, the former Liberal prime minister, lamented that the Wilson defense plans would add to the world's armament burdens and heighten the tragedy of the war. 'I know nothing more disheartening,' he said, 'than the announcement recently made, that the United States — the one great country left in the world free from the hideous, bloody burden of war — is about to embark upon the building of a huge armada destined to be equal or second to our own.' At home, William Lyons Phelps, the famous Yale professor of literature, in a letter to the *New York Times* interpreted Wilson's speech as evidence that the United States was ready to embark on 'the dance of death.'[25] A similar view was expressed by Emma Goldman, the celebrated anarchist, who saw preparedness as 'the road to universal slaughter.' Voicing her disappointment that Wilson had succumbed to the same methods and techniques used forty years ago in Germany by Bismarck, she concluded sadly that there was little essential difference between Theodore Roosevelt, 'the born bully who uses a club,' and Wilson, 'the history professor who wears the smooth polished university mask.'[26]

In the President's own party in Congress, there was intense opposition to his new view, and Wilson's December 1915 preparedness message was, in the words of his official biographer, 'generously though not enthusiastically received.' A week after the President's message, Representative Clyde H. Tavenner delivered a detailed and elaborately documented speech exposing the ties between the Navy League and the private munitions industry. Tavenner, who was a long-standing advocate of taking the profit out of war and preparation for war, now declared his belief 'that if this Republic is in danger, it is in danger not from the people beyond the seas, but from a clique of men within this country who would tax the people until their backs break, simply that

ey might make profit supplying battleships, armor and guns.'
avenner tried to make it clear that he opposed the Navy League,
ot because it advocated preparedness, but because it advocated
kind of preparedness in which the government and people of
e United States were defrauded by selfish interests. 'In tracing
e business connections of the men behind the Navy League one
annot avoid being impressed,' he asserted, 'by the number of
stances in recent years in which those identified with the steel
nd armor making concerns find their way into the official life of
e Navy Department, the Department of Justice, and even the
epartment of State.' [27] Tavenner's attack on its big business
ffiliations hit the preparedness movement in its most vulnerable
ot. Secretary of the Navy Josephus Daniels had already tangled
ith Navy League interference in his department, and the gen-
ral attitude of the Wilson administration had been hostile to the
usts. The theme of Tavenner's speech was often repeated on the
oors of Congress, and his printed remarks were widely circulated
y peace groups.[28]

Aware of this feeling and faced with revolt in Congress, Presi-
ent Wilson tried to disassociate his concept of preparedness
om that espoused by the Navy League and big business. Soon
fter his message to Congress and its disappointing reception
ere, the President decided to go before the country in order to
rouse public opinion and prevent the Republicans from taking
ver leadership in the preparedness battle. In a series of addresses
elivered in January and February 1916, the President argued
he thesis that preparedness, conceived in terms of defense and
ith adequate safeguards to insure civilian control, was not mil-
aristic. Emphasizing industrial and vocational as well as military
raining, he declared that militarism was limited to 'preparing a
reat machine whose only use is for war and giving it no use
pon which to expend itself.' [29]

The President's tour met with considerable popular enthusiasm
nd the general support of the nation's newspapers. West of the
Iississippi Valley, however, editors often expressed the fear that
reparedness might lead to militarism. In this section, there was
lso much sentiment for government ownership of the munitions
ndustry. Although the President refrained from a direct endorse-

ment of compulsory military training, there was some concern lest preparedness culminate in conscription. The San Francisco *Chronicle*, in opposing the President's program, observed:

> Every army officer who has spoken on the subject has urged conscription, and, indeed, unless that is resorted to, it would be impossible to increase the size of the Army materially. This being the case, there is no escape from militarism, which means enforced military service and all that the word implies.[30]

William Jennings Bryan in his *Commoner* charged that if the President's words meant anything at all, they seemed to indicate that the 'preparedness for which he asks is not for the purpose of preventing future wars, BUT IS FOR USE IN THE PRESENT WAR, if he thinks it necessary.' [31]

In Washington, Congressional opposition to Wilson's diplomacy and preparedness, though weakened by the President's speaking tour, was by no means completely undermined. Scores of anti-preparedness petitions were received, chiefly from agricultural Midwestern communities, or from socialist and labor groups. William S. Kenyon, Senator from Iowa, presented a petition signed by a million citizens which called for a United States embargo on the export of munitions of war.[32] Members of Congress were particularly hostile to the preparedness schemes of Secretary of War Garrison, who was calling for a 'Continental Army' of four hundred thousand trained militiamen. Some Republican Congressmen, willing to go farther than Garrison, followed Representative Gardner in his advocacy of full-scale military training and conscription. In this way, as one such Congressman pointed out, the high cost of a standing army would be avoided. 'The armies of Germany are not,' he declared, 'made up of professional soldiers. They are citizen soldiers, fighting for little or no pay.' The House refused to accept either Gardner's conscription or Garrison's Continental Army, substituting in their stead the Hay bill which provided a greater measure of federal control over the National Guard and financial support for the citizens' training camps. This alternative was favored by the strong National Guard lobby and it was also regarded by the House as a less drastic departure from tradition than the Garrison plan.[33]

In the Senate, in 1916, the proposed legislation for the army
is presented in the form of the Chamberlain bill. This bill called
r a thorough reorganization of the army and a gradual increase
its enlisted strength up to a maximum of two hundred and
ty thousand men as contrasted with the previous figure of one
indred thousand. During the spring of 1916, the Chamberlain
ll was subjected to heavy attack by a group of western Senators.
ilbert M. Hitchcock of Nebraska submitted a minority report
iestioning the increase in the General Staff and the re-enlist-
ent of men at a higher rate of pay. Charles S. Thomas of Colo-
do, who began the debate in the Senate, recalled the work of
irl Liebknecht, the German socialist, and his exposure of the
unitions trust in that country. In the same way, Thomas charged
at big-business interests in the United States were pushing the
eparedness movement, hoping thereby to forestall the Wilson
ogram of government regulation. The East Coast, already
runk' with the money received from war orders and overseas
ipping, was now actively fomenting a war from which it would
iin further profits. Although Thomas likened preparedness to 'a
ommercial enterprise,' he also recognized that the whole nation,
ot just the munitions makers, had become infected with its
iirit. 'When guns and glory go hand in hand, patriotism waxes
ot in the crowded marts of commerce only, but in the highways
id byways everywhere.' Senator Wesley L. Jones of Washington
xpressed a typical Congressional view in accusing United States
iilitary authorities of taking advantage of the European war
tuation to stampede the people into preparedness.[34]

The President, in the face of Congressional sentiment, did not
ive his full support to the Garrison conscription plan; but his
eneral backing of preparedness forced the opposition upon the
efensive. Confronted by the President's changed views as to
Inited States policy and by the increasingly serious international
.tuation, the antipreparedness forces made a desperate attempt
1 the spring of 1916 to arouse the people and thus encourage
'ongress to vote down the pending Hay-Chamberlain bills. A
irge part of the leadership and initiative in this struggle against
reparedness came from a small band of liberals and pacifists who
ad joined together in the early days of the war to organize the

American Union against Militarism and the Woman's Peace Part
The Woman's Peace Party, although stressing 'organized oppos
tion to militarism in our own country,' devoted the greater sha
of its attention to co-operating with peace groups abroad in a
effort to end the war.[35] The American Union against Militarisr
on the other hand, was the outgrowth of an effort by a group o
social workers and religious leaders to resist the preparedne
movement.

In November 1914, at a meeting in the Henry Street Settleme
House in New York City, an informal Anti-Militarism Committe
was formed. Lillian Wald, John Haynes Holmes, Stephen Wis
and Paul U. Kellogg were among the original members, and Mi
Wald, director of the Settlement House, was elected presiden
Adopting the name Anti-Preparedness Committee, the organiz
tion, which later became known as the American Union again
Militarism, attained a membership of six thousand persons an
spent thirty-five thousand dollars during its first year as part o
its bold attempt to compete with the much more lavishly finance
preparedness campaign.[36] Later Henry Ford was persuaded b
the A.U.M. to contribute funds for the circulation of antimi
itarist literature, and Ford himself signed a full page advertis
ment denouncing preparedness, which appeared in newspape
over the United States on 23 February 1916.[37]

As a part of their 'protest against the attempt to stampede th
nation into the adoption of a dangerous program of military an
naval expansion' a group of the A.U.M., leaders including Lillia
Wald, Paul U. Kellogg, John Haynes Holmes, Stephen Wis
Louis Lochner, Max Eastman, Florence Kelly, and George W
Kirchwey formed the Washington Anti-Militarism Committee a
an 'on the scenes' lobbying body.[38] Members of this committee
along with the representatives of the Woman's Peace Party, th
Society of Friends, and spokesmen for educational, farm, an
labor organizations took the lead in testifying against the Hay
Chamberlain preparedness bills at the Congressional hearings i
January and February 1916.

One of the first to offer a statement at the hearings was Jan
Addams, President of the Woman's Peace Party, who made a
urgent plea that Congress await the end of the war and the pos

ble disarmament of Europe before giving up the prized Amer-
an heritage of a small standing army. Both Miss Addams and
liss Wald, who represented the A.U.M. at the hearings, mini-
ized the possibility of an attack on the United States. They
:oposed that Congress, before appropriating more funds, in-
estigate the waste and inefficiency already existing in the army's
xpenditures. Oswald Garrison Villard, publisher of the New York
vening Post and the Nation, and a longstanding critic of mil-
arism, admitted in the course of the hearings that he had very
rong feelings about an increase in the military establishment
ecause I have watched the development of militarism in Ger-
any ever since my boyhood there, and have seen how insidi-
usly a militaristic spirit can affect a nation.' Farm leaders, repre-
enting the various state Granges and Farmers Unions, cited the
esolutions opposing preparedness, which had been adopted the
revious year by their national organizations. They particularly
riticized press propaganda for preparedness and raised the ques-
on of the cost of the whole program. Labor opposition was
eakened by the absence of Samuel Gompers, President of the
.F. of L., who had joined President Wilson in support of pre-
aredness. Other Federation officials, however, expressed labor's
esentment over the selfish, big-business pressure for a larger army
nd a more efficient National Guard.[39]

The hearings on the Hay-Chamberlain bills revealed the lack
f organized opposition to preparedness on the part of the nation's
chools, churches, and labor unions. President Gompers's con-
ersion to preparedness, announced in a speech before the Na-
ional Civic Federation in January 1916, was a blow to the anti-
nilitarist cause. In the years before the World War, Gompers
ad encouraged American workers to co-operate with the inter-
ational labor movement in giving full support to arbitration and
lisarmament, and in this period Gompers considered himself a
doctrinaire pacifist.' Like most labor leaders in the United States,
e favored American neutrality and regarded the war in Europe
s against the best interests of the workingman. Although support
f the war by various European national labor groups cast some
loubt on this assumption, a more important factor in Gompers's
onversion was his realization of the increasing dependence of

American labor upon the war orders of the Allied Powers. I November 1915, the Executive Committee of the A.F. of L. re ported that American neutrality, carried to the point of an em bargo on arms and munitions, would be disastrous to the Ame ican workingman, then just recovering from the effects of th 1914 economic set back. The committee concluded that, despit all its evils and horrors, war was no worse than the type of de potism that sought to prevent a people from working out the own economic destiny. Gompers, preferring the prosperity of pre paredness to the economic hardships of real neutrality, helped t wean labor away from its traditional hostility to a large army an navy.[40]

By the spring of 1916, the antipreparedness cause was becom ing an increasingly forlorn hope. The growing seriousness of th events in Europe and Mexico, mounting defections in their ow ranks, and the far greater resources of their opponents all com bined to place the antimilitarist forces on the defensive. As th popular newspapers and magazines began to confine their co umns to propreparedness writings, criticism was forced to find it way into print through the socialist and radical press. The ol *Masses* published a stream of bitter articles attacking variou aspects of militarism. Art Young in his cartoons satirized prepared ness as a selfish scheme concocted by the special interests to de fraud the American people. Max Eastman pointed out in a typica editorial that

> . . . we are not keeping our heads, when we denounce 'German Militarism' in one breath, and advocate 'Military Preparedness' in the other. These two things are one and the same.
> Militarism is not a trait of any one race or nation. It is a certain way of spending human life and energy, and has exactly the same character wherever it appears. German militarism is simply highly expert, effective militarism in rather large quantities.[41]

Finally, in a last desperate drive to reach the public while th army and navy legislation was still pending in Congress, th American Union against Militarism launched its April 1916 'Truth About Preparedness Campaign,' with mass meetings scheduled in the larger cities of the East and Middle West. The decision to make this appeal had come as a result of a White House inter view, in which President Wilson told representatives of the Union to hire halls if they wished to discern the American people's feelings toward preparedness. The President, confident that the country was substantially united behind his program, was impatient of the continued A.U.M. type of opposition.[42]

Despite Wilson's hostile attitude, at the conclusion of its April campaign another group of the A.U.M. saw the President to present their findings on antimilitarist sentiment in the country and to ask him to clarify his own peace position. The delegates requested Wilson to lead an attack upon the sordid and selfish interests behind the preparedness drive. But the President refused to accept the contention that preparedness was an equivalent of militarism, and he also criticized the point of view that linked military training with military service. The delegates, in opposition to Wilson's position, pointed out that training would lead to service. The current war madness in Europe, they pleaded, was all the more reason why the United States should try to keep a sane balance in military planning.[43]

In the late spring of 1916 it was becoming apparent that most of the country was no more ready than the President to listen to antimilitarist arguments. The American people seemed to agree with Wilson that his version of preparedness was not militaristic. Even if this were not admitted, it was still true, as Wilson's supporters contended, that the President's ideas about defense were less militaristic than those of Garrison or Wood or Theodore Roosevelt. What the President's supporters did not realize, however, was that the trend of events tended increasingly to favor the more extreme militarist position espoused by Wilson's political enemies. Thus the President would be drawn into a situation from which he could not retreat. Whether or not Wilson actually agreed with the extremist view, he helped to insure its success when he carried on his 1916 campaign for re-election by marching at the head of the preparedness parades.

On 3 June the President signed the National Defense Act, thus incorporating the Hay and Chamberlain bills into law. Although this measure was a compromise, not acceptable to either the militarist or pacifist point of view, it made a fundamental change in the status of the militia and also provided a precedent for more drastic legislation in the future. Under the terms of the act th regular army was increased to 175,000 men, and provision wa made for taking the militia or National Guard into the service c the United States whenever Congress authorized 'the use c troops in excess of those in the regular army.' Persons so drafte were no longer members of the state militia, and the President ir stead of the state governors appointed the officers from amon the members of the National Guard. By this law, the states wer eliminated as checks on the power of the federal government t determine military policy, and the basis for further centralizatio in the army was established. In addition, funds were provide for the R.O.T.C. program in the colleges, and later a Council o National Defense was created.[44]

The new, federalized National Guard, though less offensive t pacifists than the Garrison reserve army, was regarded in man circles as a militaristic device. The *Scientific American* saw danger in the possibility of political activity by the Guard, and i pointed out that 'The Constitutional safeguards around the Reg ular Army can have no application to this new army.' It predicte that the passage of the National Defense Act would substitut militarism for representative government. 'And so the menace o a great standing army, so dreaded by our fathers, will be an ac complished fact.' The Socialist *New Review* in describing 'th dangers of a citizen army' noted that the attitude of the worke was changed after service in the militia. Large armies increase the possibility of militarism and war, and the call to the colors ha ever been an effective means of breaking strikes.[45] In Congress Senator William E. Borah, who was in close touch with the peac organizations, charged that the real purpose of federal pay wa 'to build up a dominant and aggressive military organization in the States.'[46]

In the midst of this nationwide concern over military prepared ness, the major parties assembled in the convention cities of Chicago and St. Louis to draft their platforms and nominate their candidates for the Presidency. Both the Democratic and Re publican parties espoused preparedness, while the expiring Pro gressives called for universal military training in addition to a navy of at least second rank and an army of a quarter of a million men. The Republican nomination of Charles Evans Hughes rather than Roosevelt, the Progressive's choice, represented a partial set-back to the militarist element. Although the Wilson leaders at the Democratic convention included a ringing preparedness plank in the party platform, peace sentiment was strong among the rank and file of the delegates. The keynote address of Governor Martin H. Glynn of New York was devoted to showing the numerous in-stances in which the United States had settled serious interna-tional disputes without resort to war. His thesis that peace was not incompatible with honor was wildly cheered by the conven-tion crowd whose feelings were given a measure of recognition in the campaign slogan, 'He kept us out of war.' [47]

Although both Wilson and Hughes denied that the type of pre-paredness they advocated would lead to militarism,[48] the country was whipped into a high state of excitement by the preparedness parades and patriotic motif of the campaign. Organized opposi-tion to preparedness was left in the hands of the Socialist party, with some additional support from the Prohibitionists who also denounced militarism and universal military training. Allan L. Benson, the Socialist candidate, made an able attack on the pre-paredness movement emphasizing the danger of militarism, but the party was not united on the issue and suffered a decline of three hundred thousand votes as compared to the totals in 1912. The Socialists undoubtedly suffered, too, from the popular feeling that the best hope of peace was a vote for Wilson.[49]

Midway in the Presidential campaign, Congress passed the im-portant Naval Act of 29 August 1916. This measure took the ad-ministration's five-year naval building program, at that time with-out precedent, and compressed it into three years. Appropriations for the first year, totaling well over three hundred million dollars, were more than double the amount expended for the preceding year. Congressional approval of so ambitious a program, designed to make the United States navy second only to that of Great Britain, had come after several months of hearings and bitter de-bate. Members of Congress protested in vain that vast future projects of naval construction could not bear any possible rela-tionship to the legitimate defense needs of the United States in 1916 and 1917. Discerning other motives for the bill, Congressmen repeated their former denunciations of the Navy League and the various business and propaganda interests co-operating in the preparedness drive. Walter L. Hensley of Missouri, a leader of the fight against the navy bill in the House, cited the rise in Bethlehem Steel stock from $30 to $530 a share as evidence of the extent to which the munitions makers were 'capitalizing patriotism.' [50] In the Senate, George W. Norris of Nebraska introduced a bill to defer the entire building program until after the President had an opportunity to convene a disarmament conference. Albert B. Cummins of Iowa urged the passage of an amendment providing for United States attendance at a peace and arbitration conference after the war, while Robert M. La Follette, Asle J. Gronna, and others attacked the private business interests which were using preparedness as a cloak for more profits.[51]

The skepticism entertained by some Congressmen regarding naval preparedness of such vast proportions was overcome in part by their feeling that a large navy, unlike a large standing army, did not involve the threat of militarism. As the editor of the *Saturday Evening Post* commented: 'Most of them, no doubt, are honest in saying that they do not want militarism — being too excited to perceive the obvious fact that a huge navy and conscription are militarism.' Senator Borah, for example, in contrast to his fight against the army increase, accepted the naval bill as an alternative to worse forms of militarism.[52]

Powerless to defeat the Naval Act of 1916, the adversaries of the program were still able to force the inclusion of a provision stating that the United States approved in principle the reduction of armaments. The President was authorized and requested to invite, at a date not later than the close of the war in Europe, all the great powers of the world to a conference to consider plans for a court of arbitration, as well as to discuss the general question of disarmament. If the proposed international gathering were successful in achieving these ends, the President was empowered to suspend such United States naval construction as was inconsistent with the disarmament agreement.[53]

The Naval Act of 1916, together with the army legislation embraced in the Hay-Chamberlain bill passed that spring, indicated the complete triumph of the preparedness forces. In a minority now, even within the ranks of the clergy, schoolmasters, and labor leaders, the fast-dwindling pacifist and liberal forces turned their efforts toward preventing the war which they saw as the almost inevitable culmination of an emerging American militarism.

XII

Conscripting America for War

THE ADVOCATES of preparedness talked in terms of the defense o
the United States, but the real question implicit in the great pre
paredness debate of the spring and summer of 1916 was the pos
sibility of American entrance into the European war. The Wilso
campaign slogan 'He kept us out of war,' though factually co
rect, gave a misleading impression with regard to the future. Al
ready the Wilson policy concerning Mexico and Germany ha
carried the nation to the brink of war. The President's firm stan
against German methods of submarine warfare, coupled with in
creasing American sympathy for the Allied cause, had deprive
his diplomacy of the neutral point of view necessary to kee
America at peace. As Wilson himself seems to have realized lon
before the elections in November, if the European war did no
come to an abrupt close, the United States eventually would b
drawn into the conflict on the side of the Allies.[1] War, even to th
point of militarism at home, seemed preferable to facing th
consequences of a German victory in Europe.

Not all advocates of preparedness thought in terms of war, an
many of those that did, because of the lingering popular desir
for peace, were careful to refrain from voicing their opinion
publicly. Among the few unafraid to speak out and admit tha
preparedness was not primarily a defensive measure was Herbe
176

Croly, editor of the *New Republic* and an early apostle of Wilson's New Freedom. Croly believed that the preparedness program of 1916, although it violated America's historic traditions, was necessary because of President Wilson's decision in the summer of 1915 that there was a threat of war. Croly pointed out that the United States, following in the stream of European history, could hardly avoid adopting some of the features of European life, including a certain degree of militarization. 'The American nation,' he declared, 'needs the tonic of a serious moral adventure.' While he criticized the army legislation of 1916 as a militaristic measure, providing troops primarily for offensive action, he also expressed the hope that the new army, despite its danger to American traditions and institutions, might introduce a useful ferment into national life and give it a necessary 'tonic effect.' 'The usual explanation that the United States is preparing only for defense, which is a policy on which all good citizens can agree, merely begs the question,' Croly asserted, because, in the case of a large nation like the United States, 'no sharp line can be drawn between defensive and aggressive armament.' Thus the 'dubious aspect' of preparedness lay not in its cost, but 'in the ambiguity of its underlying purpose.' Croly also frankly admitted that 'there is a very real probability that the new Army and Navy will be used chiefly for positive and for aggressive as opposed to merely defensive purposes.' [2]

Croly, interestingly enough, made much the same analysis of the implications of the preparedness legislation as did its most bitter opponents. The latter, however, did not share Croly's pro-Wilson conclusions. While he, and other less outspoken advocates of preparedness, looked with equanimity upon the possibility of American intervention in the war, the antimilitarist forces campaigned to prevent such an outcome. The *Nation* and the *Masses* provided the mediums through which Oswald Garrison Villard, John Reed, and others published their attacks upon the militarization of America and the drift toward war. [3] The example of Europe with its long history of wars and preparations for war was cited again and again. Reference was made to the famous indictments of war and militarism by Mark Twain, Randolph Bourne, Bertrand Russell, and Karl Liebknecht. [4] Peace leaders as varied in their background as William Hull, Quaker professor of history, Frederick Howe, Wilson's Commissioner of Immigration in the Port of New York, and Scott Nearing, the socialist economist, published detailed attacks on the selfish business and economic interests engaged in pushing the preparedness program.[5] William E. Dodd, the historian, compared American preparedness advocates to the German militarists of Bismarck's time. Wilson, he said, had been forced to parade in the late campaign, and now, he feared, the President had become convinced by the preparedness propaganda.[6]

On 31 January 1917 Germany proclaimed the resumption of submarine warfare, and on the afternoon of 3 February Wilson went before Congress to announce the breaking off of diplomatic relations. The more uncompromising pacifists now united in final effort to avert the war, which they knew was near and which they feared would take the American people further along the road to militarism. Supplementing the work of the American Union against Militarism and the Woman's Peace Party, an Emergency Peace Federation was established. With the aid of socialist and other radical groups, antiwar demonstrations were held in the larger cities. Using the slogan 'A few cents now may save many dollars in taxation and possibly a son,' people were urged to write their Congressmen. William Jennings Bryan and David Starr Jordan addressed mass meetings and used their waning influence among wavering politicians and intellectuals. Late in February a delegation of the American Union against Militarism saw the President for an hour and came away momentarily hopeful of peace.[7]

Despite all efforts, the bitter struggle against preparedness and war was approaching an end. On 2 April, Wilson delivered his fateful message, and after a brief period of debate Congress passed the joint resolution declaring war upon Germany with only a few dissenting votes — fifty in the House and six in the Senate. The state of war, which began 6 April when the President signed the declaration, produced a varied effect upon the peace leaders who had fought preparedness. The greater share, including most of the clergy, went along with William Jennings Bryan in offering their services to the government. Henry Ford and the older peace societies had already yielded to the war tide, but Jane Addams and most of her associates in the American Union against Militarism remained resolute. Her speech 'Patriotism and Pacifists' delivered in Chicago in June, though bitterly criticized in the press, encouraged many pacifists to maintain their cherished convictions.[8] Vachel Lindsay in his correspondence with the founder of Hull House apologized for the militarist tone of his new poems and promised another set paying tribute to Bryan's earlier peace efforts. The dilemma facing many of those who hated war, but who felt impelled to support their country, was illustrated by Lindsay's letter to Miss Addams, asking:

> What shall I do? This war breaks my heart. Send me what you have written since Bryan enlisted — for instance. Are you with Bryan?
> Do you accept President Wilson's war message on its face value? Is that final with you?
> I hate a hyphenated America. I hate war. But I owe no one in Europe a grudge. I would rather be shot than shoot anybody. If I had been in Congress I would have voted with Miss Rankin and would have considered it a sufficient reason to say 'I will not vote for war till she does.'[9]

Although Randolph Bourne castigated the intellectuals for their acceptance of the war — 'A war made deliberately by the intellectuals!' — a few, including Bourne himself, stood firm. Oswald Garrison Villard, editor of the *Nation* and the New York *Evening Post,* and a member of the American Union against Militarism, refused to support the war. In a letter written a week after the declaration of war to Joseph Tumulty, the President's secretary, he asserted: 'Believe me, I am ready for any concentration camp, or prison, but I am *not* at war and no one can *put me into war.*'[10] The Socialist party, at an emergency convention called in St. Louis for the week of 7 April, adopted a resolution reiterating its opposition to militarism and war, and calling for the preservation of free speech and no conscription. While this stand expressed the sentiments of the majority, it resulted in the withdrawal of a large group of prominent Socialist leaders including Allan Benson, the party's Presidential candidate in the 1916 elections.[11]

Defeated in their major effort, antimilitarists turned their attentions to new problems. Those staunch pacifists who refused to accept the war, with the aid of some nonpacifist but antimilitarist sympathizers, attempted to win support for the concept of a war without militarism, to be fought in accordance with the high ideals expressed in Wilson's war message to Congress. But the extreme difficulty of attaining this lofty goal was recognized by no one more clearly than the President himself. On the eve of delivering his fateful call to arms, the President was reported as saying to Frank Cobb of the *World:*

> 'Once lead this people into war,' he said, 'and they'll forget there ever was such a thing as tolerance. To fight you must be brutal and ruthless, and the spirit of ruthless brutality will enter into every fibre of our national life, infecting Congress, the courts, the policeman on the beat, the man in the street.' Conformity would be the only virtue, said the President, and every man who refused to conform would have to pay the penalty.
>
> He thought the Constitution would not survive it; that free speech and the right of assembly would go. He said a nation couldn't put its strength into a war and keep its head level; it had never been done.[12]

Understanding better than most of his fellow citizens the virtual impossibility of waging modern war without the repressive features of the militarist state, President Wilson was at first deeply concerned by the problem. Gradually, however, he seemed to give up any serious effort to curb the growth of wartime militarism. In the face of the tremendous pressures and responsibilities of the war years, Wilson and other exponents of the New Freedom substituted propaganda and coercion for liberalism and reform. Opponents of preparedness had predicted this unhappy result during the great debate of 1916. Now, after the actual declaration of war, they were faced with the difficult task of trying to prevent their own forecast from coming true. In the brave and hopeful words of the Collegiate Anti-Militarism League, 'The mere fact that war has been declared does not mean that we who have been opposed to it must cease activities. We could not keep the militarist faction from forcing America into the war but we can work to prevent war from overwhelming her.'[13] The struggle centered first in the attempt to prevent such legislation

as the Draft and Espionage Acts. Failing in that endeavor, antimilitarists and their liberal allies worked hard to gain justice and
recognition for conscientious objectors to military service as well
as to preserve the right of free speech for all opponents of the
war.

These problems, especially conscription, had been a matter of
grave concern to liberals for at least some months prior to American entrance into the war. John Reed had written early in 1915
that the worst thing in Europe, was the lack of dissent and the
way in which soldiers and civilians alike were conditioned to
endure unspeakable conditions. Proclaiming his own hatred of
the militarism he had found in Europe, Reed warned his American readers against accepting the proposition that 'a conscript
army is Democratic, because everybody has to serve.' [14] A few
days after Reed's attack on conscription and militarism, Ralph
Barton Perry, a Harvard professor and disciple of William James,
published in the *New Republic* the manifesto of the protagonists
of universal service. Entitling his essay 'The Free Man and the
Soldier,' Perry asserted that the terms were in no way contradictory and that conscription would not destroy the free individual.[15]
Other exponents of universal service described the Swiss and
Argentine forms of conscription as examples of democratic military systems, thus hoping to overcome the traditional American
identification of conscription with Prussian and European militarism.[16] Charles Eliot, former President of Harvard, and at first
an outspoken foe of preparedness, on the eve of the elections of
1916 published an article in which he termed universal military
service 'a grave but necessary choice.' Believing that the United
States must give up its former isolation because of its industrial
expansion, he envisaged universal military service as a prerequisite to American world leadership. If conscription were of the
Swiss type, he concluded that it would give the United States
safety without militarism.' [17]

With some few exceptions, such as General Nelson A. Miles
who had testified against it before a Congressional committee,[18]
military men were enthusiastic backers of the principle of conscription. General Leonard Wood, a longtime advocate of conscription, had helped popularize citizens' military service through

his Plattsburg camps. General Hugh L. Scott, Wood's successor as Chief of Staff, included an argument for a draft in his official report in 1916, and a group of younger officers were already busily engaged in propaganda for universal military service.[19] These efforts received considerable additional support from the National Service League organized by Grenville Clark, a New York attorney. The first volume in its projected National Service Library was a collection of General Wood's writings and speeches in behalf of preparedness and conscription.[20] From February to July 1917, *National Service*, a magazine edited by Clark, Theodore Roosevelt, and Willard Straight, published the arguments for universal military training contributed by Wood, Charles W. Eliot, Ralph Barton Perry, Jacob Gould Schurman, Newton D. Baker, and others.

Well-equipped financially and deriving much strength from the parallel drives for American preparedness and belligerency, the agitation for conscription still faced strong hurdles. President Wilson and Secretary of War Baker had been converted to some type of universal service even before the United States declaration of war, but Congress remained unconvinced. Encouraged by this attitude and by the strong undercurrent of popular opposition, opponents of conscription organized their counterpropaganda. In the spring of 1916, the American Union against Militarism noticed the increasing attempt by draft proponents to win over American opposition by using the argument that the draft was democratic. This all opponents of conscription emphatically denied. Oswald Garrison Villard, a prominent member of the A.U.M., assumed a key role in the struggle to keep conscription from the United States. Pointing out that it was democratic only in the sense that all must serve, Villard asked his readers to look at the operation of the draft in Germany, Russia, France, or even Switzerland. From his own observations of the trends in European life Villard perceived a similar transformation taking place in America. 'Once,' he stated, 'we valued American self-assertiveness, independence of thought and action, mental alertness. . . . Now we are to prefer men cast in one mould, drilled in one way of thinking, and into obedience to their rulers.'[21]

Although not prepared to follow Villard and the A.U.M. into

ie ranks of the antiwar opposition after April 1917, many Ameri-
an liberals were reluctant to accept the degree of militarism and
egimentation implied in conscription. Universal compulsory
iilitary training or service was especially resented in educational
nd labor circles. Labor traditionally feared a large army, while
ducators disliked seeing American youth turned over to the harsh
iscipline of military life. Although voluntary drill and officers'
aining had become well-established in American colleges and
niversities by 1917, most educators opposed military training in
ie public school system and hesitated to endorse the principle of
niversal military conscription.[22] They particularly resented the
xtravagant claims of General Wood and the army in behalf of
mscription as an educational device. John Dewey found this a
'pical militarist illusion, and he asserted that 'Military service is
ie remedy of despair — despair of the power of intelligence.' [23]
lexander Meiklejohn, also famous as a progressive educator.
ointed out that a draft law forced through Congress before the
merican people were convinced of its desirability or necessity
ould not foster American patriotism or unity. These values, he
sserted, could be achieved far better through mutual understand-
g than through compulsory military drill and standardization.[24]

Considerable support for the Dewey-Meiklejohn position was
und among college students. Undergraduates organized anti-
ill leagues and college peace clubs, protesting both military
aining on the campus and conscription in the nation. In January
)17 a group of young men, including Wayne V. Myers, Edward
[. Earle, and Robert Dunn, testified before a House subcommit-
e on universal military training. Myers, who was president of
ie Collegiate Anti-Militarism League, argued that universal
iilitary training was unnecessary and its supposed benefits illu-
iry. Earle, president of the Columbia University Students Board
' Representatives, attacked U.M.T. as bad for education and as a
ppression of the individual. Dunn, a student at Yale University,
ported on the undergraduates' lack of interest in courses on
orld peace or international relations after they had experienced
session at the summer military training camps.[25]

Strenuous opposition to all projected plans for conscription was
insistently registered by farm and labor groups, even after they

had come to espouse a large measure of preparedness. Along wit
support of Wilson's general defense program, the National Grang
in November 1916 went on record 'as emphatically opposed to th
draft clause of the new Army Reorganization Act.'[26] Matthe-
Woll, Vice President of the American Federation of Labor, a
serted in July 1916 that 'compulsory military service is now neith
legal, constitutional, nor justified.' At the same time John P. Whit
President of the United Mine Workers, called the proposal t
establish the draft 'the saddest and most abject surrender of Ame
ican ideals ever made in this country.'[27] Labor leaders, togethe
with representatives from various peace organizations, comprise
the bulk of the opposition to conscription at the House and Senat
hearings in April 1917. Samuel Gompers of the A.F. of L. state
the opposition of the American labor movement to compulsic
and to militarism 'in all its forms.' 'We have not changed,' Gon
pers declared.[28]

Public feeling against a draft for overseas service continue
strong even after the United States entered the war. Some of th
nation's newspapers bitterly attacked the idea of adopting col
scription before the volunteer system had been given a chanc
Oswald Garrison Villard's New York *Evening Post* believed tha
conscription, when half a million volunteers were available, wa
an unwise measure which would precipitate the issue of consciei
tious objection to military service. The San Francisco *Bulleti*
likening conscription to Prussianism, saw in it 'a demand that v
put limitations upon our democracy; an advertisement of lack o
faith in the common people; a false confession that we have bee
unable to make our Government such as to command unhesitatii
allegiance.'[29] But, by the end of April 1917, many newspape
had been won over to full support of conscription.

Despite approval by most of the press and pressure from th
White House, Congress was reluctant to consent to a draft bi
Until April 1917, neither Congress nor the American people ha
expected that large United States armies would be required f
overseas service, and they wondered whether conscription w
really needed. Congressional unwillingness to rush into conscri
tion was also related, at least in the case of some members, to
conviction that the President had dragged the country into a

unnecessary war. In the midst of wartime appeals for patriotic unity, it was obviously difficult to express such sentiments publicly. But the draft bill, which was not intrinsically a popular measure, offered to dissident Congressmen an ideal vehicle for launching a general attack upon the entire idea of the war.

Opposition was especially strong in the House, where a majority of the Committee on Military Affairs, including chairman Stanley H. Dent, was unfavorable to the principle of a draft. In the midst of committee hearings President Wilson had gone to the Capitol to confer with Democratic leaders Claude Kitchin and Champ Clark, and Secretary Baker had written to Dent assuring him that there need be 'no alarm on the subject of militarism in America, and particularly no fear of any such consequences from the impending measure, temporary as it is, and designed for the emergency.' Because of Dent's opposition, the House conscription bill was sponsored by Republican Julius Kahn of California, a Congressman who was a firm believer in preparedness and a strong admirer of the German military system.[30] On the floor of the House a number of members, particularly those from the South and West, urged that the draft be deferred until the volunteer system proved itself a failure. George Huddleston of Alabama in a long speech attacked the selfish business interests behind conscription. Big business and finance, he charged, needed a large army and navy to protect their investments abroad and to suppress labor discontent and industrial disorder at home. Representatives Slayden and McLenmore of Texas criticized the conscription propaganda coming from the Eastern seaboard, while others predicted that the draft would lead to militarism. In a statement typical of many in the House, Thomas U. Sisson asserted:

> I see more danger to America in establishing the conscription system than I do from any German invasion or any German Army. I am unwilling by any vote of mine to surrender any American ideals of freedom, liberty, and justice and adopt the Prussian ideals of force, strength, oppression and injustice.[31]

Although the draft bill enjoyed a greater measure of support in the Senate, Kenneth McKellar of Tennessee submitted for the Committee on Military Affairs a minority report, signed also by

Senators Thomas, Reed, and Kirby, which called for the preserv
tion of the volunteer system. In the floor debate that began on 2
April a small group of Senators launched a bitter attack upo
every aspect of conscription. James K. Vardaman of Mississip]
asked why the conscription of men was not paralleled or precede
by a measure to draft wealth. Lawrence Y. Sherman of Illino
criticized the hysteria of the conscription campaign and the inte
lectual conscription coming to the fore in the espionage bil
Western progressives, including La Follette, Norris, Borah, an
Gronna, expressed the fear that conscription would Prussiani
America. Charles S. Thomas of Colorado, who had signed th
committee minority report, denied the contention that conscri]
tion was democratic. He told his colleagues that he was not ab
to change a lifelong conclusion that the draft and democrac
were incompatible.

> Call it anything else but that and I may make no protest. You
> say it is based upon equality. But democracy does not mean equal-
> ity and that alone. The terms are not interchangeable. . . . If the
> reasoning in favor of this bill be sound, Germany is the most demo-
> cratic of nations. And Austria also.[32]

The Selective Service Act, which became a law on 18 Ma
authorized the President to increase the regular army to 287,0(
men, to call all members of the National Guard into federal ser
ice, and to raise by selective draft an army of a million men. Ce
tain classes of citizens might be exempt or deferred from th
draft, but all men between the ages of twenty-one and thirty i
clusive had to present themselves for registration on the date s
by the President.[33] The passage of this act produced a vari
effect upon the American people. As Frederick Palmer, the bio
rapher of Newton D. Baker, later wrote, 'America for the fir
time had regimentation on the European system, naïvely unawa
of its effects.' Although Palmer saw the workings of selective ser
ice as 'an exhibition of democracy triumphant,' he also noted th
it was 'our first great standardization of human material in ma
production.'[34] The *New Republic* was surprised to see 'the succe
of selective service' despite the fact that it went beyond the ori
nal public understanding of a draft only for home defense. B

the liberal weekly also warned that excessive coercion in the enforcement of the draft might result in a reaction against the whole idea of conscription.[35] This warning went unheeded as the relatively small numbers of dissidents who continued to oppose the war and conscription became engulfed in a wave of popular hysteria and official suppression. And so, as Frederic L. Paxson has pointed out, American democracy in the World War, deprived of the challenge of an effective minority, soon degenerated into a mob and invoked the rule of mob psychology against all dissenting elements in the population.[36]

The full force of this mass repression was felt by those pacifists and socialists who attempted to organize and demonstrate against conscription in the brief interval leading up to 5 June, the date fixed for the initial registration. In the larger cities, their parades and meetings were broken up by enraged groups of soldiers and civilians. In all areas, individuals were subjected to a variety of social pressures designed to exact obedience to the draft. On 31 May, a stir was created by the arrest of two young Columbia University students on the charge of having written a pamphlet in which prospective draftees were urged to choose prison sentences instead of army service. The individuals involved, Charles F. Phillips and Owen Cattell, the latter a son of the famed psychologist and Columbia professor James McKeen Cattell, were the first persons in New York to be accused of violating the draft laws. Actually no copies of their manuscript had left the printer, but the metropolitan newspapers carried sensational front page stories setting forth the view that their arrest had averted a serious, nationwide conspiracy. A few hours after the arrest of Phillips and Cattell, the police interfered with a pacifist and socialist meeting in Madison Square Garden, and a 'no conscription mass meeting' at Hunt's Point Palace on 4 June was broken up by police and soldiers.[37]

Although there were similar disturbances elsewhere and actual riots among miners in Montana and Michigan and among some of the Indian tribes, the compulsory registration of almost ten million men on 5 June was accomplished with a surprisingly small amount of disorder or protest. There was some truth, however, in the contention of the *American Socialist* that the more than six

million men claiming exemption constituted 'an overwhelmin
vote against war, by those who must do the fighting.' The mos
serious organized resistance occurred in several Oklahoma coun
ties during the summer of 1917. A rural people, deeply religiou
and much impressed by the socialist propaganda which ha
reached a peak in Oklahoma during the prewar years, their resent
ment against the draft flared into open violence before it wa
suppressed and the leaders arrested.[38]

General acquiescence in the draft was due to various factors
the chief of which was probably the wartime psychology tha
conditioned people to accept sacrifices no matter how great. Also
as Newton D. Baker suggested: 'An important motivating influ
ence in the public acceptance of the draft in 1917 had been tha
it was a means to win "the war to end war."' [39] In addition, th
World War draft law unlike that of the Civil War, was skillfull
drawn to win public approval. Authority resided with the loca
board, deferments were on the whole fair, and there were n
substitutes. Finally, the pressure of public opinion and the threa
of prosecution under the Espionage Act made agitation agains
the draft impossible although the amount of draft evasion, as dis
tinct from organized resistance, was comparatively large. At th
conclusion of the war official army figures indicated a total o
363,022 net desertions of which 295,184 remained outstanding.[4]
The draft evader, or deserter as he was called by the army, cer
tainly exhibited little enthusiasm for the service, but his opposi
tion to militarism was less clear-cut than the avowed rejection o
war on the part of those who became conscientious objectors.

Public sympathy with the latter, or with any sort of resistanc
to the draft, was confined almost exclusively to the radical pres
conducted by left-wing socialists and anarchists. Emma Gold
man's magazine *Mother Earth* published its June issue bordere
in black under the masthead 'June 5th In Memoriam America
Democracy.' Contributors in *Mother Earth*, counseling resistanc
to conscription, argued that registration was the first compromis
with the draft. The *International Socialist Review* called for sup
port of the party's antiwar and anticonscription stand through
program of labor strikes. Individuals were urged to take a stan
as conscientious objectors, whether or not they fulfilled the tech

nical requirements of the Draft Act or met the government's limited definition governing such a position. In the *Masses* and the *Seven Arts,* Max Eastman and Randolph Bourne avowed their own opposition to the draft and called attention to the plight of the individual objector. Bourne, who desired to face jail as a C.O. but who was prevented by disability, analyzed the problem of the young man 'coerced every step of the way,' who was without definite religious convictions against war but who was unenthusiastic about fighting and opposed to all militarism.

Although the Draft Act provided noncombatant service for religious objectors who were members of the Society of Friends or other sects traditionally opposed to war, it failed to recognize the situation of those few men who, like Bourne, might object as individuals to all wars or to a particular war which they felt to be unjust. This question had already arisen in England, and the documentary accounts of the harsh experiences suffered there by political objectors had been published in America.[41] At the Congressional hearings on conscription, Norman Thomas pleaded without success for a more liberal exemption clause to include all sincere C.O.s whether or not they were members of a historic peace church. Continuing his efforts to secure a broader exemption policy, Thomas and a group of thirteen avowed conscientious objectors signed a public appeal addressed to the President which was published in the *New Republic.* Thomas also tried to explain to the American people the varied types of conscientious objectors. He recalled the American emphasis upon individualism and appealed to critics of the C.O. to recognize their idealism and deal with the problem in the spirit of American democracy and liberalism. A man in jail added no strength to the nation, and justice to the C.O., Thomas argued, would secure, rather than imperil, the safety of a democratic state.[42]

While many members of Congress were opposed to the wartime suppression of all dissenting points of view, Representative Carl Hayden of Arizona was one of the few who dared to speak out against the persecution of the individual C.O. Hayden was not convinced of the sincerity of the humanitarian or socialist objector, but he believed the problem they posed should be resolved in such a way as to avoid their martyrdom from barbaric treatment in army camps or in federal penitentiaries. His advocacy o comparative mildness in punishment of C.O.s, he declared, wa

> not so much for their sake as from a belief that, in order not to sin
> against the principles of liberty those in authority should show a
> decent respect for an honest conviction, no matter how erroneous.
> It can be said with truth that it was only by firm and conscientious
> resistance to the will of the State that the political and religious
> freedom which we now enjoy was won. It is, therefore, the part of
> wisdom to recognize the larger expediency of tempering justice
> with mercy.[43]

On the part of President Wilson and the administration ther was little disposition to deal sympathetically with the individua objector. While the draft bill was still pending in Congress, Wil son wrote that 'it has seemed impossible to make the exemption apply to individuals because it would open the door to so mucl that was unconscientious on the part of persons who wished t escape service.' Along with Secretary of War Baker, his chief con cern was to prevent any sizable number of C.O.s, and he believec the problem could best be solved by placing the men in regula military camps, segregated from the rest but close enough to b indoctrinated and converted into good soldiers.[44]

In contrast to Wilson's attitude, Charles Evans Hughes believec that it would be 'a sound policy on the part of Congress to provid for the discharge of conscientious objectors.' 'Nothing,' he told th annual meeting of the American Bar Association, 'is gained for th country by overriding the claims of conscience in such cases. Hughes, however, did not support the argument that conscriptio was unconstitutional. This view was based on the contention tha a draft or universal service destroyed the militia power of th states and denied to individuals the right of freedom guaranteec by the Thirteenth Amendment. With regard to the question o conscription and of federal versus state authority over the militia the Constitution itself was vague. Although it was extremel doubtful that the founding fathers at Philadelphia would hav considered federal conscription for overseas service constitutional the Supreme Court in the Selective Draft cases disallowed all o the antimilitarist arguments. The Court thereby upheld its ow tradition of supporting the government in wartime, and its deci ion likewise illustrated Hughes's remark that, as the Constitution marches with the times, 'So, also, we have a *fighting* constitution.' [45]

The federal courts again sided with the government in its rigorous prosecution of individuals accused of violating the provisions of the espionage laws. The Espionage Act of 15 June 1917, together with the far more drastic amendments added by the Sedition Act of 16 May 1918, authorized severe penalties for anyone convicted of obstructing the draft or of expressing disloyal sentiments in regard to the government's methods of carrying the war to a conclusion. Designed to curb sedition, these measures, as Norman Thomas and the American Union against Militarism pointed out, could also be used against conscientious objectors, Quakers, and other pacifist groups. While the Espionage Acts were invoked to prosecute dissenters of all sorts, the Committee on Public Information headed by George Creel was established to enlist mass support for the government's policies in wartime. Uniting in this fashion propaganda with repression, the Creel Committee performed the task of unifying the home front behind the war. In the words of the leading students of the committee, it was 'charged with encouraging and then consolidating the revolution of opinion which changed the United States from anti-militaristic democracy to an organized war machine.' [46]

Open opposition to the war thus became impossible. The antiwar stand of the I.W.W. was undermined by state criminal syndicalism laws and by federal espionage legislation. Meetings of the People's Council, an antiwar organization founded in June 1917, were broken up and its leaders subjected to various forms of terrorism. In favor of 'an early just and democratic peace,' and opposed to conscription and the wartime suppression of civil liberties, the Council was denied an opportunity to present its stand.[47] The American Union against Militarism, because of its continued antiwar position, suffered several resignations including that of Lillian Wald, its chairman, and Paul U. Kellogg, one of its founders. Both felt that the A.U.M. support of the C.O. position in the war had set the organization against the government and deprived it of all influence. In September 1917 this feeling resulted in the establishment of the Civil Liberties Bureau of the A.U.M.

as a separate organization which later became known as the American Civil Liberties Union. The new body then assumed the task of advising and defending those individuals who dared to challenge the government's espionage and draft laws.[48]

The small minority of conscientious objectors and political prisoners did not include those religious pacifists who were willing to accept induction into the army and assignment to non-combatant duties. These men, over fifty thousand in number, presented no great problem to the government, and their stand, although important as a personal religious manifestation or witness, had little significance in the broader aspects of the struggle against militarism. The men actually classified as conscientious objectors, those who refused to accept any form of service within the army, numbered about four thousand. After a year of conscription, a special board of inquiry headed by Harlan F. Stone, Dean of the Columbia University Law School, was set up to investigate their cases.[49] Of the more than two thousand individuals examined by the board, the overwhelming majority were found to be sincere and were offered release from the army on agricultural or industrial furloughs. Approximately thirteen hundred more men, who had originally claimed exemption as C.O.s, did not wait for hearings but accepted the army noncombatant service which was finally made available by the President. These two types of alternate service took care of the majority of the C.O.s who had been kept against their will in army camps, but an additional group of some four hundred refused to accept any form of alternate service or furlough. These absolutists were court-martialed and sentenced to long terms in army prisons, chiefly at the disciplinary barracks at Fort Leavenworth.[50]

Although classified by the government as draft evaders, many of those who refused to register or report for the draft were motivated by a sincere individualistic or political opposition to the war, which merited their consideration as conscientious objectors. These men, who included socialists, I.W.W.s, and humanitarian objectors, were usually sentenced to a year in a federal penitentiary. They were then forcibly registered and inducted into the army where, if they continued to refuse military service, they were subject to court-martial. Denounced as slackers and cowards many of the conscientious objectors underwent harsh and barbaric treatment. Some relief came after these conditions were called to the attention of President Wilson and Secretary Baker, but the President rejected the suggestion that he grant a blanket pardon to those violators of the conscription law who were not consciously disloyal in their stand.[51] Convinced that the successful prosecution of the war required an extraordinary degree of centralization and unity, Wilson also gave his support to the prosecution of the small band of radicals charged with conspiring against the government. Unlike the C.O. whose plight attracted little attention until after the war, the trials of such well-known anarchists or socialists as Emma Goldman, Max Eastman, Victor Berger, and Eugene Debs created a stir and further aroused the militaristic spirit already pervading the nation.

In general, the government concerned itself only with the more militant minority who spoke out in public against the war. There were, however, numerous instances of overzealous district attorneys prosecuting inconspicuous people for antimilitarist convictions expressed in private conversations. Untold numbers also suffered persecution of one sort or another as a consequence of their pacifist views. Ministers lost their pulpits or were forced to take leaves of absence. Teachers were subjected to various restraints, and many pacifist instructors, especially in public schools and colleges, were summarily dismissed. At Columbia University, two of the leading members of the faculty had to resign their positions because of their antimilitarist opinions.[52]

Despite the wave of wartime hysteria, the prosecution of prominent individuals under the guise of stamping out disloyalty aroused some protest. Led by Senator La Follette, members of Congress spoke out against enforcement of the Espionage Act.[53] Although the subsequent passage of the more drastic Sedition Act and the Debs trial indicated that little could be done until the close of the war, there was an outcry against some of the more flagrant instances of militarism. The Justice Department's dragnet methods of detecting draft-law evaders, culminating in the famous slacker raids' in New York City on 3 September 1918, created much indignation. A New York *World* editorial entitled 'Amateur Prussianism in New York' led to the demand for an official investigation. The *World*, a Wilson organ, likened the raid to the 'kind of treatment that the Prussian commanders impose upon the helpless inhabitants of a conquered province.' Observing that 'all this has been done under pretext of inspiring public respect for military conscription,' the *World* concluded: 'The arrest of any number of slackers could not excuse this rape of the law — this wanton ravishing of the very spirit of American institutions.' [54]

The *World's* strong criticism was an indication of a coming reaction to the militarism of the war years. Many of the idealists who had followed Wilson into the war for democracy and the war to end all wars were about to experience a progressive disillusionment, culminating in their desire to retreat to older peacetime allegiances. As Randolph Bourne observed, the liberal realists who accepted the war paid the penalty of seeing the reasons for their acceptance disappear one by one.[55] Although the continued hold of wartime attitudes was amply demonstrated in the hysteria of the immediate postwar years, the antimilitarist traditions of the country had not been completely extinguished. The rejection of army plans for permanent conscription, and the popular demand for disarmament, were to be among the outstanding instances of a return to the ways of peace after the Armistice.

XIII

Disillusionment and
Partial Disarmament

THE END OF THE Great War, which had cost the world untold billions of dollars and millions of lives, was hailed in America as a victory of democracy over militarism and autocracy. Frank Cobb, editor of the New York *World*, believed that Germany's defeat exposed the fallacy of militarism. 'The disciplined forces of militarism yield at every point to the hurriedly assembled hosts of democracy,' he wrote two days before the Armistice. 'A peace of peoples,' from which 'militarism is stripped bare,' concluded the *World* on the morning after the Armistice was signed.[1]

Both the Central Powers and German militarism had been defeated, but there still remained the difficult problem of translating victory into the framework of a just and durable peace. The preliminary outlines of such a settlement had been offered to the world by Woodrow Wilson in his famous Fourteen Points address before Congress on 8 January 1918. Stressing the idealism that had motivated America to enter the war, Wilson called for a peace that would bring an end to militarism, nationalism, and imperialism. Whether Wilson's kind of peace settlement could be achieved in the atmosphere of heightened nationalism and chauvinistic patriotism that characterized the postwar world was, however, open to serious question. Even before the conclusion of the war, doubt was being expressed over the type of peace envisaged by the Allied Powers. Colonel Edward M. House, Wilson's intimate adviser, had predicted in May 1916 that a situation might arise, if the Allies defeated Germany, 'where they may attempt to be dictatorial in Europe and elsewhere. I can see quite clearly where they might change their views on militarism and navalism. It depends entirely on what nation uses it, whether it is considered good or bad.'[2] On the eve of the Armistice, General Tasker H. Bliss, destined to be one of the American delegates to the Peace Conference, in a frank letter to Secretary of War Baker observed:

> Judging from the spirit which seems more and more to animate our European Allies, I am beginning to despair that the war will accomplish much more than the abolition of *German* militarism while leaving *European* militarism as rampant as ever. I am one of those who believe that the absolute destruction of all militarism, under any of its evil forms, is the only corner stone of the foundation of any League.[3]

Bliss's criticism seemed substantiated when the Allies refused to follow the disarmament of the Central Powers with similar reductions in their own land and naval forces. The attempt to eliminate or modify conscription was also given up, although the draft of a league covenant proposed by General Jan Smuts, the South African leader, had included this as the most essential part of disarmament.[4] Smuts's argument that conscription was 'the taproot of militarism' was echoed by prominent Americans,[5] and President Wilson, himself, in his first Paris draft of the League Covenant, included the Smuts clause abolishing conscription. Later, the President, in deference to the wishes of the French and Italian delegations, yielded the anticonscription provision and substituted a vague disarmament statement in its stead. From the standpoint of the French and Italians, who feared a German *revanche,* it seemed that Smuts and Wilson were willing to see the European land powers divested of their conscript armies, while the British Empire and the United States maintained intact their own sea power. Only Germany, which now had nothing to lose, was agreeable to a League of Nations based on complete disarmament and the abolition of conscription.[6]

In his fight to gain Senate approval for the League and the Versailles Treaty, President Wilson posed two alternative possibilities for the United States: adoption of the League, or the pursuit of a program of militarism and increased naval building. The latter policy, he predicted, would turn the United States into a despotism, its industries mobilized, its manpower conscripted, the President and the General Staff co-dictators, and freedom suppressed by a network of spies of 'a system of intelligence.' [7] Wilson, Oswald Garrison Villard wrote to Ramsay MacDonald, the English Labour party leader, 'has stated frankly that if he does not get the League, he will recommend that the United States be placed on the German basis prior to the war as the only proper way to live. This from the man who commanded us to destroy the wicked old German order!' [8]

Despite the alarming picture of the fate in store for the country if it rejected the League, many liberals who would ordinarily have been convinced by the President's plea refrained from giving their full support to a peace treaty that fell so short of Wilson's own original program. In contrast to narrowly nationalist or isolationist objections to the Versailles Treaty, dissenting liberals complained because its severe terms would not lead to the establishment of the lasting peace that they had hoped to see come out of the war. The *New Republic,* one of Wilson's staunchest supporters, broke with him on the question of ratification of the Versailles Treaty. The *Nation* under Oswald Garrison Villard was even more critically outspoken. William MacDonald, its foreign affairs expert, in an article entitled 'The Madness at Versailles,' attacked the failure of the Paris Conference to secure a general disarmament among the victor powers.[9] Harold Stearns, in his book *Liberalism in America,* took the point of view that, even if the League worked, it would result only in a war between East and West. Otherwise, he felt it was merely another nationalistic instrument for the exploitation of the weaker peoples of the world.[10] Also included in the ranks of the liberal opposition were several of the leading progressives in the Senate, men like Hirar Johnson, William E. Borah, George W. Norris, and Robert M La Follette.

Wilson, in addition, lost the support of a good many liberal and pacifists, not because they doubted the efficacy of the League but because they distrusted the sincerity of Wilson's own devotio to the cause of liberalism and peace. While the President threat ened Congress and the American people with a future militarisr if they did not espouse the League, militarism, with the encour agement of the Wilson administration, was already achieving strong hold in the United States. In the inexorable process of win ning the war and making the peace, Wilson had very largely give up the struggle against militarism at home. The preservation an reassertion of the historic American tradition of antimilitarisr owed very little to the man looked up to by European people as 'the great peacemaker.'

Deserted in high places, the revival of antimilitarism was th work of a few old-line liberals and pacifists aided by the risin tide of popular disillusionment with the war. Pacifist and libera forces were particularly concerned over the fate of those con scientious objectors and political prisoners who were still confine after the Armistice on charges of violating the Draft or Espionag Acts. However justified in 1917 and 1918, the continued imprison ment of these individuals seemed to many to reflect only a desir to perpetuate the vindictive spirit of the war. The League fo the Amnesty of Political Prisoners, in urging the prompt releas of Emma Goldman, Eugene Debs, Roger Baldwin, and their fel lows, asserted that, even if it were granted 'that their imprison ment was necessary to preserve wartime morale, how can it b justified now that peace is declared?' [11] The editors of the *Dia* pointed out that peacetime imprisonment would not solve th problem of conscientious objection to war. They appealed to th President, busily engaged in deliberation at Paris, to exercise jus tice at home and grant the release of C.O.s and political prison ers.[12] Some of the members of Congress, with Senator Borah i the lead, co-operated with the amnesty campaign,[13] but mos legislators were indifferent or hostile despite the introduction o

.ocumentary reports showing brutal treatment of C.O.s in army
amps or prisons.

Lack of sympathy with the C.O. did not mean that Congress
vas willing to extend over into peacetime the policy of conscrip-
ion adopted at the outset of the war. This Congressional antip-
thy toward peacetime concription was the logical product of
he country's traditional reliance upon a small standing army,
•acked up in time of need by volunteers and state militia. The
Jnited States, after all, had never drafted men for military service
.uring peacetime, while firsthand experience with army life dur-
ng the World War had not dissipated the historic American
•rejudice against a soldier's career.[14] With the Armistice, the
ituation that had led to conscription was removed, and most
\mericans now saw little excuse for compulsory military training.
'he threat of future conflict seemed remote, and the postwar mood
f the American people, so overwhelmingly hostile to the idea
f war, made the possibility of another expeditionary force un-
hinkable.

In his annual report for 1917, Secretary of War Baker was care-
ul to point out that the War Department had no intention of
eeking legislation for universal military training until there was
n opportunity to observe 'the arrangements consequent upon the
ermination of the present war.' Baker's report reflected the offi-
ial and also popular view that the World War would end in the
.estruction of all militarism and conscription.[15] In Congress, Sena-
or John Sharp Williams attacked a proposal to train nineteen to
wenty-one year-olds on grounds that American victory should be
ollowed by the general abolition of all conscription. Endorsing
Villiams's speech, Senator Asle J. Gronna pointed out that to 'fas-
en upon the people of this country and other nations a com-
•ulsory military system is simply to indorse the system we are
.ow fighting.' [16]

Widespread recognition of the inconsistency of adopting a sys-
em of permanent conscription in the midst of waging a war to
nd militarism gave real hope to the opponents of universal mili-
ary training. The American Union against Militarism, at its an-
ual meeting in New York City on 27 February 1918, elected

Oswald Garrison Villard as chairman, voted unanimously to re
open its Washington headquarters, and decided to 'direct all it
energies against the propaganda for compulsory military train
ing.' In a special letter to members and contributors, Villard an
Charles T. Hallinan, the executive secretary, explained that dur
ing the past year the Union had been forced to mark time, bu
now, they declared, it was the A.U.M.'s intention to fight univer
sal military training 'and that alone.' [17] During the war, th
A.U.M. had been almost the only organization to maintain con
sistent opposition to the draft law. But now, in 1919, it was abl
to secure the support of groups that had traditionally oppose
an expansion of military power. The American Federation o
Labor, in its annual convention, reaffirmed its 1916 resolution op
posing militarism and conscription.[18] The National Farmers Unio
adopted a declaration stating its hostility 'to any system of mili
tary organization that includes universal military training.' [19] Th
National Grange passed a report from its standing committee o
militarism which asserted:

> We are opposed to militarism, universal military training and a
> large standing army. We deplore any effort to develop in Amer-
> ica a caste of authority which has its sole excuse in a shoulder
> strap, and any tendency in thought which would substitute armed
> force for moral ideals. The invincible character of a citizen army
> when equipped with justice and Americanism has again been
> demonstrated. We favor the preparedness of right, rather than the
> preparedness of might.[20]

Other critics of U.M.T. set forth its potential dangers to societ
and the individual. Pacifists, for example, felt it would encourag
future wars and prevent United States co-operation for worl
peace, while educators questioned the value of the type of physi
cal training and discipline it would inculcate.[21] Liberals warne
that the mobilization of trained army reserves could be used t
break strikes and strengthen reactionary groups. They also gav
consideration to the historic role of liberalism in opposing com
pulsion of the individual. The New Republic, which announce
that it assumed a middle ground between the pacifist and mili
tarist, gave a good expression of the liberal's case against U.M.T
Believing the United States secure for at least ten years, the editor

eclared that it was not needed as a military measure, and its
:her functions could be achieved more cheaply and easily with-
ıt it.[22]

There was also growing opposition to compulsory military train-
ıg in the nation's press. As early as September 1918 the Ameri-
ın Union against Militarism noted that, in contrast to the two
ındred newspapers definitely known to have been opposed to
.M.T. at the outbreak of the war, seven hundred daily and
eekly papers now printed materials sent out by the Union. By
ebruary 1920, when the A.U.M. felt able to say that U.M.T. was
ɛfinitely defeated for the present, it was being denounced by
ɛwspapers as 'another Prussianized proposal' and as a 'scheme
› Prussianize America.' The *Springfield Republican* commented:
f England will not stand for such a system, why should America,
hich is carrying a war-debt of thirty billions?'[23]

In Congress, the question of universal military training was in-
mately related to the general problem of the size and character
˙ the postwar military establishment. Here there was strong
ɔposition to executive proposals for a large regular army backed
ɔ by some form of compulsory military training. At hearings
ɛfore the Committee on Military Affairs of the House in January
)19, Secretary Baker was asked if the creation of a recommended
ırce of five hundred thousand men would not repudiate the
resident's declared purpose of seeking disarmament after the
ar. Baker saw no inconsistency and he also denied, at this time,
ıat the administration had any immediate intention of sponsor-
ıg a conscription bill. Congress, rejecting the advice of Secretary
aker and the War Department, refused to vote the necessary
ınds for five hundred thousand enlisted men. Unable as yet to
ɡree on the army's future size, it approved an establishment tem-
ɔrarily fixed at 175,000 men, the prewar figure, and later, at a
ɛecial session of the succeeding Congress, made provision for
ı army of 325,000 men. On 3 August 1919, Secretary Baker fol-
·wed up his original recommendations and sent to Congress the
lministration's plan for a permanent army policy. In addition
› a regular force of half a million men, Baker now came forward
ith a scheme for the three-months compulsory military training
˙ all eighteen and nineteen year-old youths.[24]

Bills embracing Baker's plan together with others calling fc longer periods of service were introduced in both branches c Congress. There they met with the strong opposition of member determined upon a policy of economy. Objection to U.M.T. wa also expressed on grounds that it would result in militarism an bring over to the United States the very system defeated in Ger many. Senator Kenneth D. McKellar of Tennessee, one of th most active opponents of conscription, expressed this feeling i the typical remark: 'If it is a bad thing for Germany to hav universal military training now — and we say so in our treaty – how does it happen that it is a good thing for free America t have it now?' [25] The administration contention that rejection c the League would require the United States to keep up a larg army made little impression on members of Congress resolved t have no further part of European wars. Senator James A. Reed c Missouri, a bitter foe of the League and of U.M.T., declarec 'We ought to get the blood out of our heads. We should kno that the war is over and that America is out of it.' [26] But the exter of the Congressional revolt against Wilson's military policy wa perhaps, best indicated by the action of members of his ow party. Despite a letter of endorsement from the White Hous House Democrats on 9 February 1920 adopted by a vote of 1c to 17 a resolution stating 'that it is the sense of this caucus tha no measure should be passed by this Congress providing for un versal compulsory military service or training.' [27]

As the war receded into memory, sentiment in the country ra more strongly against the adoption of any form of peacetime co scription. Newspapers in the South and West were almost unan mously hostile. Support for a draft seemed to be confined largel to the War Department and to leaders of the recently organize American Legion. The Army Act of 4 June 1920, adopted in th form of amendments to the National Defense Act of 1916, wa a complete defeat for Secretary Baker and the administratio Universal military training was not included, the centralized co trol of the Secretary of War was limited, the independent stat militia organizations as modified by the Act of 1916 were r tained, and, finally, the size of the regular army was fixed ; 280,000 men, although Congress made appropriations for onl

75,000. Ignoring this indication of Congressional intention as to the proper size of the army, Baker authorized the continued recruiting of men until the legislators in exasperation passed over Wilson's veto a resolution directing the Secretary of War to stop all further enlistments.[28]

Decisive rejection of conscription and reduction of the army were followed by public demands for action to limit the large naval armaments that burdened the postwar world. Such armaments, along with conscription, were once more regarded as the twin evils that had led to the coming of the late war. Although not in itself a cause of war, an extensive and powerful military or naval establishment had long been viewed as evidence of militarism and as a threat to world peace. In the years before the war, the idea of an international agreement to limit armaments had enjoyed extensive support from church and peace groups as well as a certain amount of official recognition in the form of Congressional resolutions and executive pronouncements by Presidents Taft and Wilson. Heartened by the defeat of peacetime military training, the emerging liberal and pacifist forces of the postwar period were ready to renew the campaign for general world disarmament.

In the United States, problems of disarmament and of militarism involved the navy far more than the army. While the latter was being demobilized and U.M.T. defeated, the admirals had been busy laying plans for increasing United States naval power and influence. Prewar legislation for the navy had reached its climax with the passage in 1916 of a three-year building program designed to give the United States a fleet equal to the largest in the world. The even more ambitious plans suggested by naval authorities after American entrance into the war had been gradually scaled down as existing British and American units proved adequate for the task of bottling up the German fleet in the North Sea. Although the rate of building had been retarded as the war neared its conclusion, the American navy in November 1918 was inferior only to that of the British, and the termination of the war by no means indicated the eclipse of the program of 'a navy second to none.'

A month after the Armistice big-navy advocates were suddenly

given new encouragement as President Wilson and Secretar
Daniels presented to Congress a second three-year building pro
gram designed to be placed on top of the existing, but uncom
pleted, 1916 program. This recommendation of increased nava
construction, coming from a supposedly peace-loving natior
'aroused amazement and consternation abroad.' The Japanese an
British were particularly affected. Although in no position to d
so financially, both nations felt that they had to keep pace wit
American expansion. United States policy accordingly contribute
heavily to the naval race that followed the Armistice. While Japa
nese naval expenditures tripled in the years from 1917 to 192
the United States 'built in the three years after the Armistic
many more ships of war than the rest of the world combined.'
This American and Japanese naval competition heightened th
mutual distrust with which each nation regarded the other's as
pirations in the Pacific and the Far East. The transfer of one hal
the American fleet to the Pacific, and the construction of nava
bases there, also added to growing tension and helped increas
Japanese suspicion of Wilson's peace aims.

Although Americans were less inclined to regard Great Britai
as a potential rival or enemy of the United States, anti-Britis
feeling increased after the war. In order to secure British an
European backing for a peace based on the Fourteen Points an
the League of Nations, the President urged Congress to approv
the new three-year naval program. Armed with this threat, h
hoped to dictate the peace at Paris. Such tactics, although we
in accord with the power politics practiced by great nations, wer
hardly consistent with visions of an idealistic peace. Wilson'
policy not only antagonized Congressional foes of a big navy, bu
it also gave opponents of the League and the Treaty of Versaille
ample opportunity to question his sincerity. To many observers i
seemed as though the President was permitting himself to b
placed in the paradoxical position of espousing militarism at hom
in order to defeat it in Europe.[30] William Jennings Bryan reflecte
a popular view when he wrote in his *Commoner* that 'a peace tha
would require us to build a larger navy than we had before th
war would hardly be worth the twenty-two billions that it cost.'

Henry Cabot Lodge, a bitter foe of the President but always a big-navy advocate, told the Senate that

> it seems to me extraordinary that we should enter on a scheme for eternal peace throughout the world by proposing to build a Navy which in seven years is to be equal to that of England. . . . How it fits in with the policy of reduction of naval and military forces or with the high objects of a league of nations I can not conceive.[32]

Congressional opposition prevented the passage of the Wilson three-year naval program, and late in May 1919, it was withdrawn. The following year, the Wilson administration again tried to secure support for the League of Nations by invoking the threat of naval expansion. Secretary Daniels, discussing the future of the navy in dramatic terms for a popular magazine, told the American people that, if the United States did not join the League, 'we must become a super-Prussia. Militarism and navalism must be interwoven with the warp and woof of our industrial life. It must dominate our education and to some extent our religion.' [33] Congress, however, refused to be stampeded into building the Wilson-Daniels navy, and the naval appropriations bill for 1921 was confined to rounding out and completing the old 1916 program. The feeling grew that the real solution was an agreement to disarm on the part of Great Britain, the United States, and Japan. In this way the Wilsonian alternative of the League or militarism and navalism could be avoided, and the popular desire for peace and disarmament could be given a measure of recognition.

By the fall of 1920, high prices and mounting unemployment were creating a strong demand for retrenchment in governmental expenditures. This interest in economy strengthened popular opposition to large-scale naval appropriations and brought new recruits to the agitation for disarmament. In addition to aid received from farm and labor organizations and religious groups, the American Union against Militarism observed that 'For the first time in its history the Union is in a position to obtain strong business support.' Some business and industrial interests, it is true, in cooperation with the Navy League and the National Security

League, continued to lobby for increased naval building and pre
paredness. And a group of New York businessmen formed th
Army and Navy Club to combat what Rear Admiral Bradley A
Fiske called 'the tide of anti-preparedness and pacifism which i
already moving over the country.' Nevertheless, as the A.U.M. ha
noted, a large part of the business community was beginning t
doubt the wisdom of preparedness if it was going to result i
eventual national bankruptcy. The general insecurity and mount
ing tax burdens, which paralleled the world armament race, wer
viewed in some quarters as a threat to private capitalism and
free society.[34]

The desire for economy played a large part in detaching busi
ness, at least temporarily, from its old alliance with a big navy
Private bankers and Treasury officials, including Secretary Andrev
W. Mellon, came out in favor of a reduction in arms expenditures
Leading financial journals echoed the popular press in calling fo
economy. Chambers of Commerce and trade associations adopte
resolutions supporting a disarmament conference. Even the arma
ment manufacturer and steel producer joined in the econom
drive. Elbert H. Gary of the United States Steel Company an
nounced in an interview that he favored an international agree
ment on naval disarmament. James Bower, President of the Gul
States Steel Company, was even more outspoken. He felt it 'almos
criminal' for the United States to keep arming when England ha
already stopped its naval expenditures, and he called upon th
American government to set an example 'in drastic military an
naval reductions.' [35]

Especially surprising was the enthusiasm for disarmament ex
hibited at this time by leading American military figures. In a
address in New York before the European Relief Council, Genera
John J. Pershing expressed alarm over increasing expenditure
for preparedness. 'It would appear,' he declared, 'that the lesson
of the last six years should be enough to convince everybody o
the danger of nations striding up and down the earth armed t
the teeth. But no one nation can reduce armaments unless al
do.' [36] Pershing concluded that if some move in the direction o
disarmament were not made, civilization would face a future o
destructive wars and an accompanying reversion to barbarism

his same theme formed the subject of a series of lectures deliv-red in Philadelphia by General Tasker H. Bliss. Calling attention o the fact that other powers had not followed up the disarma-nent of Germany with a reduction in their own armed forces, Bliss predicted that continuation of the preparedness race would ventuate in war. 'We know,' he said, 'that neither the individual preparedness of nations nor the alliances of nations so prepared revented war.' Bliss believed a disarmament conference should be held in the United States so that visiting nations could see the threat of America's potential strength. Unless the United States ed the world from militarism and war, he asserted, the sole result f the late world struggle would be limited to the defeat of Ger-nan militarism. 'You will have killed one giant only to set up five nore in his place.'[37]

In Congress, leadership of the arms limitation movement was ssumed by Senator Borah, who on 14 December 1920 introduced a resolution authorizing the President to call a conference on this ubject with Great Britain and Japan. Borah's proposal served to ring to a focus the public demand for disarmament which had lready been reflected in growing newspaper attention to the roblem. At the same time, hearings on 'World Disarmament' held by the House Military Affairs Committee afforded an opportunity or further publicity. In their testimony before this Committee in anuary 1921, Generals Pershing and Bliss agreed with peace and abor leaders in recommending a conference.[38] In Congress and in he country at large, Borah's proposal appealed to a variety of in-erests. Peace and economy-minded Congressmen gave it their acking. Opponents of the League of Nations, as well as former upporters, united behind the idea of a conference sponsored by he United States, while Senators, particularly those from the Western states, launched bitter attacks upon the continued high evel of United States naval building.[39]

In a detailed study of public opinion and the conference, C. L. Hoag has shown how the churches and peace organizations as vell as farm, labor, and educational groups marshaled public entiment behind the demand for thoroughgoing disarmament. nfluenced by the business drive for economy and by the interests of their readers, the popular press, with a few exceptions such as

the Hearst newspapers, was almost unanimously in favor of nava
limitation. After the invitations to the conference had been issued
two of the most widely circulated popular magazines, *Collier*
and the *Saturday Evening Post*, appealed for effective disarma
ment. *Collier's* especially created a stir by urging its readers t
'Tell the President.' The coupons which were attacked for thi
purpose soon poured into Washington at the rate of a thousand
day. This constant stream of propaganda in the months imme
diately preceding the conference and during the period of it
actual deliberations was often resented by the Harding admini
tration, which felt that it placed the United States government a
a disadvantage in dealing with the other powers. At the sam
time, public pressure did much to counteract the feeling, ex
pressed abroad as well as among liberals at home, that the Unite
States was becoming militaristic. American opinion thus helpe
to provide an atmosphere favorable to the idea of disarmamen
and in that way was a major influence upon the success of th
deliberations.[40]

On the eve of the Washington Conference, an effort was mad
to unite the various groups supporting disarmament. Acting a
the suggestion of Frederick J. Libby, a number of Philadelphi
Quakers formed the Friends International Disarmament Counci
Following President Harding's invitation to the nations, member
of this Friends Council, after confering with the Foreign Polic
Association, decided to form a national organization composed o
all groups favoring the reduction of armaments. The result o
these efforts was the establishment of the National Council on th
Limitation of Armaments, which attracted a wide range of par
ticipating organizations with a membership numbered in th
millions. Serving as a co-ordinating body and as a center for th
distribution of literature, the National Council was highly suc
cessful in its educational work and withstood the bitter attacks o
those who objected to its thoroughgoing opposition to all form
of militarism. Together with the Women's Committee for Worl
Disarmament, the National Council contributed importantly t
the success of the deliberations at Washington.[41]

The American people accepted the results of the Washingto
Conference with an enthusiasm at least equal to that which char

acterized their original demand for such a gathering. Those organizations which had played a prominent role in arousing the public's interest now conducted a drive for the ratification of the treaties that had come out of the deliberations. Although these treaties contained important provisions dealing with American interests in the Pacific and Far East, public imagination was captured by the disarmament clause and the 5-5-3 ratio for the navies of the United States, Great Britain, and Japan. The general populace, however, as both pacifists and big-navy advocates realized, had little understanding of the actual impact of the treaty upon the United States navy. Capital ships alone were affected by the 5-5-3 ratio, and reduction by the American government was in ships of this category, either over-age or under construction but not yet completed. In other words, the conference achieved a limitation on future building, stopping the naval race in capital ships, but accomplishing no great over-all reduction in existing total strength. While pacifists feared that Congress would now feel compelled to keep American strength at the maximum allowed by the treaty, naval officers were concerned lest the public misconception of a drastic limitation in the navy might lead to actual far-reaching reductions in the future. As Senator Borah and others pointed out in the course of the debate over the treaty, large armaments still existed both on land and sea, and only a preliminary step against militarism had been taken.[42]

Disarmament therefore remained a vital issue. Although the organized antimilitarist and peace forces had made great gains in the period of their campaign for a disarmament conference, they continued to be a minority group. The support they had received from economy-minded industrialists could easily prove to be only temporary. At the same time, big-navy advocates, though momentarily subdued by the clamor for disarmament, were by no means permanently reconciled to the defeat of their expansionist program. The General Board of the navy continued to hold the view that it was the policy of the United States 'To create, maintain, and operate a Navy second to none,' and 'To support in every possible way American interests, especially the expansion and development of American foreign commerce.' With the backing of President Harding and Secretary of State Hughes, the

Navy Department in the spring of 1922 launched an intensive
campaign to gain Congressional support for an expanded per
sonnel program. A successful attempt was made to spread the
navy view throughout the country, and a survey of newspaper
favoring the personnel program showed that they 'closely fol
lowed the line of argument used by the professional officers.
Business and patriotic organizations, including the Nationa
Chamber of Commerce, National Association of Manufacturers
National Security League, and American Legion, also espoused
the cause of the navy in its conflict with an economy-minded
Congress. The Navy Department itself encouraged the Interna
tional Association of Machinists, representing navy yard worker
threatened with the loss of their jobs, to send a delegation to
Washington to protest any reduction in appropriations. Army and
Navy clubs were organized in larger cities to promote the con
cept that defense interests be placed above politics.[43]

The most telling propaganda device was the celebration of
National Navy Day, begun in 1922. The possibility of such an
event had originally been advanced by a member of the Navy
League and of the Navy Club in New York City. The Navy
League, enthusiastically adopting the suggestion, selected 27
October, Theodore Roosevelt's birthday, as an appropriate date
Colonel Henry Breckinridge, a former Assistant Secretary of War
was placed in charge of organizing a program and securing pub
licity. All available agencies of information were utilized, and
for perhaps the first time, the entire country was covered in a
radio network devoted to a single theme when the Navy Day
program went on the air. The weekly newsreel was another idea
device for presenting the Navy to the public, while newspapers
especially those in the larger Eastern seaboard cities, gave val
uable editorial support. Over half the state governors also called
attention to Navy Day in special proclamations.[44]

Despite the patriotic fervor generated in behalf of Nationa
Navy Day, there was much outspoken criticism of the incon
sistency of holding such a celebration less than a year after the
Washington Conference. Governor Percival P. Baxter of Maine
who with Governor John J. Blaine of Wisconsin declined to
sponsor the day, declared 'the present is no time for naval ex

pansion and our country should and will live up to both the letter and the spirit of its reduction-of-armaments agreement.' Approving this statement, the New York *World* in an editorial 'Why a Navy Day?' observed: 'No possible excuse can be offered for working up popular sentiment over the size and prestige of the navy unless it is intended that the Washington Treaty is to be scrapped and the battle-ship building program dug out of the discard.' The *World* also attacked the duplicity of the Harding administration in encouraging 'new preparedness propaganda' at home while it advised Europe to reduce armaments.[45]

The counterattack upon the navy's attempt to discredit the work of the Washington Conference received new support when Calvin Coolidge became President. Aware of the continued popular interest in disarmament and prodded by Congressional criticisms of continued large naval appropriations, the President in his annual messages to Congress repeatedly denounced the policy of 'competitive armaments.' Deprecating the scare stories 'of the magnitude of the military equipment of other nations,' Coolidge stated his belief that the United States was in general well prepared. The one weak place in our national defense, he noted in 1926, 'is our still stupendous war debt.'[46] In support of the President's assertion, the report of the Treasury Department for 1927 showed that military functions and the interest on the public debt together accounted for over eighty per cent of the national budget.[47]

President Coolidge did not hesitate to express his antimilitarist views before gatherings not commonly regarded as friendly to such a stand. In June 1925, he urged the graduating class of the Naval Academy at Annapolis to devote their first attention to the civilian life of the nation. 'I am not unfamiliar,' he said, 'with the claim that if only we had a sufficient Military Establishment no one would ever molest us.' But, he added: 'I know of no nation in history that has ever been able to attain that position. I see no reason to expect that we could be the exception.' Later that year, in an address before the American Legion Convention, the President called attention to the fact that the army and navy were costing almost twice as much as ever before in peacetime. Under the world policy of competitive armaments no nation was secure

regardless of the size of its military establishment. The only solu
tion was real economy and disarmament. 'Our people,' the Presi
dent warned, 'have had all the war, all the taxation, and al
the military service that they want. They have therefore wished
to emphasize their attachment to our ancient policy of peace.'
President Coolidge also reviewed the traditional respect of the
American people for the principle of civil authority, and he
pointed out that, 'Whenever the military power starts dictating
to the civil authority, by whatsoever means adopted, the liberties
of the country are beginning to end.' Calling finally for a new
spirit of toleration to put an end to the persecution of minorities
the President told the Legion that there 'should be intellectua
demobilization as well as a military demobilization.' [48]

The President's conviction of the need for disarmament wa
made all the more realistic because of the new naval race de
veloping in classes not restricted by the Washington Treaty. Con
gress in 1924 provided for the construction of eight ten thousand
ton cruisers, at the same time empowering the President to sus
pend this program if a successful international naval agreement
could be negotiated. From 1922 to 1925, successive naval acts
authorized the President to call such a disarmament conference
and on 10 February 1927 President Coolidge took the step of
issuing formal invitations for a meeting to be held in Geneva that
summer. Meanwhile Congress, despite the earnest pleas of the
President, refused to postpone completion of the eight-cruiser
program until after the Geneva Conference had first had an op
portunity to present some plan for international disarmament.
Representative Burton L. French of Idaho, chairman of the House
Subcommittee on Naval Affairs, warned that this action by Con
gress would arouse the navalists of Japan and England. Citing
Lord Grey's denunciation of preparedness and militarism as the
chief causes of the World War, French argued: 'Moderate pro
grams for the United States will be answered by conservative
programs for Japan, and conservative programs by Japan will be
matched by moderate programs in Great Britain.' [49]

In the months before the opening of the Geneva Conference, a
variety of competent observers joined in giving the American peo
ple pessimistic accounts of developments in Europe that seemed

bear out the urgent need for world disarmament. Ambassadors Alanson B. Houghton and Hugh Gibson reported the League of Nations to be ineffective. A dispatch to the New York *Evening Post* asserted: 'At the end of the course Europe is pursuing, the administration learns from its European advisers, nothing can be forecast but war.' Paul Scott Mowrer cabled the Baltimore *Sun:* 'Europe has learned nothing from the war and does not want to disarm. It has prepared the agenda for the forthcoming disarmament conference in such a way that it is bound to fail.' [50] Looking back upon the pre-World War period, writers discovered disconcerting parallels. Professor Wayne E. Stevens, a former army officer, contributed to *Current History* an excellent analysis of the way in which military preparedness in 1914 had carried Europe to a point where it was practically impossible to prevent war. Believing that 'militarism in its true sense is not essentially different today from what it was in 1914,' Stevens concluded that any effort toward peace must embrace the regulation of arms, the subordination of expert military opinion to civil authority, and the alteration of the old diplomacy of the balance of power. [51]

Despite the considerable public support for extensive disarmament, the Geneva Conference proved a complete failure. The American and British delegations were unable to agree upon a formula limiting naval cruisers, and the conference was soon stalemated. Peace and church organizations, which had helped to stiffen the resolve of delegates at the earlier Washington Conference, were unable to play the same role in a meeting held abroad. The munitions and big-navy interests, however, were not so handicapped. The lobbyist, William B. Shearer, it was later revealed, had been employed by three American shipbuilding concerns to wreck the conference. Though it is doubtful that the Geneva meetings would have succeeded even without Shearer's propaganda, still his activities made it more difficult for British and American delegates to arrive at some workable compromise. [52]

The futility at Geneva encouraged Congressional protagonists of a big navy, but in the Senate a bipartisan group of progressives was able to postpone passage of any naval bill pending the outcome of the Kellogg-Briand negotiations looking toward the outlawry of war. This pact, which was signed in 1928, was at least a

partial recognition of the long-standing pacifist demand that al
war be declared a violation of international law. Just how th
actual outlawry of war could be enforced and made effective wa
not at all clear. Even as a symbol, it was by no means certai
whether the Kellogg-Briand Pact was designed to arouse publi
support for peace, or merely to allay popular protests over a fast
developing world militarism. American public opinion, though
was clearly in favor of the pact, and in the party platforms o
1928, Republicans stressed the contribution to peace made b
President Coolidge and Secretary of State Frank B. Kellogg
while Democrats called for the 'Outlawry of war and abhorrenc
of militarism, conquest, and imperialism.' [53]

The 1928 elections were barely over when President Coolidg
astounded an Armistice Day audience with an address callin
upon Congress to pass the fifteen-cruiser bill already rejected b
the Senate. When the Senate assembled in December both th
cruiser bill and the Kellogg Pact were on the agenda at the sam
time. As one historian has remarked: 'It was a miraculous cham
ber, debating the rosy-tinted pledges for the renunciation of wa
and in the next moment urging appropriations for fightin
ships.' [54] Senator William C. Bruce of Maryland criticized th
pact as unrealistic and hopelessly weakened by the reservation
attached by the various signatories. Pointing to the constantly in
creasing armaments which existed side by side with the pact, h
declared: 'The only way really to renounce war is to renounc
the instruments of war.' Since this did not seem likely, Bruce an
nounced that he would support the cruiser bill. On the othe
hand, Senator Gerald P. Nye of North Dakota denounced th
propaganda of the naval experts who were advocating the cruise
bill. Both Senator Nye, who likened armaments and peace to
companionate marriage, and Senator Norris made strong pleas fo
the United States to take the lead in disarmament. The majorit
of the Senators, however, were more interested in achieving nava
parity with the British than in listening to arguments for disarma
ment. With a navy equal to Great Britain's, the United State
could compete on equal terms for foreign markets and resist an
repetition of the English World War I policy of violating neutra
rights. In February 1929, the cruiser bill was approved with th

added provision that the program might be suspended if the United States government was able to negotiate a successful agreement for naval limitations. This the President was 'requested to encourage.' [55]

In 1929, the inauguration of Herbert Hoover and victory of Ramsay MacDonald and the Labour party in England brought into leadership two men who were personally devoted to peace and who also desired to avoid the tremendous costs of an Anglo-American naval race. On July 24, Prime Minister MacDonald and President Hoover announced the cessation of work on the new cruisers being built in each country. And on that same historic day, President Hoover proclaimed the adherence of the United States to the Kellogg-Briand Treaty. It was also announced that the President intended to check the rising rate of United States expenditures for armaments. 'The American people should understand,' the President declared, 'that current expenditure on strictly military activities of the army and navy constitutes the largest military budget of any nation in the world today, and at a time when there is less real danger of extensive disturbance to peace than at any time in more than half a century.' [56] Later that year, Prime Minister MacDonald paid a visit to the United States, and in 1930 a new naval disarmament conference met at London. Although the United States achieved parity with Great Britain, the London Treaty was denounced in big-navy circles because of the increased ratio in noncapital ships granted to Japan. On the other hand, there was also much disappointment over the lack of any real disarmament provisions. The Baltimore *Sun,* which termed the treaty a 'fantastic travesty,' declared: 'It is a surrender of the most childish nature to our fetish of parity, and an ignoble bow to our chauvinists.' The Portland, Maine, *Evening News* maintained, 'If we must give up reduction or parity, let us give up parity.' [57] Especially noteworthy was the cable of protest signed by 1200 prominent American citizens, including eight governors and over two hundred college heads, who urged the delegates at London not to abandon their efforts to achieve an effective disarmament agreement.[58]

In spite of criticisms from all sides, the Hoover administration accepted the treaty. Secretary of State Henry L. Stimson attacked those naval officers who denounced the London Agreement as men imbued with the war system. 'They are handicapped by a kind of training which tends to make men think of war as the only possible defense against war.' [59] President Hoover, in his message on the treaty to the special session of the Senate, affirmed that, while opposition could naturally be expected from the small minority who believed in unrestricted military strength as an objective of the United States, most of the American people desired naval limitation. 'It is folly,' he declared, 'to think that because we are the richest nation in the world we can outbuild all other countries.' [60]

Although the more extreme demands of the navalists had been resisted during the Hoover administration, the threatening world situation and President-Elect Roosevelt's enthusiastic support of a big navy spelled the end of America's partial disarmament. While advocates of a larger navy argued the merits of an aggressive foreign policy — looking toward United States participation and intervention in world affairs — peace forces, despite some leanings toward a policy of collective security, protested that a navy for such purposes would exceed the legitimate defense needs of the country and plunge the nation into militarism and imperialism. A large navy would also be a step in the preparation of the United States for entrance into another world war.[61] The failure of disarmament therefore was a bitter blow to both the antimilitarist and the complete pacifist.

Despite the revival of war talk, the American people, profoundly disillusioned by the experience of 1917 and 1918, remained confident that the United States, at least, could avoid the chaos and destruction of a new struggle. Opposition to participation in another world conflict was especially strong among American youth despite their increasing contact with militarist influences, particularly those received in the army's well-developed postwar program of military training. In the period between wars, liberal educators and pacifists, well aware of the implications of such devices as the R.O.T.C., waged a strong campaign against all evidences of militarism in education.

XIV

Militarism in Education

ᴛᴛᴀɪɴᴍᴇɴᴛ ᴏꜰ ᴛʜᴇ lofty goals of universal disarmament and ıtlawry of war presupposed a high degree of both international nity and popular support. Because of its great economic and olitical strength the United States was expected to assume lead-·ship in the world struggle against militarism and war. Many berals and idealists in the 'twenties and 'thirties did not give p the hope that the United States might co-operate with the eague of Nations, join the World Court, and participate more :tively in the movement for disarmament. Peace societies in merica also worked to substitute a policy of international co-peration for war. In their concern with the world situation, merican liberals and pacifists did not, however, forget the threat f militarism at home nor the danger that it represented to the reservation of peace.

Particularly distressing to these groups was the increasing mil-arization of American education. The war itself had greatly en-anced military influence over the schools. In 1916, for example, ıe National Education Association under pressure from General eonard Wood modified some of its original objections to military aining in the schools.[1] In New York state, the legislature ap-roved three hours of physical education along military lines, ·hile a more extensive scheme put into practice by a Western

high school was widely publicized as the 'Wyoming idea.' [2] Eve
after the Armistice, the school system was frequently dominate
by a wartime spirit of intolerance and hate. Teachers continue
to be dismissed or rebuked for expressing pacifist or antimilitari
views, while the American Legion and other superpatriotic o
ganizations attempted to control the content of textbooks an
otherwise interfere with the curriculum and teaching. The Legio
was especially active in the effort to indoctrinate American youtl
subsidizing their various leisure activities and coming to the ai
of the R.O.T.C. whenever it was criticized by pacifists and edu
cators.[3]

In protesting such outside interference with the school systen
American liberals and antimilitarists enjoyed the firm backing o
most educators. Regardless of their feelings on the general issu
of preparedness, educators very largely agreed that military dri
should be kept out of the schools. As one of them exclaimed t
the military office at the time of American entrance into the wa
'In the name of Jehovah and the little red schoolhouse on the hi
keep your hands off the American boy until he is at least ninetee
years of age.' [4] The United States Bureau of Education als
pointed out in 1917 that, despite the war, European educato
continued to view military training 'as an anomaly in the scho
system, justified only by the exigencies of national defense. Th
enthusiastic support they lend this work comes more from pa
triotic than from pedagogic motives.' [5] Militarism, whether in th
form of military training or of pressure from veteran's organiza
tions, was viewed as incompatible with a philosophy of educatio
that sought, in the spirit of James and Dewey, to encourage th
potentialities of the individual and the well-being of society. A
though all phases of militarist encroachment were resisted, th
chief effort of the postwar years was directed against the Reserv
Officers' Training Corps units established in high schools and co
leges throughout the country.[6]

Military drill in the high school was a carry-over from the wa
period when more than one hundred thousand boys had been en
rolled. By 1926, this figure had declined to less than one half th
original number, but educators continued a strong campaign t
eliminate all Junior R.O.T.C. units or other forms of military dri

in the public high schools. Gradually the public school system began to emerge from the sway of wartime militarism. Governor Alfred E. Smith of New York state vetoed a bill to add military training to the physical education program. In Cleveland, Ohio, military drill was abolished in all the city schools. In Massachusetts, in 1926, a special commission recommended that compulsory drill be given up in the eighteen schools and two colleges where it was still required. Voluntary training was also subject to attack, and during the 'twenties schoolboy military drill remained popular only in the South.[7]

In contrast to its decline in the high school, military education in the colleges had been increasing since the close of the war. Developed originally as a result of the Morrill Land Grant Act of 1862, the training in the period before the World War was confined largely to state agricultural colleges receiving federal subsidies. During the nineteenth century military training was limited in extent, heartily disliked by many students, and often performed in perfunctory fashion. The important expansion of this restricted system of military education came only after the passage of the National Defense Acts of 1916 and 1920. Under this legislation, the War Department was authorized to provide funds and detail officers to act as teachers in any college or university that would agree to institute a two-year course in military training and tactics. The successful completion of the course, plus some additional study and service, qualified students for a commission in the reserve.[8]

Although the Defense Acts did not stipulate that the R.O.T.C. should be administered on a compulsory basis, by 1925 eighty-three of the one hundred and twenty-three colleges and universities offering the program made it a required subject.[9] The only real exception to the practice of compulsion was that some states and educational institutions exempted conscientious objectors who were members of religious sects opposed to war. In most institutions, the policy of compulsory military training remained unchallenged until 1923 when the Wisconsin state legislature broke with precedent and directed that all such drill be put on an optional basis in the university.[10] Despite some talk of withdrawal, the War Department continued to administer the Wiscon-

sin R.O.T.C. unit, and Secretary of War John W. Weeks supported
the contention of those who argued that the army could not in-
sist on compulsion as a prerequiste for the granting of federal
funds.[11]

Encouraged by Wisconsin's action, an increasing number of
college professors and students, together with sympathetic allies
in the churches and peace societies, began a far-reaching campaign against military training in schools and colleges. To co-
ordinate this effort and to help arouse public interest, a group of
liberal educators and pacifists formed the Committee on Militarism in Education, or the C.M.E. Educators and leaders of the
peace movement had long agreed that, if war was to be abolished,
American youth would have to be trained to think in terms of
peace and internationalism. The presence of military training in
schools and colleges was hardly compatible with this ideal. In
1925, therefore, the group that had formed the C.M.E. issued
under the name of the Committee on Military Training a pamphlet denouncing the R.O.T.C. written by Winthrop D. Lane.

The Lane pamphlet, which was published with the endorsement
of over fifty prominent citizens, including Jane Addams, John
Dewey, Mary E. Woolley, and Senator Borah, was a detailed and
documented attack upon the War Department's effort to spread
military training through the use of the R.O.T.C. and the Citizens'
Military Training Camps. Lane especially criticized the War Department's methods of enlisting popular support for the R.O.T.C.
For example, in War Department literature circulated to parents
and the public, the R.O.T.C. was depicted as a kind of demil-
itarized training in citizenship. At the same time, the manuals
being used by the officer-instructors in the classroom gave a far
different, much more militaristic picture of training for war and
the life of a soldier. Another aspect of the R.O.T.C. program denounced in the Lane pamphlet was the intense economic and
social pressure 'to join up' that was placed upon high school and
college youth. Even in those institutions where training was not
compulsory, the War Department could offer such potent attrac-
tions as cash subsidies and good quality uniforms, cavalry troops
and polo ponies, parades, and pretty girls to serve as honorary
regimental officers.[12]

The American people, having defeated postwar conscription, were largely unaware that the army was achieving almost the same result through the R.O.T.C. The Lane pamphlet marked the beginning of a long campaign by the C.M.E. to arouse the public over the compulsory military training issue. Lane warned that the R.O.T.C. was becoming the nucleus of a sizable military bureaucracy. If allowed to spread further in the colleges, it could seriously undermine freedom of thought and freedom of teaching. When made compulsory, it violated the individual's freedom of conscience. Finally, in direct contradiction of the widespread popular feeling against war, the R.O.T.C. was indoctrinating American youth with a psychology of militarism, thereby helping to prevent the disarmament and international co-operation that were viewed as vital avenues to peace.[13] Lane's pamphlet also provided the factual basis for criticisms of the R.O.T.C. that began to appear in various periodicals having a national circulation,[14] and a second edition was issued by the C.M.E. in March 1926.

In the midst of the interest aroused by the Lane publication, Representative George A. Welsh of Philadelphia presented in Congress a bill 'prohibiting any course of military training from being made compulsory as to any students in any educational institution other than a military school.' The Welsh bill, which was sponsored in the Senate by Lynn J. Frazier of North Dakota, had been drafted by Kenneth Walser and Walter Longstreth in co-operation with the C.M.E.[15] Longstreth, an attorney in Philadelphia, had already prepared for the Society of Friends a pamphlet in which he argued that there was no legal basis for compelling college students to take military training.[16] At public hearings on the Welsh bill, church and peace groups testified against the continuance of compulsory drill, and Edward F. McGrady, legislative representative of the American Federation of Labor, predicted that the United States would fast become a militarist nation 'unless something is done at once to curb the activities of the War Department and the propaganda of the military saber rattlers from making goosesteppers out of the school boys in America.'[17]

In the course of the hearings, unexpected approval for the abolition of compulsory R.O.T.C. came from William Bradley

Otis, Professor of English at City College in New York and, unti
three months before his testimony, director of the National Secu
rity League. Otis had been head of this organization for eigh
years, and he still believed in universal military training of the
Swiss militia type. But compulsory R.O.T.C., he felt, would create
a military caste and a bureaucracy which would threaten democ
racy in the nation and freedom of teaching within the college
Though admitting that he had not entertained such views in the
past, he declared: 'Now I am coming to the belief that physica
preparation for modern war is impossible; that if we are to be
saved at all, we have to be saved quickly through intellectual anc
moral preparedness.' In concluding his remarks the former direc
tor of the National Security informed the startled Committee or
Military Affairs that he would prefer to see his son in Leaven
worth prison rather than have him enrolled as a member of a
compulsory R.O.T.C. unit.[18]

Actually, the Welsh-Frazier resolutions had no chance of ap
proval, at this time, when the movement against compulsory
R.O.T.C. was just getting started. In addition, many members o
Congress, including some of those opposed to enforced drill, fel
that the entire question should be left to the states and the col
leges to decide for themselves as Wisconsin had already done
The failure to secure Congressional action, though disappointing
was not unexpected; it served to emphasize all the more strongly
the importance of a thorough campaign of education among the
public. With people often unaware that compulsory military
training existed in so many colleges, the C.M.E. felt that its firs
task involved the presentation to the public of the facts of the
growing militarist penetration of American education. If Congres
and the American people could be convinced that the R.O.T.C
was essentially a militarist device, and only incidentally a measure
for national defense, then the compulsory feature, at least, migh
be eliminated.

Despite a limited budget, the C.M.E. was highly successful ir
spreading its views. Educators and clergymen, who comprised a
good share of its support, had easy access to public opinion, and a
News Letter kept members informed of developments in college
where the R.O.T.C. was an issue. The peace societies and publica

tions naturally extended their aid, issuing materials based on the literature of the C.M.E.[19] The committee itself prepared a number of well-documented pamphlets, which set forth the purposes and methods of the War Department's college military training program. One of the more important of these, a sequel to the Lane pamphlet entitled *Militarizing Our Youth*, was written by Roswell P. Barnes of the Federal Council of Churches and published in 1927 with an introduction by John Dewey. In praising the C.M.E.'s efforts to acquaint the American people with the facts of militarist control over the school system, Dewey predicted that 'Nothing will be as fatal to the success of the militaristic attempt as knowledge of the facts.' Indignant at efforts to discredit the earlier Lane pamphlet and its sponsors, Dewey charged that 'To suppress the dissemination of this knowledge is the logical course for the militaristic interest to pursue.' [20]

Inspired in part by the C.M.E.'s campaign of education, criticism of the army's efforts to maintain compulsory drill in the colleges began to appear more frequently in the public press. President Coolidge was quoted by the *New York Times* as opposed to compulsory military training or any other device that stimulated the military spirit. Praising the President's position, the New York *Evening World* declared:

> It was time that some one should voice a vigorous protest against the bullying methods and impudence of those military fanatics who have set out to exclude from the advantages of an education such students as do not care to take military training. That is an intolerable, an un-American program.[21]

Earlier, the *Commercial and Financial Chronicle* had denounced military training in the schools as an attempt to expand the federal bureaucracy and elevate military above civilian influences in American life. Distrustful of the blind obedience exacted of the soldier, the *Chronicle* pointed out that the essence of militarism was a type of authority that was in conflict with the ideals of education and free government alike.[22]

In Congress, Ross A. Collins of Mississippi, a Democratic member of the House Committee on Military Affairs, made extensive use of C.M.E. materials in his speeches criticizing the R.O.T.C.

Of the War Department custom of using pretty girls as honorary R.O.T.C. officers, he remarked: 'It is the old game of playing sex appeal on youngsters for the purpose of helping to popularize this activity of "playing at war." ' [23] Collins and other members at tacked the R.O.T.C. as a propaganda device utilized for building a public opinion favorable to preparedness and war. In support of their charges, they cited the militaristic philosophy expressed in the training manuals used by the R.O.T.C. The most notorious of these was a text on citizenship prepared in 1928 under the direction of the Chief of Staff. Along with an unflattering defini tion of democracy and a highly conservative view of American history, the 1928 manual included the usual militarist defense of preparedness and denunciation of internationalism.[24] Progressive Senators were outraged by the manual's attack on public owner ship or government regulation of property as well as by the de scription of democracy as 'mobocracy.' [25] Although public pres sure forced the War Department to withdraw the manual, it continued to be much attacked as an illustration of the type of education that the army desired to give American youth in R.O.T.C. units.[26]

Another example of propaganda used in behalf of the R.O.T.C was *A Study of the Educational Value of Military Instruction in Universities and Colleges* conducted by Major Ralph Chesney Bishop with the co-operation of the United States Office of Edu cation. Questionnaires were sent to eighteen thousand R.O.T.C graduates of the period from 1920 to 1930 and, of the ten thou sand replies received, the great majority were favorable to the R.O.T.C. In answer to the question of whether their training had tended to instill an attitude of militarism inimical to world peace 93.6 per cent said 'No.' The few affirmative replies indicated that only a small percentage of the students believed they were being trained for the next war, and that such training kept alive a mil itaristic spirit at a time when the United States was officially working for peace.[27] Critics of the Bishop poll pointed out that there was little likelihood that R.O.T.C. graduates, many of whom had become officers in the army and were naturally prejudiced in favor of military training, would be at all critical of the educa tion provided in the R.O.T.C. The New York *World Telegram*, in an editorial comment on the Bishop study, remarked:

A symposium for a selected group, whose favorable opinion of military training could have been known in advance, is of doubtful value even as propaganda. Instead of settling an argument Mr. Bishop's survey has merely wasted the time and money of whoever paid for it.[28]

By the early 1930s, the rising tide of opposition to War Department propaganda convinced the C.M.E. that it had accomplished the educational phase of its work. Educators were particularly aroused at the army's efforts to silence all hostile criticism while it pushed its own campaign for the preservation of compulsory drill on the campus. Annoyed at War Department interference in the schools and colleges, teachers had increasing difficulty in accepting at face value the army view that the R.O.T.C. was purely a defense measure, or exercise in civic training, devoid of any militaristic implications. In revealing to the public the conflict between the real and pretended purpose of the army R.O.T.C. program, the basis had been laid for a new drive against compulsory military drill on the campus.

Before undertaking this campaign, the C.M.E. explored the possibility of a merger with the National Council for the Prevention of War, a more inclusive peace organization which was also devoting a large part of its work to the drive against the R.O.T.C. A proposal in 1931 whereby the N.C.P.W. would take over the staff of the C.M.E. and assume its budget proved unsuccessful. The National Council, although in sympathy with the program of the C.M.E., was reluctant to undertake the full responsibility for carrying out the fight against military training. Despite the educational work already done, the N.C.P.W. felt that its constituent membership might not be ready to embark on a struggle, 'which did not offer greater chances of immediate success.'[29] The C.M.E. therefore continued its own campaign against a compulsory R.O.T.C., devoting particular attention to colleges where the great majority of the students and their professors had already been won over to the case against compulsion. Their strong protests, backed up by outside pressure from churches and peace organizations, would, it was hoped, persuade university officials and state legislatures to abolish the compulsory system.

Among college students, who were naturally the group most directly affected, the traditional opposition to required drill broke out again soon after the close of the war. College antidrill leagues, petitions for abolishing compulsory R.O.T.C., and student polls were some of the means used to express undergraduate sentiment. Like their older contemporaries, college students were disillusioned over the results of the late war. H. L. Mencken, a campus idol in the 'twenties, debunked the army with such comments as: 'We survive because soldiers are simple-minded men with a preference for stereotyped nonsense. . . . Of all the arts practiced by man, the art of the soldier seems to call for the least intelligence and to develop the least professional competency.' [30] Although comparatively few college students embraced an extreme pacifist position, the rabid militarist was also rare. An investigation of undergraduate opinion during the early 'twenties indicated that the greater part of American college youth were opposed to large armaments and compulsory military service, including enforced drill in the colleges.[31]

Polls taken from time to time in individual colleges also showed a large proportion of the undergraduates in opposition to a compulsory R.O.T.C. Although this hostility was often a personal objection to any sort of a required course, it also reflected the students' hostility to war and their belief that the R.O.T.C. was basically a militarist institution. In February 1932, a poll of college students by the Intercollegiate Disarmament Council revealed that 92 per cent favored disarmament and 63 per cent believed the United States should take the initiative in disarming, while 81 per cent opposed a compulsory R.O.T.C. and 38 per cent favored the elimination of all military drill on the campus.[32] At Ohio State University, where a long but unsuccessful campaign was fought against the R.O.T.C., the campus newspaper summed up the student's case against the R.O.T.C. in its statement that 'compulsory drill has no educational value but rather is opposed to education. It is not in accord with American tradition as is claimed by its adherents.' [33]

While campus agitation against a compulsory R.O.T.C. was naturally most intense in the large publicly supported universities, it was also in these same institutions that the faculty and administrative officers were most subject to the pressure of outside patriotic and veteran's organizations. At City College in New York where the president attempted to suppress both faculty and student disapproval, compulsory military training was abolished in 1926 only after a bitter and widely publicized debate. In Nebraska, a group of citizens that organized to have the R.O.T.C. placed on a voluntary basis found themselves assailed by the American Legion and various patriotic societies. Professors and army officers were recruited by these groups to travel about the state defending the compulsory system.[34]

At Ohio State University in the spring of 1931, the faculty, after making a special study of the problem, voted to make military drill optional. This decision was presently reversed by a vote of 144 to 9 after administration disapproval became known and after the colonel in charge of the R.O.T.C. unit accused the opponents of compulsion of having communist sympathies. The Board of Trustees on 23 May passed a resolution pointing out that student and faculty opponents of a compulsory R.O.T.C. 'were under no compulsion to come here and are under none to remain unless they can subscribe to the fundamental purpose of this university.' Two days later the president accused several members of the faculty of failing to support University policies, and on 25 May a sociology professor who opposed compulsory military training was summarily dismissed over the protests and petition of some two thousand students and one hundred and fifty-three faculty members.[35]

In the privately endowed and church-affiliated colleges where the R.O.T.C. was seldom compulsory, a strong effort was made to eliminate military drill entirely. By 1926, many churches and associated youth organizations were taking great interest in the problem. The churches and clergy seemed especially anxious to retreat from their late wartime militarism. Liberal Protestant churchmen came close to the peace position long held by the Quakers and other pacifist sects. Led by the Federal Council of Churches, the major Protestant religious bodies were ready by

1926 to accept the challenge posed in the *Christian Century* by Paul Blanshard, who had written regarding the R.O.T.C.:

> Here is a job for the church. The church has the voters. The students in many states are ripe for a new movement against military rule. The American people do not want conscription. They would defeat overwhelmingly any effort to extend to the whole nation the system now used in our agricultural colleges. The church can clean the Prussian system out of every university in America in ten years if it will fight conscription as it fought the saloon.[36]

In December 1925, the Evanston Interdenominational Student Conference, attended by seven hundred delegates from one hundred and eighty colleges, also called upon the churches to work for the abolition of all military training in schools and colleges. Similar resolutions were adopted by various groups within the Methodist, Baptist, and Presbyterian Churches.[37]

The Methodists' opposition to militarism in education was reflected in the successful campaign against military training carried out in two of their leading educational institutions, De Pauw and Boston Universities. Abolished at Boston University only after a bitter fight in which the campus newspaper was suppressed for opposing the R.O.T.C., the compulsory feature was terminated at De Pauw in 1929 by its new president, G. Bromley Oxnam. President Oxnam, who severely criticized the army's attempt to breed a student psychology which would accept war as inevitable, declared that he would 'refuse to compel students to take courses in military science when the course material is prepared by the War Department and is not subject to faculty review.'[38]

The churches were also much concerned with the problem of the individual student who objected to compulsory military training on grounds of conscience or religious belief. Although, of course, such persons did not have to attend a college with a compulsory R.O.T.C., the fact that so many of the state institutions required it worked a hardship on youths without the financial resources to enroll in a private university. The exemption from the R.O.T.C. granted to members of such traditional peace churches as the Friends was not customarily extended to other individuals, even when they belonged to denominations that had taken a rong stand against war and military training. The Methodist Episcopal Church, for example, in its General Conference in 1932 issued an official statement opposing all military training in high schools, and compulsory training and drill in colleges and universities. At the same time, it petitioned the federal government for a ruling that would extend to members of the Church the same exemption from military instruction accorded members of the Society of Friends. Other Protestant church bodies took similar positions but were unable to secure for their members any official recognition of their status as conscientious objectors.[39]

At first, the C.O. issue was avoided, students and universities making concessions or compromises. But, by the early 1930s, the antiwar convictions of many students, bolstered by the antimilitarist campaign carried on by liberals and pacifists, resulted in a desire to test the constitutionality of the whole program of compulsory military training in American colleges. This seemed all the more necessary as the army continued to use its influence in trying to prevent the state universities from placing their R.O.T.C. units on a voluntary basis. In 1932, a Methodist and a Unitarian student were expelled from the University of Maryland because of their refusal to take the compulsory R.O.T.C. course. One of the students, Ennes H. Coale, took his case to court on the grounds that the university charter permitted exemption of C.O.s. A decision in his favor by the Maryland Superior Court was reversed by the Maryland State Court of Appeals. With the full backing and financial support of the Methodist Episcopal Church and the C.M.E., Coale then carried his case to the United States Supreme Court where his appeal was dismissed in November 1933 'for the want of a substantial federal question.'[40]

A similar but more important case, reaching the Supreme Court a year later, involved two Methodist students, Albert Hamilton and Alonzo Reynolds, who had been suspended by the University of California because of their conscientious objections to military service. The students claimed that the University action denied to them their equal rights under the Constitution, and on this basis they appealed an unfavorable California court decision to the United States Supreme Court. The Court held that the exaction of military training by the University did not violate freedom of

conscience nor the free exercise of religion. The right to exemption from military service on conscientious grounds, the Court
ruled, was not a constitutional privilege or immunity of citizens
of the United States. The decision in the Hamilton and Reynolds
case was in general accord with the Supreme Court's upholding
of wartime conscription, and with its denial of citizenship to non-
naturalized pacifist aliens. In effect, it established the law to be
that the conscientious objector has no right under the federal
Constitution to exemption from military service.[41]

The Court ruling was discouraging to the large numbers who
had hoped to see a compulsory R.O.T.C. declared unconstitutional. On the other hand, there was ground for hope in the Court's
verdict that the states, despite their acceptance of federal aid
were the sole judges of the type and extent of the military training to be provided. The C.M.E., which along with the Methodist
Episcopal Church had raised funds to carry the Maryland and
California cases to the Supreme Court, viewed the Court's clarifi-
cation of the problem as 'a gain, not a loss.' [42] The *Literary Digest*
observed that the Supreme Court decision, though correct in law
nevertheless calls attention to the revolt of American youth
against being 'tin soldiers.' In sympathy with those who opposed
the R.O.T.C. on grounds of educational policy, the *Digest* pointed
out that the R.O.T.C. was enrolling one hundred thousand undergraduates each year, an extraordinary figure to those who remembered the pre-World War college campus.[43] The New York *World
Telegram* and other Scripps-Howard newspapers criticized the
Supreme Court decision and condemned 'compulsory military
training as unwise, illiberal and unfair' as well as 'inefficient and
wasteful of the taxpayers' money.' Believing that the 'battle
against compulsory militarization of the students of State universities should go on,' the editorial concluded that 'the fight will have
to be made in Congress' and 'in the States.' [44] The C.M.E. came
to the same conclusion. In a confidential bulletin to its members
and friends, it commented regarding the Supreme Court stand
'The clear implication of this is that henceforth our campaign
must be promoted along legislative lines, both State and Federal.' [45]

Under the leadership of the C.M.E., antimilitarist forces ac-

ordingly launched a new campaign for a law that would deny
federal funds to any civil institution of learning that compelled
its students to take military training courses. In 1926, such a bill
had been drafted by the C.M.E. and introduced in Congress by
Representative Welsh and Senator Frazier. Five years later, Representative Fiorello H. La Guardia of New York sponsored an
amendment to the Army Appropriation Act prohibiting any ex-
enditures for R.O.T.C. units in which student enrollment was
compulsory. During the early years of the depression, Congress
approved some reductions in funds that had been voted the army
for use in maintaining R.O.T.C. units, but in March 1935, Congress passed a bill providing a million dollars for new R.O.T.C.
units. At the same time, amendments similar to the one supported
by La Guardia in 1931 were rejected by both Houses.[46]

In the face of this rather discouraging legislative background,
the C.M.E. attempted in the summer of 1935 to gain Congressional backing for a new onslaught upon compulsory military
training. The original C.M.E. intention of sponsoring a bill to completely abolish the R.O.T.C. had to be given up, because of world
conditions, and the war psychology that was beginning to grip
Congress. At a meeting of representatives of the C.M.E. and other
liberal and pacifist organizations in December 1934, Kenneth
Walser presented a draft of a bill to amend the National Defense
Acts of 1916 and 1920 by striking out the words 'or compulsory'
and adding the provision that no R.O.T.C. unit was to be established or maintained until the Secretary of War was satisfied 'that
enrollment in such units (except in the case of an essentially
military school) is elective and not compulsory.' Various Congressmen, including Senators Borah, Frazier, Holt, Norris, Nye,
and Shipstead, and Representatives Bierman and O'Day, were
mentioned as possible sponsors for the Walser-C.M.E. proposal
before the bill was actually introduced in July 1935 by Senator
Gerald P. Nye and Representative Paul J. Kvale. Strong War
Department objections to the bill were brought forward at once
by Secretary George H. Dern, who contended that the bill would
infringe on state rights and weaken the defenses of the United
States.[47] In reply to Dern's criticism, the C.M.E. sent a letter to
President Roosevelt in which it argued that the change in the

R.O.T.C. from a compulsory to a voluntary basis would actually strengthen the national defense by permitting the army to concentrate its efforts upon those students who were not indifferent or hostile to a military-type training.[48]

Proponents of the Nye-Kvale bill were careful to stress the limited nature of their object. The St. Louis *Star Times,* recalling the row over compulsory drill at the University of Missouri until the faculty abolished it, reminded its readers that the Nye-Kvale bill involved no question of pacifism. 'It merely stops the making of soldiers against their will in time of peace.' The *New Republic* pointed out that the supply of officers for the United States army would not be diminished 'because the last two years of training necessary to get an actual commission, are already voluntary at all institutions.' The *Christian Science Monitor,* in praising those who were carrying on the fight for the Nye-Kvale bill, observed that it is 'the soundness of their cause, both from the point of view of the objector and with respect to the efficiency of the military corps, that promises ultimate success.'[49] Editorials in the New York *Evening Post,* Baltimore *Sun,* and Washington *Post* also came out in opposition to a compulsory R.O.T.C.[50] In the New York *Evening Post,* for example, Ernest L. Meyer charged that the army maintained the R.O.T.C. chiefly as a militarist indoctrination course and as a check on radical activities within the colleges.[51]

At the Senate hearings on the Nye-Kvale bill, prominent educators and church spokesmen took the lead in supporting what Senator Nye called an amendment to the National Defense Act 'for the single and entirely reasonable purpose . . . of eliminating compulsory enrollment in R.O.T.C. units in civil schools and colleges.' Representative Kvale presented to the Senate Committee on Military Affairs the letters and petitions of hundreds of college educators who opposed a compulsory R.O.T.C. Dean Guy Stanton Ford of the University of Minnesota, whose statement was the first to be read, informed the committee that as an observer for thirty years of student drill, he was skeptical of the claims made for it in regard to individual student improvement and also doubted its contribution to national preparedness. Replying to the charge that the Nye-Kvale bill constituted federal dication over the states, Dean Ford asserted that, even if so, 'I am free to say it is the kind I should welcome in behalf of the freedom it confers on the students who come to an educational institution for an education.' The real dictation, he charged, was the impression given to the colleges that they had to make the R.O.T.C. compulsory.[52]

Final defeat of the Nye-Kvale bill in 1936, despite its widespread backing by educators and churchmen, brought to a close a decade in which the C.M.E. had organized and led the fight against a compulsory R.O.T.C. Despite the failure to secure federal legislation, substantial gains were made in the number of colleges abolishing or modifying military instruction and compulsory drill. At the same time, the development of Junior R.O.T.C. units in high schools had been largely averted.[53] The only peace organization that concentrated exclusively upon the problem of militarism in education, the C.M.E. budget had never been large, seldom exceeding ten thousand dollars. In its last years Edwin C. Johnson, the executive secretary, and Oswald Garrison Villard, the treasurer and chief contributor, were its most important figures. But throughout its active life, the membership list included many of the most prominent college educators in the United States.[54]

Until late 1940, the C.M.E. preserved its organization, continuing actively to oppose both militarism in education and the surge of preparedness legislation in Congress. Although there was some question of the validity of its program in a time of crisis and war, the first intention of the executive committee was to carry on in spite of the outbreak of war in Europe.[55] In July 1940, the C.M.E. sponsored a manifesto of prominent educators that attacked the proposal to enact the first peacetime conscription law in American history.[56] The membership, however, was becoming increasingly divided over the question of the American position with regard to the war in Europe. While most of the committee were still loyal to the original ideals of the organization, they recognized the futility of trying to maintain its existence. As Oswald Garrison Villard remarked in his letter of resignation to Edwin C. Johnson: 'With conscription and complete militarization here, I cannot conscientiously ask people to contribute money for a futile work.'[57]

XV

The Hope of Isolation and Neutrality

THE 1930s WERE a period of uncertainty and confusion. Inaugu rated in the midst of a severe economic collapse, and continuing through the rise of totalitarian states abroad, the decade closed with the onset of World War II. In attempting to cope with these problems of depression, dictatorship, and war, the American people and government moved from a policy of isolationist pacifism to an interventionist war program. This shift seriously divided the liberal and peace forces in the United States. Opponents of militarism and war came to be confronted with a direct conflict of loyalties, forcing them to choose between their love of peace and their hatred of totalitarian dictatorships.

In spite of this fundamental dilemma and the growing split within their own ranks, the peace organizations were able to maintain a considerable measure of influence throughout the 'thirties. The American people remained largely pacifist in outlook. In the two decades between wars, they absorbed the litera ture of disillusionment — novels and plays by such men as John Dos Passos, Ernest Hemingway, Maxwell Anderson, and Erich Remarque depicted the stupidity and horror of war. At the same time, historical research provided an account of the origins of World War I that departed significantly from the official story, while revelations of the role played by Allied propagandists and by selfish economic interests in the United States added to general disillusionment and strengthened the American resolve to remain neutral in any future conflict. A poll of more than one hundred thousand clergymen in 1934 revealed that, of the twenty thousand from whom replies were received, over sixty per cent expressed the feeling that the churches should sanction no war. A majority of the larger Protestant churches in their annual conferences went on record during the 'twenties and 'thirties as opposed to war and in favor of a drastic reduction in armaments. In 1935, the *Literary Digest* distributed ballots to three hundred and fifty thousand college students to learn the extent of undergraduate feeling against war and jingoism. The one-third of the ballots returned showed a majority of the students claiming they would bear arms for defense but not for invasion of another country. Most of the students believed that the United States could stay out of a future war. They accepted a strong air force and navy as insurance against hostilities and favored government control of the munitions industry and conscription of wealth in the event of a war. Throughout the 'thirties, many college students took the Oxford Pledge to refuse to fight in any war, while liberal and left-wing campus organizations made a strong stand against militarism and the doctrine of preparedness.[1]

Encouraged by these signs of mass support from the churches and the schools, the antimilitarist and peace forces entered the 'thirties in a spirit of optimism. *The Turn Toward Peace, Men Conquer Guns, Religion Renounces War, The Supreme Cause,* and *Revolt Against War* were titles of some of the volumes that summed up the case against militarism and war in realistic, but still hopeful, fashion. Skeptical of this confidence, Ernest L. Meyer, in an article entitled 'Pacifists in the Next War,' warned that the situation would be even less favorable than in 1917 when only a small minority had held fast to peace convictions. The New Deal, Meyer pointed out, was already curbing the freedom of the individual, while President Roosevelt 'is, by background and conviction, a man far more militaristic than the late Princeton doge. He is definitely a "big navy" and preparedness for defense apologist. He is definitely a nationalist.' [2] Increasingly, pacifists in the 'thirties had to face the fact that economic depression, totalitarian dictatorship, and New Deal preparedness expenditures were at one in giving encouragement to militaristic thinking and talk of war. As Norman Thomas observed:

> Ours is a generation which reads Remarque, weeps over *Journey's End*, signs a Kellogg pact to outlaw war, knows the deadliness of modern means of destruction, and then with an amazing degree of unanimity accepts large-scale violence as inevitable or in some circumstances almost desirable. It is this psychological attitude, this pre-disposition to a kind of collective suicide, which makes the future so dark.[3]

The sad spectacle of a world outlawing war while, at the same time, it increased its armies and navies in the expectation of war was not, of course, a new phenomenon. In the period before 1914, a strong peace movement had developed in the midst of preparations for war. This same curious paradox, aptly described by historian Carl Becker as 'Loving Peace and Waging War,' prevailed again in the 1930s.[4] By 1937, a veteran pacifist leader was forced to conclude that while 'we have more pacifism in the world today, there is also more militarism than before the World War.' [5]

In the United States, the confused and conflicting tendencies of the decade received their most important illustration in the policies pursued by the Franklin D. Roosevelt administration. As a candidate for the Presidency and during his first years in office, Roosevelt adhered closely to the dominant isolationist mood of the country. The American people, in turn, regarded Roosevelt as a man of peace, opposed to intervention in foreign wars. In the 1932 elections, held in the midst of the severe economic depression, Roosevelt's old World War role as Assistant Secretary of the Navy was forgotten along with his earlier championship of the League of Nations. In so far as foreign policy was an issue, Roosevelt, rather than Hoover, was viewed as the isolationist, antimilitarist candidate.

Not everyone, of course, accepted this picture. For example, Oswald Garrison Villard in an article, 'The Pot and the Kettle,' called 'Roosevelt and Hoover Militarists Both.' Dismissing the

former as a long-standing enthusiast for the navy, Villard also deprecated Hoover as 'a sham Quaker' who 'believes in going on
peace missions to other countries on battleships.' [6] In the long run,
Roosevelt was to substantiate Villard's pre-election charge of militarist sympathies, but in his first years of office he enjoyed the confidence of large numbers of liberals and pacifists. Without exception, each of the active peace groups was able to find in the New
Deal program at least one item it had wanted. Their faith seemed
justified by the administration's 'good neighbor' policy toward
Latin America, recognition of Soviet Russia, passage of the Philippine Independence bill, and proposed entrance into the World
Court. Mildly internationalist, these measures did not conflict
seriously with the dominant isolationist spirit of the country, and
they were accepted enthusiastically by most liberals and peace
supporters, whether isolationists or internationalists.[7]

Despite these early gestures toward international conciliation,
the basic policies of the New Deal were strongly nationalistic. By
refusing to commit the United States to an international currency-
stabilization program, President Roosevelt disrupted the London
Economic Conference in the summer of 1933. The conference itself might not have been able to reverse the prevailing world trend
toward economic nationalism, even if it had been accorded full
United States support. In any event, the failure at London 'dealt
a heavy blow to international co-operation, and markedly acceler-
ated the drift toward isolation, big-navyism, and extreme nationalism.' [8] Although liberal, pacifist opinion generally regarded Roosevelt's handling of the London Economic Conference as his 'one
conspicuous instance of bad faith,' the majority of the American
people, still strongly isolationist, applauded the President's action
and professed to see no threat to world peace in the vigorous program of domestic economic recovery initiated under the New
Deal.

During his first term, President Roosevelt supported many measures valued by the peace cause, but realistic observers, both within
and outside the pacifist ranks, could not ignore what a writer in
the *Nation* called 'Drifting Into Militarism.' [9] Accepting as a fact
the improbability of the success of any world disarmament and
aware of the need to encourage American industry, Roosevelt pur-

sued a policy of building up a strong army and navy. A few days
after the inauguration ceremonies, Secretary of the Navy Claude
Swanson announced the administration's intention to bring the
fleet to treaty strength and station the bulk of it in the Pacific. Although the United States was only following the course already
charted by Japan and other world naval powers, it was discouraging to antimilitarists to see the country plunged into a general
naval race. In Japan, the militarist elements used the American
naval program to influence their own people and to gain approval
for increased appropriations. By the time of the London Naval
Conference of 1935, the Japanese government and people refused
to be bound any longer by the inferior status implied in the 5-5-3
naval ratio. While the Japanese bore the major share of responsibility for the failure of the conference, the United States by 1935
was also moving toward rearmament. On the eve of the London
meetings, President Roosevelt, according to Secretary of State
Cordell Hull, was already convinced that the United States needed
a larger navy.[10]

Although there was little reason to doubt the President's sympathy with a big army and navy policy, the 1932 campaign promises of economy in government, and the political danger involved
in any sudden adoption of a larger military budget, resulted at first
in a program of rearmament by indirection. In June 1933, the President allocated over two hundred million dollars from the N.R.A.
appropriation to the construction of new battleships. Funds intended for the Public Works Agency were used to bolster up the
army and navy, and aircraft carriers, military airplanes, airports,
highways, airtunnels, and hospitals were constructed from P.W.A.
money.[11] In 1935, public opposition to this policy persuaded Congress to state the specific purpose for which appropriations were
made. In the case of some agencies of the New Deal, little change
resulted. As the biographer of Harry Hopkins has noted, 'despite
the prohibitions against any military activities which had been
written into the Work Relief Bill, W.P.A. accomplished a great
deal of construction — airports, highways, bridges, etc. — that
had deliberately strategic importance.'[12]

Unable to halt the flow of New Deal funds for military purposes,
the public was somewhat more successful in its protest against

attempts to militarize the Civilian Conservation Corps. Established as a depression measure to give employment to some three hundred thousand young men, the camps helped to save many youths from the hazards of delinquency and to give some income to their families. In other respects the C.C.C. was open to suspicion as a militarist device. Closely paralleling the work camps established in Europe, it was like them a means of keeping the national manpower physically fit and partially trained for eventual military service. Army officers, backed up by Secretary of War Harry H. Woodring and American Legion spokesmen, favored a frank militarization of the C.C.C. under army control, but such proposals were objectionable to labor and peace opinion. Robert C. Fechner, director of the C.C.C., repeatedly denied that there was any direct military training in the camps. He admitted though that, 'While C.C.C. men are not militarized in the ordinary sense of the word, their training is such that they are about 85 per cent prepared for military life.' It was not surprising therefore that the army eventually became enthusiastic over the C.C.C., accepting it as 'an admirable substitute for military training.' [13] But, despite mounting war tension in Europe and increasing pressure to turn the C.C.C. over to the army, Congress and the Roosevelt administration refrained from including military training of C.C.C. boys as a part of the expanded national defense program.[14]

Rebuffed in the case of the C.C.C., the encroachment of the military upon the civil sphere was otherwise encouraged by the Roosevelt administration's practice of using army organization and personnel to implement its policies. The army was often the most convenient, economical, and efficient agency available, and as one writer pointed out: 'In the breakneck pace of the New Deal it was impossible to examine closely the principle that it is better for civilians to run their jobs poorly than for Army men to run civilians well. That is something we may have to take up later.' [15] By these devices, Roosevelt was able to develop the army and navy, keep its officers busy, and yet appear as a champion of economy and peace because the actual military budget for 1934 had been slightly trimmed. Such subterfuges gradually became less necessary as people were conditioned to the heavy spending of the New Deal. Business and labor alike welcomed large appropriations for naval construction. The American Legion and other patriot groups stressed the need for increased military preparedness. Couched always in terms of the defense requirements of the country, the Roosevelt preparedness program was well calculated to appeal to American nationalistic sentiments.

Although rearmament in the mid-1930s was not linked as yet to an avowedly interventionist foreign policy, isolationists were becoming more wary of the eventual purpose of a larger army and navy. The fear the preparedness might again prove the prelude to war was an important factor in the isolationist drive for strong neutrality legislation. Some observers saw in the Roosevelt defense program the beginnings of a new chapter in the twentieth-century imperialist expansion of the United States, with war as the most likely outcome.[16] Liberal and labor groups were fearful of the import of Secretary Woodring's appeal, in a widely read magazine, for a larger army in order to 'cope with social and economic problems in an emergency.' The army, Woodring wrote, 'is our secret insurance against chaos. It is our "ace in the hole" for peace as well as war.'[17] Left-wing elements called for an investigation of the connection between national preparedness and business profits. Referring to the alleged tie-up of General Hugh Johnson's N.R.A. and the War Department, the American League against War and Fascism concluded: 'The alimentary canal of the Blue Eagle is a sixteen-inch gun.'[18]

The seeming paradox of the reformist New Deal embracing militarism was disillusioning to those idealists who had not as yet accepted Albert Jay Nock's pessimistic view of the future as 'a steady progress in collectivism running off into a military despotism of a severe type.'[19] *Fortune Magazine*, which had already published a sensational account of the role of the munitions industry in fomenting wars, pointed out in the fall of 1935 that

> when the vested interests were running the country, from 1920 to 1930 or thereabouts, they let military appropriations slide to the point where procurement officers had difficulty in raising the money to buy a rifle. When the great liberal, Franklin D. Roosevelt, took over the White House and the job of Commander-in-Chief, he and his Chief of Staff gave the Army its first big break since the Shipping Board ships began to rot in the Hudson.[20]

In a conclusion subtitled 'Why Defense?,' *Fortune* cited Lloyds of London's odds of 500 to 1 against any invasion of the United States. Seeing the United States army chiefly as a nucleus for a future aggressive war to protect America's economic position, the *Fortune* writer decided that, 'If the citizen is defending himself from anything at all with his poor army it is from the crazy ideas that seize upon him from time to time and persuade him that a war ought to be fought. These ideas come along every so often and they are the open doors to war.' [21]

Members of Congress, irrespective of party label or conventional badges of liberalism or conservatism, also expressed alarm over the Roosevelt army and navy program. Such ultraconservative Congressmen in each party as Republican Harold Knutson of Minnesota and Democrat John E. Rankin of Mississippi agreed that the increasing rate of American expenditures for arms meant involvement in a future world war.[22] In the Senate, William H. King, a conservative Democrat from Utah, joined the two North Dakota radical Republicans, Senators Nye and Frazier, in leading the attack on the big-navy program of the first Roosevelt administration.[23] These men, along with many fellow Congressmen, pointed out that the United States was preparing for a war with Japan. In the light of the far greater rate of United States naval expenditures as compared with either Japan or Great Britain, some Congressmen found it difficult to justify the United States claim that its preparations were merely for defense. In a typical outburst, Senator Frazier declared:

> When we see a nation increasing its armament, spending in peacetime, in preparation for war, more money than is being expended by any other civilized nation on earth, it is difficult for me to believe it is being done for any Sunday school purpose, for so-called 'adequate defense,' or anything of that kind. When a nation increases its army and navy, it is done for war purposes either at home or abroad.[24]

Although President Roosevelt made speeches criticizing the resurgence of competitive world rearmament, he was reluctant to advocate retrenchment in the United States military and naval program. Apprehensive of the international situation and not unmind-

ful of the effects of government spending to stimulate prosperity
the President preferred to continue the nationalistic policy o
building up the armed strength of the United States. Opponent
of militarism were often perplexed by the administration policy
Secretary Hull's denunciation of 'the military spirit' and 'the arma
ment race' in a speech before the Chamber of Commerce in Wash
ington was quoted by the *United States News* as part of an articl
which demonstrated that 'In the matter of naval expenditures th
United States is far ahead of other nations. The bill now goin
through Congress calls for outlays of $531,068,707 compared with
planned expenditures of $396,336,200 for the British navy and
$169,000,000 for the Japanese navy.' President Roosevelt's own
1935 disarmament speeches provoked the *Christian Century* to
make the comment: 'Not as the Pharisee.' [25] Unperturbed by criti
cism of his sincerity or consistency, the President continued to de
vote himself to the disarmament theme. In an address before the
Inter-American Conference for the Maintenance of Peace at Bue
nos Aires in December 1936, he condemned in severe terms the
nations which resorted to armaments to solve the problems of de
pression and unemployment. 'We know,' the President asserted
'that Nations guilty of these follies inevitably face the day when
either their weapons of destruction must be used against their
neighbors or when an unsound economy, like a house of cards, will
fall apart.' [26]

Despite his verbal onslaughts upon the rearmament drive of the
fascist powers, President Roosevelt during his first term in office
gave little evidence of a desire to see the United States participate
in new adventures overseas. The bulk of the American people
however, remembering Wilson's promises before 1917, desired
some guarantee of peace not dependent solely upon executive will
or policy. While many pacifists and internationalists continued
to work for United States entry into the World Court or League
of Nations, the controlling isolationist sentiment of the country
was more concerned in keeping the United States out of war and
all European entanglements. To this end schemes were suggested:
(1) to make it more difficult to declare war; (2) to eliminate or
control the profits from war and preparedness; and (3) to pre
serve American neutrality through an embargo on the export of

munitions. The roots of these ideas extended far back into the American past, but the vigorous campaign in their behalf began only after the collapse of the disarmament efforts of the 1920s and after the renewal of the threat of war in Europe and the Pacific seemed to end all hope of lasting world peace. Still profoundly disillusioned over the results of the First World War, the American people's isolationist feelings were reinforced by the sensational published accounts of the exorbitant profits and flagrant unneutrality of American munitions makers and international bankers in the months leading to the United States declaration of war in 1917.

As a result of these disclosures, various groups demanded a Congressional investigation of the munitions industry. Peace organizations, led by the Women's International League for Peace and Freedom, brought pressure to bear upon Congress. The American Legion gave its support, and even militarists and army and navy men were not averse to the idea of an investigation. Properly conducted, they hoped it might lead to the conscription of industry in wartime and the enforcement of complete militarist controls over the American economy. Unable to resist the widespread public outcry against the traffic in arms, Secretary of State Hull and President Roosevelt gave administration backing to what they hoped would be a limited investigation. This expectation was rudely shattered when the Senate appointed Gerald P. Nye of North Dakota to head its Investigating Committee. A staunch isolationist and Senator from a state without any apparent economic interest in the munitions industry, Nye gathered an able corps of assistants and carried the investigation far beyond the intentions of the Roosevelt administration.[27]

In the midst of the Munitions Investigation, war broke out again between Bolivia and Paraguay, and Italy launched its attack upon Ethiopia. It was feared that these two wars, and especially the Italo-Ethiopian conflict, might eventually involve the United States. Aroused by the findings of the Nye Committee and determined to avoid any repetition of the pattern of events that had preceded American belligerency in 1917, the American people supported the movement for some sort of neutrality legislation. The Neutrality Act approved by Congressional joint resolution in August 1935 provided for an embargo on the export of arms and munitions to all belligerents whenever the President proclaimed the existence of a state of war. This measure was a compromise between the automatic, mandatory embargo, sought mainly by the Senate, and the State Department's desire for an embargo that the President could apply at his own discretion to any or all belligerents.[28]

The revelations of the Nye Committee, showing laxity and corruption in awarding munitions contracts, not only buttressed American support for neutrality, but also strengthened the movement to take the profits out of war. Legislation to conscript wealth as well as men and to equalize the burdens of war had long been popular with the veterans of 1918. The American Legion formulated such a bill and urged it upon Congress as early as 1922. No action was taken until two years later when the Capper-Johnson Universal Draft bill was introduced in Congress but not brought out of committee. In succeeding years, Legion pressure for a universal draft was intensified, but the purpose behind such a bill changed from the goal of peace to that of war preparedness. The militarist element, with which the Legion had become increasingly identified, was now primarily interested in legislation that would make war, or preparation for war, cheaper and more efficient. This shift in emphasis from peace to war preparedness was disillusioning to liberals and pacifists who had long favored legislation to curb wartime profits because of their belief that the prospect of a profitless war would be, in itself, a powerful deterrent to the outbreak of war. Peace groups now saw that legislation to limit profits might also facilitate the conscription of American industry for war purposes. Under the War Department's Industrial Mobilization Plan, business firms were to be offered tentative contracts on a noncompetitive basis, with a guarantee of full production and satisfactory prices in the event of war.[29]

To explore these conflicting demands in regard to war profits, Congress in 1930 created a joint Congressional-Cabinet Committee under the title, a commission 'to promote peace and to equalize the burdens and to remove the profits of war.' Headed by Secretary of War Patrick Hurley, and generally known as the War Policies Commission, there is little doubt that the abbreviated title was a better description of the commission's major interest and function.

At public hearings before the commission in the spring of 1931, army plans for industrial mobilization, including the conscription of all manpower, were presented in detail. Such prominent World War I figures as Newton D. Baker and Bernard Baruch, although differing in their testimony as to the possibility or desirability of preparing too carefully or too far in advance for war, were agreed that it might not be feasible to try and fight a successful war without the lure of profits. Along with other critics of the War Department schemes, Norman Thomas, the leader of the Socialist party, expressed the belief that the constitutional amendment required for the effective conscription of wealth would bring about fascism and the full-scale regimentation of every detail of American life. Reinforcing Thomas's point of view, Tucker Smith, Secretary of the Committee on Militarism in Education, stressed the fact that the causes of war lay deeper than the profiteering of Wall Street capitalists. Peacetime policies of militarism and imperialism, he argued, were the real causes of war. Dorothy Detzer of the Women's International League for Peace and Freedom expressed her fellow pacifists' concern over the commission's emphasis upon conscription and preparation for war. John Nevin Sayre, Secretary of the Fellowship of Reconciliation, called the attention of the commission to the international declaration against conscription issued the previous fall under the auspices of a notable list of signers including Albert Einstein, H. G. Wells, Romain Rolland, and Jane Addams.[30]

The War Policies Commission's interest, however, lay in other directions. As former Congressman Richard Bartholdt told its members, the absence of State Department officials and the deference paid to War Department spokesmen at the hearings 'seems to indicate that you are concerned in preparations for the eventuality of war rather than those for peace.'[31] Liberal and pacifist skepticism over the kind of war profits bill that would emerge from the commission seemed justified when the majority submitted a report which proposed that the army be entrusted with a large measure of control over American industry. Representative Ross A. Collins alone, in his minority report, protested vigorously against permitting price controls to be set by army officers, and he also pointed out that the original function of the commission, to ascertain ways to take the profits out of war, could be achieved only by a constitutional amendment.[32]

The hearings before the War Policies Commission brought out the variety of conflicting interests involved in any attempt to remove the profits from war. Although highly suspect as means of preventing either militarism or war, the commission's proposals nevertheless continued to arouse interest on the part of Congress. Thus in 1935 the House of Representatives passed the McSwain War Profits bill, calling for a hundred per cent tax on profits, and permitting the government to take over industrial plants and to fix prices. Further action was delayed by the Senate, while the dubious nature of the proposed legislation caused antimilitarist groups to qualify their support. Jeanette Rankin, representing the National Council for the Prevention of War, told the House Military Affairs Committee that both she and the Council were

> very much in favor of taking the profits out of war, but they do not want to be disillusioned later by a bill which is futile, and legislation is futile which waits until war comes to be put in operation.
> The only way to take the profits out of war is to take them out in peacetime.[33]

In 1937, a universal service measure calling for the conscription of both labor and capital was widely denounced as 'a war dictator bill.' Senators Gerald P. Nye and Ernest Lundeen, who refused to sign the Senate Committee Report recommending such a draft bill, called it a device to 'build for a greater militarism.' [34] Under the impetus of the Nye Munitions Investigation, the drive to prevent profiteering in wartime had reached its peak without achieving its goal. Diverted to militarist purposes, the numerous proposals to conscript or tax wealth could no longer be considered as peace measures. Mobilization of a nation's economic resources and conscription of its manpower had become essential to preparedness for modern war. Opponents of militarism, as well as War Department strategists, realized this, and they were also fully aware of the tremendous social and economic changes that a new war would entail. While army planners accordingly proceeded on the frank assumption of militarist controls over the national life and economy in the event of war, antimilitarist liberals strove to avert

the coming of a war which they feared would bring militarism in
its wake.

In the twentieth century, the idea of a war without militarism
was a contradiction in terms. Recognizing the necessity of peace if
civilian democracy was to be preserved, liberal and antimilitarist
forces were badly divided over the means of attaining their goal.
In the face of embittered national rivalries, and of totalitarian governments abroad, the American people were confused by the conflicting arguments of the proponents of peace by collective security
or peace through isolation. Both groups stressed the dangerous alternative of militarism. Isolationists saw an American militarism as
the inevitable outcome of United States entrance into a world war,
while the advocates of collective security feared a world-wide militarism if the aspirations of the totalitarian states remained un-
checked. At a time when they should have stood together, liberal
and antimilitarist ranks were split between the poles of an uncompromising isolationist pacifism and an increasingly war-minded
internationalism.

By the summer of 1937, questions of American neutrality and
preparedness, debated by isolationists and internationalists
throughout the 1930s, were assuming a new and more serious import. That July, Japan embarked upon a full-scale invasion of
China. Taking advantage of the fact that war had not been officially declared, President Roosevelt refused to invoke the Neutrality Act and thus halt the export of munitions to the Far East.
Proponents of the Stimson doctrine of American pressure upon
Japan applauded the President's decision, which made possible
the continuance of aid to China. Then in October 1937, the President, yielding completely the isolationist views that he had publicly expressed during his first term in office, delivered his famous
'quarantine' speech attacking so-called aggressor nations. Roosevelt's now evident sympathy for collective security as against isolation had the effect of forcing liberals and antimilitarists to take
a stand on this question. Terminating the uneasy united front
hitherto maintained between pacifists and the New Deal, the quarantine speech further disrupted the peace movement in the United
States.[35] 'Isolationists only with respect to war,' the peace societies

and antimilitarist liberals were forced into co-operation with isola
tionist groups by the increasing belligerency of the Roosevelt ad
ministration. In other words, unless a collective security polic
were intended only as a colossal bluff or meaningless verbal threa
it required the United States to build up its military strength fo
possible use against those powers regarded as aggressor nation
This, as the peace groups fully realized, meant preparedness, mil
tarism, and ultimately, war.[36]

Although supporters of the Roosevelt foreign policy argued tha
the clear abandonment of isolation by the United States would b
sufficient to deter the Japanese and the European totalitaria
powers from aggressive action, the American people remained un
convinced. President Roosevelt himself complained of the hostil
reaction to his Chicago quarantine speech, which stood in marke
contrast to the 'overwhelmingly favorable response from press an
public' that had greeted his Chautauqua 'I hate war' address
year earlier. Public opinion polls in 1937, as the administratio
knew, showed an equally strong opposition to the abandonmen
of neutrality or to the use of sanctions against an aggressor natio
Recognizing the prevalence and depth of American feeling agains
war, Sumner Welles, Under Secretary of State, suggested tha
President Roosevelt call a peace and disarmament conference
Cordell Hull, however, was able to persuade the President that thi
would be a futile gesture and the administration seemed to b
wholly committed to the militarist policy of meeting force wit
force.[37]

In marked contrast to the bellicose attitude of the administratio
was the strong isolationist, antiwar feeling on the part of th
American people. This divergence in views helped to explain th
President's opposition to the popular Ludlow war referendum res
olution pending in Congress. Ludlow's proposal called for a
amendment to the Constitution which, except in cases of actua
invasion, would require a majority vote before a declaration of wa
could be made. Introduced in the House of Representatives onl
two days after the United States navy gunboad *Panay* had bee
fired upon by Japanese airplanes, it was defeated in January 193
by a close vote, and only after intense administration pressur
was brought to bear on Congress.[38]

A few days after the defeat of the Ludlow amendment, President Roosevelt sent a special message to Congress calling for further increases in naval armaments and for legislation aimed at the prevention of profiteering in time of war and the equalization of the burdens of possible war.' The President, alarmed over the threat to the peace of Europe coming from Hitler's Germany, had taken the first real step in the direction of implementing his quarantine speech of the previous October. Members of Congress realized that the President's message represented the first fruits of the policy of collective security. In the matter of taking the profits out of war, Congress refused to heed the President's suggestion, and legislation for a universal draft, which had been defeated in the past, was again rejected. Three members of the House Committee on Military Affairs in a minority report stigmatized such a measure as a 'bill to take democracy out of America upon the declaration of war.' [39] This hostile view won widespread acceptance in both the conservative and liberal press, where it was termed 'the war dictator bill.' [40]

The President's other recommendation of an increased naval building program was accorded a more favorable reception in Congress despite the fact that both Houses, one week before Roosevelt's special message, had already passed the largest appropriation for the navy ever adopted in peacetime. Protagonists of a still greater American navy refused to admit any connection between the new increases and the President's shift in foreign policy. Seeking to disarm the isolationist opposition, the text of the bill was amended to include a statement of naval policy in terms of the defense of the continental United States, its island possessions, and its commerce and citizens abroad. The sincerity of this view was questioned by the four members of the House Committee on Naval Affairs who signed a minority report. Authorization of three more seventy-five million dollar battleships when the old naval program was still not completed was, they alleged, a diplomatic not a naval program. It had no relation to the legitimate defense needs of the United States but was calculated to provide joint action with the British naval forces in the Pacific. Under the head 'This Bill is a Blank Check,' the minority concluded: 'If this bill is passed the President will have a blanket authorization after Congress adjourns to apply the universal-quarantine policy and Asiati interventionist policy.' [41]

Opponents of the Roosevelt naval program believed that it wa a step toward militarism and war. In the course of public hearing on the bill, liberal and pacifist spokesmen accordingly took issu with the testimony of publicist Walter Lippmann, Secretary c State Hull, and Admiral Leahy, all of whom supported a larger nav on grounds that it was needed to defend the United States. Bruc Bliven, editor of the *New Republic*, charged that the administra tion contemplated co-operation with Great Britain to defend th *status quo* in the Far East, and he asserted:

> I am not so rude as to think these gentlemen really mean the contradictory nonsense they have told us. I believe they know very clearly what they are about, but refuse to make public either their intentions or the reasons behind those intentions.
> I submit that the United States now possesses a Navy not in-tended for defense of our own shores, but for aggressive action in all parts of the world.[42]

On the floor of the House, Maury Maverick of Texas, a leadin New Dealer, bitterly attacked the policy of building more battle ships. Charging 'that the admirals of the Navy are the ones who ar directing our foreign policy,' he pointed out that the cost of two battleships just about equaled the Standard Oil Company's invest ment in China. Maverick noted the strange combination of group supporting the bill — pacifist internationalists, radicals, and mili tarists. The interest of the latter was obvious; the pacifists favore collective security as a internationalist device, and the radical wanted to aid Russia in China by helping to defeat Japan. Maver ick also denounced the President's special message as an abandon ment of the idealistic phase of the New Deal in favor of a policy of using battleship construction to end unemployment. Observin the revival of the old argument of a war to end war and make th world safe for democracy, Maverick suggested that the Presiden should call a disarmament conference before succumbing to mili tarism or embarking upon an armaments race.[43]

In the Senate, the debate on the naval bill brought to the for the whole question of the conduct of United States foreign polic and the slow drift toward war. Senator David I. Walsh of Mas

achusetts, who took the lead in defending both the bill and the
dministration's foreign policy, admitted that the latter 'depends
pon the state of mind of the President and the State Department
t any given time under a given state of facts.' Walsh, although
opeful of such a result, did not claim that the naval bill would
prevent war or keep the United States at peace. Critics of the bill
vere interested in knowing why the President had suddenly called
or a billion dollars of additional construction one week after the
House and Senate had passed the regular naval bill of over half a
pillion dollars. Senator Walsh replied that the Naval Affairs Com-
nittee understood that the navy itself had taken the initiative and
hat Admiral Leahy 'said he himself approached the President.' [44]

   The Senatorial opposition, including Nye, Vandenberg, Norris,
La Follette, Johnson, and King, was united in regarding the naval
bill as a measure that bore little relation to defense. Edwin C.
ohnson, Democrat of Colorado, saw the tremendous naval out-
ays as only 'a drop in the proverbial bucket if America is contem-
plating an aggressor policy.' He added that, in his opinion, the
Senate in deciding on the bill should understand that 'we are not
dealing with navies; we are dealing with American foreign policy.
Make no mistake about that.' William H. King of Utah, an old
advocate of the League of Nations, denounced the friends of the
bill as 'apostles of militarism and of so-called preparedness.' Robert
M. La Follette called attention to the tendency of armaments
appropriations to increase in periods of economic depression. He
ecalled in this regard the European powers' traditional use of
varlike gestures and fear of an outside enemy to conceal troubles
at home. Unless the United States intended to go ahead with the
President's 'quarantine policy,' the naval bill was unnecessary. This
he Senators realized, and hence the significance of their debate.
As George W. Norris summed it up, the United States was 'not
now in danger. We are sufficiently armed, if we defend only our-
elves, to meet any opposition the world can produce.' [45]

   Students of international affairs understood that the mounting
ide of world rearmament, in which the United States was being
wept along, could only result in war. A *Report* of the Foreign
Policy Association in 1938 estimated current world arms expendi-
ures at four times the 1913 figure, even after due allowance was

made for the price rise in the twenty-five year period. This in
crease, it was pointed out, had contributed to rising international
tension even before the Czechoslovakian crisis. Its effect upon the
domestic economy in all countries could be seen from the world-
wide decline in the standard of living, accompanied always by
more and more state controls over the people. 'For the democra
cies, the ultimate cost of unlimited armament competition may
be the loss of their free economies and the undermining of democ
racy itself.' [46] In the United States, rearmament was advocated as
a means of national defense through strengthening the collective
security of the democratic nations. But, as William E. Rappard
Director of the Graduate Institute of International Studies at
Geneva, pointed out in 1940, for collective security to work there
must be some measure of national disarmament. A product of na
tional insecurity, armaments 'are bound, in turn, to generate such
insecurity. The professional interest of soldiers and the economic
interest of those who supply them with arms and munitions can
not be expected to make for peace.' [47]

Former President Hoover, in an address delivered before the
Council on Foreign Relations at Chicago early in 1939, stressed
the close ties between a nation's military and foreign policies. In
creased armaments accordingly were a good indication of warlike
diplomacy. Strongly opposing the administration's indirect coer
cion of other nations 'as the straight path to war itself,' Hoover
added: 'No husky nation will stand such pressures without bloody
resistance. Those who think in terms of economic sanctions should
also think in terms of war.' Believing that the Roosevelt adminis
tration was leading the country into war, but confident that the
people still desired peace, Hoover warned that modern war 'means
that our country must be mobilized into practically a Fascist state
It would be so organized. It went some distance in the last great
war, although we did not use that term at the time.' [48]

Hoover's address was in reply to President Roosevelt's January
message to Congress in which he had asserted that the democra
cies 'must proceed along practical, peaceful lines. But the mere
fact that we rightly decline to intervene with arms to prevent acts
of aggression does not mean that we must act as if there were no
aggression at all.' Roosevelt followed his message with a call for

revision of the Neutrality Act and repeal of the mandatory embargo on arms. Mindful of the way in which the President had already seized the initiative in American foreign relations, and fearful of American involvement in the war already looming in Europe, Congress voted down the repeal measure in June 1939.[49]

At the time of the Congressional action on the embargo, war in Europe was only a few weeks away. Thus the decade of the 1930s, which had begun in the high tide of the crusade for peace, came to a close with the world again sinking into the abyss of war. American isolationist sentiment, though still strong, was more hopeful than it was certain that the United States could avoid participation in another world struggle. The sense of security and spirit of optimism of the nineteenth century, momentarily revived during the 1920s, succumbed again to fear and uncertainty. Opposed to war, and yet apprehensive of its coming, many isolationists united with interventionists to support American rearmament. However interpreted, whether as a means of isolationist defense or of positive American intervention in a future conflict, the extensive United States army and navy rebuilding program was a potential threat to the antimilitarist traditions of the republic. Whatever the fate of the world, so fraught with tragedy in the summer of 1939, it seemed clear that the new decade of the 'forties would be a period of crisis and of growing militarism.

XVI

Immersion in Total War

ON 1 SEPTEMBER 1939 the long-expected open conflict in Europe began as Hitler marched his legions into Poland, and England and France responded by declaring war on Germany. President Roosevelt immediately issued the proclamation of neutrality required by international law and by the Neutrality Act of 1937. But, in a radio address to the country, the President stated that he did not expect Americans to be neutral in their feelings. His acceptance of a frank unneutrality in thought contrasted with Wilson's 1914 admonition to the American people to be 'impartial in thought as well as in action.' Motivated by sympathy for the Allies, the President called Congress into special session to revise the Neutrality Act and repeal the embargo on the export of munitions. At the same time, Roosevelt gave his personal assurance 'that by the repeal of the embargo the United States will more probably remain at peace than if the law remains as it stands today.' [1]

The guiding idea behind repeal was, of course, the desire to extend American aid to England and France in their struggle against Nazi Germany. Such help, it was said, would keep the war from spreading to the Americas and insure peace for the United States. Opponents of repeal, on the other hand, argued that it was the first step along the road to war and the future militarization of America. Sending munitions to the Allies, it was believed, would

be the prelude to further intervention in their behalf until ultimately the United States entered the war as an avowed cobelliger-
ent. Senator Arthur H. Vandenberg predicted that, if this came
true, 'we would get such a regimentation of our own lives and livelihoods, 20 minutes after we entered the war, that the Bill of
Rights would need a gas mask, and individual liberty of action
would swiftly become a mocking memory.' [2] Although unsuccessful in preventing repeal of the embargo, Congressional isolationists
were able to strengthen those features of the original neutrality
legislation which were designed to keep American citizens and
shipping out of the war zone. As a result the United States, while
avoiding the danger of some incident that might lead to war, was
yet able to supply the Allies on a cash-and-carry basis.

The most important organized expression of the American desire for peace plus an Allied victory was the William Allen White
Committee to Defend America by Aiding the Allies, formed in the
spring of 1940. White himself accepted the chairmanship only on
the condition that 'no munition-makers' money, no international
bankers' money, and no money from the steel interests would be
used in the campaign.' From the outset, however, there was an
inner conflict between White and prowar Eastern members of the
committee. When Robert Sherwood, a member of the latter group,
wrote the famous 'Stop Hitler Now' advertisement, which appeared under the committee's name in all leading newspapers
over the country in June, White became indignant. In his call to
arms, Sherwood attacked all isolationists as imbeciles or traitors.
Opposed to this sort of slander, and to the idea of old men telling
young men to fight and be conscripted for war, White resigned
in December 1940 from the committee he had helped to found.
Before this break White had been able to head off an attack on the
committee's interventionist policies scheduled to appear in the
Scripps-Howard newspapers. To this end he wrote a letter to
publisher Roy Howard in which he accepted the motto, 'The Yanks
Are Not Coming.' [3]

White considered aid to the Allies a means of defeating Hitler
without bringing the United States into the war. This limited
interventionist position was difficult to maintain in the face of
German victories in the spring of 1940. President Roosevelt, stress-

ing the danger to the United States if Hitler should overcome
Great Britain, urged additional appropriations for national defense. By the end of the summer, Congress had approved a total
of some thirteen billion dollars for the army, navy, and air force —
an amount exceeding by more than three times the appropriations
made in 1917 after the United States had actually entered the
war.[4] The World War I Council of National Defense was revived,
and Republicans Henry L. Stimson and Frank Knox joined the
Cabinet as Secretary of War and Secretary of the Navy.

During the summer of 1940, fears of American intervention in
the war, already aroused by the Roosevelt rearmament program,
were given further substance with the addition of conscription to
the long list of proposed defense measures. Never intrinsically a
popular resort, conscription had been invoked only twice before in
American history — during the Civil War and again in the First
World War. After the Armistice, a strong effort was made to
continue the selective draft in the form of universal military training. Although all such schemes were rejected decisively in 1919
and 1920, the army continued to work for the renewal of Selective
Service and to urge various stand-by general mobilization plans.[5]
Actually, there had been no real opportunity to revive the draft
issue until after the outbreak of the war in Europe in 1939. Even
then, original army plans for an increase in its size did not include
conscription as an immediate resort. The initiative for a revival of
Selective Service seems to have come instead from Grenville
Clark and his associates in the old World War I Military Training
Camps Association. On 8 May 1940, at a dinner of this group in
New York City to celebrate the twenty-fifth anniversary of the
first Plattsburg Camp, Clark made a plea for preparedness and
conscription. With the editorial support of the *New York Times*
and the backing of a number of prominent citizens including
Henry L. Stimson, Robert P. Patterson, William J. Donovan, and
Elihu Root, Jr., Clark sought to persuade the War Department to
call upon Congress for the necessary legislation.

In Washington, meanwhile, General George Marshall's suggestion of an all-out drive for volunteers was squashed by Stimson,
the newly designated Secretary of War, who had a strong preference for conscription. While Marshall and the army stayed in the

background, Clark's circle of military-minded civilians took the lead in lobbying for a draft law. This strategy was not due to any hostility or lukewarmness on the part of the army toward the idea of compulsory military service. It was rather a result of the army's awareness that charges of militarism, plus the traditional American dislike of conscription, might jeopardize the administration's whole preparedness program. President Roosevelt's own reluctance to act officially, despite his strong personal enthusiasm for Selective Service, was tied to his growing concern over the forthcoming Presidential election. When administration Democrats in the Senate refused to present a draft measure, the appropriate bills already prepared by Clark and his associates were introduced into Congress late in June by Senator Edward R. Burke, a conservative, anti-New Deal Democrat from Nebraska, and Representative James W. Wadsworth, a militant Republican from upstate New York who had been in the forefront of the movement for universal military training in 1919. This sponsorship of the draft by non-New Dealers gave it a 'bipartisan appearance, and the words "Selective Service" provided an effective euphemism.' [6]

Presented as legislation to defend and protect the United States by instituting a system of military training, the Burke-Wadsworth bill, as it was popularly called, was more comparable to the World War I Selective Draft Act than to the short-term, peacetime training plans suggested after the Armistice. As a war measure, it forecast the sending of an American army to Europe or Asia as soon as the United States became an avowed belligerent. Conscription also held out far-reaching implications for the United States, and the ranks of the opposition included a wide range of American opinion.[7] This adverse feeling, though eventually overborne by arguments of defense and patriotism, was responsible for the long debate in Congress during the summer of 1940.

At the Congressional hearings on conscription in July 1940, the peace organizations, by now largely isolationist, took the lead in testifying against the Burke-Wadsworth bill. Catherine Fitzgibbon, representing the Women's International League for Peace and Freedom, pointed out that freedom meant freedom of individuals as well as of nations. Frederick J. Libby of the National Council for the Prevention of War argued that the emergency was not sufficiently grave to justify the dangers involved in the adoption of conscription. Edwin C. Johnson, Executive Secretary of the Committee on Militarism in Education, read a statement signed by some three hundred prominent educators, authors, clergymen, business and professional leaders, in which peacetime military conscription was denounced as totalitarian and unworthy of the spirit of American democracy. Johnson also quoted from a variety of newspaper editorials in which the need and advisability of a draft law were questioned. Oswald Garrison Villard believed it both unnecessary and impractical from a military point of view. John Nevin Sayre, Secretary of the Fellowship of Reconciliation, warned that conscription would accomplish an ideological invasion of the United States and bring Hitlerism over here. Norman Thomas pointed out that conscription had been Hitler's method of solving the depression and unemployment. In the United States, he feared that it would serve as a wedge for a labor draft. George F. Zook, President of the American Council on Education, announced the reluctant support of educators if Congress felt that conscription were warranted by the emergency, but he opposed taking eighteen year-olds.[8]

Congressional debate upon the Burke-Wadsworth bill took place in the midst of the bitter Roosevelt-Willkie 1940 Presidential campaign. Wendell Willkie's endorsement of conscription, in his speech accepting the Republican nomination, prevented it from becoming a real election issue and probably killed all hope of defeating the bill in Congress, although the antiwar, isolationist group in both parties conducted a strong delaying fight. Senator Vandenberg saw 'these militarizing proceedings' as the collapse of a one hundred and fifty-year tradition of American individual liberties. Senator Norris contrasted the atmosphere of militarism, which would follow a permanent draft, with life in the United States as he had known it. A review of the sponsors of conscription was given by Bennett Champ Clark, Senator from Missouri, who named Grenville Clark, Secretaries Stimson and Knox, and Julius Ochs Adler, publisher of the *New York Times*, as advocates dating back to World War I days.[9] Other Senators attacked the economic interests behind the draft. Rush Holt of West Virginia accused prominent interventionists and draft advocates of being large investors in aircraft companies enjoying government contracts. Burton K. Wheeler pointed out the paradox of 'the great economic royalists,' who had been clamoring about balancing the budget, but who now were willing to go to any expense for so-called national defense. Wheeler also noted that at the time of the passage of the eighteen billion-dollar armaments bill, the cry was for weapons, since men are no good without arms. Now this had been neatly transformed into the argument that the weapons are no good without men! The Senators opposed to the draft believed that it threatened the United States with the very European totalitarianism it was designed to help defend against. 'Political militarism,' declared Edwin C. Johnson, 'is American democracy's enemy No. 1. It threatens its future even more than does the current crop of European dictators.' [10]

The arguments against the Burke-Wadsworth bill expressed in committee hearings and on the floors of Congress were given a wide range of outside support. Both the A.F. of L. and C.I.O. were critical of conscription and the contrast it offered between a prospective draftee's wages of twenty-one dollars a month and big-business profits from rearmament.[11] While labor saw military training as a means of governmental tyranny, some business spokesmen, not yet thoroughly won over by the promise of an armaments boom, viewed conscription as another New Deal totalitarian measure. The *Commercial and Financial Chronicle*, which had greeted the Burke-Wadsworth bill with the caption, 'Involuntary servitude must not be restored,' asked: 'Does not this defense program in some of its aspects take on the appearance of another New Deal project tainted with the philosophy of totalitarianism and heavy with risk of further infringement of individual liberty?' With regard to the talk of a two million-man army, the *Chronicle* asked:

> Can any one explain what we should do with an army of that size if we are not to engage in a war on foreign soil . . . ? Would not such exaggerated militarism on our part be much more likely to convince Germany, Japan, Italy, and the others that we had aggressive designs of our own . . . ? [12]

Harry Emerson Fosdick, representing the antiwar wing of the Protestant clergy, under the title, 'Conscripts for Conquest?,' concluded that the draft was for an expeditionary force to lead an offensive war in Europe and the Orient. The Catholic magazine *Commonweal* believed the Burke-Wadsworth bill 'is obviously a long leap toward entry into the war.' [13]

Responding to public anxiety on this issue, Roosevelt and Willkie outdid each other in making lavish promises that American boys would not be sent to fight across the oceans. However impressive to the voters, such assurances were meaningless in view of the increasingly interventionist foreign policy advocated by both candidates.[14] The draft, as some of its supporters frankly admitted, was justifiable only to the extent that United States participation in the war was viewed as necessary and desirable. This was the position of Freda Kirchwey, editor of the *Nation,* who wrote somewhat reluctantly: 'There Is No Alternative.' In its same issue the *Nation* also published an attack on conscription by Maxwell S. Stewart, the associate editor.[15] Almost as badly divided was the *New Republic,* which at first believed that the United States should limit itself to continuing as the arsenal of democracy, and then in September announced: 'It is with heavy hearts that the editors of The New Republic endorse the principle of compulsory service at this time, though rejecting many aspects of the Burke-Wadsworth bill.' [16]

Supporters of Roosevelt's foreign policy could not logically refrain from endorsing the militarism needed to back it up. By the same token, the isolationist and pacifist opposition hoped that the defeat of the draft might weaken or reverse the trend toward United States intervention. In the midst of the long debate in which the real issue was often avoided, one editor effectively summed up the essential significance of conscription: 'As a measure of national defense, peacetime conscription remains unconvincing. As a device to strengthen the President's control of foreign affairs, it is an inspiration.' [17] The bitter legislative fight was concluded in September when the House, by a vote of 233 to 124, and the Senate, voting 47 to 25, gave their approval to the Burke-Wadsworth Selective Service bill.[18]

Although in reality a war measure envisioning an expeditionary force, popular opposition to another A.E.F. exacted an amendment limiting the draftees to duty in the Western Hemisphere, territories, and possessions of the United States. There was also some doubt among legal scholars as to whether conscription for foreign service was constitutional. One outstanding authority noted that 'it is by no means certain that the Constitution was originally thought to permit conscription for such a purpose.' [19] The possibility that the courts would rule against a draft law was precluded by the long line of cases in which the Congressional authority to raise an army had been treated as virtually unlimited.

In the United States, as in Europe, conscription and modern war had become inseparable. Defended by its proponents as the only democratic means of raising an army, conscription and democracy had developed together since the days of the *levée en masse* of the French Revolution. Yet a universal draft was fraught with undemocratic implications. In time of war, it forestalled the type of hostility to an unpopular struggle traditionally manifested in a dearth of volunteer soldiers. In peacetime, it was a powerful bulwark of militarism.[20] Even those who distinguished between so-called totalitarian and democratic conscription could not ignore the dangers of long-time service and of the permanent continuance of powers granted to a government in the heat of war.[21]

Putting into effect the first peacetime conscription law in the nation's history, President Roosevelt on 16 September 1940 signed the Selective Service Act requiring all men between the ages of 21 and 35 inclusive to register for an eventual year of military service. 'It is,' said the President, 'a program obviously of defensive preparation and of defensive preparation only.' [22] The period of service under the original Draft Act was for one year, but by the summer of 1941 there was a growing movement to keep the draftees in uniform for an additional six months. Strong popular opposition to this revision of the draft law almost gave the anti-militarist forces a belated victory as the House approved the extension by a margin of only one vote. While the people wanted the boys back home, the soldiers who had been promised a one-year tour of duty were often the most bitter of all. The slogan

O H I O, 'over the hill in October,' chalked on the walls of military installations, conveyed their feelings and indicated the low morale prevailing in the army.[23]

The extension of the draft law, together with the further amendment of the Neutrality Act in November 1941, carried the United States as far as it was possible to go, short of war. Admirers of the Roosevelt leadership realized that the President had done all he could to aid the Allies. 'He had no more tricks left. The hat from which he had pulled so many rabbits was empty.' [24] A month later the Japanese attack on Pearl Harbor resolved the President's dilemma. It also plunged the American people into a war that was to bring an unprecedented transformation in the historic antimilitarist traditions of the republic.

A period of warfare is always full of grave risks for such essential features of liberal democracy as the preservation of minority rights and civilian control of the government. Thus, in 1941, the United States, despite its antimilitarist tradition, could hardly expect to defeat the Axis nations without an understanding and at least a partial application of the German and Japanese militarists' concept of total war.[25] In conscription and large-scale rearmament, the United States had already embraced two of the more obvious and essential features of militarism and total war. Other measures, adopted back in the 1930s, also contributed their influence to bringing about an American militarism in wartime. Throughout the decade of the 'thirties, depression at home and dictatorship abroad had combined to instill in the American people a profound sense of crisis. New Deal reforms with their emphasis upon paternalistic government had also provided an ideal background for military control of production and manpower. Then, in 1940, the Alien Registration Act or Smith Act broadened the scope of all previous sedition legislation, making it unlawful to encourage disaffection in the armed forces, to advocate or teach the desirability of overthrowing a government of the United States, or to organize or affiliate with any group advocating such a policy.[26]

Finally, the circumstances of the coming of the war were well-suited to strengthening the military organization and to overcoming all lingering remnants of opposition. Believing the climax at Pearl Harbor to be an entirely unprovoked attack, the American people at once discarded their antiwar feelings in a burst of patriotic unity. Pearl Harbor likewise persuaded isolationist leaders that any attempt to assume the role undertaken by La Follette and Debs in World War I would mean political suicide. Among all the members of the House and Senate, only Jeanette Rankin, who had been one of the small group that had voted against American entry into the First World War, refused to give her assent to the President's call for a declaration of war against Japan and the European members of the Axis.

In general, the protest against war and militarism in 1941 was much weaker than in 1917. This was attributable not so much to popular enthusiasm for the war as to a kind of public apathy that settled over the American people once they had recovered from the initial shock of Pearl Harbor. As Robert Sherwood has noted, 'Morale was never particularly good nor alarmingly bad. There was a minimum of flag waving and parades. It was the first war in American history in which the general disillusionment preceded the firing of the first shot.' [27] Of the radicals who had stood out against war in 1917, the socialists were divided and less effective. There was also no counterpart in the labor ranks of the mass protest carried out in World War I by the I.W.W. On the extreme left, American Communists, who had been active in the peace movement of the 'thirties, strongly supported the Roosevelt policies after Russia entered the war in June 1941.

Of all the liberal elements traditionally identified with an opposition to militarism and war, the conscientious objectors were the only ones who carried their pacifist convictions to the point of open resistance. Although the small number of actual C.O.s was to prove disappointing to those pacifists who had taken seriously the antiwar pledges of college youth in the 'thirties, the prospect of even a few thousand objectors was disquieting to the government. The army solution for the C.O. was essentially a system of segregation and seclusion with as little publicity as possible. World War I experience had already demonstrated the folly of forcing the C.O. into the army or of confining them in federal penitentiaries. This harshness had made the objectors of 1918 the heroes of the disillusioned postwar college generation. What the army desired, instead, was a device that would discourage conscientious objection without creating a new set of martyrs to the cause of peace and antimilitarism. The Selective Service Act of 1940 accordingly contained the provision that any person 'who, by religious training, and belief is conscientiously opposed to participation in war in any form' and whose claim to exemption was sustained by his local draft board or by appeal to a higher authority should be assigned to noncombatant service, or if sincerely opposed to that, 'to work of national importance under civilian direction.' [28]

The Draft Act removed the C.O. from direct control by the army, but at the same time it tended to limit recognition to those objectors who were members of some established church. Congress refused to follow the English example and accept as sincere those objectors who were motivated primarily by ethical, social, humanitarian, or nonsectarian religious beliefs.[29] It also refused to consider the plea that complete exemption be granted those absolutists who objected, not only to war service, but to the entire principle of conscription and military regimentation. While the 1940 law was an advance over the World War I legislation and practice, pacifist spokesmen at the draft hearings warned the Congressmen that they were enacting a measure which, in providing insufficient protection for religious freedom and the cause of conscience, would again fill the federal jails with sincere objectors to war and militarism.[30] This prediction was in part realized as many C.O.s were either denied such a classification on technical grounds or themselves refused to comply with the strict provisions of the act. Although 16 October, the date set by Presidential proclamation for the mass registration of all eligibles, passed with little incident and practically none of the opposition manifested in 1917, instances of avowed nonregistrants soon attracted much attention. Conspicuous in this regard was the case of eight theological students at Union Seminary in New York City, who persisted in their carefully thought-out decision not to register despite the fact that, as potential ministers, they were entitled to a complete deferment.[31]

Those conscientious objectors who complied with the law and were adjudged sincere by their draft boards had the alternative of going into the armed forces as noncombatants, or of entering he Civilian Public Service Camps established jointly by the churches and the government. In all, approximately twelve thousand C.O.s were assigned to these Civilian Public Service units. This figure represented only a small percentage of those originally seeking classification as conscientious objectors, but who were deferred for other reasons, or who finally went into the army. The number of C.O.s granted noncombatant status in the army was far larger, variously estimated at from twenty-five to one hundred thousand men. The failure of the Selective Service Act to meet the problem of the absolutists of World War II was illustrated by the fact that some six thousand C.O.s were convicted of Draft Act violations and sentenced to prison terms of as much as five years. Of this number, over four thousand were Jehovah's Witnesses who had been denied a classification as ministers.[32]

The conscientious objectors who were in prison as a result of their protest against war and conscription were the most uncompromising of the opponents of militarism. The small number of these absolutists did not mean that other Americans were without any concern over the problem of militarism. Although recognizing the importance of patriotic loyalty to the nation in wartime, many Americans were alarmed at the lengths to which the doctrine of military necessity could be carried. Members of Congress, despite their desire to give the armed forces everything they needed, could not conceal their anxiety over the tremendous military appropriations of the war years. Revelations of waste and inefficiency stimulated Congressional criticism, and in June 1943 Harry S. Truman, chairman of the Senate's Special Committee to Investigate the National Defense Program, declared that the armed services

> know how to waste money better than any other organization I have ever had anything to do with. They do an excellent job on the waste side. . . .
> I could stand here all afternoon and give example after example showing that tremendous sums of money are simply being thrown away with a scoop shovel.[33]

Huge military expenditures and the argument of military necessity were also useful devices for furthering the army's effort to gain command of the nation's economy. Desirous of controlling the allocation of all industrial output, the army carried on a long-drawn-out struggle with the War Production Board headed by Donald Nelson. Nelson himself later wrote bitterly that the army people 'did their best to make an errand boy of WPB.' Although he had the backing of President Roosevelt, who was concerned lest the armed forces acquire too much authority and undermine democracy, Nelson was unable to prevent the army from holding up the gradual reconversion of American industry to the increased manufacture of civilian goods. His belief that the state of war production and the growing supply of labor in 1944 made this transition possible came into conflict with army aspirations for a national war service bill that would include a full-scale labor draft to match military conscription.[34]

Secretary of War Stimson and Under Secretary Robert P. Patterson were long-time protagonists of such a measure, and the idea of a universal draft bill was also a favorite with those business leaders who followed Bernard Baruch in advocating close ties between industry and the armed forces. Liberal groups and labor organizations viewed these schemes as threatening to bring about the complete triumph of a militarist philosophy. Oswald Garrison Villard, writing in the *Christian Century*, charged that Stimson's insistence on universal conscription would make the United States a nation of slaves.[35] At the Senate hearings early in 1944, William Green, President of the American Federation of Labor, refuted the army argument that a national war service bill would equalize the sacrifice of the soldier and the civilian.

> There can be no true comparison between drafting citizens to serve in the armed forces for the defense of their country and drafting other citizens to work by compulsion in industries operating for private property. Neither can there be any Nation-wide draft of labor without a correspondingly drastic draft of capital. Such measures are abhorrent to the American way of life, fatal to the free enterprise system and clearly violative of the Constitution, because they involve involuntary servitude and confiscation.[36]

The considerable public feeling against the adoption of a national war service bill was also instrumental in the defeat of army plans for the enactment of a system of compulsory military training for use after the war. With the backing of President Roosevelt, Secretary Stimson, and top army figures, the advocates of peacetime conscription hoped to persuade Congress to pass the requisite legislation while the country was still in the grip of the war spirit. Early in 1943 and again in January 1944, bills were introduced in Congress providing for a year of military training for all American youths. After the Presidential elections in November, these measures were brought out into the open and, in the midst of considerable public debate in the spring of 1945, hearings were held by the House Select Committee on Post War Policy.[37] The churches and peace societies, together with prominent educators, took the lead in organizing resistance to a peacetime draft, and the 'mail of Senators and Representatives was flooded with protests.' The churches seemed to feel that the adoption of U.M.T. would be the equivalent of what Harry Emerson Fosdick, minister of Riverside Church, called 'Worshipping the Gods of a Beaten Enemy.'[38] Educators joined the clergy in urging that all consideration of peacetime conscription be postponed until after the war when military needs could be seen in their relation to the peace settlement. The educators were especially critical of the argument that U.M.T. was desirable as a health measure or teaching device.[39] Although presented in such terms by President Roosevelt, its more candid proponents admitted that 'A great deal of the educational and social claims for the program are fantastic.'[40]

Liberals on all sides were alarmed at the totalitarian implications of peacetime conscription and the break that it made with past American traditions. They also questioned whether postwar conscription was compatible with the principles of the Atlantic Charter or necessary to the maintenance of world peace. Peace groups argued that the passage of U.M.T. would surrender the goals of the war and lead to future conflicts. Conservatives as well as radicals attacked Mrs. Roosevelt's suggestion that every one give a year of his life to the government. Thus the *Commercial and Financial Chronicle* saw U.M.T. as the climax of statism, while John Chamberlain, writing in the *Progressive*, pointed out that, 'If the United States War Department wants an authoritarian State, then it is going about it in the right way when it advocates compulsory peacetime conscription.'[41] In general, Congress and the country seemed to agree with the point of view that peacetime conscription, with all its far-reaching implications for the future course of American life, might better await the close of the war. Mindful of the hasty World War I adoption of the Eighteenth Amendment, there was strong sentiment against making any decision until the veterans could return home and cast their votes.

Largely successful in their opposition to the armed forces' plans to control all American manpower, liberals and antimilitarists were, however, unable to counter the most conspicuous instance of authoritarian military procedure during the war. The victims of this wartime hysteria were the Japanese-Americans on the Pacific Coast and in Hawaii. Although there was no case of espionage or sabotage by a single Japanese, citizen or noncitizen, all Americans of Japanese descent were evacuated from the Pacific Coast, and military government was imposed upon the Hawaiian Islands, where Japanese-Americans formed the largest single element in the population. Later, after the close of the war, the Supreme Court declared the army rule of Hawaii to have been an illegal invasion of the rights of the inhabitants. But, in the case of the removal of the West Coast Japanese-Americans, the Court refused to interfere. With the authority of a Presidential order to the army, allowing the commanding general on the Pacific Coast to designate military areas from which any or all civilians could be excluded, General John L. DeWitt, on the plea of military necessity, gave over one hundred thousand Japanese-Americans, two-thirds of whom were citizens of the United States, five days in which to leave their homes and be transferred to government relocation or detention centers. As a staunch advocate of evacuation, General DeWitt played the key role in the affair, but his decision enjoyed the approval of both President Roosevelt and Secretary of War Stimson. In the post-Pearl Harbor mood of anti-Japanese feeling, no attempt was made to distinguish between citizens or aliens, or between the loyal or disloyal. The few protests emanating from such organizations as the Fellowship of Reconciliation and the American Civil Liberties Union were ignored, and even the latter organization at first approved, or at least condoned, the evacuation.[42]

Gradually liberals perceived the falsity of the blanket charges of disloyalty directed against the Japanese-Americans, and the harsh injustice of depriving them of their homes, property, and means of future livelihood. In 1943, the Supreme Court, although refusing to rule against the army decision, expressed its grave suspicion of the necessity of evacuation. After the war, the Court decided that the evacuees must be permitted to return to their Pacific Coast homes. Still another judicial criticism of the army's procedure was handed down by the Circuit Court of Appeals in 1949. Affirming the restoration of citizenship to those Japanese-Americans who had renounced it during their incarceration in the wartime relocation centers, Judge William Denham wrote a decision, which the *New York Times* described as 'a blistering denunciation of Lieut. Gen. John L. DeWitt.' The Judge likened the relocation centers to German concentration camps and denounced the General's doctrine of enemy racism as similar to the Nazi philosophy.[43]

In the retrospect of the postwar years, it became apparent that militarist thinking, race prejudice, and economic discrimination, rather than opposition to the United States war effort, had forced the Japanese-American citizens into the virtual category of enemy aliens. After the war, legal scholars did not hesitate to denounce what one of them called 'the most drastic invasion of civil rights in the United States which this war has evoked, the most drastic invasion of the rights of citizens of the United States by their own government that has thus far occurred in the history of our nation.'[44] But, during the period of hostilities, there was little specific criticism and practically no overt opposition to the administration's conduct of either civil or military affairs.

This almost universal acquiescence helps to explain what most students have accepted as the improved record of the government in the matter of civil liberties as compared with the situation in the First World War. Assured of general support, the Roosevelt administration could afford to be tolerant of its few rather academic and intellectual critics. The sensational raids and vindictive prosecutions of the World War I period were on the whole avoided. An attempt to convict a group of American pro-Nazi sympathizers in a mass sedition case resulted in a mistrial. Except for a few disloyal individuals, the alien population in the United States proved no great problem and only a few hundred were interned besides the Japanese-Americans.

Although the Roosevelt wartime record in the matter of civil liberties and civilian control appears superior to that of Presidents Wilson and Lincoln, it is doubtful that President Roosevelt personally equaled their deep concern over these issues. In the instances where the government's policy was subject to criticism — the army's evacuation of the West Coast Japanese-Americans, the military's attempt to dominate war production and manpower, and Selective Service's attitude toward the conscientious objectors — the Roosevelt administration pursued a policy of expediency, offering little permanent opposition to the extravagant demands of the military establishment.

In general, American public opinion followed the lead of the administration. Under the impact of World War II, the American people largely discarded the antimilitarist convictions of the past. On all matters involving war and preparedness — including a navy and air force second to none, peacetime military training, and skepticism of any peace teaching — there had been a complete change in opinion as against the 1930s.[45] With regard to isolationism and internationalism, American thinking was less clear, sharing much of the confusion involved in the propaganda use of the two terms, but in theory at least Americans were overwhelmingly internationalist. Sure of their conversion to internationalism, the American people were not aware of the way in which they often made the world's future hopes conform to American national values. The task of securing a genuine internationalism, based on the ideals of peace and world patriotism, instead of militarism and war, was to be the chief heritage and the continuing problem of the postwar years.

XVII

Toward the Garrison State

WORLD WAR II has not receded far enough into the past for us to perceive its more lasting influence on the course of human events. But the historian of the future who ventures to specify militarism as an important outcome of the war will certainly find ample evidence to support his conclusion. Thus the United States, hitherto among the least military of the great nations, emerged from the war a powerfully armed state; and the reaction in the direction of peace that had succeeded earlier wars was slow to take effect.

In part, delay in the return to peace was a result of the tremendous scope and intensity of the Second World War. The collapse of Hitler's armies in the spring of 1945 and the Japanese surrender the following August brought to a close the most widespread and devastating war in the annals of modern history. Extending over a period of some five years, the conflict left an inheritance of astronomical costs and of millions killed on the battlefields or in the rubble of bomb-torn cities. Before the end of this great struggle while its horrors were still fresh in men's minds, the representatives of the United Nations gathered at San Francisco to draft the charter of a new international organization. Shortly thereafter, the war terminated as the first atomic bombs were exploded over Japan without preliminary notice or direct warning. The initial use of the tremendous forces of atomic energy for war purposes, though hailed as speeding the surrender of Japan and bringing an end to all hostilities, gave rise to the accompanying fear that civilization itself might be destroyed in the event of some future world struggle. Most Americans as well as other peoples refused to accept such a pessimistic outlook. The defeat of the Axis powers and the organization of the United Nations temporarily renewed men's hopes of a lasting peace, and for a brief moment after the close of the war, the world seemed ready to demobilize its armies and resume a civilian pattern of life.

In the United States, public pressure forced the administration to modify its plans for keeping the country on a war footing. In the matter of the army, for example, G.I. riots and demonstrations, plus the complaints of the men's families, speeded up the return home and release from military service of the millions of draftees. Although there were charges that the G.I. protests were Communist inspired, the rank and file of the men, disliking police duty or just plain homesick, needed little encouragement to agitate for a speedier demobilization. As the sympathetic *Nation* pointed out, the bulk of the American troops were 'not mercenaries or career soldiers; they are citizens of the United States who, willingly or not, left their homes, their families, and their livelihoods to fight a war.' [1]

The discharge of the greater part of the United States armed forces was paralleled by a partial relaxation of the economic controls adopted in wartime. The Republican party victory in the 1946 Congressional elections reflected a popular impatience with continued governmental authority. The desire for peace and 'normalcy,' so similar to the demand of 1920, was in direct conflict, however, with the heritage of the late war. That struggle, together with the whole background of events since at least the turn of the century, had fostered a spirit of militarism that was almost certain to make the return to civilian ways a difficult task.

Demobilization of the world's great war machines was rendered immeasurably more complicated by the series of postwar disagreements between the United States and Soviet Russia. Confronted with the so-called 'cold war,' the United States never really experienced any considerable postwar reaction but continued to be held in the grip of wartime thinking. Except for the brief period of demobilization in 1946, military policy and legislation after the war was indistinguishable from that of the war years. Official American thinking came more and more to be dominated by the belief that the best way to secure peace was through the maintenance of a strong military force. Only the threat of superior American armed power, it was felt, would restrain Soviet expansion. The United States government, accordingly, proposed to keep relatively large armies of occupation in Germany and Japan, while naval and airbases were scattered at strategic points throughout the world. At the same time, plans were made to revive the military controls exercised during wartime, and the armed forces were maintained at a level of over a million and a half men, with almost an equal number of civilian employees and a much larger number of men in the National Guard and organized reserves.

To support the largest peacetime military establishment in American history approximately one third the federal budget, or some twelve billion dollars, was appropriated directly for the army and navy in 1947. Such vast military expenditures naturally gave the armed forces increasing influence within the government, and top military men moved into key positions in federal agencies. Admiral William D. Leahy stayed on at the White House as President Truman's personal military adviser or private chief of staff. General Marshall replaced James Byrnes as Secretary of State, and the department itself came more and more under military control. Abroad in overseas posts, General Walter B. Smith, United States Ambassador to Russia, General Lucius Clay, High Commissioner of the American occupied zone in Germany, and General Douglas MacArthur, Supreme Allied Commissioner for Japan, gave a militarist cast to our postwar policy. At home, unification of the armed forces in a single department and establishment of the National Security Council enabled the Secretary of National Defense to work with the State Department in determining foreign policy.[2]

The practical results of the new integration of American foreign and military policy was the continued acceptance of the doctrine of peace through strength. The first step in this direction had been the wartime Allied insistence on the unconditional surrender of the Axis powers and the military occupation of their territory. Along with occupation went the trials of the Axis civil and military leaders as war criminals and the attempt to indoctrinate the German and Japanese people with the ideologies of the victor powers. In the portion of Germany under United States control, the difficult task of administering the military occupation was rendered even more complex by the deterioration of United States relations with Russia and by the growing doubt in all circles, military as well as civilian, as to the original wisdom of insisting on unconditional surrender. Observers of the United States army in Germany criticized the operation of the 'military mind' and the inability of the American military government to deal adequately with the problems of displaced persons, denazification, the black market, and the health and morale of American soldiers. In the summer of 1949, the State Department took over the technical responsibility of administering Germany, but the army of course remained as a garrison force, and military thinking and personnel continued to dominate the occupation.[3]

The army itself was not responsible for the war crimes trials of the Axis leaders, but the procedures used in the prosecution were regarded by many Americans as another example of the attempt to carry out a militaristic or Carthaginian peace settlement. Soon after the German surrender, President Hutchins of the University of Chicago warned that 'We should hesitate to punish Germans for acts which we have committed or may commit.'[4] Already in the Far East, General MacArthur, in his desire to anticipate the Nuremberg trials in Europe, had secured the conviction and execution of General Yamashita, Japanese commander in the Philippines, on charges of atrocities committed by his troops. Although the United States Supreme Court refused to reverse the military judgment, Justices Murphy and Rutledge issued minority opinions sharply criticizing both the fairness of Yamashita's trial before a United States military commission and the justice of convicting an enemy general for his conduct during hostilities.[5]

In the case of both the Nuremberg and Tokyo war crimes trials, some segments of American opinion, although in no way sympathetic with the Axis leaders who had been such conspicuous proponents of militarism in their own countries, nevertheless opposed the continued prosecution of the defendants by methods reminiscent of the Nazi courts. This feeling, together with the changing world political situation, led to a new policy of leniency toward former German and Japanese officials, and in the spring of 1950 John J. McCloy, United States High Commissioner in Germany, established a War Crimes Clemency Committee.

American modification of the concept of a harsh peace came chiefly as a result of the growing antagonism with Soviet Russia, which emphasized the desirability of some sort of rapprochement with Germany and Japan. In this way United States postwar policy, though continuing to be based on military considerations, underwent a drastic change in direction. Proceeding on the assumption that the expansion and interests of the Soviet Union could be contained by building up a sufficient counterforce, the United States under the Truman Doctrine and Marshall Plan pursued a policy of granting military and economic help to anti-Communist nations. The North Atlantic Treaty, signed in April 1949, was the first step in a series of measures that brought the United States into close military alliance with Western Europe. In Asia, the United States also extended considerable material aid to governments resisting Communist upheavals.

American military commitments and responsibilities of such a vast scope could not fail to have important effects at home as well as abroad. Military control of American foreign policy, as a wide variety of critical observers pointed out, involved not only a sharp break with the American past but also posed a strong threat to peace and democracy. The military's lifelong identification with the use of force and contempt for the workings of diplomacy was viewed in the long run as likely to lead the United States into war. Even if such a contingency were avoided, there was the danger that the almost exclusive reliance on armed power in the conduct of American foreign relations would go far to stifle the workings of democracy at home. Centralization of authority, military control over the economy, and conscription of manpower were looked upon as probable results of a policy of peace through strength.[6]

Opponents of militarism were disturbed to see the armed forces' new role in foreign affairs paralleled by increasing military encroachments into other civilian areas, both public and private. In the important field of atomic energy, for example, military leaders were only barely defeated in their attempt to take control from the hands of the civilian commission headed by David Lilienthal, former chairman of the Tennessee Valley Authority. Even so, the concentration of the work of the commission upon the problem of producing atomic bombs insured a preponderant military influence in the future development of nuclear power.[7]

Over science and industry as a whole the role of the military underwent a dramatic expansion after 1946. On the assumption that modern total war requires a state of continued advance preparation, Congress was persuaded to pass the comprehensive and unprecedented National Security Act of 1947. This act, which provided for the unification of the armed forces and at the same time created the National Security Council to integrate foreign and military policy, had still other features that made possible increasing military control over the civilian economy. Under the terms of the act a series of special boards, both military and civilian, were established with broad authority and ample funds to direct scientific research and to allocate industrial production along military lines.[8] With the close liaison between science and the armed forces, so necessary for war in a technological age, freedom of inquiry for the scientist and the free circulation of scientific ideas were restricted and governed by considerations of military security. It was also doubtful whether a free and competitive economic system could survive the governmental controls dictated by vast military spending.

Military predominance over science and industry extended also into the realm of culture. American higher education, for example, became dependent to a great extent upon military funds. A large proportion of university research activities in the sciences was subsidized by the army and navy. The armed forces also offered attractive scholarships to the better students and greatly expanded the size and activities of their prewar R.O.T.C. program. In the immediate postwar years, veterans under the G.I. aid bill crowded the campus, while a number of military men, led by General Dwight D. Eisenhower as President of Columbia University, gained influential positions in American colleges and universities.[9]

Underlying these specific instances of the extension of military power into civilian fields, and an even greater threat to civil supremacy, was the growing ability of the military to influence both public and Congressional opinion. Flourishing in the atmosphere of perpetual crisis and war hysteria pervading Washington, the military expert with his argument of military necessity usually took first rank at Congressional hearings. Utilizing their new-found prestige, the armed services also conducted effective lobbying campaigns and spent large sums on public relations.[10] Much of the military office's propaganda had as its object the enactment of some system for the compulsory peacetime training of all American youths. Such a measure, whether in the form of military training or a universal service law, was calculated to give the army virtual control of American manpower. This, together with the direction already exercised over industrial production, would bring the United States to the edge of the total mobilization for war so long desired by militarists within and outside the armed services. Faced with all the variety of circumstances in the postwar world that contributed to this end of a 'garrison state,' old-line liberal and pacifist believers in the American antimilitarist tradition were forced to fight a defensive battle. But in the struggle against peacetime conscription, which they regarded as a key issue, their efforts, however futile in other directions, met with some success.

By no means an exclusive criterion of militarist influence within a society, conscription is among the more obvious and important evidences of such influence. In the period after World War II, no other issue attracted more attention from both militarist and antimilitarist spokesmen. Army lobbying and propaganda for peacetime conscription went so far as to attempt to exert pressure upon the President's Advisory Commission on Universal Military Training. A House investigating committee, which included staunch advocates of U.M.T., unanimously reported

> its firm conclusion that, on the basis of the evidence at hand, the War Department, its personnel and civilian employees have gone beyond the limits of their proper duty of providing factual information to the people and the Congress and have engaged in propaganda supported by taxpayers' money to influence legislation now pending before the Congress.[11]

Another example of army propaganda for U.M.T., which escaped general notice, was the elaborate effort of the Selective Service System to provide an account of the historical background of conscription. Under the title, *Military Obligation: The American Tradition*, Selective Service published for the period from 1609 to 1789 facsimile reproductions of every colonial and state law that exacted any measure of military compulsion. By including newly compiled editions of the same statutes the collection was elaborately padded and gave a misleading impression of the extent to which conscription existed in the American colonies.[12]

The opposition to conscription, which was carried on in an atmosphere of official hostility, included such established pacifist groups as the Fellowship of Reconciliation, War Resisters League, National Council for the Prevention of War, and the Society of Friends, as well as a broad range of liberal and antimilitarist opinion drawn from the churches, labor organizations, and educational bodies. In addition to the special anticonscription committees organized within the older peace societies, new groups such as the Post War World Council and the National Council Against Conscription were created with a membership and contributors that included prominent liberals, pacifists, and antimilitarists. The Post War World Council, under the leadership of Norman Thomas, stressed the necessity of complete and universal disarmament, while the National Council Against Conscription sought to co-ordinate the antimilitarist fight against U.M.T. Over the endorsement of a group of prominent citizens headed by Albert Einstein, the Council issued well-documented pamphlets on the militarization of America [13] and also published a semimonthly bulletin, *Conscription News.*

The drive for peacetime military training was a relic of wartime militaristic thinking carried over into the postwar period. In the hope that a satisfactory bill might be enacted before a postwar reaction could set in, a plan for U.M.T. had been presented to Congress as early as 1943. Majority sentiment, however, favored postponement of the question until after the war, and Congress could see little justification for new legislation and new expenditures while the wartime Selective Service law was still in operation. Soon after the close of the war, the campaign for a training law was renewed with emphasis upon the peacetime or nonmilitary benefits of such a system. Although couched in these terms, conscription of any sort continued to be regarded by the American people as a war measure, justifiable only in so far as there was real danger of an impending international conflict. Unable to see any great merit in the conscriptionist argument that universal military training in peacetime and Selective Service in wartime were two different things, the average citizen seemed to feel that there was little point to training unless it carried a presumption of active duty. Unless absolutely necessary, the American people, in accord with their historic attitude, wished to avoid both military training and military service.

As a concrete proposal, it was doubtful that conscription was any more popular with the American people after World War II than it had been previously in American history. The favorable verdict periodically recorded by opinion polls was open to question on grounds that it necessarily presented the issue of U.M.T. as an abstract question cloaked with an aura of preparedness and patriotism — two intangibles on which there was never any popular disagreement or opposition. But, despite the intense pressures in its behalf and the ever-present danger that continued differences with Russia might lead to open conflict, it is significant that Congress preferred to extend the wartime Selective Service law rather than pass a permanent measure for compulsory military training in peacetime. The postwar controversy over a system of peacetime conscription added few new arguments to those already presented on each side of the question in the period of World War I, or again in 1940. The two World War Selective Service laws were generally considered temporary measures. Postwar military training or service, on the other hand, was a long-range program with all sorts of implications for the future. While the proponents of conscription, thinking in terms of peace by force, emphasized the need for a large conscript army to support American commitments under the United Nations, its opponents pointed out the folly of pursuing ideals of peace through the time-honored militarist device of universal compulsory military training or service.

Proposals to abolish conscription aroused little official enthusiasm, either in the United States or abroad. Even though the American people were by no means wholly convinced that U.M.T. was in any sense a peace measure, they were attentive to the argument that it was necessary for national security in a world faced by the threat of war. Opponents of conscription in the United States could no longer count on the automatic support of public opinion. They also had to face the fact that military training and universal service were integral parts of a world-wide trend toward greater regimentation of the individual by authoritarian governments. As a nationalizing device, conscription offered advantages which all modern governments seemed increasingly unwilling to forego. Even England and the United States, the only major powers hitherto without peacetime conscription, adopted it in some form after World War II.

In the United States, Congress turned to a serious consideration of various peacetime conscription schemes in the fall of 1945. That November, the House Committee on Military Affairs began hearings on the May bill calling for a year of training for all youths upon reaching the age of eighteen. Ranged against the favorable testimony of army officers and War Department spokesmen at the hearings was the practically unanimous opposition of representatives of labor, the churches, and the schools. Affirming that educators were two to one against U.M.T., Ralph McDonald, representing the large and influential National Education Association, explained the paradox of the people through their organizations opposing U.M.T., while the Gallup public opinion polls indicated a popular percentage in its favor. The average man, he pointed out, was apathetic and tended to confuse the problem of the defense of the country, which of course he favored, with U.M.T. Thus he automatically voted 'yes' in the opinion polls.[14]

As a result of the widespread critical discussion of the purposes of U.M.T., military men were forced to abandon their extravagant claims for conscription as a health measure or educational device. Shifting their ground, advocates of conscription proposed to secure a limited measure of military training through the device of extending the wartime Selective Service Act. Congressional approval was gained largely as an outcome of the members' concern over mounting international tension in Europe. Opponents of peacetime conscription, on the other hand, charged that a war scare had been used to put across a measure otherwise certain to be defeated. They raised the question of whether the United States was working for peace or adopting conscription in preparation for war.[15]

Selective Service, as a direct means of securing men for the army, was at first little used, although its backers felt that it accomplished its purpose by stimulating volunteering. The extension of the draft law also served to keep the issue of compulsory service or training before the American public until such time as Congress might be persuaded to agree to the permanent peacetime conscription that was at the center of all militaristic thinking and planning. President Truman, an enthusiastic advocate of conscription, co-operated with the drive for a permanent law by appointing in December 1946 a Presidential Advisory Commission on Universal Training. Sometimes mistakenly considered by the public as an impartial scientific committee to study the merits of U.M.T., the commission was rather a body whose members were already wholly convinced of the necessity of such training. In his informal introductory remarks to the newly formed commission, President Truman stressed the desirability of U.M.T. as a disciplinary and educational measure, valuable for instilling a spirit of patriotism in American youth. 'I don't like to think of it as a universal military training program,' the President declared. 'I want it to be a universal training program.'[16]

In broadening the scope of the training to include nonmilitary as well as military service, the President argued that in modern total war security no longer depended solely on the armed forces. But the idea of universal service to the state, which the President urged his Advisory Commission to recommend, was also a totalitarian concept that had been much used by fascist and communist regimes. The Advisory Commission in its report denied the charge of totalitarianism and contended that universal training was no more un-American, militaristic, or compulsory than public education. But the commission's emphasis upon the responsibility of the individual to the state, though fully in accord with European practice, represented a relatively new idea in the United States. Whatever the mutual obligations of the citizen and his government, the American tradition had always been one in which the state was considered the servant, and not the master of the people. The universal service advocated by the Presidential Commission not only contradicted this tradition, but it also envisaged a type of service that, no matter how disguised, was basically for military purposes.[17]

Challenging the whole philosophy on which the report was based, the editors of the *New Republic* asserted that the Presidential Commission had been stampeded by diplomatic events into giving the army and the American Legion all they wanted. Proposed in the context of the Truman Doctrine, the *New Republic* saw U.M.T. as a part of the age-old process of preparation for war leading to war. 'UMT is no call for a stronger UN and a better democracy. It is a call to outworn values that have always led to war and always will. The way to keep America out of war is to keep war out of the world.' [18]

The publication of the Report of the President's Advisory Commission in May 1947 marked the beginnings of a new drive to pass a peacetime conscription law. President Truman hoped to persuade a reluctant Congress to enact such a measure before the temporarily extended Selective Service Act expired in May 1948. By the spring of 1948 the debate on U.M.T. was again in full swing. Meanwhile, Congress continued its investigation of extensive army propaganda in behalf of conscription, and a subcommittee of the House charged that pamphlets had been issued by the army in wholesale numbers at a cost of over a million dollars. The pioneer experimental U.M.T. unit maintained by the army at Knoxville, Tennessee, was found to be a show place calculated to give a misleading impression of the type of training camp the drafted men could expect to find. Army Secretary Kenneth C. Royall admitted the charge of using public funds to sell the American people the idea of military training but, believing U.M.T. desirable, he affirmed that he had 'no apology' to make.[19]

Public indignation at the army's illegal use of its funds for propaganda purposes was comparatively slight. Concerned over the problem of national security in an era of intense international disagreement, the American people seemed less and less disposed to turn down any program sought by the armed services or to question the premises on which military thinking was based. In the existing temper of American public opinion, opponents of U.M.T. faced an uphill struggle. Although the number of volunteers seemed sufficient to meet army needs, there was talk of conscription to meet future threats of war abroad or chaos at home. Nevertheless, church, educational, and labor groups still bitterly contested the claims advanced for U.M.T., and Congress continued reluctant to approve a draft bill.[20] In May 1948, the antimilitarist point of view scored a brief success when the wartime Selective Service Act was allowed to expire. But, a month later, Congress approved another Selective Service Act for two more years. The new draft law was passed in the midst of American alarm over the Russian blockade of Berlin, and after the receipt of what were later shown to have been mistaken army intelligence reports relating to Russian troop movements. Although there was comparatively little debate in Congress while the Selective Service bill was under consideration, a final dramatic filibuster led by Senator Glen H. Taylor of Idaho pointed up the significance of the passage of America's first real peacetime draft law.[21]

The 1948 Selective Service Act, although similar to the wartime law that had already expired, was in reality a temporary two-year peacetime conscription law, later extended and amended, that could be used either as a means of universal military training or as a service measure to expand the regular army. Requiring registration for all youths between the ages of eighteen and twenty-six and a period of twenty-one months of active duty for those inducted into service, it was a measure without precedent in American history. With respect to conscientious objectors, the provisions of the Selective Service Act were similar to those in force during World War II. The limitation of these provisions to the individual 'who by reason of religious training and belief, is conscientiously opposed to war in any form,' excluded from consideration for deferment the objector whose motivation was primarily political and ethical rather than religious. The Act of 1948 further narrowed the grounds for conscientious objection by defining religion as the belief in a Supreme Being. Finally, severe penalties were provided for anyone guilty of advising resistance to the law or of otherwise interfering with the operations of the act.[22]

Prosecution of infringements of the act varied greatly, but there was a small number of absolutists and political objectors who were tried for their open refusal to register. Even more significant, perhaps, were the extremely large numbers who gave only a grudging acceptance to the draft law. Norman Thomas's prediction that many Americans would disobey a peacetime draft was partially borne out as many youths were slow to register or present themselves for induction. Although a threatened campaign of civil disobedience among Negroes was called off, a group of ninety-nine Protestant clergymen called upon the nation to observe 'a day of mourning and repentance' on the eve of the first draft registrations in August 1948.[23]

The prosecution of conscientious objectors who refused to register or report for military service raised again the wartime issue of the individual versus the state. It was especially disheartening for the many liberals and pacifists who sympathized with the C.O.s to have to turn to this new problem before the status of the old World War II objectors had been satisfactorily settled. After the war, all objectors had gradually been released from the Civilian Public Service camps and federal penitentiaries. While the men from C.P.S. were able to resume their normal life, the C.O. who had been in prison was classed as a felon and subject to the permanent loss of his civil rights. An organized protest movement in behalf of the prison C.O.s finally persuaded President Truman to appoint a special Presidential Amnesty Board headed by former Supreme Court Justice Owen J. Roberts. On the basis of this board's findings, the President in December 1947 granted Christmas Eve executive pardons to 1,523 Selective Service Act violators. These pardons covered only a small proportion of the over fifteen thousand convicted draft violators and also included only a minority of the six thousand men considered by the Justice Department as conscientious or religious objectors.[24]

Disappointed in their failure to gain a more liberal Presidential pardon policy, the peace groups, with considerable outside support from a number of prominent citizens, continued to campaign for a general amnesty for all conscientious objectors.[25] Although these pleas attracted the editorial support of a significant section of the nation's press, by 1949 the idea of an amnesty for World

War II conscientious objectors was coming into conflict with the rising war temper of the country. In the midst of renewed government prosecution for violations of the peacetime draft act there was little likelihood of a general amnesty. The peace societies accordingly turned to the problem of helping the new conscientious objectors, who were again being sent to federal prisons for their infringements of the Selective Service Act of 1948.

American conscription and postwar rearmament were part of a general world-wide armaments race in which the United States and the Soviet Union exercised military leadership over two rival blocs of nations. With the countries on each opposing side insisting that their expanded military establishments were necessary to national security and world peace, the obligation of the United Nations to seek out some means for the regulation and reduction of armaments and armed forces was largely ignored. Although the growing gulf between Russia and the West seemed to preclude any real hope of disarmament, public uneasiness over the specter of atomic warfare helped to keep the disarmament issue from being completely forgotten.

In the United States, official thinking, though by no means unaware of the danger of a war waged with atomic weapons, continued to advance the thesis of preparedness to prevent war. This point of view which, of course, had never won acceptance by pacifists or antimilitarists, was subjected to increasing re-examination as the costs of the United States armaments burden rose and as it appeared that Russia also had been able to produce an atomic bomb. Conservatives, by no means friendly to Soviet Russia, joined liberals and pacifists in voicing a concern over America's military program. Former President Hoover, in an address in the summer of 1949, pointed out that the average citizen must work thirty-five days a year in order to pay the taxes to cover the costs of past or future wars.[26] Later in the year, the Committee for Economic Development, a nonpartisan business group, made public a report attacking the nation's defense program as a threat to individual freedom and civil supremacy in government.[27] The widespread publicity given the C.E.D. Report was paralleled by expressions on the part of thoughtful and influential journalists of concern over United States militarism and arms expenditures.

The reviving American interest in disarmament was brought to the attention of Congress early in 1950 in the important speeches made by Senators Brien McMahon of Connecticut and Millard Tydings of Maryland. Senator McMahon's remarks were inspired by President Truman's decision directing the Atomic Energy Commission to continue its work on the hydrogen bomb, a weapon theoretically without limit in its destructive capacity. Accepting the decision as a necessary substitute for unilateral disarmament, Senator McMahon nevertheless argued that the United States must take the lead in a new moral crusade for peace and disarmament. The only alternative, he warned, was an intensification of the cold war and a degree of military spending that would add significantly and perhaps fatally to the 'restrictions on freedom already brought about by the atomic bomb and by its pressures upon us to accept loyalty checks, espionage counter measures, and widening areas of official secrecy.' [28]

Going beyond Senator McMahon, who called for a system of international inspection to outlaw atomic and hydrogen bombs, Senator Tydings stressed the need for 'disarmament all the way down the line to rifles.' Otherwise, the Senator pointed out, just as soon as a war started with conventional weapons, international inspection would cease, and each belligerent would immediately resume building atomic or hydrogen bombs. Noting that the United States was already spending, out of a total budget of forty-two billion dollars, some thirty billions for war — past, present, or future — Senator Tydings again urged the President to heed his repeated resolutions calling for a disarmament conference. Assailing the State Department for its 'mountainous . . . defeatism' in committing the United States to a policy of continued cold war with Russia, Tydings warned that the significance of Dr. Albert Einstein's remark that 'Annihilation of any life on earth is within the range of technical possibilities' had been overlooked by American policy-makers. 'Like Nero,' he concluded, 'we seem to show a willingness to fiddle while our world burns.' [29]

Encouraged by the growing recognition in Congress and throughout the country of the need for some check on militarism and the race to rearm, the peace forces in the United States sought to arouse popular support for the idea of a disarmament conference with Russia. The Society of Friends published for a wide audience their conclusions regarding the sources of disagreement between the United States and Russia. Confident that war need not be inevitable, the Friends questioned the assumption of security through competitive rearmament.[30] The National Council against Conscription, continuing to bring together a numerous body of pacifists and liberals, began a pamphlet series on disarmament and also published a detailed historical survey, *America Russia and the Bomb*.[31]

By the spring of 1950, leaders of American foreign policy were showing a new concern over charges of United States militarism. John Foster Dulles, adviser to the State Department and subsequently Secretary of State, in his book *War or Peace* pointed out that while 'Military needs are important, and a strong military establishment is a necessity . . . we shall fail in our search for peace, security, and justice unless our policies, in reality and also in appearance, give priority to the hopes and aspirations for peace of the peoples of the world.' Afraid that 'As a result of excessive zeal to give the military whatever they professionally suggest, we have let it appear that we have gone militaristic,' Dulles urged the United States not to yield its moral birthright as a peaceloving and antimilitaristic nation.[32]

In his Memorial Day address at Arlington National Cemetery, General George C. Marshall emphasized the need for the United States to lead the way to world peace through the United Nations. Opposed to a policy of weakness as inviting aggression, Marshall warned that 'we should not place complete dependence on military and material power.'[33] Walter Lippmann saw Marshall's words as an attempt to counteract the growing feeling that 'the Administration's foreign policy has during the past year created the impression here and abroad that it places virtually complete dependence on military and material power.' Believing that the United States seriously weakened itself in world opinion 'by explaining that everything we do, every decision we take, is based on a strategical calculation about war,' Lippmann concluded: 'This damnable obsession has gotten to the point where we can hardly send milk to babies abroad without explaining that this is an important action in our cold war with Russian communism.'[34]

Before this movement for disarmament could achieve any tangible results, war broke out in Korea and other parts of the Far East. The United States decision to defend South Korea resulted in new calls for combat troops and a defense budget approximating that of the World War II years. In the 1950s the armed forces exceeded three million men, with half that number stationed abroad in hundreds of bases. Congress, upset over inadequacies in the American military machine despite the fifty billion dollars already spent in the four years of the cold war, approved new annual appropriations to almost that amount for each single year throughout the early '50s. After the Korean War, it passed a special law to permit General George C. Marshall to become Secretary of Defense, making an exception to the rule that a civilian secretary should be over the armed services. Marshall, as well as Generals MacArthur and Eisenhower, was again discussed as a possible nominee for the Presidency, and in 1952 Dwight D. Eisenhower, despite his refusals four years earlier, was elected to the nation's highest office.

Top professional soldiers were often less militaristic than military-minded civilians, and Eisenhower's victory at the polls was due as much as anything to public feeling that he could terminate the unpopular Korean War. Though this was accomplished by the truce agreement of 1953, the heavy costs of the Korean struggle added to those of World War II, and the continued cold war in Asia and Europe, gave the American people little hope of any sudden return to real peacetime modes of living. Whether American democracy would be able indefinitely to survive a perpetual war economy or garrison-type state was an unanswered question. But peace or war, dictatorship or democracy, it was difficult to believe that the society of the future would be governed by the antimilitarist traditions that had guided three centuries of American history. Even if such a prospect were not accepted as evidence of a decline in American and world civilization, it pointed to one of the grave problems and tragedies of our time. Two world wars, instead of lessening the dangers of militarism and war, had only brought the Western world closer to catastrophe.

Speculation over the fate of civilization was a grim task that had increasingly absorbed the attentions of philosophers and historians since the beginnings of the twentieth century. The gloomy pictures of the future set forth in the period of the First World War by such philosophic historians as Henry Adams in the United States and Oswald Spengler in Germany were repeated in the 1930s in the midst of depression and impending war. Lewis Mumford, in his widely read *Technics and Civilization,* noted Herbert Spencer's prediction of a coming world regression toward militarism and imperialism. In similar fashion, Mumford saw Western society 'relapsing at critical points into pre-civilized modes of thought, feeling, and action because it has acquiesced too easily in the dehumanization of society through capitalist exploitation and military conquest.' [35] The machine, instead of rendering militarism archaic, had failed to provide properly for human activity and had thus opened the way for a return to barbarism through the medium of militarism. Karl Mannheim, the German sociologist, viewed society as moving through the stages of crisis, dictatorship, and war, or from unorganized insecurity into an organized insecurity directed along militarist lines.[36]

Also during the 'thirties Arnold Toynbee, the most scholarly of the philosopher-historians, completed the first six volumes of his monumental *A Study of History.* Challenging the militarist thesis of the efficacy of armaments and war, Toynbee demonstrated that, historically, military victory was self-defeating with the vanquished countries only stimulated to still greater military efforts in order to be able to fight again in an attempt to reverse the verdict of their late defeat. Toynbee also questioned the assumption that democracies were automatically more peace-loving or antimilitaristic than other forms of government. Conscription, for example, had developed along with democracy, and the 'compulsory recruitment of manpower for "cannon-fodder," which autocracies do not lightly attempt, becomes practicable in a democratic community when it is fighting a national war in a popular cause.' Toynbee, moreover found in 'the suicidalness of militarism' by far the commonest cause of the breakdowns of civilizations.[37] Although first published in the 1930s, *A Study of History* enjoyed its greatest popularity in the United States in the condensed one-volume edition made available after the war. Disturbed at the mounting menace of militarism among living nations, Toynbee authorized a second selection from his original work, and in 1950 those portions of the *Study* that were devoted especially to an analysis of the disastrous effects of militarism and war upon civilization were published in the United States.[38] Though impressed by Toynbee's emphasis upon the need of Christian idealism to supplant the evils of war and militarism if civilization were to be saved, Americans were reluctant to apply his analysis of militarism to the postwar scene.

Between the two World Wars thoughtful American scholars had alluded to the danger that the United States, with the passing of the frontier and the end of the relative isolation of the nineteenth century, might become an aggressive imperialist and militarist power. While Frederick Jackson Turner, the historian of the frontier, felt it 'inconceivable that we should follow the evil path of Europe and place our reliance upon triumphant force,' his associate Frederic Logan Paxson posed the problem of whether the United States would turn to true internationalism, or: 'Shall we, in the foreign field, develop our nationality, take advantage of our growing wealth, and become the world menace of the next century, — for no imperial power has ever stopped itself thus far. . . .'[39] Writing after American entrance into the war, Charles A. Beard, the leading American philosophic historian, raised the question of whether the United States would embrace the militarism of the totalitarian states of Europe and resort to a war economy to avert a postwar depression.[40]

Thus by mid-century, the American people faced a future clouded with uncertainty. The age of the common man seemed limited in its achievement to the guarantee of temporary material comforts, while the progress of science had culminated in the hydrogen bomb. Everywhere there was the overshadowing specter of war and the tremendous reality of vast military establishments. The new-style, perpetual mobilization for war made all the more imperative the return of that general world peace which alone could restore any vestige of normal civil life. Only in such an atmosphere could the American tradition of antimilitarism, peace, and democracy flourish and continue to be a vital, living force for the future.

Bibliographical Comment

MATERIALS USED in writing this volume are cited in detail in the
NOTES. They include a wide range of sources, both official and unof-
ficial. In addition to the standard bibliographical guides, particular
mention should be made of the specialized lists of references, dealing with military subjects, compiled by the Division of Bibliography
of the Library of Congress. Also useful are the similar-type lists issued by the Carnegie Endowment for International Peace. The
Social Science Research Council has sponsored the publication
of two valuable works, covering recent research materials: *Civil-
Military Relations: Bibliographical Notes on Administrative Problems of Civilian Mobilization* (Chicago: Public Administration
Service, 1940); and *Civil-Military Relations: An Annotated Bibliography 1940–1952* (New York: Columbia Univ. Press, 1954).

Records of most of the pacifist and antimilitarist organizations,
as well as other pertinent manuscript materials, are conveniently
brought together in the Swarthmore College Peace Collection
(S.C.P.C.). A *Guide* to the Collection was published in 1947.
Additional important manuscript data and correspondence, shed-
ding light on American antimilitarism since the First World War,
may be found in the Oswald Garrison Villard Papers in the Houghton Library of Harvard University, and in the Amos Pinchot
Papers in the Manuscripts Division of the Library of Congress.

For background the best works are Alfred Vagts, *A History of Militarism* (New York: Norton, 1937), and Merle Curti, *Peace or War: The American Struggle, 1636–1936* (New York: Norton, 1936). There are a number of volumes on the history of American military and naval policy, but superior to any of them are Howard White, *Executive Influence in Determining Military Policy in the United States* (Urbana: Univ. of Illinois, 1925), and Harold and Margaret Sprout, *The Rise of American Naval Power* (Princeton: Princeton Univ. Press, 1939). Louis Smith, *American Democracy and Military Power* (Chicago: Univ. of Chicago Press, 1951), is an excellent study of administrative and constitutional problems. Of the general histories, John Bach McMaster, *A History of the People of the United States* (New York: Appleton, 1907–1913), devotes the most attention to antimilitarism and is also useful as a guide to public opinion. The published records of the United States government, and especially the Congressional debates and Hearings are, of course, invaluable.

Notes

Introduction

1 Hans Speier, 'Militarism in the Eighteenth Century,' *Social Research,* III (Aug. 1936), 304–36.

2 C. B. Rogers, *The Spirit of Revolution in 1789* (Princeton, 1949), 125–6. See also John U. Nef, *War and Human Progress* (Cambridge, Mass., 1950), 312–15.
The relationship between the rise of democracy and conscript armies is pointed out in S. B. McKinley, *Democracy and Military Power* (New York, 1934); Hoffman Nickerson, *The Armed Horde* (New York, 1942).

3 Alfred Vagts, *A History of Militarism* (New York, 1937), 15, and Introd.

4 Harold Laski, *Liberty in the Modern State* (New York, 1949), 20. See also A. T. Lauterbach, 'Militarism in the Western World,' *Journal of the History of Ideas,* v (Oct. 1944), 446–78.

Chapter I

1 G. M. Trevelyan, *England under the Stuarts* (London, 1925), 143; C. M. Clode, *The Military Forces of the Crown* (London, 1869), I, 1, 16–21, 31ff.

2 William Haller and Godfrey Davies (eds.), *The Leveller Tracts* (New York, 1944), 324, 327; S. R. Gardiner (ed.), *The Constitutional Documents of the Puritan Revolution* (Oxford, 1906), 368.

3 W. E. H. Lecky, *A History of England in the Eighteenth Century* (New York, 1887–90), I, 550ff.; J. S. Omond, *Parliament and the Army* (Cambridge, 1933), chaps. 1–2; E. A. Miller, 'Some Arguments Used by English Pamphleteers, 1697–1700, concerning a Standing Army,' *Journal of Modern History,* XVIII (Dec. 1946), 306–13.

4 Lecky, *History of England,* II, 533.

5 Allen French, 'The Arms and Military Training of Our Colonizing Ancestors,' Massachusetts Historical Society *Proceedings,* LXVII (1941–44), 3–21.

6 H. L. Osgood, *The American Colonies in the Seventeenth Century* (New York, 1904-7), I, 496-8, 506.

7 M. E. Hirst, *The Quakers in Peace and War* (New York, 1923), chap. 13; Isaac Sharpless, *A Quaker Experiment in Government* (Phil., 1898), chap. 7.

8 E. I. McCormac, *Colonial Opposition to Imperial Authority* (Berkeley, 1911); L. H. Gipson, *The British Empire before the American Revolution* (Caldwell, Idaho, and New York, 1936-54), VII, 32-4, 44-5, 69-70, 140ff.

9 C. E. Carter, 'The Significance of the Military Office in America,' *American Historical Review*, XXVIII (Apr. 1923), 476.

10 *Considerations on the Propriety of Imposing Taxes in the British Colonies* (North America, [1766]), 35-6.

11 To Richard Jackson, 10 June 1768, Massachusetts Historical Society *Collections*, 5th ser., IX (1885), 288.

12 To Samuel Cooper, 8 June 1770, *Writings* (A. H. Smyth, ed., New York, 1905-7), V, 259; see also ibid. VI, 334-5.

13 Quoted in T. C. Hansard (ed.), *The Parliamentary History of England* (London, 1813), XVI, 987.

14 O. M. Dickerson, *Boston under Military Rule* (Boston, 1936), xi.

15 *Writings* (H. A. Cushing, ed., New York, 1904-8), I, 257, 264-5.

16 Ibid. I, 340-42, II, 79, 362.

17 Ibid. III, 104.

18 *Orations Delivered at the Request of the Inhabitants of the Town of Boston* (Boston, 1807), 6, 19, 38, 47-8, 110, 180.

19 *Journals of the Continental Congress* (Wash., 1904-37), I, 70, 73, 116.

20 Ibid. II, 188-9. See also F. V. Greene, *The Revolutionary War* (New York, 1911), 283ff.

21 E. C. Burnett (ed.), *Letters of Members of the Continental Congress* (Wash., 1921-36), I, 360-61.

22 F. N. Thorpe (comp.), *The Federal and State Constitutions* (Wash., 1909), V, 3083.

23 Ibid. VII, 3814, V, 2637, IV, 2455.

24 *Journals Cont. Cong.*, XI, 640, 649, 654.

25 Merrill Jensen, *The Articles of Confederation* (Madison, 1948), 194.

26 *Writings* (P. L. Ford, ed., New York, 1892-9), II, 129; Jonathan Smith, 'How Massachusetts Raised Her Troops in the Revolution,' Massachusetts Historical Society *Proceedings*, LV (1921-2), 352ff.

27 Allen Bowman, *The Morale of the American Revolutionary Army* (Wash., 1943), 30ff., 62ff.; L. C. Hatch, *The Administration of the American Revolutionary Army* (New York, 1904), 51, and chap. 7.

28 M. B. Macmillan, *The War Governors in the American Revolution* (New York, 1943), 35, and chap. 8; John C. Miller, *Triumph of Freedom* (Boston, 1948), 233ff.

29 *Writings* (J. C. Fitzpatrick, ed., Wash., 1931-44), VI, 4-7, 106-16.

30 E. C. Burnett, *The Continental Congress* (New York, 1941), 233; Burnett, *Letters*, II, vii-viii, 262.

31 Ibid. II, 263, 269.

32 Ibid. III, 99ff., 110, 132ff., v, xii; Washington, *Writings* (Fitzpatrick), XI, 291; *Journals Cont. Cong.*, X, 190–203, XVI, 36–7.

Chapter II

1 For an excellent account of 'the politics of demobilization,' see Merrill Jensen, *The New Nation* (New York, 1950), 67–84.

2 Hamilton to Washington, 25 March 1783, in Burnett, *Letters*, VII, 102–3; *Journals Cont. Cong.*, XXV, 607.

3 W. H. Glasson, *Federal Military Pensions* (New York, 1918), 20–34; Hatch, *American Revolutionary Army*, chap. 5.

4 George Greene, *The Life of Nathanael Greene* (New York, 1867–71), III, 470–72. See also contemporary pamphlet signed Tullius, *Three Letters Addressed to the Public* (Phil., 1783), 12–14.

5 Louise Dunbar, *A Study of 'Monarchical' Tendencies in the United States* (Urbana, 1922), chap. 3; John Fiske, *The Critical Period* (Boston, 1890), 112ff.; Hatch, *American Revolutionary Army*, chap. 9.

6 *Journals Cont. Cong.*, XXIV, 93ff., 207–10, 291ff., XXV, 926, 938. See also Glasson, *Federal Military Pensions*, 41ff.; J. B. McMaster, *A History of the People of the United States* (New York, 1907–13), I, 176ff.

7 Washington, *Writings* (Fitzpatrick), XXVII, 225; *Journals Cont. Cong.*, XXV, 837–8.

8 *Writings* (Fitzpatrick), XXVI, 374ff., 483ff.; Burnett, *Letters*, VII, xxvii.

9 Madison to Edmond Randolph, 17 June 1783, *Writings* (G. Hunt, ed., New York, 1900–1910), I, 478–9; Monroe to Lee, 16 Dec. 1783, *Writings* (S. M. Hamilton, ed., New York, 1898–1903), I, 23; Lee to Monroe, 5 Jan. 1784, *Letters* (J. C. Ballagh, ed., New York, 1911–14), II, 287; *Journals Cont. Cong.*, XXV, 722–25, 736–41.

10 Ibid. XXVII, 428–35, 512ff., 539–40. See also E. B. Wesley, "The Military Policy of the Critical Period,' *Coast Artillery Journal*, LXVIII (Apr., 1928), 281–90.

11 11 Aug. 1786, *Writings* (Memorial Edition, Wash., 1904), V, 386.

12 To Benjamin Vaughan, 14 March 1785, *Writings* (Smyth), IX, 296–8; To Jane Mecom, 20 Sept. 1787, ibid. IX, 612–13.

13 Edgar E. Hume, 'Early Opposition to the Cincinnati,' *Americana*, XXX (1936), 597–638; W. E. Davies, 'The Society of the Cincinnati in New England,' *William and Mary Quarterly*, 3rd ser., V (Jan. 1948), 3–25; John Marshall, *The Life of George Washington* (Phil., 1804–7), V, 24ff.; McMaster, *History*, I, 167ff.

14 *Considerations on the Society or Order of Cincinnati* (Phil., [1783]), 8.

15 Jefferson to Washington, 16 Apr. 1784, *Papers of Thomas Jefferson* (J. P. Boyd, ed., Princeton, 1950–   ), VII, 105–10; Washington, *Writings* (Fitzpatrick), XXIX, 222–3.

16 Edgar E. Hume, *General Washington's Correspondence concerning the Society of the Cincinnati* (Baltimore, 1941), 152–4, 170–74; 'Journal of the General Meeting of the Cincinnati in 1784 by Major Winthrop Sargent,' Historical Society of Pennsylvania *Memoirs* (Phil., 1858), VI, 79ff.; Hume, 'Early Opposition,' loc. cit. 612–13.

17 Max Farrand (ed.), *The Records of the Federal Convention of 1787* (New Haven, 1911), I, 25.

18 Ibid. I, 165, 256, 285, II, 8–9; Charles Warren, *The Making of the Constitution* (Boston, 1928), 171–2.

19   Farrand, *Records*, II, 318–19.

20   Ibid. I, 465.

21   Ibid. II, 329–30.

22   Ibid. II, 388. Debate on the militia is summarized conveniently in J. B. Scott, *The Militia* (Wash., 1917), 28–38.

23   Farrand, *Records*, II, 334–35, 341, 505, 508.

24   Warren, *Making the Constitution*, 704–5.

25   J. B. McMaster and F. D. Stone (eds.), *Pennsylvania and the Federal Constitution* ([Phil., 1888]), 480–81; Jonathan Elliot, *The Debates in the Several State Conventions on the Adoption of the Federal Constitution* (Wash., 1836), II, 542ff.

26   Ibid. II, 136–7; S. B. Harding, *The Contest over the Ratification of the Federal Constitution in the State of Massachusetts* (New York, 1896), 25, 30, 36, 53, 64.

27   Elliot, *Debates*, I, 326–30, 335–6, II, 406, IV, 244.

28   *Observations . . . in a Number of Letters from the Federal Farmer to the Republican* ([New York], 1787), 15ff., 23–4.

29   Elliot, *Debates*, III, 47–53, 169, 379–85.

30   Ibid. III, 659–60.

31   Jefferson to Madison, 20 Dec. 1787, and 31 July 1788, *Writings* (Ford), IV, 476, V, 47.

32   *Annals of Congress*, 1 Cong., 1 Sess., 434, 749–51. See also E. B. Greene, *Religion and the State* (New York, 1941), 137–8.

33   *The Federalist*, Nos. VIII, XVI, XXV–XXVII (H. C. Lodge, ed., New York, 1902), 39ff., 91ff., 146ff.

34   Nos. XXIV, XXVIII–XXIX, ibid. 141ff., 163ff.

35   No. XLI, ibid. 251.

36   Charles Beard, *The Republic* (New York, 1943), 21.

Chapter III

1   John M. Palmer, *Washington Lincoln Wilson* (Garden City, 1930), Part I; and his *America in Arms* (New Haven, 1941), chaps. 1–2.

2   *American State Papers, Military Affairs* (Wash., 1832–61), I, 7. Useful at this and many subsequent points is Howard White, *Executive Influence in Determining Military Policy in the United States* (Urbana, 1925), chap. 6.

3   *American State Papers, Military Affairs*, I, 8, 11.

4   *Annals of Congress*, 1 Cong., 2 Sess., 1818–24; 2 Cong., 1 Sess., 112, 205, 208.

5   Act of May 8, 1792, *U.S. Statutes at Large*, I, 271–4; Palmer, *America in Arms*, 51; White, *Executive Influence*, 128–35.

6   James Monaghan, 'Opposition to Involuntary Military Service in the United States' (MS. M.A. thesis, Univ. Pennsylvania, 1918), summarizes the state laws.

7   White, *Executive Influence*, 98–9.

8   *The Journal of William Maclay* (Charles Beard, ed., New York, 1927), 227, 234.

9   Ibid. 233; J. D. Richardson (comp.), *A Compilation of the Messages and*

Papers of the Presidents (Wash., 1896–9), I, 104. See also James R. Jacobs, *The Beginnings of the United States Army* (Princeton, 1947), 50–51.

10 *Annals of Congress,* 2 Cong., 1 Sess., 328, 337ff.

11 To Archibald Stuart, 14 March 1792, *Writings* (Ford), V, 454.

12 White, *Executive Influence,* 102.

13 *Annals of Congress,* 3 Cong., 1 Sess., 433ff.

14 Madison, *Writings* (Hunt), VI, 215–19; Monroe, *Writings* (Hamilton), I, 286–7, 297.

15 *Annals of Congress,* 4 Cong., 1 Sess., 1418–21.

16 Mifflin to Washington, 5 Aug. 1794, *Pennsylvania Archives,* 2nd ser. (Harrisburg, 1890), IV, 88, 91.

17 *Writings* (Fitzpatrick), XXXVI, 6. See also Leonard White, *The Federalists* (New York, 1948), 150ff.

18 To James Monroe, 4 Dec. 1794, *Writings* (Hunt), VI, 221.

19 William Findley, *History of the Insurrection* (Phil., 1796), 143. See also McMaster, *History,* II, 190–203; L. D. Baldwin, *Whiskey Rebels* (Pittsburgh, 1939), chap. 12.

20 *Writings* (Fitzpatrick), XXXIV, 159–60.

21 Richardson, *Messages and Papers,* I, 216.

22 E. P. Link, *Democratic-Republican Societies* (New York, 1942), 177ff.

23 Harold and Margaret Sprout, *The Rise of American Naval Power* (Princeton, 1939), 38ff. This work is valuable at all points touching on naval policy.

24 D. R. Anderson, *William Branch Giles* (Menasha, Wisc., 1914), 73; *Annals of Congress,* 5 Cong., 3 Sess., 2870. See also Monroe to Jefferson, 4 May 1798, *Writings* (Hamilton), III, 120.

25 White, *Executive Influence,* 154ff.

26 *Time-Piece and Literary Companion,* 1 (9 June 1797), 155.

27 *Annals of Congress,* 5 Cong., 2 Sess., 1525ff., 1634, 1640–41, 1650ff., 1754; 5 Cong., 3 Sess., 3022ff. See also Thomas Cooper, *Political Essays* (Phil., 1800), 28–9.

28 To James McHenry, 22 Oct. 1798, *Works* (C. F. Adams, ed., Boston, 1850–56), VIII, 613. See also Edward Channing, *A History of the United States* (New York, 1905–25), IV, 179, 190–200; Gilbert Chinard, *Honest John Adams* (Boston, 1933), 278ff., 293ff.; Claude Bowers, *Jefferson and Hamilton* (Boston, 1925), chap. 18.

29 *Annals of Congress,* 6 Cong., 1 Sess., 247ff., 298.

30 *Works* (C. F. Adams), IX, 596, X, 113.

31 *Essays Literary Moral and Philosophical* (Phil., 1798), 183–8. Although Rush's Plan was first published obscurely in Benjamin Banneker's *Almanack for 1793* (Phil., 1792), it was little known until included among the *Essays*. See *Letters of Benjamin Rush* (L. H. Butterfield, ed., Princeton, 1951), I, 542, fn. 6.

Chapter IV

1 Jefferson to Madison, 6 Sept. 1789, *Writings* (Mem. Ed.), VII, 461.

2 To Samuel Adams, 26 Feb. 1800, *Writings* (Ford), VII, 426. L. M. Sears, *Jefferson and the Embargo* (Durham, 1927), 5–25, contains a good summary of Jefferson's views.

3 To Elbridge Gerry, 26 Jan. 1799, *Writings* (Ford), VII, 327–8.

4 Richardson, *Messages and Papers*, I, 321–4. See also Jefferson's first annual message to Congress, 8 Dec. 1801, ibid. I, 329; and his letter to Thomas Paine, 18 March 1801, *Writings* (Mem. Ed.), X, 223–5; John P. Foley, *The Jefferson Cyclopedia* (New York, 1900), 54–5.

5 Ibid. 550–51; *Writings* (Mem. Ed.), X, 365–6; Richardson, *Messages and Papers*, I, 382–8.

6 See, for example, Sidney Forman, 'Thomas Jefferson on Universal Military Training,' *Military Affairs*, XI (Fall 1947), 177–8.

7 Henry Adams, *History of the United States* (New York, 1890–91), I, 431, 445; Sears, *Jefferson and the Embargo*, 4, 18; Sprout, *Rise of American Naval Power*, 53.

8 *Annals of Congress*, 9 Cong., 1 Sess., 555ff.; 9 Cong., 2 Sess., 362ff., 389, 489, 598. Brief summaries of some of the key debates in Congress may be found in E. S. Bates, *The Story of Congress* (New York, 1936).

9 *Annals of Congress*, 10 Cong., 1 Sess., 834ff., 1136, 1169.

10 Richardson, *Messages and Papers*, I, 410.

11 McMaster, *History*, III, 327ff.

12 *Annals of Congress*, 11 Cong., 1 Sess., 61ff., James R. Jacobs, *Tarnished Warrior* (New York, 1938), chap. 10; Act of June 28, 1809, *U.S. Statutes at Large*, II, 552.

13 *Annals of Congress*, 12 Cong., 1 Sess., 832ff.; 876, 999; Sprout, *Rise of American Naval Power*, 68–70.

14 *Annals of Congress*, 12 Cong., 1 Sess., 45–6, 107ff. See also J. W. Pratt, *Expansionists of 1812* (New York, 1925), 144ff.; Henry Adams, *History*, VI, 147ff.

15 *Annals of Congress*, 12 Cong., 1 Sess., 422, 441–2, 447, 450–55.

16 McMaster, *History*, III, 438; White, *Executive Policy*, 21, 173–6.

17 *Annals of Congress*, 12 Cong., 1 Sess., 297, 1637ff., Appendix 2196ff.

18 Fisher Ames, *Works* (Boston, 1854), II, 382.

19 To Thomas McKean, 21 June 1812, *Works* (C. F. Adams), X, 17.

20 'Address,' *Niles' Weekly Register*, II (29 Aug. 1812), 417–19.

21 *Proceedings of a Convention of Delegates* (Worcester, 1812), 19–20. See also McMaster, *History*, III, 551–2; H. P. Prentiss, 'Timothy Pickering,' *Essex Institute Historical Collections*, LXX (Apr. 1934), 105–46.

22 *American State Papers, Military Affairs*, I, 324, 604–23; *Annals of Congress*, 13 Cong., 3 Sess., Appendix 1744–95; McMaster, *History*, V, 407–8.

23 *Annals of Congress*, 12 Cong., 2 Sess., 549, 619, 629–31, 649, 681, 781ff.

24 *American State Papers, Military Affairs*, I, 514–19. See also Monroe to Madison, Dec. 1813, *Writings* (Hamilton), V, 275–77.

25 18 June 1813, *Writings* (Mem. Ed.), XIII, 261. See also Jefferson's letters, ibid. XII, 365–9, XIV, 184–6, 207, 227, 242, and *Writings* (Ford), IX, 484–5.

26 To Correa de Serra, 27 Dec. 1814, *Writings* (Mem. Ed.), XIV, 221–5. For an important expression of traditional Jeffersonian antimilitarism at this time, see John Taylor, *An Inquiry into the Principles and Policy of the Government* (Fredericksburg, Va., 1814), 175–84.

27 *Annals of Congress*, 13 Cong., 3 Sess., 73, 79–80, 100.

28 Webster's unpublished speech on the conscription bill is printed in C. H. Van Tyne, *The Letters of Daniel Webster* (New York, 1902), 56–68. See also G. T. Curtis, *Life of Daniel Webster* (New York, 1870), I, 138–9; Henry Adams, *History*, VIII, 269ff.

29 *Annals of Congress,* 13 Cong., 3 Sess., 775–6, 782. See also the detailed analysis in J. F. Leach, *Conscription in the United States* (Rutland, Vt., [1952]), chaps. 2–7.

30 *Niles' Weekly Register,* VII, Supplement 106–8. See also J. T. Adams, *New England in the Republic* (Boston, 1926), 286–7; McMaster, *History*, IV, 240ff.

31 John T. Horton, *James Kent* (New York, 1939), 237ff.

32 *The Proceedings of a Convention of Delegates* (Hartford, 1815), 11, and *passim.*

33 Theodore Dwight, *History of the Hartford Convention* (New York, 1833), 332.

Chapter V

1 To Matthew Lyon, 7 May 1816, *Writings* (Henry Adams, ed., Phil., 1879), I, 700.

2 *Forty Years of American Life* (London, 1864), I, 39, 63.

3 *History*, IX, 226–7.

4 Sprout, *Rise of American Naval Power*, 89–92.

5 *Annals of Congress,* 16 Cong., 1 Sess., 2142; Sprout, *Rise of American Naval Power*, 97.

6 E. B. Wesley, *Guarding the Frontier* (Minneapolis, 1935), 65.

7 *Annals of Congress,* 14 Cong., 1 Sess., 829ff.; Reports of 1818 and 1820 in *American State Papers, Military Affairs*, I, 779–82, II, 188–98. See also Calhoun, *Works* (R. K. Crallé, ed., New York, 1851–6), V, 25–40, 80–93.

8 29 Apr. 1821, *Correspondence of John C. Calhoun* (J. F. Jameson, ed.), Annual Report, Am. Hist. Assoc. 1899 (Wash., 1900), II, 185.

9 *Annals of Congress,* 14 Cong., 2 Sess., 845; 15 Cong., 2 Sess., Appendix 2401–8; *American State Papers, Military Affairs*, I, 642–4, 663–6; Dorothy Goebel, *William Henry Harrison* (Indianapolis, 1926), 214–19.

10 *Annals of Congress,* 15 Cong., 2 Sess., 549; 17 Cong., 2 Sess., 565.

11 William H. Sumner, *An Inquiry into the Importance of the Militia* (Boston, 1823), 69–70, and *passim*. See also Sumner's *A Paper on the Militia* (Wash., 1833).

12 *Annals of Congress,* 16 Cong., 2 Sess., 771ff., 792–4.

13 W. H. Channing (ed.), *Memoir of William Ellery Channing* (Boston, 1848), I, 329.

14 'War,' *Works* (Boston, 1855), III, 35–7.

15 *Friend of Peace,* II, (1821), 14–22.

16 H. T. Mook, 'Training Day in New England,' *New England Quarterly,* XI, (Dec. 1938), 675–97; Everett Dick, *The Dixie Frontier* (New York, 1948), chap. 25.

17 *Niles' Weekly Register,* XI (30 Nov. 1816), 211–15. See also W. F. Galpin, *Pioneering for Peace* (Syracuse, 1933), 5.

18 *A Declaration of the Society of People Commonly Called Shakers* (Albany, 1815), 15.

19   C. Z. Lincoln (ed.), *Messages from the Governors* (Albany, 1909), III, 84–5.

20   John R. Commons *et al.* (eds.), *A Documentary History of American Industrial Society* (Cleveland, 1909–10), V, 29, 120, 160–61; Commons *et al.*, *History of Labour* (New York, 1926), I, 180, 221–2, 281–2; *Working Man's Advocate*, IV (5 Jan. 1833), 1.

21   Commons, *History of Labour*, I, 296, 329–30.

22   Joseph Story, *Commentaries on the Constitution* (Boston, 1833), III, 746, and chap. 21.

23   Sidney Forman, *West Point* (New York, 1950), 61ff.

24   *American State Papers, Military Affairs*, II, 5ff., 21–2, 30, 138–9.

25   *Annals of Congress*, 16 Cong., 1 Sess., 1627, 1630–32.

26   *Works* (C. F. Adams), X, 201–4, 419–20.

27   J. Q. Adams, *Memoirs* (C. F. Adams, ed., Phil., 1874–7), VII, 214–15.

28   *American State Papers, Military Affairs*, V, 307, VII, 89; *Register of Debates*, 24 Cong., 1 Sess., 4569–76; 'Military Academy,' *House Report No. 303*, 24 Cong., 2 Sess., 14ff., 31.

29   *Congressional Globe*, 27 Cong., 2 Sess., Appendix 442–4; 28 Cong., 1 Sess., 205, 272–4, 323–4, 357, 473–4, 478; *North American Review*, LVII (Oct. 1843), 287.

30   *Congressional Globe*, 29 Cong., 1 Sess., 806, and Appendix 585.

31   Ibid. 31 Cong., 1 Sess., 1450ff., 1781; T. H. Benton, *Thirty Years View* (New York, 1854–6), I, 182–6, 638–41, II, 466–8.

32   *Oeuvres de Condorcet* (Paris, 1847), VIII, 27–8.

33   Isaac Candler, *A Summary View of America* (London, 1824), 498. See also Isaac Holmes, *An Account of the United States* (London, [1823]), 118; James Stuart, *Three Years in North America* (Edinburgh, 1833), I, 152–3; Henry Tudor, *Narrative of a Tour in North America* (London, 1834), I, 132; Frederick von Raumer, *America and the American People* (New York, 1846), 226–7.
Useful guides to the travel literature are Jane Mesick, *The English Traveller in America* (New York, 1922), 195–6; W. E. Chace, 'The Descent on Democracy' (MS. Ph.D. dissertation, Univ. North Carolina, 1941), 216–18, 326–9; F. P. Prucha, 'The United States Army as Viewed by British Travellers, 1825–60,' *Military Affairs*, XVII (Fall 1953), 113–24.

34   *Views of Society and Manners in America* (New York, 1821), 267–8. See also James Flint, *Letters from America* (Edinburgh, 1822), 174–5.

35   *Men and Manners in America* (Phil., 1833), II, 31–2.

36   *Democracy in America* (P. Bradley, ed., New York, 1945), I, 228.

37   Ibid. II, 270, and chaps. 22–6.

38   *The Eastern and Western States of America* (London, 1842), I, 26–9, 501, II, 514; *The Slave States of America* (London, 1842), I, 126, 355.

Chapter VI

1   *Works* (C. Colton, ed., New York, 1904), IV, 111–12, VI, 308–9.

2   Washington *Daily National Intelligencer* (4 Aug. 1827), 3.

3   *Register of Debates*, 21 Cong., 1 Sess., 756ff., 819; *American State Papers, Naval Affairs*, III, 352.

4   *Writings and Speeches* (National Edition, Boston, 1903), ɪɪ, 124; McMaster, *History*, vɪ, 153.

5   To John Floyd, 16 Jan. 1833, in O. P. Chitwood, *John Tyler* (New York, 1939), 113.

6   *Register of Debates,* 22 Cong., 2 Sess., 405–6; *Examiner and Journal,* ɪ (Oct. 1833), 89–91.

7   R. L. Watson, 'Congressional Attitudes toward Military Preparedness, 1829–35,' *Mississippi Valley Historical Review,* xxxɪv (March 1948), 611–36; Claude Bowers, *Party Battles of the Jackson Period* (Boston, 1922), chap. 14.

8   J. F. Rippy, *Joel R. Poinsett* (Durham, 1935), chaps. 12, 14; *American State Papers, Military Affairs,* vɪɪ, 571–9; White, *Executive Influence,* 197–8.

9   *House Ex. Doc. No. 2,* 26 Cong., 1 Sess., 43–4. See also the contemporary comments in *New York Review,* vɪɪ (Oct. 1840), 277–305; *North American Review,* ʟɪɪ (Jan. 1841), 1–30.

10   *Writings* (Natl. Ed.), ɪɪɪ, 48. See also Webster's speech before the Whig Convention at Richmond, ibid. ɪɪɪ, 95.

11   *Works* (J. B. Moore, ed., Phil., 1908–11), ɪv, 304–8.

12   Bancroft, 'The Office of the People' (1835), *Literary and Historical Miscellanies* (New York, 1855), 426; Wayland, *The Elements of Political Economy* (Boston, 1840), 432; Hickok, *The Sources of Military Delusion* (Hartford, 1833), 10ff.; Mann, *Life and Works* (Boston, 1868), ɪɪɪ, 15–17, 646; and *Lectures on Education* (Boston, 1850), 238ff.

13   *Congressional Globe,* 27 Cong., 2 Sess., 585–6; 28 Cong., 1 Sess., 75–6. See also White, *Executive Influence,* 199–200.

14   *Works,* ɪɪ, 216–17, ɪv, 139–40, 241ff.

15   William Jay, *War and Peace* (first pub. 1842; New York, 1919), 6–11.

16   Charles Sumner, *The True Grandeur of Nations* (Boston, 1845), 2, 28ff., 52ff., 58ff.

17   Ibid. 65–6; E. L. Pierce, *Memoir and Letters of Charles Sumner* (Boston, 1893), ɪɪ, chap. 28.

18   Richardson, *Messages and Papers,* ɪv, 413.

19   *Writings* (Natl. Ed.), ɪv, 31–2.

20   H. V. Ames (ed.), *State Documents on Federal Relations* (Phil., 1906), 241–2.

21   *Congressional Globe,* 29 Cong., 2 Sess., 34–6, Appendix 213; 30 Cong., 1 Sess., Appendix 198. See also Bates, *Story of Congress,* 177–8.

22   'The War for Texas,' editorial New York *Evening Post* (13 May 1846), 2; H. N. Aizenstat, 'New England Public Opinion on the Mexican War' (MS. M.A. thesis, Clark Univ., 1936), 19–20; Allan Nevins, *Ordeal of the Union* (New York, 1947), ɪ, 8.

23   *American Review,* v (Jan. 1847), 3; vɪɪ (Jan. 1848), 3–14; vɪɪ (May 1848), 437–52.

24   'Civil Disobedience,' *Writings* (Manuscript Edition, Boston, 1906), ɪv, 359–61. See also Francis Wayland, *The Duty of Obedience to the Civil Magistrate* (Boston, 1847), 21ff., 37–8; Theodore Parker, *Works* (Centenary Edition, Boston, [1907]), ɪx, 288–325, xɪ, 21–31; Theodore Sedgwick, *The American Citizen* (New York, 1847), 31–2; William Jay, *A Review of the Causes and Consequences of the*

Mexican War (Boston, 1849), 213ff.; Abiel Livermore, *The War with Mexico Reviewed* (Boston, 1850).

25   *Congressional Globe,* 29 Cong., 1 Sess., Appendix 946ff.; 29 Cong., 2 Sess., 140.

26   Ibid. 30 Cong., 1 Sess., 96ff.; Nevins, *Ordeal of the Union,* I, 8.

27   Channing, *History of the United States,* v, 596–9. On the problem and extent of desertion, see Annual Reports of the Secretary of War, 1830 and 1831, *American State Papers, Military Affairs,* IV, 585, 708.

28   The Democrats' dismay over the Whig generals is illustrated in 'Military Presidents,' *United States Magazine and Democratic Review,* XXVI (June 1850), 481–98.

29   *Congressional Globe,* 29 Cong., 2 Sess., 13, 20.

30   9 Howard, 614.

31   Nevins, *Ordeal of the Union,* I, 4–5.

32   Excerpts from Pierce diary, July 1847, in Roy Nichols, *Franklin Pierce* (Phil., 1931), 156.

33   *Congressional Globe,* 33 Cong., 1 Sess., 803. See also Benton, *Thirty Years View,* II, 452, 573–7; Sprout, *Rise of American Naval Power,* 140ff.

34   *White-Jacket* (New York, 1855), 165, 196–7, 245–6; *Man-of-War Life* in *Nine Years A Sailor* (Cincinnati, 1857), 140–41. Melville also commented on the spirit of war and militarism in his satire on expansionism, *Mardi,* in *Works* (Constable Edition, London, 1922–4), IV, 242ff. See also Nevins, *Ordeal of the Union,* I, 120–21.

Chapter VII

1   *Speeches, Lectures and Letters* (Boston, 1863), 421–2. See also Merle Curti, *Peace or War* (New York, 1936), chap. 2.

2   Pierce, *Memoir and Letters,* IV, 144; Laura White, 'Charles Sumner and the Crisis of 1860–61,' *Essays in Honor of William E. Dodd* (Avery Craven, ed., Chicago, 1935), 187ff. Nathaniel Hawthorne was also dismayed at the military spirit. See his 'Chiefly about War-Matters by a Peaceable Man,' *Atlantic Monthly,* X (July 1862), 43–61.

3   *Senate Doc. No. 1,* 37 Cong., 1 Sess., 27. See also Harry Williams, 'The Attack upon West Point during the Civil War,' *Mississippi Valley Historical Review,* XXV (March 1939), 491–504; Kenneth Stampp, *And the War Came* (Louisiana State Univ., 1950), 28–30.

4   See, for example, H. C. Burnett and J. C. Breckinridge of Kentucky. *Congressional Globe,* 37 Cong., 1 Sess., 73, 137ff. See also White, *Executive Influence,* 211–12.

5   Quoted in H. C. Perkins, *Northern Editorials on Secession* (New York, 1942), II, 801. See also S. D. Brummer, *Political History of New York State during the Civil War* (New York, 1911), 152ff.

6   James G. Randall, *Constitutional Problems under Lincoln* (New York, 1926), 152.

7   *Federal Cases* (St. Paul, 1895), XVII, 152. See also Carl Swisher, *Roger B. Taney* (New York, 1936), chap. 26.

8   'Some Papers of Franklin Pierce, 1852–1862,' *American Historical Review,* X (Jan. 1905), 368. See also Nichols, *Franklin Pierce,* chap. 74; Charles Warren, *The Supreme Court in United States History* (Boston, 1935), II, 369–72.

9 Maryland House of Delegates, *Report of the Committee on Federal Relations* (Frederick, Md., 1861), 8, and *passim*.

10 J. F. Rhodes, *History of the United States from the Compromise of 1850* (New York, 1893–1906), III, 553ff.

11 Donaldson Jordan and E. J. Pratt, *Europe and the American Civil War* (Boston, 1931), 21–2.

12 *Executive Power* (Boston, 1862), 13, 16, 20–24, 29. See also William Whiting, *The War Powers of the President* (Boston, 1862); Josiah Warren, *True Civilization* (Boston, 1863), 22ff.

13 Lincoln, *Messages from the Governors*, v, 445–84; Rhodes, *History*, IV, 169 fn. 4, 235–6.

14 *Speeches* (New York, 1864), 494, and *passim*.

15 Quoted in Stewart Mitchell, *Horatio Seymour* (Cambridge, Mass., 1938), 293.

16 Quoted in George F. Milton, *Abraham Lincoln and the Fifth Column* (New York, 1942), 171–2. See also Gideon Welles, *Diary* (J. T. Morse, ed., Boston, 1911), I, 321–2; Rhodes, *History*, IV, 253.

17 4 Wallace, 127. See also Samuel Klaus (ed.), *The Milligan Case* (New York, 1929).

18 Washington *Daily National Intelligencer* (1 Jan. 1867), 2. See also Warren, *Supreme Court*, II, 427; Carl Swisher, *American Constitutional Development* (Boston, 1943), 320.

19 'The Draft,' *Harper's Weekly*, VI (6 Sept. 1862), 562. Emory Upton called attention to the significance of the Civil War draft as a nationalistic device. *The Military Policy of the United States* (Wash., 1904), 443.

20 Fred Shannon, *The Organization and Administration of the Union Army* (Cleveland, 1928), I, 272ff., 285–6.

21 Ibid. I, 295ff. See also J. F. Leach, *Conscription in the United States* (Rutland, Vt., [1952]), chaps. 9–16.

22 *Congressional Globe*, 37 Cong., 3 Sess., 976ff., 989. See also the defense of conscription by the former pacifist Caleb Sprague Henry, 'Something We Have to Think of, and to Do,' *Continental Monthly*, II (Dec. 1862), 657–61.

23 *Congressional Globe*, 37 Cong., 3 Sess., 1214, 1224ff., 1250, 1255, 1363ff.

24 Rhodes, *History*, IV, 320ff.

25 James G. Randall, *The Civil War and Reconstruction* (Boston, 1937), 607. See also Greeley, 'Progress of the Nation,' *Independent*, XIV (7 Aug. 1862), 1; and his *The American Conflict* (Hartford, 1864–6), II, chap. 21.

26 To Kate Field, 23 Aug. 1862, in Michael Sadleir, *Trollope A Commentary* (London, 1927), 227. See also Trollope's *North America* (New York, 1863), 178–9, 335–7, 385–7.

27 Roger B. Taney, 'Thoughts on the Conscription Law,' *Tyler's Quarterly Magazine*, XVIII (Oct. 1936), 74–87; *Pennsylvania State Reports*, XLV, 238–43, 323, 334. See also the comments of James Buchanan, *Works*, XI, 340–41, 346; John J. Freedman, *Is the Act . . . Constitutional?* (New York, 1863).

28 E. N. Wright, *Conscientious Objectors in the Civil War* (Phil. 1931), chaps. 2, 4; Shannon, *Organization of the Union Army*, II, 247ff.; *Bulletin of the Friends Historical Society*, IV (March 1911), 12–27.

29 *Congressional Globe*, 38 Cong., 1 Sess., 254ff.; Arthur C. Cole, *The Irrepressible Conflict 1850–1865* (New York, 1934), 313.

30   Wright, *Conscientious Objectors,* chap. 3, and 135ff.; F. G. Cortland, *Southern Heroes or the Friends in War Time* (Cambridge, Mass., 1895); Shannon, *Organization of the Union Army,* II, 175.

31   Lincoln, *Messages from the Governors,* V, 445–84; Horatio Seymour, *Public Record* (New York, 1868), 120–21; Shannon, *Organization of the Union Army,* II, 175–243; W. B. Weeden, *War Government Federal and State* (Boston, 1906), chap. 7; W. B. Hesseltine, *Lincoln and the War Governors* (New York, 1948), chap. 14.

32   Seymour, *Public Record,* 141–2.

33   Lincoln, *Messages from the Governors,* V, 551.

34   Randall, *Civil War and Reconstruction,* 411.

35   Ella Lonn, *Desertion during the Civil War* (New York, 1928), chap. 9, and Appendix 231–6; Bell I. Wiley, *The Life of Billy Yank* (Indianapolis, 1952), chap. 11.

36   R. G. Osterweis, *Romanticism and Nationalism in the Old South* (New Haven, 1949), 91–4, 125ff.

37   Dunbar Rowland (ed.), *Jefferson Davis* (Jackson, Miss., 1923), V, 363; Bell I. Wiley, *The Life of Johnny Reb* (Indianapolis, 1943), chap. 8.

38   Randall, *Civil War and Reconstruction,* 667, 674.

39   W. C. Ford (ed.), *A Cycle of Adams Letters 1861–1865* (Boston, 1920), I, 151, 182–3, 165.

Chapter VIII

1   C. R. Fish, 'Back to Peace in 1865,' *American Historical Review,* XXIV (Apr. 1919), 441. See also Dixon Wecter, *When Johnny Comes Marching Home* (Cambridge, Mass., 1944), 182ff.

2   Randall, *Civil War and Reconstruction,* 745; E. P. Oberholtzer, *History of the United States since the Civil War* (New York, 1917–37), I, 417–18; Mary R. Dearing, *Veterans in Politics: The Story of the G.A.R.* (Baton Rouge, 1952).

3   W. E. Woodward, *Meet General Grant* (New York, 1928), chap. 6.

4   Dorothy and Julius Goebel, *Generals in the White House* (New York, 1945), 242. See also Hugh McCulloch, *Men and Measures of Half a Century* (New York, 1888), 297.

5   Kirk H. Porter, *National Party Platforms* (New York, 1924), 99.

6   *North American Review,* CXLVII (Dec. 1888), 622.

7   Richardson, *Messages and Papers,* VI, 548. See also Joel Parker, *The Three Powers of Government* (New York, 1869); Howard Beale, *The Critical Year* (New York, 1930), 170–72.

8   *Congressional Globe,* 39 Cong., 2 Sess., 1380–81, 1448ff., Appendix 124–9.

9   *Ibid.* 39 Cong., 2 Sess., Appendix 85, 92–4.

10   Randall, *Civil War and Reconstruction,* 757.

11   Lincoln, *Messages from the Governors,* VI, 255–60.

12   J. F. Rhodes, *The History of the United States from Hayes to McKinley* (New York, 1919), 101ff.; Allan Nevins, *Abram S. Hewitt* (New York, 1935), 403ff.; Bates, *Story of Congress,* 281ff.

13   *Report of the Secretary of War, Nov. 22, 1865* (Wash., 1865), 22.

14   *Congressional Globe*, 40 Cong., 2 Sess., 155–6. For similar resolutions, see ibid. 40 Cong., 1 Sess., 780, 784, 798.

15   Ibid. 40 Cong., 2 Sess., 1232ff., 2033ff.; 40 Cong., 3 Sess., 927.

16   Ibid. 40 Cong., 3 Sess., Appendix 182ff.

17   Ibid. 41 Cong., 2 Sess., Appendix 147–8, 2275ff.

18   White, *Executive Influence*, 223.

19   L. B. Priest, *Uncle Sam's Stepchildren* (New Brunswick, 1942), chap. 2.

20   *Congressional Record*, 43 Cong., 1 Sess., 986.

21   Priest, *Uncle Sam's Stepchildren*, 23ff.; G. W. Manypenny, *Our Indian Wards* (Cincinnati, 1880), 175ff., 388ff.

22   *Council Fire*, I (Dec. 1878), 189; II (Jan., Apr. 1879), 5–6, 60.

23   James C. Sylvis, *The Life of William H. Sylvis* (Phil., 1872), 127ff., 294. See also Jonathan Grossman, *William Sylvis* (New York, 1945), chap. 3.

24   B. M. Rich, *The Presidents and Civil Disorder* (Wash., 1941); R. S. Rankin, *When Civil Law Fails* (Durham, 1939); M. S. Reichley, 'Federal Military Intervention in Civil Disturbances' (MS. Ph.D. dissertation, Georgetown Univ., 1939), chap. 5; F. T. Wilson, *Federal Aid in Domestic Disturbances 1903–1922* (Wash., 1922); Leon Whipple, *The Story of Civil Liberty in the United States* (New York, 1927), chap. 6.

25   Rhodes, *Hayes to McKinley*, 48ff.; 'The Army of the United States,' *North American Review*, CXXVI (March–June 1878), 193ff., 442ff. During the Civil War, Garfield resisted attempts to expand the powers of military commissions. T. C. Smith, *The Life and Letters of James Abram Garfield* (New Haven, 1925), II, 825–6.

26   *Congressional Record*, 45 Cong., 2 Sess., 3538.

27   Henry George, Jr., *The Life of Henry George* (New York, 1911), 577.

28   John P. Altgeld, *Live Questions* (Chicago, 1899), 675–6. See also Almont Lindsey, *The Pullman Strike* (Chicago, 1942), chap. 8; Edward Berman, *Labor Disputes and the President of the United States* (New York, 1924), chap. 1.

29   *American Journal of Education*, XI–XIV (1862–4), *passim*.

30   'Military Drill in Schools,' *Christian Examiner*, LXXVI (March 1864), 232–40; [Henry Lee and J. F. Clarke], *The Militia of the United States* (Boston, 1864), 97ff., 118–28; T. W. Higginson, 'Our Future Militia System,' *Atlantic Monthly*, XVI (Sept. 1865), 371–8.

31   Willard Nash, *A Study of Military Science in the Land-Grant Colleges* (New York, 1934), chap. 3.

32   *Congressional Globe*, 39 Cong., 1 Sess., 1381. See also Margaret Gearhart, 'Military Instruction in Civil Institutions of Learning' (MS. M.A. thesis, State Univ. Iowa, 1928), chap. 1.

33   *Congressional Globe*, 40 Cong., 3 Sess., 1528–9.

34   Ibid. 40 Cong., 2 Sess., 967, 1497; 41 Cong., 2 Sess., 1850; *Congressional Record*, 44 Cong., 1 Sess., 1336; 54 Cong., 2 Sess., 1204ff.

35   John Gazley, *American Opinion of German Unification* (New York, 1926), 351, 377.

36   Quoted in *Peacemaker*, II (Dec. 1883), 83.

37   Carl Wittke, *Against the Current: The Life of Karl Heinzen* (Chicago, 1945), 17, 50–51, 253–4.

38 Charles Sumner, *Works* (Boston, 1870–83), XIV, 15, 54ff., 78ff. See also Gazley, *American Opinion*, 377; Elizabeth White, *American Opinion of France* (New York, 1927), chap. 6.

39 D. S. Freeman, *R. E. Lee A Biography* (New York, 1934–5), IV, 278, 497; J. William Jones, *Personal Reminiscences of Gen. Robert E. Lee* (New York, 1874), 93–4.

40 *Congressional Record*, 46 Cong., 3 Sess., 187; Assoc. Am. Agricultural Colleges, *Proceedings 3rd Annual Convention* (Wash., 1890), 126–30.

41 *Century*, XLVII (Jan. 1894), 468–9; XLVIII (June 1894), 318–19. See also *School Review*, II (May 1894), 281–5; *Education*, XV (March, Apr. 1895), 398, 473.

42 *American Journal of Politics*, V (July 1894), 209.

43 *Arena*, X (Aug. 1894), 427–8.

44 Lincoln, *Messages from the Governors*, IX, 628.

Chapter IX

1 *Nation*, LI (3 July 1890), 4–5.

2 Donald Dozer, 'Anti-Expansionism during the Johnson Administration,' *Pacific Historical Review*, XII (Sept. 1943), 253–75. See also Dozer, 'Anti-Imperialism in the United States, 1865–95' (MS. Ph.D. dissertation, Harvard Univ., 1936).

3 *Congressional Globe*, 42 Cong., 1 Sess., 294ff.; 42 Cong., 2 Sess., 953.

4 *Report of the Secretary of the Navy* (Wash., 1876), 6–7.

5 Ibid. (Wash., 1877), 8–9.

6 *Congressional Record*, 47 Cong., 1 Sess., 5639ff., 5647.

7 Sprout, *Rise of American Naval Power*, 194.

8 W. E. Livezey, *Mahan on Sea Power* (Norman, 1947), 68ff., 263ff. See also W. D. Puleston, *Mahan* (New Haven, 1939); E. M. Earle, 'The Navy's Influence on our Foreign Relations,' *Current History*, XXIII (Feb. 1926), 648–55; Sprout, *Rise of American Naval Power*, 227ff.

9 Ibid. 207–11.

10 *Congressional Record*, 51 Cong., 1 Sess., Index 498, lists some two hundred petitions. See also George T. Davis, *A Navy Second to None* (New York, 1940), 99.

11 *Congressional Record*, 52 Cong., 1 Sess., 5236–7, 5294. See also Sprout, *Rise of American Naval Power*, 211–12.

12 *Congressional Record*, 52 Cong., 1 Sess., Appendix 417–18; 52 Cong., 2 Sess., 1877.

13 Ibid. 52 Cong., 1 Sess., 3364–5, 3390–91.

14 Ibid. 52 Cong., 1 Sess., 3360–63.

15 Claude Fuess, *Carl Schurz* (New York, 1932), 351.

16 *Harper's Magazine*, LXXXVII (Oct. 1893), 745. See also Schurz, *Speeches, Correspondence and Political Papers* (Frederic Bancroft, ed., New York, 1913), V, 398ff., 477ff., 494ff.

17 *Scientific American*, LXXIV (28 March 1896), 194. See also Moorfield Storey, *A Civilian's View of the Navy* (Wash., 1897); Andrew Carnegie, 'Americanism versus Imperialism,' *Complete Works* (B. J. Hendrick, ed., New York, 1933), 153–86.

18 Edward Berwick, 'American Militarism,' *Century*, XLVII (Dec. 1893),

316–17. See also E. L. Godkin, 'The Absurdity of War,' ibid. LIII (Jan. 1897), 468–70; N. S. Shaler, 'The Last Gift of the Century,' *North American Review*, CLXI (Dec. 1895), 674–84; A. B. Ronne, 'The Spirit of Militarism,' *Popular Science Monthly*, XLVII (June 1895), 234–9; Franklin Smith, 'Peace as a Factor in Reform,' ibid. LIII (June 1898), 225–40.

19 'The Policy of Annexation for America,' *Forum*, XXIV (Dec.̃ 1897), 385–95. See also Bryce, *The American Commonwealth* (London and New York, 1889), II, 443–4.

20 Quoted in John D. Hicks, *The American Nation* (Boston, 1941), 313. See also Charles Beard, *The Open Door at Home* (New York, 1934), chap. 3.

21 *Watson's Jeffersonian Magazine*, V (Oct. 1910), 817. See also Watson, *Life and Speeches* (Nashville, 1908), 218–31; J. W. Pratt, *Expansionists of 1898* (Baltimore, 1936), chap. 7; C. Vann Woodward, *Tom Watson* (New York, 1938), 334.

22 Guglielmo Ferrero, *Militarism* (London, 1902), chap. 1; Edward Dicey, 'The New American Imperialism,' *Nineteenth Century*, XLIV (Sept. 1898), 487–501; Richard Heindel, *The American Impact on Great Britain, 1898–1914* (Phil., 1940), chaps. 4–5.

23 Maria C. Lanzar, 'The Anti-Imperialist League,' *Philippine Social Science Review*, III (1930), 29. See also Fred Harrington, 'The Anti-Imperialist Movement in the United States, 1898–1900,' *Mississippi Valley Historical Review*, XXII (Sept. 1935), 211–30.

24 'The Issue of Imperialism,' *Speeches* (Bancroft), VI, 23. See also Schurz to Bjornson, 22 Sept. 1898, ibid. V, 514.

25 *Imperial Democracy* (New York, 1901), 27, 35–6, 109. See also Goldwin Smith, *Commonwealth or Empire* (New York, 1902), 2, 6–7, 19ff.

26 *The Conquest of the United States by Spain* (Boston, 1899), 25, and *passim;* and Sumner, 'The Predominant Issue,' *International Monthly*, II (Nov. 1900), 505–6.

27 *Atlantic Monthly*, LXXXV (March 1900), 289–301.

28 Bryan, *Speeches* (New York, 1911), II, 14.

29 Ibid. II, 27ff.; Merle Curti, *Bryan and World Peace* (Northampton, 1931), 130ff.; Porter, *National Party Platforms*, 211.

30 *Commoner*, I (13 Feb.; 22 Nov. 1901), 1; 3.

31 'Affairs in the Philippine Islands,' *Senate Doc. No. 331,* 57 Cong., 1 Sess., 884, 949ff., 1428ff., 1969ff., 2251ff. See also Elihu Root, *The Military and Colonial Policy of the United States* (Cambridge, Mass., 1916), 56ff.; Lanzar, 'The Anti-Imperialist League,' *Philippine Social Science Review*, IV (1931), 182, 239ff.

32 White, *Executive Influence*, 237–8.

33 *Congressional Record,* 56 Cong., 1 Sess., Appendix 295.

34 Ibid. 55 Cong., 3 Sess., 338ff.; 56 Cong., 2 Sess., 1117.

35 Richardson, *Messages and Papers*, X, 188–9. See also Merze Tate, *The Disarmament Illusion* (New York, 1942), Parts II, III.

36 Davis, *A Navy Second to None*, 160fn.

37 W. D. Vandiver of Missouri, *Congressional Record*, 56 Cong., 1 Sess., 4320.

38 *The Philippines* (no date or place, published by Anti-Imperialist League), 8.

39 Schurz, 'Militarism and Democracy,' *Speeches* (Bancroft), VI, 48ff. See also

Joseph May, *Militarism* (Phil., 1899); W. M. Salter, *The New Militarism* (Phil., 1899).

40   'Militarism,' *American Federationist,* v (Dec. 1898), 203–4.

41   *Nation,* LXVII (14 July; 15 Sept. 1898), 34–6; 198–9; LXIX (12 Oct. 1899), 273–4. See also Wallace Rice, 'Some Current Fallacies of Captain Mahan,' *Dial,* XXVIII (16 March 1900), 198–200.

42   *Nation,* LXXV (7 Aug. 1902), 105; LXXVI (23 Apr. 1903), 324–5.

43   Ibid. LXXVI, 324.

Chapter X

1   Richard Hofstadter, *The American Political Tradition* (New York, 1948), 206.

2   Howard Hurwitz, *Theodore Roosevelt and Labor* (New York, 1943), 255. See also Henry Pringle, *Theodore Roosevelt* (New York, 1931), 4, 578, 589–90; Pringle, *The Life and Times of William Howard Taft* (New York, 1939), II, 748–9; Howard Hill, *Roosevelt and the Caribbean* (Chicago, 1927), chap. 8; A. B. Hart and H. R. Ferleger, *Theodore Roosevelt Cyclopedia* (New York, 1941), 338ff.

3   Elihu Root, *Five Years of the War Department* (Wash., 1904), 58, 266.

4   Philip Jessup, *Elihu Root* (New York, 1938), I, 261. See also Otto Nelson, *National Security and the General Staff* (Wash., 1946), 44ff., 55ff.; J. D. Hittle, *The Military Staff* (Harrisburg, 1944), 176, 187; Frederic Paxson, *American Democracy and the World War: Pre-War Years 1913–1917* (Boston, 1936), 111ff.

5   M. T. Reynolds, 'The General Staff as a Propaganda Agency, 1908–1914,' *Public Opinion Quarterly,* III (July 1939), 391–408; Hermann Hagedorn, *Leonard Wood* (New York, 1931), II, 100–104.

6   *U.S. Statutes at Large,* XXXV, 400.

7   Root, *Military and Colonial Policy,* 147. See also S. T. Ansell, 'Legal and Historical Aspects of the Militia,' *Yale Law Journal,* XXVI (Apr. 1917), 471–80.

8   E. H. Crosby, 'The Military Idea of Manliness,' *Independent,* LIII (18 Apr. 1901), 873–4; J. D. Miller, 'Militarism or Manhood?,' *Arena,* XXIV (Oct. 1900), 379–92. On labor's attitude, see Jessup, *Root,* 268–9.

9   Urbain Gohier, 'The Danger of Militarism,' *Independent,* LII (25 Jan. 1900), 233–6; Gustave Hervé, 'Anti-Militarism in France,' ibid. LIV (11 Sept. 1902), 2170–73.

10   Eugene Hale, *Congressional Record,* 58 Cong., 3 Sess., 1390.

11   Ibid. 57 Cong., 1 Sess., 3348ff.; 58 Cong., 2 Sess., 1005.

12   *The Campaign Text Book of the Democratic Party* (1904), 39; *Commoner,* IV (11 Nov. 1904), 1.

13   *Works* (National Edition, New York, 1926), XV, 467.

14   Pringle, *Theodore Roosevelt,* 165ff.; Sprout, *Rise of American Naval Power,* 229ff.

15   Ibid. 258.

16   Ibid. 261. See also C. E. Jefferson, 'The New Navy,' *Independent,* LVII (27 Oct. 1904), 972–4; John D. Long, 'Shall the Navy Be Increased?,' ibid. LVIII (23 March 1905), 639–41.

17   *Congressional Record,* 58 Cong., 2 Sess., 2223–4.

18 Ibid. 58 Cong., 3 Sess., 2937, 2590.

19 Ibid. 58 Cong., 3 Sess., 2667, 2747, 3486.

20 Sprout, *Rise of American Naval Power*, 261–4; Elting Morison, *Admiral Sims and the Modern American Navy* (Boston, 1942), 173ff.

21 *Congressional Record*, 60 Cong., 1 Sess., 2360–62, 2717–19, 2952–3, 4586–7, 4611, 4781, 4789. See also C. E. Jefferson, 'Some Fallacies of Militarism,' *Independent*, LXIV (27 Feb. 1908), 457–60; L. A. Mead, 'Some Fallacies of Captain Mahan,' *Arena*, XL (Aug.–Sept. 1908), 163–70; 'Thirty Reasons Why Our Navy Should Not Be Enlarged,' *Advocate of Peace*, LXXI (Feb. 1909), 32–5.

22 *Senate Doc. No. 378*, 60 Cong., 1 Sess., *passim*. See also B. J. Hendrick, *The Life of Andrew Carnegie* (Garden City, 1932), II, 320.

23 Eleanor Tupper and G. E. McReynolds, *Japan in American Public Opinion* (New York, 1937), 41ff., 90; *Literary Digest*, XXXVI (22 Feb.; 2 May 1908), 253–4; 631–2; Sprout, *Rise of American Naval Power*, 267–8.

24 LXXXVI (25 Apr. 1908), 1010.

25 *Proceedings 13th Annual Convention* (New York, 1908), 16.

26 *Current Literature*, XLVI (March 1909), 238–45.

27 *Present Day Problems* (New York, 1908), 54–9; *Peace Addresses by President Taft* (New York, [1911]); Pringle, *Life of Taft*, II, 736–7.

28 Sprout, *Rise of American Naval Power*, 283–5.

29 *Congressional Record*, 61 Cong., 2 Sess., 3779, 3831.

30 Ibid. 61 Cong., 2 Sess., 4068, 4426–7, 6593, 6729; 61 Cong., 3 Sess., 3077.

31 Ibid. 61 Cong., 2 Sess., 6595.

32 Sprout, *Rise of American Naval Power*, 287.

33 *Newer Ideals of Peace* (New York, 1907), 216–22.

34 W. G. Sumner, *War and Other Essays* (New Haven, 1911), 39–40; Havelock Ellis, *The Task of Social Hygiene* (Boston, 1912), chap. 10; V. L. Kellogg, 'Eugenics and Militarism,' *Atlantic Monthly*, CXII (July 1913), 99–108.

35 Morris Hillquit, *Socialism in Theory and Practice* (New York, 1909), 296–302; George Kirkpatrick, *War—What For?* (West LaFayette, Ohio, 1910); C. E. Russell, 'For Patriotism and Profits,' *Pearson's Magazine*, XXX (Nov. 1913), 545–6. See also Edmund Silberner, *The Problem of War in Nineteenth Century Economic Thought* (Princeton, 1946), Part III.

36 *Proceedings 1st Convention* (New York, 1905), 269.

37 *Mother Earth*, VI (Aug.; Dec. 1911), 165–6; 298–301. See the same type of criticism by William Allen White, 'The Proud Army,' *Emporia Gazette*, 27 Sept. 1913, quoted in *The Editor and His People* (H. O. Mahin, ed., New York, 1924), 313–14.

38 U.S. Bureau of Educ., *Report of the Commissioner, 1898–1899* (Wash., 1900), 480ff.; Francis Walker, *Discussions in Education* (New York, 1899), 272; W. A. Bancroft, 'A Word for Military Training,' *New England Magazine*, XLV (Nov. 1908), 365–7; G. Stanley Hall, *Educational Problems* (New York, 1911), I, 641ff.; Ira L. Reeves, *Military Education in the United States* (Burlington, 1914), 90ff.

39 *House Doc. No. 1207*, 60 Cong., 2 Sess., *passim;* Roosevelt, 'Letters to His Children,' *Works* (Natl. Ed.), XIX, 458.

40 House Comm. on Military Affairs, *Hearings on H.R. 11336* (Wash., 1908), 5–8.

41 *Journal of the Military Service Institution,* XLVI (March–Apr. 1910), 172–92; *Educational Review,* XL (June 1910), 103.

42 *American Physical Education Review,* I (Sept.–Dec. 1896), 50–59; National Educ. Assoc., *Journal of Proceedings* (Chicago, 1896), 920–6; Sargent, *Physical Education* (Boston, 1906), chap. 9; and Sargent's *Autobiography* (Phil., 1927), chap. 9.

43 Merle Curti, *The Social Ideas of American Educators* (New York, 1935), 250–51. See also *An Eleven-Year Survey of the Activities of the American School Peace League* (Boston, 1919), 23, and *passim.*

44 *Congressional Record,* 59 Cong., 1 Sess., 6411; 61 Cong., 2 Sess., 3021.

45 *Survey,* XXXV (25 Dec. 1915), 342; A. C. Coolidge, *The Scoundrel of Militarism* (Worcester, 1911); A. J. Nock, 'World Scouts,' *American Magazine,* LXXIII (Jan. 1912), 275–84.

46 David J. Brewer, *The Mission of the United States in the Cause of Peace* (Boston, 1911), 3, 11.

Chapter XI

1 C. C. Tansill, *America Goes to War* (Boston, 1938), chap. 1; C. C. Cummins, *Indiana Public Opinion and the World War* (Indianapolis, 1945), 8; R. H. Hilliard, 'The Ohio Press and American Neutrality, 1914–1917' (MS. Ph.D. dissertation, Ohio State Univ., 1938), 20ff.; H. E. Snide, 'American Public Opinion on the Outbreak of the World War' (MS. M.A. thesis, American Univ., 1934), 83.

2 'Slavery and Militarism,' *Nation,* XCIX (1 Oct. 1914), 395; W. M. Shuster, 'The Breakdown of Civilization,' *Century,* LXXXIX (Nov. 1914), 51–9; *Forum,* LIII (Jan. 1915), 157.

3 *The Road toward Peace* (Boston, 1915), 66–7, 126, 153–5.

4 *Through Europe on the Eve of War* (New York, 1914), 136. For the comments of other clergymen, see C. E. Jefferson, *The Cause of the War* (New York, 1914); E. H. Crosby, *The Absurdities of Militarism* (Wash., [1914]); Peter Ainslie, *The Scourge of Militarism* (New York, [1914]); Frank Crane, *War and World Government* (New York, 1915); W. C. Allen, 'Missions and Militarism,' *Missionary Review of the World,* XXXVIII (Jan. 1915), 26–8.

5 C. E. Schieber, *The Transformation of American Sentiment toward Germany* (Boston, 1923), 222–3; H. C. Peterson, *Propaganda for War* (Norman, 1939), 46–8.

6 *U.S. Army and Navy Journal,* LII (3 Oct. 1914), 181. The 17 Oct. and subsequent issues reprint critical comments from the press.

7 Walter Millis, *Road to War* (Boston, 1935), 94–5. See also R. B. Perry, *The Plattsburg Movement* (New York, 1921), chap. 1; Leonard Wood, *The Military Obligation of Citizenship* (Princeton, 1915).

8 *Annual Report of the Secretary of War 1913* (Wash., 1913), 20; J. L. Elliott, *University Presidents and the Spirit of Militarism* (New York, 1915); C. H. Hamlin, *Educators Present Arms* (n.p., 1939).

9 *Congressional Record,* 63 Cong., 2 Sess., 16745; 63 Cong., 3 Sess., 7, 1601ff.

10 Russell Buchanan, 'Theodore Roosevelt and American Neutrality, 1914–1917,' *American Historical Review,* XLIII (July 1938), 775–90; Paxson, *American Democracy and the World War: Pre-War Years,* 199ff. The most detailed account is W. W. Tinsley, 'The American Preparedness Movement, 1913–1916' (MS. Ph.D. dissertation, Stanford Univ., 1939).

11 *Public Papers* (R. S. Baker and W. E. Dodd, eds., New York, 1925–7), III, 225; R. S. Baker, *Woodrow Wilson: Life and Letters* (New York, 1927–39), VI, 5–6.

12 Washington *Sunday Star,* Magazine Section (10 Jan. 1915), 3–4, 16; *Congressional Record,* 63 Cong., 3 Sess., 2035, 2073, 2679ff., 2721ff., 3126–7, 4325ff.

13 Ibid. 63 Cong., 3 Sess., 3633, Appendix 71–2, 417ff., 583–6, 735–7.

14 *The Preparedness of America* ([New York, 1915]), 10ff.

15 *The Menace of All Militarism* (undated pamphlet in the Columbia Univ. Library); *Literary Digest,* L (6 Feb. 1915), 242–3.

16 J. C. Crighton, *Missouri and the World War* (Columbia, 1947), 115–17.

17 *Literary Digest,* L (23 Jan. 1915), 137–8, 162ff. See also 'Pacifism and Preparedness—A Poll of the Press,' *Outlook,* CX (30 June 1915), 495–9.

18 Walter Johnson, *William Allen White's America* (New York, 1947), 254–5.

19 Curti, *Bryan and World Peace,* 191ff.; Charles Seymour (ed.), *The Intimate Papers of Colonel House* (Boston, 1926–8), I, 299.

20 *New York Times* (20 June 1915), 1, 4; (25 June 1915), 1. See also Bryan, *The Causeless War* (n.p., 1915); Curti, *Bryan and World Peace,* 223ff.

21 W. E. Dodd, *Woodrow Wilson and His Work* (New York, 1920), 177ff.; Paxson, *American Democracy and the World War: Pre-War Years,* 286ff.; 'The President and Preparedness,' *Nation,* CI (21 Oct. 1915), 485.

22 George Mowry, *Theodore Roosevelt and the Progressive Movement* (Madison, 1946), 313. For Roosevelt's preparedness views, see his *Works* (Natl. Ed.), XVIII, *passim,* and the summary of his speeches inserted in the *Congressional Record,* 64 Cong., 1 Sess., 957–62.

23 Davis, *A Navy Second to None,* 207.

24 Baker, *Woodrow Wilson,* VI, 8–9; *Public Papers* (Baker and Dodd), III, 386.

25 Tinsley, 'American Preparedness Movement,' 202ff.; Millis, *Road to War,* 238; *New York Times* (17 Nov. 1915), 1; (21 Nov. 1915), Sect. II, 18.

26 *Mother Earth,* X (Dec. 1915), 331–8.

27 Baker, *Woodrow Wilson,* VI, 24; *Congressional Record,* 64 Cong., 1 Sess., 273, 282.

28 Josephus Daniels, *The Wilson Era: Years of Peace* (Chapel Hill, 1944), chap. 34; 'Civilian Control of the Navy,' editorial, *Nation,* C (6 May 1915), 486; *Congressional Record,* 64 Cong., 1 Sess., 458ff., 1215ff., 1322ff., Appendix 665ff., 86off.

29 *Public Papers* (Baker and Dodd), IV, 12, 50–51.

30 *Literary Digest,* LII (5 Feb., 12 Feb.; 11 March 1916), 269, 359; 617–24, 647ff.

31 *Commoner,* XVI (Feb. 1916), 1.

32 *Congressional Record,* 64 Cong., 1 Sess., 933, 1185, 1612, 1753, 2250, 2490. See also J. B. McMaster, *The United States in the World War* (New York, 1918–20), I, 234.

33 *Congressional Record,* 64 Cong., 1 Sess., 4340–47; Millis, *Road to War,* 256.

34 *Congressional Record,* 64 Cong., 1 Sess., 4268, 5201ff., 6011ff.

35 Jane Addams, *Peace and Bread in Time of War* (New York, 1922), 6–7; M. L. Degen, *The History of the Woman's Peace Party* (Baltimore, 1939), 11, 38;

Yearbook of the Woman's Peace Party 1916 (Chicago, 1916), 2; Curti, *Peace or War*, 241ff.

36   Lillian Wald, *Windows on Henry Street* (Boston, 1934), 288ff.; R. L. Duffus, *Lillian Wald* (New York, 1938), 151ff.; American Union against Militarism, MS. Records (Swarthmore College Peace Collection), Box 4 includes materials on origin of A.U.M.

37   A.U.M., *Bulletin* (12 June 1916); *New York Times* (23 Feb. 1916), 7.

38   *Survey*, xxxv (1 Jan. 1916), 370.

39   House Comm. on Military Affairs, 'To Increase the Efficiency of the Military Establishment,' *Hearings*, 64 Cong., 1 Sess. (Wash., 1916), 4–5, 18–21, 65ff., 115; Senate Comm. on Military Affairs, 'Preparedness for National Defense,' *Hearings*, 64 Cong., 1 Sess. (Wash., 1916), 856ff., 1026ff.

40   Lewis Lorwin, *Labor and Internationalism* (New York, 1929), 89ff., 123–4; Samuel Gompers, *Seventy Years of Life and Labor* (New York, 1925), ii, chap. 38; A.F.L. *Labor and the War* (Wash., 1918), 11ff.

41   *Masses*, viii (March 1916), 14–16.

42   A.U.M., MS. Records (S.C.P.C.), Box 3, including Form Letter to Members, 3 Aug. 1916. See also Wald, *Windows on Henry Street*, 301ff.; *Survey*, xxxvi (22 Apr. 1916), 95–6.

43   'The President on Militarism,' *Survey*, xxxvi (20 May 1916), 198–9; Wald, *Windows on Henry Street*, 303.

44   Act of June 3, 1916, Sections 54, 57ff., *U.S. Statutes at Large*, xxxix, 194, 197ff.; Act of Aug. 29, 1916, Section 2, ibid. xxxix, 619. See also John Dickinson, *The Building of an Army* (New York, 1922).

45   'Militarism and the Militia,' *Scientific American*, new ser., cxiv (15 Apr. 1916), 396; *New Review*, iv (May 1916), 144–6.

46   *Congressional Record*, 64 Cong., 1 Sess., 5411, 6202ff., Appendix 1019–20. See also A.U.M., *Bulletin* (18 May 1916); *Survey*, xxxvi (17 June 1916), 309–10.

47   Edward Stanwood, *History of the Presidency* (Boston, 1928), ii, 348; Millis, *Road to War*, 318ff.

48   Hughes Acceptance Speech, *New York Times* (11 June 1916), 1; Wilson, *Public Papers* (Baker and Dodd), iv, 203.

49   Porter, *National Party Platforms*, 389, 403–4; Allan Benson, *Inviting War to America* (New York, 1916); Benson, 'Socialism vs. Militarism,' *Independent*, lxxxviii (30 Oct. 1916), 195–6.

50   *Congressional Record*, 64 Cong., 1 Sess., 8812, 8866ff., 8894.

51   Ibid. 64 Cong., 1 Sess., 10931ff., 11312, 11330ff., 11353. See also Sprout, *Rise of American Naval Power*, 333ff.

52   *Congressional Record*, 64 Cong., 1 Sess., 11171; 'Unconscious Militarists,' *Saturday Evening Post*, clxxxix (8 July 1916), 20.

53   Sprout, *Rise of American Naval Power*, 340–41; Davis, *A Navy Second to None*, 228.

Chapter XII

1   Seymour, *Intimate Papers of Colonel House*, ii, 84.

2   'The Effect on American Institutions of a Powerful Military and Naval Establishment,' *Annals of the American Academy of Political and Social Science*, xvi (July 1916), 157–72.

3 'A Symposium in the Present Crisis,' *Nation Supplement*, CIII (3 Aug. 1916), 1–4; *Masses*, VIII; IX (July; Nov. 1916), 7–12; 10.

4 Samuel Clemens, 'The War Prayer,' in A. B. Paine, *Mark Twain A Biography* (New York, 1912), III, 1232–4; and his *The Mysterious Stranger* (New York, 1916), 116ff., 127–9; Bourne, *The Tradition of War* (New York, 1914); Russell, *Justice in Wartime* (Chicago, 1916); Liebknecht, *Militarism* (New York, 1917).

5 Hull, *Preparedness* (New York, 1916); Howe, *Why War?* (New York, 1916); Nearing, *The Germs of War* (St. Louis, 1916); Nearing, *The Menace of Militarism* (New York, 1917).

6 *Nation*, CIV (18 Jan. 1917), 74–5.

7 McMaster, *United States in the World War*, I, 325; Millis, *Road to War*, 385, 389; *New York Times* (1 March 1917), 1.

8 Clippings and Correspondence, June 1917, Jane Addams Papers (S.C.P.C.). See also Curti, *Peace or War*, 255ff.; Ray Abrams, *Preachers Present Arms* (New York, 1933), 51ff.

9 Letters to Jane Addams, 9 Apr.; 26 June 1917, Jane Addams Papers. See also C. E. Jefferson, 'What Must We Do?,' *Independent*, XC (26 May 1917), 374; John Reed, 'Whose War?,' *Masses*, IX (Apr. 1917), 11–12.

10 Quoted in Villard, *Fighting Years* (New York, 1939), 324–5. See also Randolph Bourne, 'The War and the Intellectuals,' *Untimely Papers* (James Oppenheim, ed., New York, 1919), 23.

11 Alexander Trachtenberg (ed.), *The American Socialists and the War* (New York, 1917), 38; Morris Hillquit, *Loose Leaves from a Busy Life* (New York, 1934), 145ff.; Lillian Symes and Travers Clement, *Rebel America* (New York, 1934), 293–4.

12 John Heaton, *Cobb of 'The World'* (New York, 1924), 268–70.

13 *War*, I, no. 3 (War Number, 1917), 1.

14 *Masses*, VI (March 1915), 17–18. See also Granville Hicks, *John Reed* (New York, 1936), 152ff., 181–2; and Reed's testimony before the House Comm. on Military Affairs, 14 Apr. 1917, *Hearings*, 65 Cong., 1 Sess. (Wash., 1917), 31–2.

15 *New Republic*, VI (25 March 1916), 205–7.

16 George Marvin, 'Universal Military Service in Argentina,' *World's Work*, XXXIII (Feb. 1917), 381–92; 'Conscription,' editorial, *Independent*, XC (28 Apr. 1917), 191–3; Sidney Ballou, 'Compulsory Military Training and Service,' Navy League of the U.S., *Pamphlet No. 125* (Wash., [1917]).

17 *World's Work*, XXXIII (Nov. 1916), 16–24. See also the articles by Eliot et al., *National Economic League Quarterly*, III (May 1917); and symposium, 'Military Training Compulsory or Volunteer,' *Proceedings of the Academy of Political Science*, VI (July 1916).

18 House Comm. on Military Affairs, *Hearings*, 8 Feb. 1916, 64 Cong., 1 Sess. (Wash., 1916), 44–5.

19 Frederick Palmer, *Bliss Peacemaker* (New York, 1934), 139–40. See also E. H. Crowder, *The Spirit of Selective Service* (New York, 1920); Hagedorn, *Leonard Wood*, II, 130ff.

20 *Universal Military Training* (New York, 1917). See also Wood's testimony before various Congressional committees, collected under the title, *Universal Military Training* (Wash., 1917).

21 'The Universal Military Service Cure-All,' *Nation*, CII (11 May 1916), 510–11. This article was reprinted by the A.U.M. in 1918. See also A.U.M., *Bulletin*

(27 May, 7 June 1916); George Nasmyth, 'Universal Military Service and Democracy,' *Journal of Race Development*, VII (Oct. 1916), 208–19 (also reprinted by A.U.M.); W. T. Colyer, 'The Military Mind,' *Independent*, LXXXIX (1 Jan. 1917), 22; Amos Pinchot, 'The Commercial Policy of Conscription,' *Masses*, IX (May 1917), 6–8.

22   See, for example, the symposium at the American Sociological Society Meeting, Dec. 1915, *Papers and Proceedings 10th Annual Meeting* (Chicago, 1916), 96–101.

23   *New Republic*, VI (22 Apr. 1916), 309–10.

24   *Proceedings*, VI (July 1916), 171–8; also in *School and Society*, IV (1 July 1916), 9–14.

25   Senate Subcommittee of the Comm. on Military Affairs, 'Universal Military Training,' *Hearings*, 64 Cong., 2 Sess. (Wash., 1917), 522–31. See also Collegiate Anti-Militarism League, Constitution and other miscellaneous papers (Columbia Univ. Library), and its publication *War*.

26   *Journal of Proceedings, 50th Annual Session* (Concord, [1916]), 206.

27   *Proceedings Academy Political Science*, VI (July 1916), 136, 205.

28   House Comm. on Military Affairs, 'Volunteer and Conscription System,' *Hearings*, 65 Cong., 1 Sess. (Wash., 1917), 17, 20, 29, 33; Senate Comm. on Military Affairs, 'Temporary Increase of Military Establishment,' *Hearings*, 65 Cong., 1 Sess. (Wash., 1917), 3ff. See also *American Federationist*, XXIV (Jan., Apr., May 1917), 21ff., 269ff., 376.

29   *Literary Digest*, LIV (21 Apr. 1917), 1147–9. See also Russell Buchanan, 'American Editors Examine American War Aims and Plans in April, 1917,' *Pacific Historical Review*, IX (Sept. 1940), 253–65; Mark Sullivan, *Our Times* (New York, 1927–35), V, chap. 15.

30   McMaster, *United States in the World War*, I, 384; Frederick Palmer, *Newton D. Baker* (New York, 1931), I, 192; *New York Times* (12 Apr. 1917), 1; *Congressional Record*, 63 Cong., 2 Sess., 3973.

31   Ibid. 65 Cong., 1 Sess., 1220. See also pp. 1091ff., 1054–5, 1104ff., 1182, 1186–9, 1233–4, 1408ff.

32   Ibid. 65 Cong., 1 Sess., 996. See also pp. 907–8, 1087, 1155ff., 1354ff., 1442ff., 1490, 1623.

33   *U.S. Statutes at Large*, XL, 76.

34   *Our Gallant Madness* (New York, 1937), 111–12, 196.

35   *New Republic*, X (31 March; 14 Apr. 1917), 249–50; 311–2; ibid. XI (5 May; 9 June 1917), 7–8; 148–50.

36   *American Democracy and the World War: America at War* (Boston, 1939), chap. 13.

37   *New York Times* (1 June 1917), 1; Newspaper clippings, H. W. L. Dana Papers (S.C.P.C.), Box 1; Emma Goldman, *Living My Life* (New York, 1931), II, 602ff.; 'The No Conscription League,' *Mother Earth*, XII (June 1917), 112–4; John Reed, 'Militarism at Play,' *Masses*, IX (Aug. 1917), 18–19; McMaster, *United States in the World War*, I, 387–8.

38   *New York Times* (6 June 1917), 1; *Second Report of the Provost Marshal General* (Wash., 1919), 207ff.; *American Socialist*, III (16 June 1917), 1; Charles Bush, 'The Green Corn Rebellion' (MS. M.A. thesis, Univ. Oklahoma, 1932).

39   Palmer, *Newton D. Baker*, II, 64.

40   *Second Report of the Provost Marshal General*, 203.

41 *Survey*, xxxvii (3 March 1917), 636–8. See also the summaries of English experience in John Graham, *Conscription and Conscience* (London, 1922); Denis Hayes, *Conscription Conflict* (London, 1949).

42 Senate Comm. on Military Affairs, 'Temporary Increase of Military Establishment,' *Hearings*, 65 Cong., 1 Sess. (Wash., 1917), 3ff.; *New Republic*, xi (26 May 1917), 109–11; *Survey*, xxxviii (4 Aug. 1917), 391–4.

43 *Congressional Record*, 65 Cong., 1 Sess., 5898, 5901.

44 Baker, *Woodrow Wilson*, vii, 45, 289.

45 'War Powers under the Constitution,' *Senate Doc. No. 105*, 65 Cong., 1 Sess. (Wash., 1917), 5, 14; 245 *U.S. Reports*, 366; F. R. Black, 'The Selective Draft Cases,' *Boston University Law Review*, xi (Jan. 1931), 37–53.

46 James Mock and Cedric Larson, *Words That Won the War* (Princeton, 1939), 4, 23.

47 Paul Brissenden, *The I.W.W.* (New York, 1919), 344ff.; 'The Pacifist Pilgrims,' *Literary Digest*, lv (15 Sept. 1917), 16–17; *Bulletin* and MS. Records of the People's Council in H.W.L. Dana Papers (S.C.P.C.).

48 Minutes of the Exec. Comm., June to Sept. 1917, A.U.M. MS. Records (S.C.P.C.), Box 1; MS. Notes and Letters in 'General Correspondence, 1917,' Amos Pinchot Papers (Library of Congress), Boxes 27, 30.

49 *Second Report of the Provost Marshal General*, 57–61.

50 Secretary of War, *Statement Concerning the Treatment of Conscientious Objectors in the Army* (Wash., 1919), 19–25; Paul French, *We Won't Murder* (New York, 1940), 24, 59ff.; Norman Thomas, *The Conscientious Objector in America* (New York, 1923), 14–15.

51 National Civil Liberties Bureau, *The Facts about Conscientious Objectors in the United States* (New York, 1918), 16ff.; N.C.L.B., *Political Prisoners in Federal Military Prisons* (New York, 1918); Baker, *Woodrow Wilson*, vii, 539; French, *We Won't Murder*, 102–3.

52 Howard Beale, *Are American Teachers Free?* (New York, 1936), chap. 3; Curti, *Peace or War*, 256.

53 *Congressional Record*, 65 Cong., 1 Sess., 7878ff. See also Ellen Torelle, *The Political Philosophy of La Follette* (Madison, 1920), chaps. 14–17; Claudius Johnson, *Borah of Idaho* (New York, 1936), 214.

54 New York *World* (6 Sept. 1918), 8; Baker, *Woodrow Wilson*, vii, 385; *Second Report of the Provost Marshal General*, 202.

55 *Untimely Papers*, 99.

Chapter XIII

1 New York *World* (9 Nov.; 12 Nov. 1918), 8; 12.

2 Seymour, *Intimate Papers of Colonel House*, ii, 284.

3 Frederick Palmer, *Bliss Peacemaker* (New York, 1934), 340. See also Bliss's advice to O. G. Villard, quoted in the latter's *Fighting Years*, 457.

4 David H. Miller, *The Drafting of the Covenant* (New York, 1928), ii, 48–9.

5 See, for example, W. E. Borah in *Congressional Record*, 65 Cong., 3 Sess., 440; T. S. Woolsey, 'Freedom of the Land and Freedom of the Seas,' *Yale Law Journal*, xxviii (Dec. 1918), 155–6.

6 R. S. Baker, *Woodrow Wilson and World Settlement* (Garden City, 1922), i, chaps. 19–21; Miller, *Drafting of the Covenant*, i, 34–5, 47, 65ff., 171, 545.

7 'Speech at Coliseum, St. Louis, Sept. 5, 1919,' *Public Papers* (Baker and Dodd), v, 638. See also ibid. vi, 50–51, 392, 412–3.

8 Villard to MacDonald, 27 Sept. 1919, Villard Papers (Houghton Library, Harvard Univ.).

9 *Nation,* cviii (17 May 1919), 778. See also T. A. Bailey, *Woodrow Wilson and the Great Betrayal* (New York, 1945), 21–2.

10 Harold Stearns, *Liberalism in America* (New York, 1919), ix.

11 *Free Our Political Prisoners* ([New York, 1918]), 7. See also Ray Ginger, *The Bending Cross: Eugene Victor Debs* (New Brunswick, 1949), 404ff.

12 *Dial,* lxvi (11 Jan. 1919), 5–6. See also Norman Thomas and Albert De Silver, 'Amnesty of Political Prisoners,' *Arbitrator,* ii (Aug. 1919), 2–6; 'Forgotten "Conscientious Objectors,"' *Literary Digest,* lxiii (1 Nov. 1919), 34.

13 Johnson, *Borah of Idaho,* 217ff.; C. Vann Woodward, *Tom Watson* (New York, 1938), 476; *Congressional Record,* 67 Cong., 4 Sess., 485ff.

14 See, for example, Frank Tannenbaum, 'The Moral Devastation of War,' *Dial,* lxvii (5 Apr. 1919), 333–6; Merle Armitage, 'The Citizen Army and Militarism,' *Public,* xxii (8 March 1919), 237–8.

15 *Annual Report of the Secretary of War, Nov. 20, 1917* (Wash., 1918), i, 42–3. See also Baker, *Woodrow Wilson,* vii, 305–6, 324; and the collection of quotations compiled by the *Nation* in *Since the Night We Entered War* (New York, [1918]).

16 *Congressional Record,* 65 Cong., 2 Sess., 4262–3.

17 *Washington Bulletin,* new ser., no. 1 (2 Apr. 1918), A.U.M. Records (S.C.P.C.), Box 3.

18 *Report of the Proceedings, 39th Annual Convention* (Wash., 1919), 78.

19 *Minutes . . . 1919* (Texarkana, [1920]), 50.

20 *The Farmer's Yearbook* (New York, 1919), 149.

21 See, for example, *World Tomorrow,* i (June 1918), 132–5; *Nation,* cvii (20 July 1918), 59; *Arbitrator,* i (Feb. 1919), 7–11; *Survey,* xliii (14 Feb. 1920), 575–6.

22 'Universal Training vs. Preparedness,' *New Republic,* xxii (17 March 1920), 70–72. See also G. T. Robinson, 'Military Paternalism and Industrial Unrest,' *Dial,* lxvii (23 Aug. 1919), 137–9; Stearns, *Liberalism in America,* chap. 1.

23 A.U.M., *Bulletin,* nos. 5, 22 (17 Sept. 1918; 14 Feb. 1920); *Literary Digest,* lxiv (14 Feb. 1920), 19–20.

24 House Comm. on Military Affairs, 'Army Reorganization,' *Hearings,* 65 Cong., 3 Sess. (Wash., 1919), 17, 26–9; White, *Executive Influence,* 261; Dickinson, *Building an Army,* 323–30.

25 *Congressional Record,* 66 Cong., 2 Sess., 2754, 4074–5, 4429–30, 5276, 5318–20, 5402–3. See also 'Reorganization of the Army,' 28 Jan. 1920, *Senate Report No. 400,* 66 Cong., 2 Sess., Part ii.

26 *Congressional Record,* 66 Cong., 2 Sess., 5895–6.

27 Dickinson, *Building an Army,* 367.

28 Ibid. 364; White, *Executive Influence,* 261–5; *U.S. Statutes at Large,* xli, 759, 948, 954; *Congressional Record,* 66 Cong., 3 Sess., 2684, 2719. See also B. G. Franklin, 'The Military Policy of the United States, 1918–1933' (MS. Ph.D. dissertation, Univ. California, 1943).

29 Davis, *A Navy Second to None,* 243, 252, 268–9.

30 'America's Military Menace,' *Literary Digest,* LXIII (6 Dec. 1919), 23–4; 'Peace and Naval Policy,' *Scientific American,* CXIX (30 Nov. 1918), 432.

31 *Commoner,* XIX (Jan. 1919), 4. See also C. L. Hoag, *Preface to Preparedness* (Wash., 1941), 25.

32 21 Dec. 1918, *Congressional Record,* 65 Cong., 3 Sess., 727.

33 'The Navy's Future,' *Independent,* CI (10 Jan. 1920), 51–2, 71.

34 A.U.M., *Bulletin,* no. 30 (16 Dec. 1920), 2; Hoag, *Preface to Preparedness,* 11; Frank Cobb, 'Economic Aspects of Disarmament,' *Atlantic Monthly,* CXXVIII (Aug. 1921), 145–9.

35 Hoag, *Preface to Preparedness,* 47, 73–9.

36 *New York Times* (30 Dec. 1920), 8.

37 Bliss, 'The Problem of Disarmament,' in E. M. House and Charles Seymour, *What Really Happened at Paris* (New York, 1921), 375, 397.

38 *Congressional Record,* 66 Cong., 3 Sess., 310; Hoag, *Preface to Preparedness,* 45ff.; House Comm. on Military Affairs, 'World Disarmament,' *Hearings,* 66 Cong., 3 Sess. (Wash., 1921).

39 *Congressional Record,* 66 Cong., 3 Sess., 4145–6, 4254ff., 4281; 67 Cong., 1 Sess., 1420, 1731.

40 Hoag, *Preface to Preparedness,* 80–86, chap. 6; editorials in *Collier's,* LXVIII (17 Sept. to 5 Nov. 1921); 'The New Internationalism,' *Saturday Evening Post,* CXCIV (20 Aug. 1921), 20. See also 'Europe Thinks We Are Growing Militaristic,' *Current Opinion,* LXXI (Oct. 1921), 426–7; R. G. Brown, 'Militarism in the United States and the Conference,' *Nation,* CXIII (9 Nov. 1921), 526–8.

41 Minutes of the Exec. Board and Annual Report of the National Council for 1921 (S.C.P.C.), File Case 1; National Council, *News Bulletin,* I (1921), *passim;* F. J. Libby, *War on War Campaign Textbook* (Wash., [1922]).

42 Harold and Margaret Sprout, *Toward a New Order of Sea Power* (Princeton, 1940), 269–70, 274; Hoag, *Preface to Preparedness,* 167–9.

43 Davis, *A Navy Second to None,* 309; Hoag, *Preface to Preparedness,* 164–75.

44 Ibid. 175–6, 181–2.

45 Ibid. 178–9; New York *World* (24; 25 Oct. 1922), 12; 12.

46 Annual Messages to Congress, 1924–6, *Congressional Record,* 68 Cong., 2 Sess., 55; 69 Cong., 1 Sess., 461; 69 Cong., 2 Sess., 33–4.

47 *Annual Report of the Secretary of the Treasury 1927* (Wash., 1928), 16ff.

48 *Address U.S. Naval Academy June 3, 1925* (Wash., 1925), 5; *Address before the American Legion Convention at Omaha* (Wash., 1925), 4ff. See also *Addresses,* Kansas City, Missouri, and Trenton, New Jersey, 1926 (Wash., 1926).

49 *Congressional Record,* 69 Cong., 2 Sess., 1246–8; Davis, *A Navy Second to None,* 316–9.

50 *Literary Digest,* LXXXIX (3 Apr. 1926), 10–12.

51 'European Militarism in a New Phase,' *Current History,* XXIV (Sept. 1926), 915. See also 'Revolution via Militarism,' *New Republic,* XLII (18 March 1925), 86–8; Ludwig Quidde, 'European Militarism,' *World Tomorrow,* IX (Oct. 1926), 161–2; Kirby Page, 'The Menace of Military Preparedness,' ibid. IX (Oct. 1926), 163–5; William Allen White, *Forty Years on Main Street* (New York, 1937), 182; Carlton J. H. Hayes, *Essays on Nationalism* (New York, 1928), chap. 6.

52 Davis, *A Navy Second to None,* 323–4.

53 Ibid. 327; *Congressional Record*, 71 Cong., 3 Sess., 1801.

54 Davis, *A Navy Second to None*, 329–30. See also R. H. Ferrell, *Peace in Their Time: The Origins of the Kellogg-Briand Pact* (New Haven, 1952).

55 *Congressional Record*, 70 Cong., 2 Sess., 678–9, 2599, 2619.

56 *New York Times* (24 July 1929), 1; Davis, *A Navy Second to None*, 333ff.

57 Quoted in *Congressional Record*, 71 Cong., 2 Sess., 3443, 5967–8.

58 *New York Times* (3 March 1930), 1.

59 *London Naval Treaty*, Radio Address, 12 June 1930 (Wash., 1930), 7. See also Frank B. Kellogg, Address, Town Hall, New York City, 28 March 1930 in *Congressional Record*, 71 Cong., 2 Sess., 6426.

60 *State Papers and Other Public Writings* (W. S. Myers, ed., New York, 1934), I, 351–2.

61 Charles Beard, *The Navy: Defense or Portent?* (New York, 1932); Walter Millis, 'Prepare, Prepare, Prepare,' *Atlantic Monthly*, CXLIX (June 1932), 753–69.

Chapter XIV

1 N.E.A., *Journal of Proceedings* (Ann Arbor, 1915), 27, 38ff., 335–7; N.E.A., *Addresses and Proceedings* (Ann Arbor, 1916), 27–8, 159–65; *School and Society*, 1 (6 March 1915), 353–5; *Literary Digest*, LIII (22 July 1916), 186; *Survey*, XXXVI (15 July 1916), 418–19. See also L. P. Todd, *Wartime Relations of the Federal Government and the Public Schools, 1917–1918* (New York, 1945), 111ff.

2 See the analyses of the New York law in *School and Society*, III (15 Apr. 1916), 573–5; *New Republic*, VII (29 July 1916), 318–19; *Current Opinion*, LXI (Aug. 1916), 115–17; *Survey*, XXXVI (17 June 1916), 314. On the Wyoming Plan, see *Everybody's Magazine*, XXXIV (Feb. 1916), 150–59; *School Review*, XXV (March 1917), 145–50.

3 Beale, *Are American Teachers Free?*, chap. 4; Bessie Pierce, *Public Opinion and the Teaching of History* (New York, 1926), Part I, chaps. 4–5; Marcus Duffield, *King Legion* (New York, 1931), 25off. For the similar experience of England, see John Langdon-Davies, *Militarism in Education* (London, [1919]).

4 *American Physical Education Review*, XXII (May 1917), 304.

5 U.S. Bureau of Educ., *Bulletin No. 25* (Wash., 1917), 5.

6 An excellent summary, useful at all points in this chapter, is Doris Rodin, 'The Opposition to the Establishment of Military Training in Civil Schools and Colleges in the United States, 1914–1940' (MS. M.A. thesis, American Univ., 1949).

7 U.S. Bureau of Educ., *Bulletin No. 33* (Wash., 1927), 9, 20, 21; *Public Papers of Alfred E. Smith, Governor 1919* (Albany, 1920), 69–75; Report of the New York State Commission on Military Training, published by the A.U.M. as *New York's Sober Second Thought* (Wash., 1919), 14–15; A.U.M., *When School Boards Run Amuck* (Wash., 1920), reviews the Cleveland story; Massachusetts Committee on Militarism in Education, *Military Training* (n.p., 1926); Committee on Militarism in Education, *News Letter No. 1* (6 March 1926), 1; C.M.E., MS. Records on the organization of community opposition to R.O.T.C. (S.C.P.C.), File Cases 15–16; R. D. Meade, 'The Military Spirit of the South,' *Current History*, XXX (Apr. 1929), 55–60.

8 Sections 40 and following, Acts of June 3, 1916, and June 4, 1920, *U.S. Statutes at Large*, XXXIX, 191ff., XLI, 776ff.

9 W. D. Lane, *Military Training in Schools and Colleges of the United States* (n.p., [1925]), 10. Elbridge Colby, however, argues that the original Morrill Act implied compulsion. *Georgetown Law Journal*, XXIII (Nov. 1934), 1–36.

10 Merle Curti and Vernon Carstensen, *The University of Wisconsin* (Madison, 1949), II, 417–18.

11 Letter, 18 Nov. 1924, General Records of the Office of the Secretary of Interior (National Archives, R.G. 48), cited with other correspondence in Rodin, 'Opposition to Military Training,' 33–4.

12 Lane, *Military Training*, 12–13, 24–7, and *passim*. See also Paul Blanshard, 'Military "Glory" in the Colleges,' *Nation*, CXX (18 Feb. 1925), 183–4.

13 Lane, *Military Training*, 18, 27–31, and *passim*.

14 *Survey*, LV (15 Dec. 1925), 340–41, 384; *Nation*, CXXI (16 Dec. 1925), 694; *New Republic*, XLV (16 Dec. 1925), 100–102; *Christian Century*, XLIII (11 March 1926), 314–16; *Current History*, XXIV (Apr. 1926), 27–31.

15 *Congressional Record*, 69 Cong., 1 Sess., 2936, 6424; C.M.E. Records (S.C.P.C.), File 13.

16 *Regarding Military Training at Universities* (n.p., 1925).

17 House Comm. on Military Affairs, 'Abolishment of Compulsory Military Training at Schools and Colleges,' *Hearings*, 69 Cong., 1 Sess. (Wash., 1926), 17ff.

18 *Ibid*. 38, 29ff.

19 National Council for the Prevention of War, *Bulletin*, V, VI (1926–7); Women's International League for Peace and Freedom, *Some Facts Concerning Military Training* (Minneapolis, 1926); *Advocate of Peace*, LXXXVIII (July 1926), 425–7; *World Tomorrow*, IX (Oct. 1926), *passim*.

20 *Militarizing Our Youth* (New York, 1927), 3–4. See also C.M.E. pamphlets: *Brass Buttons and Education; The Camel and the Arab* (a survey of college catalogues); *So This Is War; The War Department as Educator*.

21 *Literary Digest*, XC (3 July 1926), 12. See also *New Republic*, LX (2 Oct. 1929), 168–70; *Christian Century*, XLVI (14 Aug. 1929), 1009–11; XLVIII (25 Feb. 1931), 266–8; LI (5 Sept. 1934), 1109–11; *Progressive Education*, XII (Jan. 1935), 12–19.

22 'Military Training in Schools,' *Commercial and Financial Chronicle*, CXXII (6 March 1926), 1222–4.

23 *Congressional Record*, 70 Cong., 2 Sess., 1158, 1161. See also other Collins speeches, 71 Cong., 2 Sess., 1388ff.; 71 Cong., 3 Sess., 1942ff.

24 'Citizenship,' *Training Manual No. 2000–25* (Wash., 1928), 1–4, 13, 91–2, 111ff.

25 Senators Norris, Costigan, Cutting, La Follette, *Congressional Record*, 72 Cong., 1 Sess., 12415ff.

26 See, for example, *Scribner's*, XCI (Apr. 1932), 220–21; *New Republic*, LXXXIX (2 Dec. 1936), 144.

27 U.S. Office of Educ., *Pamphlet No. 28* (Wash., 1932), 18.

28 28 March 1932. See also the C.M.E. News Bulletin, *Breaking the War Habit*, I (Apr. 1932), 3–4; *Nation*, CXXXV (6 July 1932), 10–11.

29 Records C.M.E., including Agenda and Minutes of Exec. Board, Apr. 7, 27, 1931, and Letter to Board Members, Apr. 17, 1931 (S.C.P.C.), File 17.

30 *American Mercury*, XVIII (Sept. 1929), 22–4. See also C. F. Thwing, *The*

American Colleges and Universities in the Great War (New York, 1920), 252–4; Oliver La Farge, 'The Colleges and War,' *Scribner's*, LXXVIII (July 1925), 13–17.

31 Eliot Porter, 'Student Opinion on War' (MS. Ph.D. dissertation, Univ. Chicago, 1926).

32 *Literary Digest*, CXII (6 Feb. 1932), 21–2.

33 Quoted in *Christian Century*, XLIII (11 Feb. 1926), 173.

34 C.C.N.Y. *Lavender*, III (Dec. 1925), 3–12; *Messenger of Peace*, LI (Jan. 1926), 40–52; C.M.E., *News Letter No. 1* (6 March 1926), 1, and C.M.E. Records (S.C.P.C.), State Files, no. 5; *Christian Century*, XLIII (27 May 1926), 678–80.

35 Ibid. XLVIII (3, 17 June 1931), 731–2, 805–7; C.M.E. Records contain much information on the campaign against a compulsory R.O.T.C., classified by states and colleges. See especially the notes on faculty opposition at Ohio State Univ. (S.C.P.C.), State Files, no. 10.

36 *Christian Century*, XLII (14 May 1925), 636–7; Commission on International Justice and Goodwill of the Federal Council of Churches, *Military Training in Schools and Colleges* (New York, [1926]); Devere Allen, *The Fight for Peace* (New York, 1930), 47ff.

37 C.M.E., *News Letter No. 1; No. 3* (6 March; 7 June 1926), 1; 3.

38 Ibid. *No. 3* (7 June 1926), 3; *Nation*, CXXV (20 July 1927), 59–60; CXXVIII (20 March 1929), 333.

39 *Literary Digest*, CXV; CXVI (18 Feb.; 9 Dec. 1933), 18–19; 18; C.M.E. Records, including File on religious and civic organizations in opposition to compulsory military training (S.C.P.C.).

40 290 *U.S. Reports*, 597. See also C.M.E. materials on Maryland (S.C.P.C.), State Files, no. 7.

41 Ibid. State Files, no. 5; 293 *U.S. Reports*, 245. See also K. E. Walser, 'What the Supreme Court Decided,' *Intercollegian and Far Horizons*, LII (Jan.–Feb. 1935), 95–7; *Christian Century*, LI (26 Dec. 1934), 1651–2; L. H. Coate, *The Conscription of Conscience* (Los Angeles, 1934).

42 C.M.E., Report 1934 (S.C.P.C.), File 17.

43 *Literary Digest*, CXVIII (15 Dec. 1934), 7.

44 New York *World-Telegram* (6 Dec. 1934), 26.

45 C.M.E., Report 1934, loc. cit.

46 *Congressional Record*, 71 Cong., 3 Sess., 2261ff.; 74 Cong., 1 Sess., 2485ff., 3109–14.

47 C.M.E., Minutes of the Exec. Board, 20 Dec. 1934 (S.C.P.C.), File 17; C.M.E. File 14 contains detailed materials on the campaign for the Nye-Kvale bill. See also *Congressional Record*, 74 Cong., 1 Sess., 11745, 11814; Rodin, 'Opposition to Military Training,' 16off.

48 C.M.E., Confidential notes on background information to be used in reply to War Dept. objections to the Nye-Kvale bill, and 'Educators' Letter to President Roosevelt Rebukes Secretary of War,' Dec., 1935 (S.C.P.C.), File 14.

49 St. Louis *Star Times* (26 July 1935); *New Republic*, LXXXIII (7 Aug. 1935), 347; *Christian Science Monitor* (2 Nov. 1935), 16.

50 Quoted in *Congressional Record*, 74 Cong., 2 Sess., 4956–7.

51 New York *Evening Post* (21 March 1936), 13.

52 Senate Subcommittee of the Comm. on Military Affairs, 'Compulsory Military Training,' *Hearings*, 74 Cong., 2 Sess. (Wash., 1936), 3, 152–3.

53 *School and Society*, LI (2 March 1940), 261–8, contains an evaluation of the work of the C.M.E. by Edwin C. Johnson, Executive Secretary. See also C.M.E., *News Bulletin* (1939–40), *passim*.

54 C.M.E., Financial Records and Reports (S.C.P.C.), File 18.

55 C.M.E., Annual Report 1939 (S.C.P.C.), File 17.

56 *New York Times* (9 July 1940), 4.

57 C.M.E., Minutes of the Exec. Board, 24 Sept.; 7 Oct. 1940, and Letter to Friends of the C.M.E., 16 Oct. 1940 (S.C.P.C.), File 17.

Chapter XV

1 *World Tomorrow*, XVII (10 May 1934), 222ff.; W. W. Van Kirk, *Religion Renounces War* (Chicago, 1934), 10–12; *Literary Digest*, CXIX (12 Jan.; 16 Feb. 1935), 38; 7.

2 *North American Review*, CCXXXVIII (Nov. 1934), 398–405.

3 *As I See It* (New York, 1932), 43.

4 *Yale Review*, XXVI (June 1937), 649–68.

5 Emily Greene Balch, quoted in Robert Bowers, 'The American Peace Movement, 1935–1941' (MS. Ph.D. dissertation, Univ. Wisconsin, 1949).

6 *Nation*, CXXXV (26 Oct. 1932), 390.

7 Bowers, 'American Peace Movement,' chap. 2.

8 T. A. Bailey, *A Diplomatic History of the American People* (New York, 1947), 733.

9 M. A. Hallgren, *Nation*, CXXXVII (4 Oct. 1933), 372–4.

10 *The Memoirs of Cordell Hull* (New York, 1948), I, 287, 451.

11 Davis, *A Navy Second to None*, 359; Harold Ickes, *The Autobiography of a Curmudgeon* (New York, 1943), chap. 15; Dixon Wecter, *The Age of the Great Depression* (New York, 1948), 78; Elias Huzar, *The Purse and the Sword* (Ithaca, 1950), 346. Allocations from emergency funds for the army and navy totaled over a half billion dollars. See tables in Davis, p. 474, and Huzar, p. 141.

12 Robert Sherwood, *Roosevelt and Hopkins* (New York, 1948), 75–6.

13 W. T. Winslow, *Youth a World Problem* (Wash., 1937); Frances Perkins, *The Roosevelt I Knew* (New York, 1946), 177–81; 'Military Value of CCC,' *Army Navy Journal*, LXXV (25 Dec. 1937), 354; Wecter, *Age of the Great Depression*, 185–6.

14 Much material on the opposition to the C.C.C. is in the Comm. on Militarism in Educ. Records on Military Training and the C.C.C. (S.C.P.C.), File 3. See also the summary in Rodin, 'Opposition to Military Training,' 167ff.

15 Samuel Grafton, 'The New Deal Woos the Army,' *American Mercury*, XXXIII (Dec. 1934), 436–43.

16 See, for example, L. M. Hacker, 'The New Deal Is No Revolution,' *Harper's Magazine*, CLXVIII (Jan. 1934), 123–33; O. G. Villard, 'We Militarize,' *Atlantic Monthly*, CLVII (Feb. 1936), 138–49; 'Millions for Defense?,' *Christian Century*, LIV (10 Feb. 1937), 175–7.

17 'The American Army Stands Ready,' *Liberty*, XI (6 Jan. 1934), 7.

18   Quoted in Seymour Waldman, *Guns Are Ready* ([New York, 1935]), 11. See also John Franklin, *National Defense* ([New York, 1936]); Rose Stein, *M-Day, The First Day of War* (New York, 1936), 303ff; Rep. Francis Shoemaker's attack on the N.R.A., *Congressional Record*, 75 Cong., 2 Sess., 1119.

19   *Our Enemy the State* (New York, 1935), 205.

20   *Fortune*, XII (Sept. 1935), 135.

21   Ibid. 144.

22   *Congressional Record*, 75 Cong., 1 Sess., 1924–5.

23   Ibid. 73 Cong., 2 Sess., 617ff., 3459ff., 3682ff., 3780, 3997; 74 Cong., 1 Sess., 3091, 8444ff.

24   Ibid. 74 Cong., 1 Sess., 3098.

25   *United States News*, IV (4 May 1936), 1, 5; *Christian Century*, LIII (11 March 1936), 397–9.

26   *The Public Papers and Addresses of Franklin D. Roosevelt* (New York, 1938–50), V, 606. For the charge that the Roosevelt administration also indulged in such practices, see Broadus Mitchell, *Depression Decade* (New York, 1947), 49–50, 368–70.

27   Hull, *Memoirs*, I, 400; Bowers, 'American Peace Movement,' 128ff.; Charles and Mary Beard, *America in Midpassage* (New York, 1939), I, 401; Dorothy Detzer, *Appointment on the Hill* (New York, 1948), 151ff.

28   Elton Atwater, *American Regulation of Arms Exports* (Wash., 1941), 203ff.

29   Duff Gifford, 'The New Conscription,' *New Republic*, LX (25 Sept. 1929), 149–51; F. R. Black, 'The Profits of War,' *Nation*, CXXXI (27 Aug. 1930), 222–3. See also Seymour Waldman, *Death and Profits* (New York, 1932), chaps. 1–3; Stein, *M-Day*, Part III; H. C. Engelbrecht, *Revolt Against War* (New York, 1937), chap. 10; H. W. Thatcher, 'Planning for Industrial Mobilization, 1920–1940,' *Quartermaster Corps Historical Studies* (Aug. 1943).

30   'War Policies Commission,' *Hearings*, 71 Cong., 2 Sess. (Wash., 1931), 30ff., 124–5, 678–9, 722–3.

31   Ibid. 489ff.

32   War Policies Commission, 'Report,' *House Doc. No. 264*, 72 Cong., 1 Sess. (Wash., 1932), 2–5.

33   House Comm. on Military Affairs, 'Taking the Profits Out of War,' *Hearings*, 75 Cong., 1 Sess. (Wash., 1937), 84.

34   'Prevention of Profiteering in Time of War,' *Senate Report No. 480*, 75 Cong., 1 Sess. (Wash., 1937), 20ff., 29. See also H. E. Fey, 'Shall Conscription Come Again?,' *Christian Century*, LIV (27 Jan. 1937), 107–9; Stephen Raushenbush, 'Kill the Conscription Bill!,' *Nation*, CXLIV (27 Feb. 1937), 236–8.

35   'The Dilemma of the Pacifist,' *Peace Digest*, VI (Spring 1937), 2–3; James Wechsler, 'War in the Peace Movement,' *Nation*, CXLVI (19, 26 March 1938), 323ff., 352ff.

36   For some critical analyses of United States military policies, see: Stephen and Joan Raushenbush, *The Final Choice* (New York, 1937); M. A. Hallgren, *The Tragic Fallacy* (New York, 1937); Norman Thomas and B. D. Wolfe, *Keep America Out of War* (New York, 1939); O. G. Villard, *Our Military Chaos* (New York, 1939).

37   Hull, *Memoirs*, I, 480, 544–6.

38 Ibid. I, 563–4; *Congressional Record,* 75 Cong., 3 Sess., 277, 282–3.

39 'Preventing Profiteering in Time of War,' *House Report No. 1870,* 75 Cong., 3 Sess. (Wash., 1938), 15.

40 *Philadelphia Record, Washington Post,* and Scripps-Howard newspapers quoted in ibid. 17. See also *Christian Century,* LV (9 March 1938), 299–301.

41 'To Establish the Composition of the United States Navy,' *House Report No. 1899, Part II,* 75 Cong., 3 Sess. (Wash., 1938), 1–11.

42 House Comm. on Naval Affairs, *Hearings on Sundry Legislation,* 75 Cong., 2 & 3 Sess. (Wash., 1938), 2146–7, and 2123ff., 2132ff. See also Senate Comm. on Naval Affairs, 'Naval Expansion Program,' *Hearings,* 75 Cong., 3 Sess. (Wash., 1938), 127ff., 142ff., 277ff.

43 *Congressional Record,* 75 Cong., 3 Sess., 776, 902–3, 1244–5, 3274, 3330.

44 Ibid. 75 Cong., 3 Sess., 5519, 5525.

45 Ibid. 75 Cong., 3 Sess., 5707, 6117, 5890–91, 5854.

46 W. T. Stone, 'Economic Consequences of Rearmament,' *Foreign Policy Reports,* XIV (1 Oct. 1938), 158, 170–72. See also Hanson Baldwin, *The Caissons Roll* (New York, 1938); C. H. Grattan, *The Deadly Parallel* (New York, 1939).

47 *The Quest for Peace Since the World War* (Cambridge, Mass., 1940), 335–7.

48 Quoted in *Congressional Record,* 76 Cong., 1 Sess., Appendix 402–4.

49 Roosevelt, *Public Papers,* VIII, 3. See also Atwater, *American Regulation of Arms Exports,* 237ff.

Chapter XVI

1 *Public Papers,* VIII, 518.

2 *Congressional Record,* 76 Cong., 2 Sess., 97.

3 Walter Johnson, *The Battle against Isolation* (Chicago, 1944), 41–2, 61, 87, 92, 177, 181–3, 195ff. See also Anthony Netboy, 'How to "Sell" a War,' *Progressive,* IX (3 Dec. 1945), 8; W. A. White to O. G. Villard, 14 June 1940, 12 Apr. 1941, Villard Papers.

4 See the analytical and statistical surveys by D. H. Popper, *Foreign Policy Reports,* XVI (1 Dec. 1940), 213–28; XVII (1 Apr.; 1 May 1941), 13–24; 37–48.

5 U.S. Joint Army and Navy Selective Service Comm., *American Selective Service* (Wash., 1939), *passim.*

6 Henry L. Stimson and McGeorge Bundy, *On Active Service in Peace and War* (New York, 1948), 345ff.; Mark Watson, *The War Department Chief of Staff* (Wash., 1950), 189–95; J. M. Palmer, *America in Arms* (New Haven, 1941), 196–9; Sherwood, *Roosevelt and Hopkins,* 157.

7 See, for example, the views quoted in the symposium on the draft in *United States News,* VIII (28 June 1940), 22–3; IX (9, 16 Aug. 1940), 24, 26.

8 Senate Comm. on Military Affairs, 'Compulsory Military Training and Service,' *Hearings,* 76 Cong., 3 Sess. (Wash., 1940), 121, 143, 182, 201, 235, 242, 255. See also House Comm. on Military Affairs, 'Selective Compulsory Military Training and Service,' *Hearings,* 76 Cong., 3 Sess. (Wash., 1940).

9 *Congressional Record,* 76 Cong., 3 Sess., 9598, 10114, 10117.

10 Ibid. 13437ff., 10233, 10959. See also the similar views of Senators Capper, Ashurst, Bulow, and Taft, ibid. 10477, 10724, 10741, Appendix 5490–92; and House debate, Sept. 3–4, 1940, ibid. 11359ff., 11415ff.

11   *American Federationist,* XLVII (Sept. 1940), 3–4, 31ff.; *United Mine Workers Journal,* LI (15 Aug.; 1, 15 Sept. 1940), 10–11; 6, 6–7.

12   *Commercial and Financial Chronicle,* CL (29 June 1940), 4027–9; CLI (3 Aug. 1940), 591–3.

13   *Christian Century,* LVII (21 Aug. 1940), 1030–31; *Commonweal,* XXXII (5, 19 July; 2, 16 Aug. 1940), 219, 258; 297, 357–8.

14   The sincerity of Roosevelt's campaign concessions to the anti-war feelings of the country are questioned in Sherwood, *Roosevelt and Hopkins,* 185ff. Willkie dismissed his promises as 'campaign oratory.'

15   *Nation,* CLI (3 Aug. 1940), 81, 85–6.

16   *New Republic,* CIII (1 July; 2 Sept. 1940), 6–7; 294–5.

17   *Uncensored,* no. 43 (27 July 1940), 4.

18   *Congressional Record,* 76 Cong., 3 Sess., 12160, 12227.

19   E. S. Corwin, *The President Office and Powers* (New York, 1940), 419. See also 'Brief Submitted by the Lawyers Comm. to Keep the United States Out of War,' *Congressional Record,* 76 Cong., 3 Sess., Appendix 5206–10; F. B. Wiener, 'The Militia Clause of the Constitution,' *Harvard Law Review,* LIV (Dec. 1940), 181–200; M. I. Baldinger, *The Constitutionality of the Selective Service System* (Wash., 1941); J. C. Duggan, *The Legislative and Statutory Development of the Federal Concept of Conscription* (Wash., 1946), chap. 5.

20   Hoffman Nickerson, *The Armed Horde* (New York, 1942), 14–17. See also F. M. Cutler, 'The History of Military Conscription' (MS. Ph.D. dissertation, Clark Univ., 1922); B. W. Knight, 'How to Round Up Cannon-Fodder,' *American Mercury,* XXXIV (Jan. 1935), 31–9; E. A. Fitzpatrick, *Conscription and America* (Milwaukee, 1940); C. C. Tansill, 'Historical Background of Compulsory Military Service,' *Thought,* XV (Dec. 1940), 623–40.

21   Herman Beukema, 'Social and Political Aspects of Conscription: Europe's Experience,' *Military Affairs,* V (Spring 1941), 21–31.

22   *Public Papers,* IX, 473–5.

23   Sherwood, *Roosevelt and Hopkins,* 366–7; Stimson, *On Active Duty,* 378–9. See also Comm. against Extension of Conscription, *Conscription and Liberty* (New York, [1941]).

24   Sherwood, *Roosevelt and Hopkins,* 383.

25   A. T. Lauterbach, 'Roots and Implications of the German Idea of Military Society,' *Military Affairs,* V (Spring 1941), 1–20. See also Pendleton Herring, *The Impact of War* (New York, 1941), chap. 1; Roscoe Pound, 'War and the Law,' *Pennsylvania Bar Association Quarterly,* XIV (Jan. 1943), 110–25; Clinton Rossiter, *Constitutional Dictatorship* (Princeton, 1948), chap. 18.

26   Act of June 28, 1940, Title I, *U.S. Statutes at Large,* LIV, 670–71.

27   Sherwood, *Roosevelt and Hopkins,* 438.

28   Act of Sept. 16, 1940, Sect 59(g), *U.S. Statutes at Large,* LIV, 889. See also *Nation,* CLI (12 Oct. 1940), 326–8; *New Republic,* CIII (12 Aug. 1940), 210–11.

29   English practice is presented in Denis Hayes, *Challenge of Conscience* (London, 1949). On Congressional reactions, see National Service Board for Religious Objectors, *Congress Looks at the Conscientious Objector* (Wash., 1943).

30   Senate Comm. on Military Affairs, 'Compulsory Military Training and Service,' *Hearings,* 76 Cong., 3 Sess. (Wash., 1940), 307; House Comm. on Military Affairs, 'Selective Compulsory Military Training and Service,' *Hearings,* 76 Cong.,

3 Sess. (Wash., 1940), 450. See also American Civil Liberties Union, *Conscience and the War* (New York, 1943).

31 W. R. Bowie, 'Some Choose Jail Rather Than Register,' *Living Age*, CCCLIX (Dec. 1940), 330–33. The A.C.L.U. at first was unwilling to defend C.O.s who refused to register but later, aroused over reports of discriminatory treatment, it established a National Committee on C.O.s to co-operate with pacifist organizations and also set up a legal-aid service. A group in the above forty-five age class that refused to register was not prosecuted. See A.C.L.U. Reports from 1940 to 1943: *Liberty's National Emergency*, 31; *The Bill of Rights in War*, 46–7; *Freedom in Wartime*, 37.

32 M. Q. Sibley and P. E. Jacob, *Conscription of Conscience* (Ithaca, 1952), 83, 464, 498; U.S. Dept. of Justice, Bureau of Prisons, *Federal Prisons* (Leavenworth, 1949), 11; N. M. Wherry, *Conscientious Objection*, Selective Service Special Monograph no. 11, vol. I (Wash., 1950), 264–70, 315.

33 *Congressional Record*, 78 Cong., 1 Sess., 6709. See also H. A. Toulmin, *Diary of Democracy: The Senate War Investigating Committee* (New York, 1947).

34 Donald Nelson, *Arsenal of Democracy* (New York, 1946), xvii, 363, chaps. 19–20. See also Jack Peltason, 'The Reconversion Controversy,' in Harold Stein (ed.), *Public Administration and Policy Development* (New York, 1952), 228ff.

35 *Christian Century*, LX (24 March 1943), 356–9.

36 Senate Comm. on Military Affairs, 'National War Service Bill,' *Hearings*, 78 Cong., 2 Sess. (Wash., 1944), 184.

37 House Select Comm. on Military Affairs, 'U M T,' *Hearings*, 79 Cong., 1 Sess. (Wash., 1945), *passim;* selections from the testimony are compiled in American Friends Service Committee, Peace Section, *America Questions Peacetime Conscription* (Phil., 1945). See also *Editorial Research Reports*, I (15 Apr. 1944), 265–81; Juliet Reeve, *et al.*, *Sourcebook on Peacetime Conscription* (Phil., 1944); Hanson Baldwin, 'Conscription for Peacetime?,' *Harper's Magazine*, CXC (March 1945), 289–300.

38 *Congressional Digest*, XXIV (Jan. 1945), 3ff.; H. E. Fosdick, *A Great Time to Be Alive* (New York, 1944), 155–62. See also the symposium conducted in the *Commercial and Financial Chronicle*, CLX–CLXI (Oct. 1944–Jan. 1945).

39 National Educ. Assoc., *Journal*, XXXIII (May, Nov. 1944), 111, 177ff.; N.E.A. Educ. Policies Comm., *Compulsory Military Training* (Wash., 1945); *Social Education*, IX (Jan. 1945), 26–8.

40 E. A. Fitzpatrick, *Universal Military Training* (New York, 1945), vii–ix.

41 *Commercial and Financial Chronicle*, CLXI (14 June 1945), 2628; *Progressive*, IX (22 Jan. 1945), 1.

42 J. G. Anthony, *Hawaii under Army Rule* (Stanford, 1955); Carey McWilliams, *Prejudice* (Boston, 1944), 3, 108–10; Dorothy Thomas and R. S. Nishimoto, *The Spoilage* (Berkeley, 1946), 7–10, 14ff.; Caleb Foote, 'Have We Forgotten Justice?,' *Fellowship*, VIII (May 1942), 79–81; A.C.L.U., *Military Power and Civil Rights* (New York, 1942), 4; A.C.L.U., *Freedom in Wartime* (New York, 1943), 29. For an analysis of the forces behind removal, see Morton Grodzins, *Americans Betrayed* (Chicago, 1949).

43 *Federal Reporter*, 2nd ser., CLXXVI, 953ff.; *New York Times* (27 Aug. 1949), 5.

44 E. S. Corwin, *Total War and the Constitution* (New York, 1947), 91ff. See also E. V. Rostow, 'The Japanese American Cases—A Disaster,' *Yale Law Journal*, LIV (June 1945), 489–533; M. R. Konvitz, *The Alien and the Asiatic in American*

Law (Ithaca, 1946), chap. 11; Clinton Rossiter, *The Supreme Court and the Commander in Chief* (Ithaca, 1951), 40–54.

45   See, for example, the survey of public opinion in T. F. Lentz, 'Opinion Change in Time of War,' *Journal of Psychology*, xx (July 1945), 147–56.

Chapter XVII

1   'Why G. I.'s Demonstrate,' *Nation*, CLXII (19 Jan. 1946), 60–61. See also Samuel Stouffer *et al.*, *The American Soldier: Adjustment during Army Life* (Princeton, 1949), 224ff., 440ff.

2   The literature on the new role of the military is extensive, but see: Blair Bolles, 'Influence of Armed Forces on United States Foreign Policy,' *Foreign Policy Reports*, XXII (1 Oct. 1946), 170–79; Hanson Baldwin, 'When the Big Guns Speak,' in Lester Markel (ed.), *Public Opinion and Foreign Policy* (New York, 1949), 97–120; W. R. Tansill, 'The Concept of Civil Supremacy over the Military in the United States,' Lib. of Cong. Legis. Ref. Service, *Public Affairs Bull. No. 94* (Wash., 1951); B. M. Sapin and R. C. Snyder, *The Role of the Military in American Foreign Policy* (Garden City, 1954).

3   There is a wealth of material, some of it critical, in *Civil Affairs in Occupied and Liberated Territory* (A weekly digest of press opinion, 1945–1948, prepared by the Analysis Branch, Public Information Division, Dept. of the Army). See also 'Investigations of the National War Effort,' *House Report No. 2740*, 31 Dec. 1946, 79 Cong., 2 Sess. (Wash., 1947); H. B. White, 'Military Morality,' *Social Research*, XIII (Dec. 1946), 410–41; J. Frank Dobie, 'Samples of the Army Mind,' *Harper's Magazine*, CXCIII (Dec. 1946), 529–35; Marshall Knappen, *And Call It Peace* (Chicago, 1947).

4   'The New Realism,' *Commonweal*, XLII (6 July 1945), 282–4.

5   327 *U.S. Reports*, 1; A. Frank Reel, *The Case of General Yamashita* (Chicago, 1949).

6   'A Militarized America,' *Christian Century*, LXIII (27 March 1946), 390–91; Cord Meyer, 'What Price Preparedness?' *Atlantic Monthly*, CLXXIX (June 1947), 27–33; O. G. Villard, *How America Is Being Militarized* (New York, [1947]), *passim*; J. G. Kerwin (ed.), *Civil-Military Relationships in American Life* (Chicago, 1948).

7   For a detailed analysis of the issues involved in the control of atomic energy, see Eilene Galloway, 'Atomic Power,' Lib. of Cong. Legis. Ref. Service, *Public Affairs Bull. No. 44* (Wash., 1946), 96ff.

8   *U.S. Statutes at Large*, LXI, 495. See also Walter Gelhorn, *Security Loyalty and Science* (Ithaca, 1950).

9   For a summary of developments see the well-documented account of the National Council Against Conscription, *Militarism in Education*, Feb. 1950. See also the Fellowship of Reconciliation, *Peace Notes*, a bulletin circulated among schools and colleges.

10   Hanson Baldwin, 'The Military Move In,' *Harper's Magazine*, CXCV (Dec. 1947), 481–9; John Swomley, *Press Agents of the Pentagon* (Wash., 1953).

11   *House Report No. 1073*, 24 July 1947, 80 Cong., 1 Sess. (Wash., 1947), 7.

12   *Backgrounds of Selective Service*, Special Monograph no. 1, vol. II, parts 1–14, comp. by Lt. Col. Arthur Vollmer (Wash., 1947), part 1, iii, and *passim*.

13   *The Militarization of America*, Jan. 1948, and *New Evidence of the Militarization of America*, Feb. 1949.

14   House Comm. on Military Affairs, 'Universal Military Training,' *Hearings, Part I*, 79 Cong., 1 Sess. (Wash., 1946), 417ff. and *passim*.

15   The literature pro and con is tremendous, but most of the arguments are summed up in House Comm. on Military Affairs, 'Extension of the Selective Training and Service Act,' *Hearings*, 79 Cong., 2 Sess. (Wash., 1946); Senate Comm. on Military Affairs, 'Selective Service Extension,' *Hearings*, 79 Cong., 2 Sess. (Wash., 1946).

16   *New York Times* (21 Dec. 1946), 5.

17   Karl Compton, *et al., A Program for National Security* (Report of the President's Advisory Commission, Wash., 1947).

18   *New Republic*, CXVI (23 June 1947), 11.

19   *House Report No. 1510*, 4 March 1948, 80 Cong., 2 Sess. (Wash., 1948); *Washington Post* (15 Jan. 1948).

20   Senate Comm. on Armed Services, *Hearings on U. M. T.*, 80 Cong., 2 Sess. (Wash., 1948); American Friends Service Comm., Peace Section, *Sourcebook— Peacetime Compulsory Military Training* (Phil., [1948]).

21   *Congressional Record*, 80 Cong., 2 Sess., 8778ff.

22   *U.S. Statutes at Large*, LXII, 604.

23   Washington *Evening Star* (20 Apr. 1948); *Washington Post* (9 Aug. 1948).

24   Committee for Amnesty, New York City, *Amnesty Bulletin* (1947). Sibley and Jacob, *Conscription of Conscience*, chap. 17.

25   Central Committee for Conscientious Objectors, Philadelphia, *News Notes* (1948).

26   Washington *Evening Star* (11 Aug. 1949), 16. See also *The Hoover Commission Report* (New York, [1949]), chap. 8.

27   *National Security and Our Individual Freedom* (New York, [1949]). See also the expanded version by Harold Lasswell, *National Security and Individual Freedom* (New York, 1950).

28   *Congressional Record*, 81 Cong., 2 Sess., 1338–40.

29   Ibid. 81 Cong., 2 Sess., 1478, 1849–50, 2272.

30   *The United States and the Soviet Union* (New Haven, 1949).

31   June 1950.

32   *War or Peace* (New York, 1950), 240.

33   *Washington Post* (31 May 1950).

34   'Today and Tomorrow,' *Washington Post* (1 June 1950).

35   *Technics and Civilization* (New York, 1934), 302.

36   *Man and Society in an Age of Reconstruction* (New York, 1940), 135–6.

37   *A Study of History* (London, 1945–6), II, 100ff., IV, 141–2, 465ff., 640–51. See also the abridgement of vols. I–VI by D. C. Somervell (New York, 1947), 190, 336–8.

38   Toynbee, *War and Civilization* (selected by A. V. Fowler; New York, 1950), *passim.*

39   Turner, *The Significance of Sections in American History* (New York, 1932), 339; Paxson, *When the West Is Gone* (New York, 1930), 134. See also J. Allen Smith, *The Growth and Decadence of Constitutional Government* (New York, 1930), chap. 10.

40   *The Economic Basis of Politics* (New York, 1945), 101–3; Charles and Mary Beard, *A Basic History of the United States* (New York, 1944), 488–9.

Index

Abolitionists, oppose Mexican War, 84, 88, 91

Adams, Charles, 105-6

Adams, Henry, 47, 60-61, 105, 289

Adams, John, 12, 14, 16, 23, 46, 53-4, 64, 69; and naval war with France, 41ff.

Adams, John Quincy, 70, 75, 80

Adams, Samuel, 9-10, 23

Addams, Jane, 152, 168-9, 179, 220, 245

Adler, Julius Ochs, 258

Agreement of the People, The, 4

Alexander the Great, 69

Alfred the Great, 3

Alger, Russell A., 141

Algiers, naval war with, 36

Alien Registration Act (1940), 262

Allies, and militarism after World War I, 196ff.; United States aid to in World War II, 254ff.

Altgeld, John P., 118

American Civil Liberties Union (A.C.L.U.), founding, 192; and Japanese-Americans, 268

American Council on Education, 258

American Federation of Labor (A.F. of L.), 138, 221; in World War I, 169-70, 184, 200; in World War II, 259, 266

American Journal of Education, 118

American League against War and Fascism, 240

American Legion, 210-11, 218, 239-40, 244, 282

American Peace Society, 122

American Review, 84

American Socialist, 187

American Union against Militarism (A.U.M.), founding, 168-9; leads World War I antipreparedness campaign, 168ff., 178ff., 191; postwar struggle against U.M.T., 199ff.; and disarmament, 205-6

Ames, Fisher, 53

Amnesty campaign, World War I, 198-9; World War II, 284-5

Anderson, Maxwell, 234

Andrew, John A., 119

Annapolis, U.S. Naval Academy, 82, 211

Anti-Imperialist League, 133, 135

Anti-Preparedness Committee, 168

Arthur, Chester A., 126-8

Arbitrary arrests, in Civil War, 93ff.

Arena, 122

Armistice of 1918, and continued militarism, 195ff.

Army, fear of standing, 4-5, 7-11; Continental, 12, 15-17; reductions of, 17, 37, 47, 62ff., 79-80, 112ff.; increases in, 35-6, 41, 78; principle of stand-

Army (*continued*)
  ing accepted, 62ff.; comments of European travelers, 71ff.; and democracy, 72; in South, 109ff.; used against Indians, 114ff.; in strikes, 116ff.; after Spanish-American War, 135–6; Root reforms, 141; New Deal funds for, 239
Army and Navy Club, 206, 210
Army and Navy Journal, 157
Arsenal, military school in South Carolina, 104
Articles of Confederation, 14, 21, 24
Atlantic Monthly, 134
Atomic energy, 276; threat of in wartime, 285ff.
Atomic Energy Commission, 286
Austin, Jonathan W., 11

Baker, Newton D., 245; role in World War I, 182, 185, 188, 190, 193; plans for postwar army, 196, 199, 201–2
Baker, Robert, 144, 147
Baker, William, 130
Baltimore *Sun,* 213, 215, 232
Bancroft, George, 79
Bank of the United States, 77
Barnard, Daniel Dewey, 84
Barnard, Henry, 118
Barnes, Roswell P., 223
Bartholdt, Richard, 150, 245
Baruch, Bernard, 245, 266
Baxter, Percival P., 210
Beall, Jack, 147
Beard, Charles A., 90, 290
Beard, Mary R., 90
Becker, Carl L., 236
Bell, John, 92
Belmont, Perry, 127
Benson, Allan L., 173, 179
Benton, Thomas Hart, 70, 87–8
Berger, Victor, 193
Bethlehem Steel Co., stock rise of, 174
Bierman, Fred, 231
Biglow Papers, 84
Bill of rights, issue in ratification of Constitution, 27ff.
Bishop, Ralph Chesney, 224
Blaine, James G., 128
Blaine, John J., 210
Bland, Theodore A., 115–16
Blanshard, Paul, 228
Bleecker, Harmanus, 54–5
Bliss, Tasker H., 196, 207
Bliven, Bruce, 250

Borah, William E., 172, 174, 186, 198, 220, 231; and Washington Conference, 207
Boston Gazette, 9
Boston Massacre, 9–11
Boston University, and compulsory R.O.T.C., 228
Boudinot, Elias, 20
Bourne, Randolph, 177, 179, 189, 194
Bower, James, 206
Boy Scouts, and military drill, 154
Braddock, Edward, defeat of, 6
Branch, John, 76
Breckinridge, Henry, 210
Breckinridge, John C., 92–3
Brewer, David J., 138, 154–5
Bruce, William C., 214
Bryan, William Jennings, 134, 144–5, 162–4, 166, 178, 204
Bryce, James, 131–2
Buchanan, James, 78–9, 88
Buckingham, James Silk, 73
Burke, Aedanus, 22–3, 34
Burke, Edward R., 257
Burke-Wadsworth bill, 257–60
Burnside, Ambrose E., 96–7
Burr Conspiracy, 49
Burton, Theodore E., 146, 150
Business, and navy, 127–8; and preparedness, 159, 162ff., 178; and disarmament, 206; and New Deal defense expenditures, 240
Butler, Benjamin F., 97, 105, 111, 113
Butler, Nicholas Murray, 153, 160–61
Byrnes, James F., 273

Caesar, Julius, 23, 27, 69
Calhoun, John C., 77–8, 85; reports as Secretary of War, 63–4
Calhoun-Harrison plan for the militia, 78
Campbell, John A., 102
Canada, as goal of 'War Hawks,' 50–52, 54, 58
Cannon, Newton, 69
Capper-Johnson Universal Draft bill, 244
Carmack, Edward W., 147
Cattell, James McKeen, 187
Cattell, Owen, 187
Century, 157
Chamber of Commerce, 210, 242
Chamberlain, John, 267
Chandler, William E., 129
Channing, William Ellery, 65–6, 80

Charles I, King of England, 4
Charleston Mercury, 85
Chautauqua 'I hate war' address, Franklin D. Roosevelt's, 248
Chesapeake affair, 48
Chicago Times, 97
Christian Century, 228, 242, 266
Christian Science Monitor, 232
Church, Benjamin, 10
Cincinnati, Society of the, 20, 22–4, 45–6
Circuit Court of Appeals, affirms citizenship to Japanese-Americans, 269
Citadel, military school in South Carolina, 104
Citizens' Military Training Camps ('Plattsburg idea'), 158, 182, 220; and World War II conscription, 256
Civil liberties, issue in World War I, 191ff.; World War II, 268ff.
Civil Liberties Bureau, 191
Civilian Conservation Corps (C.C.C.), 239
Civilian Public Service Camps (C.P.S.), for C.O.s in World War II, 265, 284
Clark, Abraham, 36
Clark, Bennett Champ, 258
Clark, Champ, 185
Clark, Grenville, 182, 256–8
Clarke, James Freeman, 119
Clay, Alexander S., 150
Clay, Henry, 73, 75, 77, 86
Clay, Lucius, 273
Clergy, in World War I, 157, 193; oppose compulsory R.O.T.C., 227ff.; polled on war, 235; oppose U.M.T., 267, 284
Cleveland, Grover, 118, 128, 134
Clinton, De Witt, 67
Cobb, Frank, 180
Cobden, Richard, 139
Cockrell, Francis M., 129
Coercive Acts, 11
'Cold war,' impact of, 272ff., 285ff.
College students, and R.O.T.C., 226ff.; polled on war, 235
Collegiate Anti-Militarism League, 180, 183
Collier's, 208
Collins, Ross A., 223–4, 245
Columbia University, and World War I, 161, 187, 193
Columbian College (Washington, D.C.), 70

Commercial and Financial Chronicle, 148, 223, 259, 267
Committee for Economic Development (C.E.D.), 285
Committee on Militarism in Education (C.M.E.), 245, 258; founding, 220ff.; administration and finances of, 233
Committee on Military Training, 220
Committee on Public Information, 191
Committee to Defend America by Aiding the Allies, 255
Committees of Safety, in American Revolution, 15
Commoner, 166, 204
Commonweal, 260
Communists, 263
Condorcet, Marquis de, 71
Confederate States of America, problems of, 104–5; and military cult of South, 104
Confederation, problems of, 20ff.; size of army during, 35
Congress of Industrial Organizations (C.I.O.), opposes U.M.T., 259
Conscientious objectors (C.O.s), rights of under Constitution, 27, 29–30, 190, 230; in Civil War, 101–2; in World War I, 189ff.; amnesty for, 198–9, 284–5; and R.O.T.C., 219, 229ff.; in World War II, 263–5; *see also* Quakers
Conscription, and militia, 3–4, 6, 14, 16, 33ff.; War of 1812, 53ff.; Monroe plan, 55–7; Civil War, 98ff.; in South, 104–5; German system, 120–21; and League of Nations, 196; of wealth and labor, 244ff.; background, 256; constitutionality, 261; and total war, 261; as post-World War II issue, 279ff.; *see also* Selective Service; Universal military training
Conscription News, 278
Constitutional Convention, 24–7
'Continental Army,' Garrison's plan for, 166–7
Continental Congress, 11ff.
Coolidge, Calvin, 211–12, 214, 223
Copperheads, in Civil War, 96–7
Corwin, Thomas, 83
Council Fire, 115
Council of National Defense, 172, 256
Cox, Nicholas M., 136
Creel, George, 191
Croly, Herbert, 177
Cromwell, Oliver, 4, 19, 23, 46

Crosby, Ernest H., 143–4
Cruiser bill, debate on, 213ff.
Cummins, Albert B., 174
Curtin, Andrew G., 96
Curtis, Benjamin R., 95

Daggett, David, 56
Daniels, Josephus, 163, 165, 204–5
Darragh, Cornelius, 87
Davis, Garrett, 86, 110
Davis, Jefferson, 102, 104–5
Debs, Eugene, 193, 198, 263
Declaration of Independence, 13–14
Declaration of Rights, by First Continental Congress, 11
Declaration of Rights, in state constitutions, 13; in Virginia, 29
Demobilization, after Civil War, 107ff.; lack of after Spanish-American War, 140; and World War II, 272
Democratic party, platform (1880), 109; (1900), 134
Denham, William, 269
Dent, Stanley H., 185
De Pauw University, and compulsory R.O.T.C., 228
Desertion, in Mexican War, 86; Civil War, 103–4
Detzer, Dorothy, 245
Dewey, George, 132
Dewey, John, 183, 218, 220, 223
DeWitt, John L., 268–9
Dial, 198
Dick Act (1903), federalizes militia, 143
Disarmament, after World War I, 203ff.; after World War II, 285–8
Dix, John A., 103
Dodd, William E., 178
Donovan, William J., 256
Dos Passos, John, 234
Douglas, Paul, 161
Douglas, Stephen A., 92
Draft riots, in Civil War, 102–3
Dred Scott case, 95, 98
Dulany, Daniel, 7
Dulles, John Foster, 287
Dunn, Robert, 183
Dwight, Theodore, 58–9

Earle, Edward M., 183
Eastman, Max, 168, 170, 189, 193
Educational Review, 153
Educators, and military training in

schools and colleges, 118ff., 217ff.; oppose U.M.T., 267
Eighteenth Amendment, compared with U.M.T., 268
Einstein, Albert, 245, 278, 286
Eisenhower, Dwight D., 276, 288
Election laws, federal troops enforce, 111–12
Eliot, Charles W., 157, 160, 181–2
Ellis Havelock, 152
Embargo, repeal of (1939), 255
Embargo Act, Jefferson's, 49
Emergency Peace Federation, 178
Eppes, John, 48, 55, 63
Espionage Act (1917), 181, 188, 191, 193, 198
Essay on Civil Disobedience, 84
Evanston Interdenominational Student Conference, 228
Examiner and Journal, 77

'Farewell Address,' Washington's, 39
'Farewell Order to the Armies of the United States,' Washington's, 20
Farmers Union, 169, 200
Fechner, Robert C., 239
Federal Council of Churches, oppose compulsory R.O.T.C., 227
Federalist papers, 28, 30–31
Federalists, 32, 35, 37, 40ff.; and War of 1812, 52ff.
Fellowship of Reconciliation (F.O.R.), 245, 258, 268, 278
Findley, William, 39
Fiske, Bradley A., 206
Fitzgibbon, Catherine, 257
Flogging, in navy, 88
Flower, Benjamin O., 122
Force Act (1808), 49; (1833), 76–7
Ford, Guy Stanton, 232
Ford, Henry, 168, 178
Foreign Policy Association, 208, 251
Fortune Magazine, 240
Forum, 157
Fosdick, Harry Emerson, 260, 267
'Fourteen Points' address, Wilson's, 195, 204
Fourth of July, as military celebration, 61, 73
France, naval war with in 1798, 40ff.; and threat of war in 1835, 77
Franco-Prussian War, 120–21
Franklin, Benjamin, 8, 22
Fraser, Leon, 161
Frazier, Lynn J., 221, 231, 241

Frémont, John C., 97
French, Burton L., 212
French and Indian War, 6–7
French Revolution, 46
Freneau, Philip, 41
Friend of Peace, 66
Friends International Disarmament Council, 208

Gage, Thomas, 8, 11
Gallatin, Albert, 41, 60
Gallup poll, 280
Gardner, Augustus P., 158, 166
Garfield, James A., 108–9, 117
Garrison, Lindley M., 158, 163, 166–7, 171–2
Gary, Elbert H., 206
General Staff, adopted in United States, 142–3
Geneva Conference, 212–13
George III, King of England, 11
George, Henry, 118
Gerry, Elbridge, 23, 25–6
Gibson, Hugh, 213
Giddings, Joshua, 83
Giles, William B., 37, 50
Glorious Revolution (1688), and English army, 4
Glynn, Martin H., 173
Godkin, Edwin L., 117, 124, 139
Goldman, Emma, 164, 188, 193, 198
Gompers, Samuel, favors preparedness, 169–70; opposes conscription, 184
Gore, Christopher, 57
Grand Army of the Republic (G.A.R.), 108, 113
Grange, state and national, 169, 184, 200
Grant, Ulysses S., 108–9, 114, 126
Greeley, Horace, 100, 102, 125
Greene, Nathanael, 19
Gronna, Asle J., 174, 186, 199

Habeas corpus, writ of, suspended in Civil War, 93
Hague Conferences, 137–9, 151
Hale, Eugene, 150–51
Hale, John P., 94
Halleck, Henry W., 97
Hallinan, Charles T., 200
Hamilton, Albert, 229
Hamilton, Alexander, 19–21, 33, 131; and Constitutional Convention, 24; *Federalist,* 30–31; in Whiskey Rebellion, 37–9; naval war with France, 40, 42
Hamilton, Thomas, 72
Hancock, John, 11
Hancock, Winfield Scott, 109
Harding, Warren G., 208–9
Harmar, Josiah, 36
Harper's Magazine, 131
Harper's Weekly, 98
Harrison, Benjamin, 108, 122, 128
Harrison, William Henry, 63–4, 73, 78–9
Hart, Albert Bushnell, 157
Hartford Convention, 58
Hawaii, military rule in World War II, 268
Hay, James, 159
Hay, John, 142
Hay-Chamberlain bills, 166–7, 169, 171, 174
Hayden, Carl, 189
Hayes, Carlton, 161
Hayes, Rutherford B., 108, 112, 116
'He kept us out of war,' campaign slogan in 1916, 173, 176
Heinzen, Karl, 121
Hemingway, Ernest, 234
Hendricks, Thomas A., 120
Henry, Patrick, 28–9
Henry Street Settlement House, 168
Hensley, Walter L., 174
Hewitt, Abram S., 112, 117
Hibben, John Grier, 158
Hickok, Laurens P., 79
Hitchcock, Gilbert M., 167
Hitler, Adolph, 254ff.
Hoag, C. L., 207
Hoffman, John T., 111
Holland, James, 48
Holman, William S., 130
Holmes, John Haynes, 168
Holt, Rush D., 231, 258
Hoover, Herbert, 215–16, 236–7, 252, 285
Hopkins, Harry, 238
Houghton, Alanson B., 213
House, Edward M., 162, 196
House Committee on Military Affairs, and West Point, 69; hearings on conscription, 185, 201, 207, 222, 246, 249, 280
House Select Committee on Post War Policy, 267
Howard, Jacob M., 110
Howard, Roy, 255

Howe, Frederick, 178
Huddleston, George, 185
Hughes, Charles Evans, 209; campaign of 1916, 173; and C.O.s, 190–91
Hull, Cordell, 242, 248, 250
Hull, William, 178
Hurley, Patrick, 244
Hutchinson, Thomas, 11

Imperialism, after Civil War, 124ff.; opposed, 125, 130ff.; in 1890s, 130ff., 155
Indian Affairs, Bureau of, 114–16
Indians, war on 1790s, 35–6; after Civil War, 114ff.
Industrial Mobilization Plan, 244–5
Industrial Workers of the World (I.W.W.), 152, 191–2, 263
Influence of Sea Power upon History, The, 127
Intercollegiate Disarmament Council, poll by, 226
International Association of Machinists, 210
International Socialist Review, 188
Ireland, John, 153
Isolationism, and New Deal, 236ff.

Jackson, Andrew, 72–8, 82, 87, 89, 126
Jackson, James, 34
James, William, 181, 218
Japan, naval rivalry with the United States, 204, 238, 241–2
Japanese-Americans, removal, 268–70
Jay, John, 23, 30, 80
Jay, William, 80
Jay Treaty, 40
Jefferson, Thomas, 36–7, 44, 77, 87; and militia, 14, 55–6; fear of standing army, 22, 46; and Society of the Cincinnati, 23, 45–6; and Constitution, 29; as President, 46ff.
Jeffersonian Republicans, 32, 37, 40ff.
Johnson, Andrew, 108, 110
Johnson, Edwin C. (Executive Secretary, C.M.E.), 233, 258
Johnson, Edwin C. (U.S. Senator), 259
Johnson, Hiram, 198, 251
Johnson, Hugh, 240
Johnson, Reverdy, 110
Johnson, Richard M., 50
Jones, Wesley L., 167
Jordan, David Starr, 133, 160, 178

Kahn, Julius, **185**

Kellogg, Frank B., **214**
Kellogg, Paul U., 168, 191
Kellogg, Vernon L., 152
Kellogg-Briand Pact, 213–15
Kelly, Florence, 168
Kent, James, 58
Kenyon, William S., 166
King, William H., 241, 251
Kirby, William F., 186
Kirchwey, Freda, 260
Kirchwey, George W., 161, 168
Kitchin, Claude, 185
Kneedler v. *Lane,* 101
Knox, Frank, 256, 258
Knox, Henry, 22–3, 33ff., **39**
Knutson, Harold, 241
Korean War, 288
Kvale, Paul J., 231

Labor, and militia duty, 67–8; and troops in strikes, 116ff.; opposes Root army reforms, 143; and World War I, 169–70; and conscription, 184, 200
La Follette, Robert M., 198, 263; in World War I, 160, 174, 186, 193
La Follette, Robert M., Jr., 251
La Guardia, Fiorello H., 231
Lane, Winthrop D., 220–21
Lea, Homer, 157
League for the Amnesty of Political Prisoners, 198
League of Nations, 196ff.; 204–5, 207, 217, 236, 242
League To Enforce Peace, 162–3
Leahy, William D., 273
Lee, Henry, 38
Lee, Richard Henry, 21, 28
Lee, Robert E., 105, 121–2
Levellers, 4
Libby, Frederick J., 208, 257
Liebknecht, Karl, 167, 177
Lilburne, John, 4
Lilienthal, David, 276
Lincoln, Abraham, 83, 90–102, 107
Lindsay, Vachel, 179
Lippmann, Walter, 250, 287
Literary Digest, 230, 235
Livingston, Robert R., 17
Lochner, Louis, 168
Lodge, Henry Cabot, 127, 130, 141, 155, 158, 205
Logan, John A., 113–14
London Economic Conference, 237
London Naval Conference, 238
Longstreth, Walter, 221

Love, Alfred H., 122
Lowell, James, 10
Lowell, James Russell, 84
Ludlow, Louis, war referendum of, 248
Lundeen, Ernest, 246
Lusitania, 162

MacArthur, Douglas, 273–4, 288
McClellan, George B., 97
McCloy, John J., 275
McDonald, Ralph, 280
MacDonald, Ramsay, 197, 215
MacDonald, William, 197
McGrady, Edward F., 221
McHenry, James, 42
McKee, Samuel, 50
McKellar, Kenneth D., 185, 202
McKinley, William, 134–5, 137, 141
McLenmore, Atkins J., 185
McMahon, Brien, 286
McSwain War Profits bill, 246
Maclay, William, 35
Macon, Nathaniel, 49, 63
Madison, James, 20–21, 34, 37–8; and
    Constitutional Convention, 24–5; Vir-
    ginia ratifying convention, 28–9;
    Federalist, 30–31; War of 1812, 49ff.,
    55, 68
Mahan, Alfred Thayer, 127–9, 132, 137,
    139, 141, 145, 149, 153, 155, 158
Mallory, Robert, 100
Manifest destiny, 74, 78, 82ff.
Mann, Horace, 79
Mannheim, Karl, 289
Marshall, George C., 256, 273, 287–8
Marshall Plan, 275
Martial law, in Civil War, 98
Martin, Luther, 25
Maryland, state courts, and compulsory
    R.O.T.C., 229
Mason, George, 13, 25–6, 28–9
Mason, Jeremiah, 56
Massachusetts, and War of 1812, 53–4
Masses, 170, 177
Maverick, Maury, 250
May bill, 280
Meacham, Alfred B., 115
Meiklejohn, Alexander, 183
Mellon, Andrew W., 206
Melville, Herman, 88
Mencken, Henry L., 226
Merryman, John, case of, 93–4
Methodist Church, and compulsory
    R.O.T.C., 228ff.

Mexican War, 70, 80ff.; Whig opposi-
    tion to, 82ff.
Meyer, Ernest L., 232, 235
Mifflin, Thomas, 38
Miles, Nelson A., 142, 181
Militarism, German, 120–21, 157, 181;
    in Europe before World War I, 156–
    7; Wilson attitude toward, 171, 180;
    after World War I, 195ff.; and New
    Deal, 238ff.; and total war, 262; in
    foreign policy, 275ff.; and science
    and education, 276; and U.M.T., 277;
    and democracy, 289–90
Military commissions, in Civil War, 93,
    97–8
Military dictatorship, feared in Ameri-
    can Revolution, 15ff., 31; and Lin-
    coln, 90ff.
Military rule, in South, 109ff.
Military training, in schools and col-
    leges, 121–3, 153–4, 183, 217ff.; *see
    also* Reserve Officers' Training Corps
Militia, English, 3–5; in colonies, 6;
    American Revolution, 12ff.; Confed-
    eration, 21–2; Constitution, 24–6;
    early plans for, 33ff.; Act of 1792,
    34ff.; Jefferson and, 47; Calhoun-
    Harrison plan, 63ff.; duty opposed,
    66ff.; Poinsett classification plan, 78–
    9; in South, 104; Dick Act, 143
Miller, Morris S., 57
Milligan case, 98
Money, H. D., 136
Monroe, James, 21–2, 37; militia plan,
    55ff., 64
Morgan, John T., 122
Morrill, Justin S., 119
Morrill Land Grant Act (1862), 119,
    122, 153, 219
Mother Earth, 152, 188
Mowrer, Paul Scott, 213
Mumford, Lewis, 289
Munitions industry, 213; and prepared-
    ness in New Deal, 240ff.; investi-
    gated, 243ff.
Mutiny Act, British, 5, 8
Myers, Wayne V., 183

Napoleon Bonaparte, 46
Nason, Samuel, 27
Nation, 117, 124, 139, 157, 177, 197,
    237, 260, 272
National Association of Manufacturers,
    149, 210

National Council against Conscription, 278, 287

National Council for the Prevention of War (N.C.P.W.), 225, 246, 257, 278

National Council on the Limitation of Armaments, 208

National Defense Act (1916), 171–2, 202, 219, 231; (1920), 202, 219, 231

National Education Association (N.E.A.), 217, 280

National Guard (U.S.), 143, 166, 172, 273

National Recovery Administration (N.R.A.), 238, 240

National Security Act (1947), 276

National Security Council, 273, 276

National Security League, 158–9, 163, 205–6, 210, 222

National Service, 182

National Service League, 182

National War Service bill, 266

Naval Act (1916), 173–4

Naval Policy Board, created, 129

Navy, and Algiers pirates, 36–7; war with France, 40–41; Jeffersonian hostility toward, 50; after War of 1812, 61ff.; reductions in, 76, 82; expansion in 1850s, 87–8; shift to steel, 126ff.; in Roosevelt and Taft administrations, 145ff.; after World War I, 203ff., 210–11; debate over 1938 appropriations bill, 249ff.

Navy Day, 210–11

Navy League, founding, 146; 147, 157, 162, 164–5, 174, 206, 210

Nazi sympathizers, trial of, 269

Nearing, Scott, 178

Negroes, and U.M.T., 284

Nelson, Donald, 266

Nesmith, James W., 99

Neutrality Acts, 243–4, 254; revised, 253ff., 262

New Republic, 177, 181, 186, 189, 197, 200, 260, 282

New Review, 172

New York Assembly, suspended, 8

New York *Evening Post*, 84, 184, 213, 232

New York Times, 157, 160, 164, 223, 256, 258

New York Tribune, 100, 102, 109, 125

New York Workingmen's party, 68

New York *World*, 96, 193–5, 211, 223

New York *World Telegram*, 225, 230

Newark, New Jersey, *Evening Journal*, 93

Newburgh Address, Washington's, 20

News Letter (C.M.E.), 222

Newspaper opinion, and British troops, 9; Mexican War, 84; Civil War, 92–3; World War I, 161, 165–6; and conscription, 184, 202; on Navy Day, 210–11

Nicholas II, Czar of Russia, 137–8

Nicholas, John, 37, 42

Nichols, Thomas Low, 60

Nicola, Lewis, 19

Nobel Prize, awarded Theodore Roosevelt, 141

Nock, Albert Jay, 240–41

Nordhoff, Charles, 88

Norris, George W., 174, 186, 198, 214, 231, 251, 258

North American Review, 117

North Atlantic Treaty, 275

Northern Pacific Railroad, defended by army, 115

Norton, James A., 144

Nullification, 76–7

Nuremberg war crimes trials, 274

Nye, Gerald P., 214, 231, 241, 243, 246, 251

Nye Committee, munitions investigation, 243ff.

Nye-Kvale bill, 232–3

Occupied territory, Mexican, 87; German, 274ff.

O'Day, Caroline G., 231

Officer caste, and American Revolution, 15, 18–20; and Society of the Cincinnati, 22ff.

Ohio State University, and compulsory R.O.T.C., 226–7

Oklahoma, draft resistance, 188

Olney, Richard, 134

Otis, William Bradley, 221–2

Outlook, 158

Oxford Pledge, 235

Oxnam, G. Bromley, 228

Pacifists and peace movement, after War of 1812, 65–6; and Mexican War, 84–5; oppose Theodore Roosevelt's navalism, 148; growth in 1900s, 151–2; World War I preparedness and conscription, 167ff., 189ff.; and disarmament, 208–9; hopes of, 217, 220, 235ff.; and New Deal, 237; on war profits, 243ff.; split between isolation and collective security, 247ff.; *see also* Conscientious objectors

Paine, Thomas, 66

Palmer, Frederick, 186

Panay incident, 248–9

Paris Peace Conference, 196, 204

Parker, Alton B., 144

Parker, Joel (Governor of New Jersey), 95

Parker, Joel (Harvard Professor), 95

'Patriotism and Pacifists,' Jane Addams's address in 1917, 179

Patterson, Robert P., 256, 266

Paxson, Frederic L., 186, 290

Pearl Harbor, impact of, 262–3

Peel, Robert, 139

Peel, Samuel W., 130

Pendleton, George, 100

Penn, John, 17

Penn, William, 6

Pennsylvania Assembly, on defense, 6–7

Pensions, for veterans of American Revolution, 18–20

Perry, Matthew, 88

Perry, Ralph Barton, 181–2

Pershing, John J., 206–7

Petition of Right, 4

Phelps, William Lyons, 164

Philippine Islands, and United States, 134ff.

Phillips, Charles F., 187

Pickering, Timothy, 42

Pierce, Franklin, 70, 87–8, 94

Pinckney, Charles, 26

Pitkin, William, 8

Pitt, William, the Elder, 5

'Plan for a Peace-Office for the United States,' Benjamin Rush's, 43

Platt amendment, 142

Poindexter, George, 76–7

Poinsett, Joel R., 78–9

Polk, James K., 82ff.

Portland, Maine, *Evening News*, 215

Post War World Council, 278

Pownall, Thomas, 8

Preparedness, in 1798, 41–2; War of 1812, 48ff.; Mexican War, 82; before Civil War, 91–2; campaign for in World War I, 158ff.; Wilson converted to, 163ff.; under New Deal, 238ff.; debate over in 1938, 249ff.

President, military powers of under Constitution, 24ff.; in Civil War, 90ff.

President's Advisory Commission on

Universal Military Training, 277, 281–2

Presidential Amnesty Board, 284

Progressive, 267

Progressive party, on U.M.T., 172–3

Prohibition party, opposes conscription, 173

Propaganda, by military establishment, 224, 277

Public Works Agency (P.W.A.), 238

Pullman strike, 118

Puritans, in England, 4

Quadruple Alliance, 61

Quakers, and militia duty, 6–7, 27, 34–5, 67; in War of 1812, 52; and Civil War draft, 99, 101–2; World War I, 168, 189, 191, 208, 221; World War II, 278, 287

'Quarantine' speech, Franklin D. Roosevelt's, 247–8

Quincy, Josiah, 54

Quitman, John A., 87

Radical Republicans, policies of, 108ff.

Raguet, Condy, 77

Randolph, Edmund, 24, 26

Randolph, John, 43, 48–51, 55, 63, 65

Rankin, Jeanette, 246, 263

Rankin, John E., 241

Rappard, William E., 252

Reconstruction Act (1867), 110–11

Reed, James A., 186, 202

Reed, John, 177, 181

Remarque, Erich, 234

Reserve Officers' Training Corps, 276; established, 172; after World War I, 216ff.

Reynolds, Alonzo, 229

Rhodes, James Ford, 100

Roberts, Owen J., 284

Robeson, George M., 126–7

Rogers, Andrew J., 111

Rolland, Romain, 245

Roosevelt, Eleanor, 267

Roosevelt, Franklin D., 216; as President, 235ff.; and World War II, 254ff.

Roosevelt, Theodore, 127, 132, 139, 153, 155, 163, 171, 173, 182, 210; as President, 141ff.

Root, Elihu, 135, 141–4, 155

Root, Elihu, Jr., 256

Roseberry, Archibald P., 164

Ross, Lewis W., 112–13

Rush, Benjamin, 16, 43
Rush-Bagot Agreement, 62
Russell, Bertrand, 177

St. Clair, Arthur, 36
St. Louis *Post Dispatch*, 161
St. Louis *Star Times*, 232
San Francisco *Bulletin*, 184
San Francisco *Chronicle*, 166
Sargent, Dudley Allen, 154
Saturday Evening Post, 174, 207
Saulsbury, Willard, 110
Saunders, R. M., 64
Sayre, John Nevin, 245, 258
Schurman, Jacob Gould, 182
Schurz, Carl, 116, 131, 133, 138
Scientific American, 131, 172
Scott, Hugh L., 182
Scott, Winfield, 86
Scripps-Howard newspapers, 230, 255
Sedition Act (1918), 191, 193, 198
Selective Draft cases, World War I, 190
Selective Service, Act of 1917, 186ff.;
in World War II, 256ff.; extension op-
posed, 261–2; and C.O.s, 264–5; pub-
lications by, 278; expiration of and
renewal in 1948, 283
Seminole Indian War, 78
Senate Special Committee to Investigate
the National Defense Program, 265
'Sentiments on a Peace Establishment,'
Washington's, 21, 33
Seton, Ernest Thompson, 154
Seven Arts, 189
Seven Years War, 5
Seymour, Horatio, 95–6, 102–3
Shakers, 67, 99
Shanklin, George S., 111
Shays' Rebellion, 18
Shearer, William B., 213
Sheffey, Daniel, 55
Sheppard, Morris, 147
Sheridan, Philip, 111
Sherman, John, 119–20
Sherman, Lawrence Y., 186
Sherman, Roger, 12, 34
Sherman, William T., 109, 114
Sherwood, Isaac R., 150
Sherwood, Robert, 255, 263
Shipstead, Henrik, 231
Simkins, Eldred, 64
Sisson, Thomas U., 185
'Slacker raids,' World War I, 193–4
Slayden, James L., 185
Smith, Alfred E., 219

Smith, Tucker, 245
Smith, Walter B., 273
Smuts, Jan Christiaan, 196
Socialism, and militarism, 152
Socialist party, 173, 179
Spanish-American War, 128, 132ff.
Spencer, Herbert, 131
Spengler, Oswald, 289
Springfield Republican, 201
Standing army, fear of British, 3–5, 7–
11; during American Revolution,
11ff.; Confederation and Constitution,
21–2, 25ff.
Stanton, Edwin M., 95, 101
State constitutions, 13
State Department (U.S.), 273
State ratifying conventions, and federal
Constitution, 27ff.
Stearns, Harold, 197
Stephens, Alexander H., 85, 105
Steuben, Baron von, 22, 33
Stevens, Thaddeus, 101
Stevens, Wayne E., 213
Stewart, Maxwell S., 260
Stimson, Henry L., 215, 256, 258, 266
Stimson Doctrine, 247
Stone, Harlan F., 192
'Stop Hitler Now' advertisement, 255
Story, Joseph, 68
Straight, Willard, 182
Sumner, Charles, 80–81, 91, 101, 121,
125
Sumner, William Graham, 133–4, 152
Sumner, William H., 64
Supreme Court of United States, and
occupation of Mexico, 87; in Civil
War, 98; Selective Draft cases, 190;
and compulsory R.O.T.C., 229–30;
and Japanese-Americans, 268–9
Swanson, Claude, 238
Sylvis, William H., 116

Taft, William Howard, 143, 203; as
President, 149ff.
Taney, Roger B., 87, 93–4, 101
Tavenner, Clyde H., 164–5
Taylor, Glen H., 283
Taylor, Zachary, 83, 86
Tennessee Valley Authority (T.V.A.),
276
Thomas, Charles S., 167, 186
Thomas, Lorenzo, 113
Thomas, Norman, 189, 191, 236, 245,
258, 278, 284
Thompson, Richard W., 126

Thoreau, Henry David, 84–5
Tocqueville, Alexis de, 72–4
Toombs, Robert, 85
Townshend, Charles, 5
Toynbee, Arnold, 289–90
Tracy, Benjamin F., 129
Travelers, European in America, 71–3
Trent affair, 94
Trollope, Anthony, 100–101
Trueblood, Benjamin F., 122
Truman, Harry S., 265, 273, 281, 284
Truman Doctrine, 275, 282
Trumbull, Lyman, 94
'Truth About Preparedness Campaign,'
     170–71
Tumulty, Joseph, 179
Turner, Frederick Jackson, 290
Twain, Mark, 177
Tydings, Millard, 286
Tyler, John, 76, 80, 82

Unconditional surrender policy, 273ff.
Union Theological Seminary, student
     C.O.s, 264
United Nations, 271–2
United States News, 242
Universal military training (U.M.T.),
     Knox-Washington plan, 33; Jefferson
     on, 47; World War I, 181ff., 200ff.;
     World War II, 267, 277ff.
Universal Peace Union, 122
University of California, and compulsory
     R.O.T.C., 229
University of Maryland, and compulsory
     R.O.T.C., 229
University of Virginia, military drill, 69
University of Wisconsin, abolishes com-
     pulsory R.O.T.C., 219–20

Vallandigham, Clement L., 96–8
Valley Forge, hardships at, 16
Van Buren, Martin, 78–9
Vandenberg, Arthur H., 251, 255, 258
Vardaman, James K., 186
Versailles, Treaty of, 197, 204
Villard, Oswald Garrison, 169, 177ff.,
     200, 233, 236–7, 258, 266
Virginia Military Institute, 104
Volunteer soldiers, in Mexican War, 86;
     Civil War, 92, 99

Waco *Times Herald*, 161
Wadsworth, James W., 257
Wald, Lillian, 168–9, 191
Walser, Kenneth, 221, 231

Walsh, David I., 250–51
War Crimes Clemency Committee, 275
'War Hawks,' 50–52, 54, 71, 82
War of 1812, 50ff.; aftermath of, 60ff.
War Policies Commission, 244–5
War Production Board (W.P.B.), 266
War Resisters League (W.R.L.), 278
Warren, Joseph, 10
Washington, George, 12, 15–17, 46, 69,
     74; and Confederation, 19–21; So-
     ciety of the Cincinnati, 22–3; as
     President, 32ff.; and Whiskey Rebel-
     lion, 37–9
Washington Anti-Militarism Committee,
     168
Washington Conference, 207ff.
Washington *National Intelligencer*, 75,
     84
Washington Post, 232
Watson, Thomas E., 130, 132
Wayland, Francis, 79
Wayne, Anthony, 37
Webster, Daniel, 57, 76–8, 83
Welles, Sumner, 248
Wellman, Wayne, 161
Wells, H. G., 245
Welsh, George A., 221, 231
Welsh, Thomas, 11
Welsh-Frazier resolutions, 222
West Point, U.S. Military Academy,
     hostility toward, 66, 69–71, 120; role
     in Civil War, 92
Wheaton, Laban, 54
Wheeler, Burton K., 259
Wheeler, William A., 115
Whigs (National Republicans), criti-
     cize Jackson, 76–7; and militia, 78–9
Whiskey Rebellion, 37–9
White, Frederick E., 130
White, John P., 184
White, William Allen, 162, 255
Wilkinson, James, 49
Williams, John, 37
Williams, John Sharp, 136, 199
Williams, Lewis, 62, 64–5
Willkie, Wendell, 258, 260
Wilson, Henry, 99, 101
Wilson, James, 12
Wilson, Woodrow, 151, 242, 254; as
     President, 159ff.; on militarism, 171,
     180; campaign of 1916, 173; and
     World War I, 178ff.; and C.O.s, 190,
     192; postwar policies, 195ff.
Wise, Stephen, 168
Woll, Matthew, 184

Woman's Peace Party, 168, 178
Women's Committee for World Disar-
    mament, 208
Women's International League for
    Peace and Freedom, 243, 245, 257
Wood, Fernando, 113
Wood, Leonard, 142, 158, 171, 181–3,
    217
Woodring, Harry H., 239–40
Woolley, Mary E., 220
Worcester, Noah, 65–6

Work Relief Agency (W.P.A.), 238
World Court, 217, 237, 242
Wright, Frances, 71
'Wyoming idea,' 218

Yamashita, Tomoyuki, 274
Yanktown *Press*, 161
Young, Art, 170

Zook, George F., 258